The Psychology of St Terrorism

This new volume explores terrorism and strategic terror, examining how the public responds to terrorist attacks, and what authorities can do in such situations.

The book uses a unique interdisciplinary approach, which combines the behavioural sciences and international relations, in order to further the understanding of the 'terror' generated by strategic terror. The work examines five contemporary case studies of the psychological and behavioural effects of strategic terror, from either terrorist attacks or aerial bombardment. It also looks at how risk-communication and public-health strategies can amplify or reduce psychological and behavioural responses, and considers whether behavioural effects translate into political effects, and what governments can do to relieve this. Ultimately, the study argues that the public is not prone to panic, but can change their behaviours to reduce their perceived risk of being exposed to a terrorist attack.

This book will be of much interest to students of terrorism studies, homeland security, social psychology and politics in general.

Ben Sheppard is an Adjunct Fellow at the Potomac Institute for Policy Studies, Washington, DC, specialising on the terror of terrorism and missile proliferation. He has a PhD from King's College, London.

Contemporary terrorism studies

Understanding Terrorist Innovation
Technology, tactics and global trends
Adam Dolnik

The Strategy of Terrorism
How it works, why it fails
Peter Neumann and M. L. R. Smith

Female Terrorism and Militancy
Agency, utility and organization
Edited by Cindy D. Ness

Women and Terrorism
Female activity in domestic and international terror groups
Margaret Gonzalez-Perez

The Psychology of Strategic Terrorism
Public and government responses to attack
Ben Sheppard

The Psychology of Strategic Terrorism

Public and government responses to attack

Ben Sheppard

Routledge
Taylor & Francis Group

LONDON AND NEW YORK

First published 2009
by Routledge
2 Park Square, Milton Park, Abingdon, Oxon OX14 4RN

Simultaneously published in the USA and Canada
by Routledge
270 Madison Avenue, New York, NY 10016

Routledge is an imprint of the Taylor & Francis Group, an informa business

Transferred to Digital Printing 2009

© 2009 Ben Sheppard

Typeset in Garamond by Wearset Ltd, Boldon, Tyne and Wear

British Library Cataloguing in Publication Data
A catalogue record for this book is available from the British Library

Library of Congress Cataloging in Publication Data
A catalog record for this book has been requested

ISBN10: 0-415-47195-8 (hbk)
ISBN10: 0-415-57810-8 (pbk)
ISBN10: 0-203-88978-9 (ebk)

ISBN13: 978-0-415-47195-4 (hbk)
ISBN13: 978-0-415-57810-3 (hbk)
ISBN13: 978-0-203-88978-7 (ebk)

Contents

Illustrations

Figures

Tables

Foreword

This book addresses one of those questions which seem obvious once asked but has been left surprisingly unanswered up to now. We have a considerable literature on the psychology of terrorists but far less on their intended victims. Any attacks directed against civilian populations, whether by air raids, rocket attacks or suicide bombers. How likely are they to succeed?

When evaluating terrorism this becomes part of a wider debate about what the terrorists are actually trying to achieve. After the 7 July 2005 attacks on London, and those that were attempted two weeks later, there were calls for fundamental changes in foreign policy, including withdrawal from Afghanistan and Iraq, in order to turn off the flow of recruits for such deadly missions. But unless attacks acquire some regularity, no government is even going to consider changing foreign policy to conciliate groups who would probably still not be conciliated. Indeed, because the objectives of these groups are often poorly articulated or seem so distant and utopian as to be unreal, the easy assumption is that the basic objective is to kill and maim and any political claims are rationalisations for an inner blood-lust. In this way, unlike most political groups which would expect to be judged by movement towards their objectives, terrorists are normally judged by far more relaxed standards. Any actual attack, which leaves people dead and others injured, everyday routines disrupted and the media fixated, counts as a success. How great a success depends on the carnage: the attacks on the United States of 11 September 2001 set the standards against which those following must judge their achievements.

This reflects the keen sense of vulnerability to terrorism felt in western democracies. Their cities are crowded, movement is easy and reports of atrocities are instantaneously transmitted. Furthermore, unlike the armed forces, civilians are not trained to expect and cope with danger. There is therefore the sneaking suspicion that the terrorists might be on to something. With sufficient organisation, especially if their militants are prepared to be suicidal, then regular attacks could play havoc with morale, so that popular pressure might soon demand of the government measures to appease the terrorists. Public opinion is considered so fragile that even occasional atrocities, perhaps with chemical or radiological weapons, are assumed to have psychological effects well beyond the original damage to life and property. Ask policy-makers and emergency planners what concerns them most in the event of a terrorist attack, the answer will often come back 'panic'. The concern is picked up in much of the academic literature which often takes the knock-on social and political effects of attacks as being as, if not more, important than the actual event. Indeed what is the point of terrorism if it can not create terror?

Against this background of uncertainty over what terrorists are hoping to achieve and how we evaluate their success, Ben Sheppard has filled a large gap in the literature by examining the available evidence from some of the most prominent attacks launched on western populations in recent times. These include a range of events from the attacks of 9/11 to the release of Sarin gas by the Aum Shinrikyo group on the Tokyo underground in 1996, to the Israeli experience of Scud missiles in 1991 and suicide bombers earlier in this decade. In general his findings are encouraging. The public is remarkably resilient. Without diminishing the significance of the direct mental as well as physical impact on those caught in the middle of atrocities, the evidence does not support the view that the public is prone to panic. People may adjust their behaviour, for example avoiding air travel until they are sure that these events are not becoming too regular, but that is prudence not panic.

Responding to terrorism is an exercise in risk management and communication. This is an area where people look to government for guidance, about what they should do in the aftermath of an attack (and following a chemical incident this could be essential advice), the dangers of a repeat performance and what they are doing to mitigate the risks. Ben Sheppard also explores this aspect of the problem. How well did the authorities explain what was going on and encourage confidence that they were in control of the situation? The answer is mixed. One example is the anthrax scare in the United States, in the weeks following 9/11, when early attempts at reassurance backfired. This is therefore a valuable contribution to the literature on risk communication as well as to that on terrorism.

Lawrence Freedman
Professor of War Studies
King's College, London
March 2008

Preface

This book marks the culmination of ten years of research into understanding the terror of strategic terrorism. This includes the psychological effects on population centres, the consequences of government and public health actions, risk communication strategies to counter the terror of terrorism, and the efficacy of terrorism as a tool of coercion. Of particular value is this book's interdisciplinary nature of incorporating psychiatry and psychology while retaining the core focus of international relations.

This research started by focusing on the psychological and behavioural effects of ballistic missile threats and attacks on population centres but evolved into examining the effect of terrorism. The origins of this book stem from research undertaken first at Aberystwyth University, and then at Jane's Information Group in the late 1990s where as a defence analyst among other duties, I first began exploring and writing on the psychological dimension in the context of ballistic missile threats and attacks on population centres. A number of these articles were published in *Jane's Intelligence Review* and some in *Jane's Defence Weekly*. The main output of this work was a *Jane's Special Report* in 2000 titled *Ballistic Missile Proliferation* which I co-authored and edited. I was also privileged to work with a number of eminent individuals in this area as part of an annual conference series which I designed and ran at Jane's. Recognising the importance of this subject matter to question the robustness of assumptions being made of the public's responses to attacks and incorporate academic rigour, I began in 2001 a part-time PhD at the War Studies Department at King's College London under the supervision of Professor Sir Lawrence Freedman. With the September 11 attacks on the World Trade Center occurring just months into my doctorate, it was Lawrence Freedman's astute insight that recommended my research incorporate terrorist attacks. Little did I realise then that two major events were to occur over the subsequent years which were to become part of the case studies: the anthrax attacks in 2001 and the Second Intifada in Israel. Towards the closing stages, the 2004 Madrid train bombings and the 2005 July 7 bombings in London provided additional evidence to incorporate and test the robustness of several assumptions made in the research. These two incidents are incorporated in the conclusion.

It was during this time at King's College London whilst working on a separate project on designing and running war game simulations for the pharmaceutical industry at the King's Centre for Risk Management that I was introduced to the area of risk analysis. The core components of risk analysis examined here are risk perception, risk communication, and the social amplification of risk. This played a significant role in formulating and influencing the structure of the doctorate research. It became apparent that while the mental health literature could provide good quantitative evidence on the consequences of attacks, risk analysis provides frameworks that help to understand why people respond as they do to risks and perceived threats. It also explores how risk communication can address occasions where individuals 'overreact' to risks that are statistically highly unlikely and the fear of the unknown. These are key aspects for understanding and engaging with the public whilst facing terrorist attacks.

In addition I was fortunate enough to be invited by Professor Simon Wessely to attend the NATO–Russia Advanced Scientific Workshop on the Social and Psychological Consequences of Chemical, Biological and Radiological Terrorism in Brussels in March 2002. This provided a valuable opportunity to be introduced to a number of key researchers and leaders in this area.

The bibliography of selected material is testimony to the interdisciplinary nature of this book and the indebtness to others who have conducted extensive research to develop frameworks that have been incorporated in this book. In particular the area of risk analysis, which for several decades, conducted studies to fit the need for industry, policy makers and regulatory bodies to enhance their dialogue between their organisations and the public over new technologies and scientific developments. Since 9/11 the field of risk analysis has conducted valuable studies on terrorism while drawing upon previous research.

I would like to acknowledge a number of seminal contributions that have played a key role in shaping this work. Those by Baruch Fischhoff, Paul Slovic and Roger Kasperson on risk analysis, Simon Wessely on mental health, and Lawrence Freedman on War Studies.

It is my intention that the publication of this book addresses the gap of understanding the terror of terrorism and advance the international relations discipline. This study is designed to be of value to students, scholars, and to the general and more specialised audiences.

Ben Sheppard
London
July 2008

Acknowledgements

I am particularly grateful to Professor Sir Lawrence Freedman who provided guidance and constructive criticism of my research at King's College London. I would also like to thank my former colleagues at the King's Centre for Risk Management who provided invaluable assistance in formulating my ideas for the book. I am indebted to Jamie Wardman who in particular provided guidance and advice and Dr Brooke Rogers who also gave constructive support in the closing stages.

I am particularly grateful to Professor Simon Wessely who, through inviting me to the NATO–Russia Advanced Scientific Workshop on the Social and Psychological Consequences of Chemical, Biological and Radiological Terrorism in Brussels in March 2002, provided me with a plethora of contacts and research content to develop this study. I would also like to thank Jane's Information Group for providing the opportunity to develop and formulate the early parts of this research.

I am deeply indebted to my wife Bonny for her love and constant support as I pursued my academic studies to see that I completed this book. I would also like to thank Simon Hewings who along with Bonny spent many hours proof reading.

I would also like to thank Palgrave Macmillan for granting permission to use some material from the *Journal of Public Health and Public Policy* where some of the ideas contained in this book first appeared.

- Ben Sheppard, 'Societal Responses to New Terrorism'. Reprinted from Simon Wessely and Valery N. Kransnov (eds), *Psychological Responses to New Terrorism: A NATO–Russia Dialogue*, pp. 205–219 (IOS Press, 2005), with permission from IOS Press.
- Ben Sheppard, G. James Rubin, Jamie K. Wardman, Simon Wessely 'Terrorism and Dispelling the Myth of a Panic Prone Public', *Journal of Public Health Policy*, Vol. 27, No. 3, 2006, pp. 219–245, reproduced with permission of Palgrave Macmillan.

Figures

Figure 2.1 reproduced by kind permission of Springer and Plenum Press. Paul Slovic, Baruch Fischhoff and Sarah Lichtenstein, 'Facts and Fears: Understanding Perceived Risks' (pp. 181–214), in Richard C. Schwing and Walter A. Albess, Jr (eds), *Societal Risk Assessment: How Safe Is Safe Enough?* (New York/London: Plenum Press, 1980), p. 201, Figure 5.

Figure 6.1 reproduced by kind permission of Gallup, Inc. Lydia Saad, 'Most Americans Say Lives Not "Permanently Changed" by 9/11', *Gallup*, 11 September 2006.

Figure 6.2 reproduced by kind permission of Gallup, Inc. Lydia Saad, 'Most Americans Say Lives Not "Permanently Changed" by 9/11', *Gallup*, 11 September 2006.

Figure 6.3 reproduced by kind permission of Gallup, Inc. Lydia Saad, 'Most Americans Say Lives Not "Permanently Changed" by 9/11', *Gallup*, 11 September 2006.

Figure 6.4 reproduced by kind permission of Blackwell Publishing. Gerd Gigerenzer, 'Out of the Frying Pan into the Fire: Behavioural Reactions to Terrorist Attacks', *Risk Analysis*, Vol. 26, No. 2 (2006), p. 349, Figure 1.

The author added the following note. 'The number of fatal traffic accidents in the United States increased after the terrorist attacks on 11 September 2001, for a period of 12 months. Numbers are expressed as deviations from the five-year base line 1996–2000 (the zero line). The error bars (shown for the 12 months following the terrorist attacks) specify the maximum and the minimum numbers for each month of the base line. Before September 11, the average of the monthly numbers of fatal traffic accidents for 2001 was close to the zero line, and the monthly values were always within the maximum and minimum of the previous five years. Yet in the 12 months following the terrorist attacks (October 2001 to September 2002), the number of fatal traffic accidents every month was higher than the zero line, and in most cases exceeded the maximum of the previous years. Data are taken from the US Department of Transportation, Federal Highway Administration: www-fars.nhtsa.dot.gov/FinalReport.cfm?stateid=0&title=crashes&title2=time&year=2002; www-fars.nhtsa.dot.gov/finalReport.cfm?stateid=0&year=2003&title=Crashes &title2=Time.

1 Introduction

On 22–23 June 2001, the Johns Hopkins Center for Civilian Biodefence Strategies ran a bioterrorism exercise in conjunction with the Analytic Services (ANSER) Institute for Homeland Security to examine America's preparedness and response mechanisms to a smallpox terrorist attack. Designed to increase awareness of the threat posed by bioterrorism among senior US national security experts and enhance preparedness and response strategies, the scenario assumed extensive civil disorder, panic buying of food, and hospitals being overwhelmed with people with common illnesses who feared they had smallpox.[1] As with subsequent TOPOFF (Top Officials) US terrorism preparedness exercises mandated by Congress, one of the aims of the exercise designs is to evaluate how public opinion can be influenced to anticipate civil unrest and panic that could ensue following a single or multiple chemical, biological or radiological (CBR) attack.[2] But to what degree is the public prone to panic or does it exhibit prudence when faced with terrorist attacks? What government and public health response measures can exacerbate or reduce the terror of terrorism, and how robust are assumptions concerning societal resilience?

This book seeks to explore, through five case studies, the psychological and behavioural effects of strategic terrorism caused by terrorist attacks on a population as a tool of coercion. This includes how the targeted populace's authorities' risk communication and public health strategies can amplify or reduce the populace's psychological and behavioural responses. The aim is to further the understanding of the so-called 'terror and disorientation' generated by strategic terrorism through incorporating key findings from the behavioural sciences (psychiatry and psychology), public opinion polls and the print media. The five case studies are:

1   The 1991 Iraqi missile strikes against Israel
2   The 1995 sarin attack on Tokyo's subway system
3   The September 11 attacks
4   The following anthrax attacks in October–November 2001
5   The Second Intifada in Israel.

The book will assess the evidence and consider how this might translate into behavioural effects, whether behavioural effects translate into political effects, and what governments can do to relieve this. The 1991 Gulf War is included to further understand how a targeted populace responds under systemic and enduring attacks, and to the threat of rocket attacks launched by terrorist groups as encountered by Israel, for instance.

The behavioural sciences and the political science and international relations literature on strategic terrorism takes two different approaches. The literature in political science and international relations provides a more historical and journalistic account of the effects of terror on populations but dos not address how successful strategic terrorism is in generating terror. The behavioural sciences are more rigorous but very focused, lacking the political context. This book brings the two together.

The psychological dimension of strategic terrorism has been touched upon in many books and articles but political science and international relations has employed terms like 'panic', 'fear' and 'anxiety' when discussing this dimension with very little, if any, evidence to back up their assumptions. This is despite the availability of empirical evidence from the behavioural sciences, together with public opinion polls to measure changes in a targeted populace's daily routines. Through the case studies this book demonstrates that the public is largely resilient to attacks and responds in a calm and reasonable way. While disorders like Post Traumatic Stress Disorder (PTSD) and related symptoms like acute stress were evident, these were fairly minimal. However there are noticeable changes in the behaviour and attitudes of civilians threatened or attacked as they seek to reduce the perceived risk to themselves. This includes altering their plans for travel, leisure, going to work and the like.

The lack of credible supporting evidence in political science and international relations means researchers need to question the robustness of some scholars' assumptions of the terror (fear, anxiety and panic) and disruption to civilian life generated by strategic terrorism. For instance, Robert Pape (2005) believes that suicide terrorist attacks generate 'immediate panic'.[3] In 1996 Walter Laqueur writing on terrorism stated that from 'the single successful [weapon of mass destruction (WMD)] one could unleash far greater panic than anything the world has yet experienced'.[4] An investigation of the 1995 sarin attack on Tokyo's subway system and the 2001 anthrax attacks suggests that panic does not break out following a chemical, biological or radiological (CBR) terrorist strike but society is reasonably resilient, although these episodes do not themselves comprehensively prove one way or the other the effect of WMD on society. Grant Wardlaw observed that the dislocation of society is an aim of terrorism, noting that the 'ultimate of the terrorisation process occurs when the individual is so isolated as to be unable to draw strength from usual social supports and is cast entirely upon his or her own resources'.[5] But can terror become so extreme that it causes the dislocation of society?

With academia and analysts increasingly drawing inferences from strategic bombing to guide their understanding on the public's resilience to terrorism, it is also worth reviewing the robustness of assumptions concerning this form of strategic terror within international relations. Martin Navias and Aaron Karp comment on the use of ballistic missiles from the Second World War to the 1991 Gulf War as weapons of terror without making reference to existing empirical evidence at the time to support their case. Martin Navias saw the Iraqi Scud missile attacks against Israel in 1991 as a 'useful means of causing terror amongst civilians' and to cause 'disruption of enemy civilian life', without providing supporting evidence.[6] Similarly Aaron Karp wrote 'where conventionally armed ballistic missiles are too few or too small to matter on the battlefield, they gain their importance from their psychological effects'.[7] Again no evidence from the behavioural sciences was incorporated. Richard Overy and Andrew Lambert observed how strategic bombing in the Second World War did not have a devastating impact on morale. Instead they concluded it only had the impact of lowering industrial production and the diversion of troops to air defence, but bombing, by itself, did not precipitate strikes or open revolt as expected by inter world war year theorists like Giulio Douhet and Hugh Trenchard.[8,9] Nor did it hasten a political termination of the war with the exception of the nuclear bombings on Japan in 1945 that arguably precipitated the end of the war on the Pacific. While Richard Overy did not look at the psychological effects of strategic bombing, Andrew Lambert provides a good assessment based on the available qualitative material to examine coping mechanisms, the change of fear with unexpected air attacks, and sensitisation to repeated attacks. Irving Janis's RAND study also provided a comprehensive account based on the fear and anxiety caused by strategic bombing in the Second World War, concluding that the air raids did not cause mass panic but the public in Britain and Germany expressed a decline in overt fear reactions as the attacks continued and the raids became more intense.[10] However, the lack of available quantitative mental health data for Lambert's or Janis's studies limited their work to mainly qualitative assessments. A more scientific approach to best capture and analyse what lessons the predominantly qualitative literature provides on the Second World War strategic bombing can be found in Edgar Jones *et al.*'s study (2004) of British civilians in the Blitz.[11]

To engage more effectively in debating the consequences and responses to terrorism, there needs to be a better understanding of what terror such threats and attacks can generate. Following the attack on the US on 11 September 2001 (9/11) and the resultant heightened concern surrounding mass-casualty, conventional, suicide bombing and CBR terrorism, the field of international relations needs to significantly advance its ability to understand and analyse the terror of strategic terrorism, and its efficacy as a tool of coercion. In the course of this book it will be demonstrated that some of the common assumptions about an often panic-prone public are not robust.

There have been some attempts to incorporate psychology and behavioural responses in international relations from Andrew Lambert's *The Psychology of Airpower* (1995) and Eric Morris and Alan Hoe's book titled *Terrorism: Threat and Responses*. Lambert and Irving made some inroads but by the nature of their case studies were limited to mainly qualitative material and limited field research on which to base their conclusions. Morris and Hoe briefly assessed the basic psychological and physical needs of individuals and how terrorist actions can potentially undermine these basic needs, but again did not go beyond this brief assessment.[12] Lambert discussed the civilian reactions as a mirror image of soldiers under enemy fire and listed the symptoms for combat stress. However, he provided only limited empirical evidence to support the effect of strategic bombing on civilians. D. P. Sharma's book *Victims of Terrorism* recognised the importance of incorporating the behavioural sciences to understand terrorism but again fell short in providing empirical evidence that existed at the time of the book's publication in 2003.[13]

More recently, Peter Neumann and M. L. R. Smith's study *The Strategy of Terrorism* (2008) makes some reference to papers on PTSD and mental health in their discussion on the utility of terrorism and to what degree it may cause disorientation among the targeted populace. This includes the Second Intifada, and the bombings in London on 7 July 2005 and Madrid in March 2004.[14] While recognising the importance of incorporating this type of material to further the field of terrorism research, their discussion only briefly touched upon these points and did not include risk analysis to increase the understanding of the public's perceptions and responses to terrorism. Since 9/11, risk communication and risk perception have gradually been integrated into the literature. For instance, Lawrence Freedman's paper 'The Politics of Warning: Terrorism and Risk Communication' examined how risk communication could be used by governments to both prepare their publics for and respond to a possible terrorist attack and the problems involved in what can and cannot be communicated.[15] Jessica Stern published an article on bioterrorism (2002–2003) that discussed applying the concepts of dread risks and risk trade-off analysis to US foreign and national security policy decision-making to reduce access to dangerous pathogens and related information.[16]

International relations has had to mainly draw upon sources like that of Andrew Silke's *Terrorists, Victims and Society*, which examines from a psychological perspective the motivations and origins of terrorists, the impact of their acts on victims and ways of combating terrorism. While it includes information related to the case studies, the section on the victims of terrorism also includes assessments of the Oklahoma bombing; protracted campaigns in Northern Ireland, Basque territory, and Palestine; and the effect on children. Evidence includes reference to DSM and psychology studies similar to those included here, but excludes risk analysis work. Another useful volume has been Simon Wessely and Valery Krasnov's book on the psychological responses to new terrorism that examined the mental health effects of terrorism and risk communication.[17]

A likely explanation to why the behavioural sciences have only marginally been incorporated can be gleaned from Paul Wilkinson. Writing on terrorism Wilkinson observed that: 'quantifying the terror of terrorism is a complex issue because of its subjectivity – a possible reason to why other commentators have not focused on the fear and anxiety of terrorism'.[18] He adds that it is the 'interplay of these subjective factors and individual irrational, and often unconscious, responses that makes the state of terror, extreme fear or dread a peculiarly difficult concept for empirical social scientists to handle'.[19] Similarly Lambert argued that the 'analysis of airpower as a psychological weapon is scarce, and the little data that is available shows much scatter and is sometimes contradictory'.[20] Lambert goes on to add that 'nor does there exist a psychological model that unerringly explains cause and effect'.[21] This study demonstrates that it is possible to add empiricism to understanding strategic terrorism in political science and international relations through incorporating information from existing research and data. From this a framework can be developed to help explain the consequences of strategic terrorism.

The remainder of this chapter will summarise each case study. The following chapter will then review the three key fields of research incorporated in this study. Terrorism in international relations, psychiatry and finally risk analysis in psychology. An essential component will be introducing to international relations the risk analysis areas of risk perception, risk communication, and the social amplification of risk. To illustrate the key themes of risk communication Chapter 2 will contain a section on cases where risk communication has not been adequately employed. Chapter 3 will outline the case study structure and why these cases were chosen. Finally, the five key assumptions tested in the case studies will be outlined.

The case studies

The five case studies draw heavily upon the behavioural sciences (psychiatry and psychology) literature, and on public opinion polls and print media information from the respective countries. The psychiatry element incorporates literature based on the discipline's diagnostic tool, the Diagnostic and Statistical Manual of Disorders third edition (DSM-III) and fourth edition text revision (DSM-IV-TR) developed by the American Psychiatric Association. A detailed overview of the DSM methodology is contained in the next chapter.

While none of the case studies has extensive evidence across psychology, psychiatry and the media, collectively they show that strategic terror has a limited effect on the targeted populace, but in the short term (days and weeks) can cause significant changes in people's daily lives as they aim to reduce the risk of being personally exposed to a subsequent attack. In the long term (months/years) the public returns to normal life and can become complacent and ignore specific time and place warnings of further attacks. Overall this book demonstrates that terror is limited and short term when generated but a minority of the populace can continue to exhibit psychological and behavioural effects from the attacks in the following months and years. Society adapts well and is fairly resilient to strategic terror.

Chapter 4 on the 1991 Scud missile strikes on Israel explores the terror conventionally armed missile strikes and threats of non-conventional warfare can induce in a population. A conventional warhead contains high explosives while non-conventional weapons are those that contain a chemical, biological, radiological or nuclear device. This chapter examines to what extent the fear of the unknown persisted in shaping Israeli perception and behaviour throughout the conflict. The findings further the understanding of society's response to strategic terror. Chapter 5 on the 1995 sarin attack on Tokyo's subway system by the religious cult Aum Shinrikyo suggests that panic is rare following the release of a chemical weapon in an urban environment. Although available data are limited in certain areas, the analysis provides a valuable case study in the assessment of the effects of a chemical weapons attack. The chapter's strength is that it includes material on those directly exposed to sarin in the subway together with the general public's reaction in assisting the injured and ferrying them to hospitals. The case study also explores to what degree the lack of effective communication with the public can exacerbate the number of individuals arriving at medical facilities incorrectly believing they have been exposed to sarin, but who physiologically did not require treatment. This is sometimes referred to as the 'worried well'.

The plethora of DSM-based research on the September 11 2001 attacks in Chapter 6 highlights the short- and long-term effects of a mass-casualty conventional terrorist attack. Of particular interest is how the perceived personal risk expressed by Americans in surveys manifested itself in changes in their daily lives. In some cases these precautionary behaviours led to further casualties in subsequent months by Americans choosing to drive rather than fly long distances within the US.

Chapter 7 on the mailing of anthrax to media and government institutions in October–November 2001 examines Americans' behaviour in comparison to some public officials' expectations of panic. Despite reports by the media of a reactive and hysterical public, the populace exhibited steadfastness in an environment of uncertainty. Behavioural changes were evident from the handling of mail through to the undertaking of unnecessary precautionary measures. The final case study chapter on the Second Intifada in Israel provides useful data on the effects an ongoing terrorist campaign can have on a populace. As with Chapter 4 on the 1991 missile strikes, the analysis examines the level of adaptation among Israelis.

As part of the conclusion, it shall be argued that poor risk communication can exacerbate adverse changes in behaviours and attitudes by individuals that can then be detrimental to the well-being of themselves and those around them. The conclusion will also assess how this study contributes to the fields of risk analysis, psychiatry and political science.

Conclusion

Despite the wide variety of sources, the differing methodologies in the compilation of the literature used and the varied case studies, a consistent theme appears. The public is not prone to panic but is resilient and adapts well to threats and attacks. While there is a small elevation of clinical symptoms like PTSD, the main effects are changes in the behaviours and attitudes of the targeted populace made to minimise the perceived risk of being personally exposed to a terrorist attack. The political effects are primarily confined to counter-terrorism legislation, and the terror generated insufficient to cause the targeted society to accede to the perpetrators' demands. Poor risk communication in advising citizens of precautionary measures can decrease public trust in the authorities, and contribute to adverse changes in behaviours and attitudes that can endanger the health of the individuals concerned and those around them.

This book is intended to improve the understanding within political science and international relations beyond the often-unsubstantiated assessments made about the effects generated by terrorism. By pulling these fields of research together, the Conclusion can provide key lessons on how governments could reduce the terror of terrorism through effective risk communication and an emergency response strategy, and how strategic terrorism can affect the political process.

2 Overview of the key disciplines

As this book takes an interdisciplinary approach, this chapter outlines the key themes from the areas of terrorism in international relations, psychiatry and risk analysis in psychology. This provides a good introduction to the fields of research that readers from various disciplines may be less familiar with. Critically this includes an overview of the risk analysis concept of risk perception, risk communication and the social amplification of risk that are used extensively. This chapter also assesses the various interpretations of definitions concerning fear, anxiety, panic and terror from these different fields that will be used in this book. The definitions will explain the methodological parameters and which aspects will not be covered.

International relations – terrorism

Strategy and strategic terrorism

In international relations literature, strategic terrorism can be viewed as a form of military strategy which terrorist groups employ to advance their political interests. As such, it is useful to evaluate how the discussion of terrorism is linked to strategic theory. Strategy describes the ways in which military power is used by an actor to achieve a political objective, with means having the capacity to maim, kill, coerce and destroy.[1] While strategy is traditionally viewed primarily as the employment of military force, strategy concerns itself with how to employ means to achieve an end; these means can be of any nature.[2] Importantly, strategy is subordinate to politics, with war a continuation of political discourse.[3] Strategy also requires at least two players both seeking to maximise their utility by understanding and anticipating the behaviour of their opponent.[4]

The analysis of the strategic dimension falls within the realist area of international relations, in particular, the understanding that power determines and influences the outcome of the interaction between actors. To realism, according to John Garnett, the 'political realities are power realities, and power must be countered with power'.[5] Military action is viewed as one means to settle disputes among selfish actors. Neo-realists like Kenneth

Waltz view power as encompassing not just the military dimension, but also the size of the actor's population and territory, available resources, economic capability, political stability and technological capability.[6] A second theme of realism is the concept of moral neutrality which argues that realists do not seek to pass judgement on an actor's cause. Realists seek to understand the behaviour of the actor from the options they are presented with, and the calculation of interest and the efficiency of the actions.[7]

To achieve the political ends, the actor does not necessarily have to employ a single blow, but can achieve the objective through a series of engagements. The gradual approach can entail a bargaining structure of manipulative incentives that conveys that the cost of complying with demands than that of resisting. As Peter Paret noted, writing on the Prussian military thinker Carl Von Clausewitz, the aim of warfare is 'to raise the price of further hostilities to such an extent that the opponent will desist'.[8] Clausewitz also recognised the importance of psychology, placing the analysis of the psychological forces at the centre to his theory of war and believed the psychological dimension should not be ignored.[9]

A good overview of the relationship between terrorism and strategy and the distinction between strategic and tactical terrorism can be found in Lawrence Freedman's analysis on the psychology of strategic terror. Freedman noted that terrorism 'is a form of strategic coercion' whereby 'the target remains a voluntary agent and so has a choice whether or not to accede to the pressure'.[10] Strategic terror, according to Freedman, 'attempts to use acts of violence to achieve political ends'.[11] This is distinct from situations where the perpetrator's aim is not to get the target to choose differently but, for instance, to remove them from the contested territory. This includes, for example, employing ethnic cleansing in Bosnia or genocide in Rwanda.

In the course of achieving political aims, terrorists engage in what is described by R. D. Crenlinstein as a form of 'political discourse' where their attacks are designed to get the attention of those in power, which is followed by the perpetrators transmitting more specific messages like a political manifesto, or particular demands.[12] This perspective echoes that of general strategic thinking outlined by Thomas Schelling in his Cold War seminal writing, *The Strategy of Conflict*. Schelling views the use and threat of violence for coercion as 'diplomacy of violence'. Terrorism is described by Neumann and Smith as the creation of fear 'to influence the political behaviour of a given target group', and is thus seen as a form of 'coercive diplomacy'.[13] With the creation of terror being an aim of the perpetrator to coerce the target to accept political demands, and terrorism being a means to induce terror, the strategic terrorism definition needs to make a distinction between the two.

Lawrence Freedman provides a succinct explanation of strategic terrorism, defining this as a 'two-stage process: first, independent deliberate acts of violence, or threats of violence against a populace, intended to produce a particular psychological effect – terror – on the assumption that, second, this will influence the target's whole political system through shifting its attitudes and behaviour'.[14] Freedman's definition echoes Thomas Schelling's view of strategic theory that examines what factors can control or influence the behaviours and of one's adversary in conflict, and identifying how these variables can be controlled.[15] Interpreting strategic terrorism as a means to influence behaviour creates a suitable context for this study to explore the behavioural and psychological effects of terrorism on non-combatants within their homeland, and how this could then translate into political effects.

Defining terrorism

As noted earlier, the political science and international relations literature rarely attempts to define terms like fear, anxiety, panic and terror beyond the endeavours by Alan Hoe, Eric Morris, Lawrence Freedman and Andrew Lambert. As Wilkinson argued the interplay of these subjective factors makes it extremely difficult for the social sciences to study. Conor Gearty rightly observed, 'terrorism is a subject rife with moral certainty but shrouded in terminological confusion'.[16] Walter Laqueur wrote that 'all specific definitions of terrorism have their shortcomings simply because reality is always richer (or more complicated) than any generalisation'.[17] Paul Wilkinson noted that terrorism is a 'special form of political violence'.[18] Similarly Bruce Hoffman defined terrorism as the 'deliberate creation and exploitation of fear through violence or the threat of violence in the pursuit of political change'.[19] The key aspect is how the political violence affects the targeted populace (non-combatants) and ultimately the political process.

As this book focuses on terrorism by non-state actors (as opposed to systemic violence conducted by a government against its own people), Thomas Thornton's definition provides the most suitable description. Thornton wrote that terrorism is 'a symbolic act designed to influence political behaviour by extranormal means, entailing the use or threat of violence'.[20] As Andrew Rathmell noted, an attraction of Thornton's definition is the inclusion of the term 'extranormal' which enables a distinction between legitimate and non-legitimate acts of violence as defined by the Geneva Convention and international agreements.[21] Rathmell defines extranormality using the definition from Brian Jenkins as 'acts of violence waged outside the accepted rules and procedures of international diplomacy and war'.[22] Consequently, this book is not concerned with direct attacks on political figures, military installations and production plants; but acts of political violence against non-combatants. This does though exclude state terror: a regime using systemic violence against its own people, for instance, Stalin's or Saddam Hussein's reigns of oppression and insurgent and guerrilla warfare against their own populations. To encapsulate the difference between guerrilla warfare and terrorism, this book will employ Laqueur's distinction that a guerrilla leader 'aims at building up ever-growing military units and eventually an army, and establishing liberated zones in which an alternative government can be put up and propaganda openly conducted'.[23]

Violent acts are viewed in this study as those executed by a non-state actor who has adopted violent means against the general populace to further their political cause (terrorism). The 'shifting of attitudes and behaviour' for political ends in the strategic terrorism definition is a key theme illustrated in several definitions of terrorism. Strategic terrorism will thus look at the psychological and behavioural effects of political violence against non-combatants conducted by a terrorist group indigenous or external to the targeted country.

Efficacy of terrorism

There is growing evidence to demonstrate that terrorism is not an effective tool to achieve political objectives. Max Abrahams noted that while the prevailing view in international relations is that terrorism can be an effective coercive strategy, he observed that there is scant empirical research to support this thesis. This view of terrorism being an effective tool has stemmed from a lack of robust evidence based on game-theoretic models, single case studies, or a handful of well-known terrorist victories.[24] Abrahams' study of data on 28 terrorist groups showed that only 7 per cent of the groups accomplished their policy objectives. This is considerably less than the success of countries imposing economic sanctions on a country of 34 per cent according to an authoritative study.[25] Abrahams concludes that terrorist groups rarely achieve their policy objectives and the poor success rate is inherent to the tactic of terrorism itself.[26]

Those who contend that terrorism is an effective strategy include Robert Pape who believes that the tactic of suicide terrorism has increased in its use due to groups recognising that 'it pays'. Six of the 13 terrorist campaigns he examined led to 'significant policy change in the target state'.[27] Pape concluded that in four of his studies, the target government's policy changes were clearly due to the coercive pressure of the terrorist group.[28] For instance, the withdrawal of US and French forces in Lebanon in 1983 following the suicide bombing of US Marines barracks in Beirut. Pape does admit that suicide terrorism can only coerce states to abandon limited or modest goals, for instance, withdrawing from territory of low strategic importance, and attacks are unlikely to cause the target to abandon goals central to their wealth and security.[29] Max Abrahams contends that Pape's argument lacks empirical evidence by only examining a few cases covering three countries, and does not examine whether terrorist groups achieved their core policy objectives.[30]

N. O. Berry suggests that terrorism can be effective 'when the target of terrorism acts in such a manner that it either loses public support for its political position or it lessens its own political capabilities'.[31] Therefore 'terrorists must know or manipulate the target's psychological perceptions to induce it to act in the way it is predisposed to act'.[32] This includes over-reaction by the target that can cause the loss of public support. If the target is unable to respond effectively to the threat, then it can lose the support of the public and reduce the government's ability to counter terrorism in the future. Banning political parties and arresting protestors can cause moderates to sympathise more or join the terrorists' cause. However Neumann and Smith suggest that the need for terrorists groups to escalate their campaign to make the targeted political authority respond in a way that can be exploited prevents terrorist groups from 'acquiring the perceived legitimacy sought in the target audience or even cause their own destruction'.[33] For this reason, strategic terrorism is a 'flawed strategy'.[34]

The limited value of terrorism as a coercive tool is underpinned by the societal resilience to attacks being greater than might otherwise be expected. Paul Wilkinson rightly pointed out that there are three assumptions about human behaviour that are either false or unproven. First, the persons faced with threats to safety will ultimately surrender their allegiances, principles or beliefs to save themselves; second, terrorism invariably leads to terrorisation of the target and victims; third, when the targeted populace has been exposed to a given quotient of coercive intimidation they will inevitably suffer a collapse of will and submit to their persecutors.[35] For these reasons, Paul Wilkinson believes terrorism as a tool of coercion has limited use, although its prolonged and intensive use can be very damaging to the democratic governments and societies that experience it.[36]

Disorientation

Unlike conventional warfare, terrorism has a strong psychological dimension that seeks to undermine societal, political and economic stability. John Garnett's observation on the utility of warfare is aptly suited for studying terrorism noting that 'human beings, their property, and the society they live in are easily destroyed. It is this fragility of human beings and their artefacts which is exploited by those who wield military power'.[37] Neumann and Smith believe that terrorism is above all a form of psychological warfare where the 'aim of the strategy of terrorism is not to kill or destroy but to break the spirit and create a sensation of fear within a target group, which will initiate political change'.[38] The intent of undermining and disrupting the stability of the target's society through terror generated by indiscriminate attacks is to coerce them into acceding to terrorists' demands. The field of terrorism in international relations posits that putting the targeted populace 'into a state of chronic fear' as Alex Schmid and Albert Jongman call it, causes disorientation.[39]

A main aim of this study is to further the international relations understanding of disorientation to explore to what degree terrorists attacks can dislocate society, a key component of a terrorist *modus operandi* (method of operating). A succinct approach to understanding how disorientation fits

into the wider context of terrorism strategy is presented by Peter Neumann
and Martin Smith. Focusing on non-state terrorist groups, they note terrorism has three distinct modus operandi:

1 Disorientation: to alienate the authorities from their citizens.
2 Target response: to induce a target to respond in a manner that is
favourable to the insurgent cause.
3 Gain legitimacy: to exploit the emotional impact of the violence to
insert an alternative political message.[40]

Neumann and Smith defined the objective of disorientation as 'to alienate
the authorities from their citizens, reducing the government to impotence in
the eyes of the population, which will be perceived as unable to cope with a
situation of evolving chaos.'[41]

The concept of disorientation has long been established in the terrorism
field. Grant Wardlaw argued that a main aim of terrorism is to 'divide the
mass society from the incumbent authorities'. He added that on one level,
terrorism seeks to 'disorient the population by showing that the government
is unable to fulfil primary security functions for its subjects: that is the provision of safety and order. On a deeper level, however, the aim is to isolate
the citizen from his or her social context.'[42] The success of disorientation
comes when 'the individual is so isolated as to be unable to draw strength
from usual social supports and is cast entirely upon his or her own
resources'.[43] Similarly, Thomas Thornton noted that the aim is to 'break the
tie that binds the mass to the incumbents within the society, and remove
the structural supports that give society its strength'.[44]

Through 'disorientation' terrorists can force authorities to impose
counter-terrorist measures that may curtail a population's freedom and civil
liberties. Grant Wardlaw remarked that pursuance of such security would
also 'raise the level of fear in the community as the impression of being
under siege would inevitably be intensified', and that 'such fear would obvi-
ously motivate some people to change their lifestyles to avoid what they see
as dangers and overall the quality of life would be adversely effected'.[45] In
the extreme form a climate of fear caused by terrorism could lead to what
Harvey Griesman called 'closure of society' where the mere threat of terrorism can trigger responses with widespread ramifications.[46] Paul Wilkinson
stated that when terrorism becomes severe and protracted it can present a
serious challenge to the well-being and security of local communities or
even entire nation states, as in Peru, Lebanon and Sri Lanka during their
experiences of extensive terrorism.[47]

A fundamental part of terrorism aimed at causing disorientation is the
perpetrators' ability to instil the fear of the unknown about when and where
the next attack might take place and what form it might take. As Schelling
observed, 'Strategy is not concerned with the efficient *application* of force but
with the *exploitation of potential force*'.[48] Schelling adds that 'most conflict

situations are essentially bargaining situations. They are situations in which the ability of one participant to gain his ends is dependent to an important degree on the choices or decisions that the other participant will make'.[49] With terrorism ultimately being a psychological mind-game, it is this fear of the unknown that can have the greatest effect in instilling disorientation and the closure of society as the public has to adapt to the ongoing terrorism threat. A well-thought-out terrorist campaign could then engender a continuous, high level of anxiety through vague warnings and unpredictable attacks which could make the targeted society more susceptible to the political message espoused by the terrorists' form of political discourse.[50] To use Schelling's expression, terrorists ultimately seek to make the possibility of non-capitulation 'terrible beyond endurance'.[51] However, very seldom can this ultimate end result be achieved. As Schmid and Jongman noted, 'non-state terrorist organisations are rarely able to develop a level of activity which places sectors of the public in constant fear of sudden victimisation'.[52]

To understand the coercive potential and the public's resilience to systemic and enduring terrorist campaigns, the terrorism literature has often made references to and drawn conclusions from civilian responses to aerial bombardment, in particular the Second World War strategic bombing campaigns. Grant Wardlaw examined individual reactions to stress caused by air raids to determine the possible psychological reactions to the varying duration and magnitude of terrorism. Neumann and Smith believe that evidence from aerial bombardment suggests that people can even adjust to high levels of violence and physical threat.[53] While such an approach is valid, the lack of available quantitative evidence from the Second World War constrains the utility of these comparisons. This book, though, addresses this gap through examining the Israelis' response to the Iraqi missile strikes during the 1991 Gulf War where there is extensive quantitative evidence to draw inferences and further inform thinking strategic on terrorism.

Despite the recognition that terrorism seeks to cause the 'closure of society' or 'disorientation' through repression combined with the onset of fear and anxiety in the targeted populace, quantifying the latter aspects can provide a detailed understanding of how these processes work. However, no previous study has set out to successfully achieve this combined with the area of risk analysis in a single volume. While the literature has developed a comprehensive framework to outline the functioning and utility of terrorism, this approach needs to be investigated further to assess to what degree disorientation is effective, and therefore address the conflicting arguments that prevail over the efficacy of terrorism.

This book seeks to significantly further the understanding of the target's behavioural response through understanding what type and degree of disorientation takes place, and how actions by a government (e.g. their law enforcement and public health authorities) may amplify or attenuate the terror of terrorism. To state that terrorism is not an effective strategy with the exception of specific circumstances overlooks the finer details of the situation. Current thinking on terrorism strategy and its consequences needs to gain greater sensitivity to its effects. It is contended here that a more subtle effect of disorientation occurs through individuals changing their behaviours and attitudes to reduce the perceived risks of terrorism. While for the majority these adverse responses are short term, there can be a large proportion who continue to change their day-to-day routines in the subsequent months and years. The level of disorientation is not necessarily sufficient to cause significant political change in line with a terrorist group's political agenda. Instead the terror of terrorism may undermine the safety and well-being of individuals by convincing them to take actions that could cause additional casualties separate to those directly caused by a terrorist attack. Given the importance of resilience and recovery, understanding these subtleties can reduce the damage that terrorism can cause to society. While the psychological effects are more pervasive and complex than might otherwise be regarded, there are a series of recommendations through the field of risk analysis that can reduce these adverse effects – and in turn further reduce the ability of terrorist groups to coerce their target into acceding to their political objectives.

Psychiatry

Psychiatry is the study of mental disorders and their diagnosis, management and prevention. The Diagnostic and Statistical Manual (DSM) of Disorders is a diagnostic tool of the profession together with the ICD-10 of behaviour disorders. Within the medical literature, psychiatry terms have been defined for disorders based on an individual's physiological and psychological symptoms.

Definitions

The following medical definitions originate from the *Stedman's Medical Dictionary* (27th edition) that focuses on the physiological conditions and the *Psychiatric Dictionary* (7th edition) that looks at both physiological and psychological attributes. This illustrates the differing interpretations dependent upon the physiological and psychological symptoms exhibited. With much of the literature used in this study taken from the medical science, the terms fear, panic and anxiety refer to the following.

There are two types of anxiety. One is a normal response to uncertainty designed to make individuals alert and ready for action, and the other is a pathological form which exists when circumstances do not warrant heightened alertness. The Yerkes–Dobson law of 1908 demonstrates both aspects of anxiety in relation to performance.[54]

According to Stedman anxiety is fear or apprehension or dread of impending danger, the symptoms of which are restlessness, tension, tachycardia and dyspnoea unattached to a clearly identifiable stimulus.[55] Fear is apprehension, dread and/or alarm having an identifiable stimulus. It is differentiated from anxiety which has no easily identifiable stimulus.[56] 'Panic' meanwhile is defined as 'extreme and unreasoning anxiety and fear, often accompanied by disturbed breathing, increased heart activity, vasomotor changes, sweating, and a feeling of dread'.[57] In these definitions, Stedman focuses very much on the physiological symptoms, whereas this book is very much interested in the psychological and behavioural symptoms. The latter can be found in the *Psychiatric Dictionary* (7th edition) by Robert Jean Campbell. While noting similar physiological conditions, the *Psychiatric Dictionary* adds that for anxiety, the psychological aspect includes:

> Specific conscious inner attitude and a peculiar feeling state characterised by
>
> 1   A physically as well as mentally painful awareness of being powerless to do anything about a personal matter
> 2   Presentiment of an impending and almost inevitable danger.
> 3   A tense and physically exhausting alertness as if facing an emergency.
> 4   An apprehensive self-absorption which interferes with an effective and advantageous solution of reality-problems.
> 5   An irresolvable doubt concerning the nature of the threatening evil, concerning the probability of the actual appearance of the threat, concerning the best objective means of reducing or removing the evil, and concerning one's subjective capacity for making effective use of those means if and when an emergency arises.[58]

Campbell goes on to say that anxiety is differentiated from fear, which lacks characteristics four and five. Fear is a reaction to a real or threatened danger, whereas anxiety is more typically a reaction to an unreal or imagined danger.

Panic, according to Campbell, is seen as an 'overwhelming anxiety; panic attack'. A panic attack is defined as an episode of intense anxiety or fear in which symptoms develop suddenly and reach a crescendo, usually within ten minutes. In addition to the physiological symptoms noted by Stedman, a panic attack also includes according to Campbell a 'fear of dying, and a fear of "losing my mind" or of doing something uncontrolled'.[59] The latter part is important as it infers that the individual suffering from a panic attack loses effective cognitive function and the ability to rationally process and act upon their surroundings leading to unreasoning behaviour. According to the mental health literature, it is rare for individuals to panic until they believe there is no escape from a life-threatening situation. Simon Wessely noted that 'people generally don't panic in the face of adversity – unless they are caught in confined spaces without any visible means of escape.'[60] David Alexander and Susan Klein caution that panic should not be confused with mass anxiety because the latter can lead to constructive action.[61]

Clinical syndromes

Illan Kutz and Avraham Bleich outline four main stages of clinical syndromes following a conventional and non-conventional terrorist attack.[62] Acute Stress Reaction (ASR), Acute Stress Disorder (ASD), acute Post Traumatic Disorder (PTSD), and then delayed-onset of PTSD. ASR occurs up to the first 48 hours. This criterion is taken from the International Statistical Classification of Diseases and Related Health Problems (ICD-10) of behaviour disorders.[63] The coding system for ICD-10 is compatible with DSM-IV.[64] Second is ASD. Drawn from the DSM-IV classification, this occurs from the second day through to the fourth week. Acute PTSD is from one to three months. Delayed-onset PTSD is six months on. Not all the surveys used in the following pages follow these criteria. While the PTSD criteria is utilised in all the case studies, ASR and ASD is used mainly in the Israeli studies.

PTSD entails a series of physiological and psychological symptoms. According to DSM-IV-TR, there are six criteria that must be met for an individual to be diagnosed as having PTSD. Stressor criteria (Criteria A) state that an individual needs to have experienced, witnessed or been confronted with an event that involved actual or threatened death or serious injury, threat to physical integrity of the individual or those around him. Re-experiencing criteria (Criteria B) list five possible symptoms of distress of which only one needs to be met for an individual to be classified as meeting these criteria. Symptoms include recurring, intense psychological distress at exposure to internal or external clues that symbolise or resemble an aspect of the trauma. Avoidance symptomatology criteria (Criteria) are divided into effortful avoidance and numbing/dissociation. These include efforts to avoid conversations, thoughts or activities related to the trauma; and an inability to recall parts of the trauma. Symptoms of physiological arousal (Criteria) require two or more symptoms that include the following: difficulty falling or staying asleep, irritability or outbursts of anger; difficulty in concentrating; hype-vigilance; and exaggerated startled response. The fifth criteria (Criteria E) require symptoms of B, C and D to persist for at least a month. The sixth criteria (Criteria F) state that all symptoms must impair the individual's social or occupational functioning. Mild or occasional symptoms that are short-lived and/or do not interfere with the person's life should be considered as falling in the range of normal reactions to stressful events. Those who exhibit insufficient or short-term PTSD B, C, D symptom criteria but still have a clinically significant response to a trauma can be classified as having Acute Stress Disorder.[65]

This book also uses the term probable PTSD. This is where the diagnosis of PTSD is made on the basis of screening instruments (e.g. a random digit telephone survey) rather than comprehensive clinical evaluations. This entails a PTSD Check List (PCL) which is a self-report measure developed for use when administration of a structured clinical interview is not feasible.[66]

One factor that needs to be considered is the distinction between medically unexplained symptoms (the somatisation of distress) and PTSD. Somatisation is when physical symptoms develop through stress or emotional problems. This is sometimes referred to as the 'worried well' or mass psychogenic illness. This entails individuals experience unexplained functional or psychological symptoms that are not PTSD. An example of this is the 1995 sarin attack where the reported ratio of those who sought medical help to those who required immediate medical care was approximately 450:1.[67] This presents challenges to the medical profession where there might be different interpretations of causation compared to the patients' understanding that they have been exposed to a contaminant when in fact physiologically they are fine. Robert E. Bartholomew and Simon Wessely referred to the presence of extraordinary anxiety with symptoms spread via sight, sound or oral communication as mass psychogenic illness. They observed that, 'No one is immune from mass psychogenic illness because humans continually construct reality and the perceived danger needs only to be plausible in order to gain acceptance within a particular group and generate anxiety'.[68] These fear-generated responses of mass psychogenic illness, mass hysteria, and the worried well have also been referred to as outbreaks of multiple unexplained symptoms (OMUS).[69] These fear responses tend to increase when non-conventional weapons are used. While the term 'worried well' has frequently been employed to describe the arrival of those at medical facilities who incorrectly believe they need treatment, Ross Pastel cautions against using this term as it suggests symptoms are not real but exist only in the mind, whereas individuals are suffering from real symptoms that cause real pain and real distress.[70] Instead, Pastel recommends, a non-judgemental term that does not imply mental illness or weakness should be used, for instance OMUS.

While the DSM criteria can serve as a useful comparison tool of data across the case studies where research using this approach has been undertaken, there is concern that using a checklist of symptoms can lead to the medicalisation of symptoms, rather than to looking at the causes of symptoms which may be regarded as normal responses. In addition, the expansion of PTSD to include subsyndromal or partial PTSD has come under criticism, which centres on the concern that liberalising the diagnostic criteria threatens to dissolve the border between disease and normative stress reactions.[71] Therefore it needs to be considered whether the statistical evidence for PTSD and related symptoms might be greater than it actually should be.

Psychology – risk analysis

Psychology is the study of people: how they think, how they act, react and interact. This book is concerned with a particular area of psychology called risk analysis that has generated a significant amount of literature from a range of studies. There are three areas of risk analysis that will be used extensively. First, risk perception. Second, risk communication and best practices for its implementation. Third, the social amplification of risk model. The three are interlinked as the interpretation by individuals of risks posed by terrorism is influenced by risk communication, institutions and groups that would be involved before, during and after terrorist attacks. This includes alert advisories and government guidance on preparedness through to information on what the public should do during and after an attack.

Risk perception

The study of risk perception aims to understand why individuals perceive certain risks and activities to be more or less risky than statistics suggest. Identifying, characterising and quantifying risk enables one to explore how people perceive and respond to risks (risk perception). This in turn provides a basis for improving dialogue with the public (risk communication)[72] Where the perception of risk is greater than the actual risk, individuals tend to 'overreact' despite evidence and reassurances by experts that a particular risk is minimal or unlikely.[73]

Defining risk is a complex task because it means different things to different audiences. According to Paul Slovic, risk, in the view of experts, correlates highly with technical estimates of annual fatalities. For lay people risk could mean assessing annual fatalities and producing their own estimates. However, the lay person's judgements of risk are more closely related to other hazard characteristics, like catastrophic potential and threat to future generations. As a result the public's perceptions differ from experts' estimates of annual fatalities.[74] A risk perceived by individuals that includes the attributes of catastrophic potential, threat to future generations and being involuntary is called 'dread risk'.

This framework can help to explain why the public is not prone to panic during and following a terrorist attack, but can calmly undertake activities that, while reducing the perceived risk of terrorism can in certain circumstances increase their exposure to another risk. This in turn can inform us on the utility of terrorism as a tool of coercion through influencing the targeted public's behaviours and attitudes, and whether this may be in line with the intended strategic goals of the terrorists of achieving their political objectives. Brooke Rogers citing Fullerton noted that risk of terrorism can be distinguished from other risks, such as man-made or natural disasters, by 'characteristic extensive fear, loss of confidence in institutions, unpredictability and pervasive experience of loss of safety'.[75]

The risk perception literature provides a valuable insight into what makes the public undertake the actions they do based on their own perceived risks versus actual risks. Studies have used this general approach and theoretical framework in what is called the psychometric paradigm. This framework assumes that risk is subjectively defined by individuals who may be influenced by a wide array of psychological, social, institutional and cultural factors. The risk matrices of the psychometric paradigm are discussed in detail below with reference to Figure 2.1. This approach enables one to question and understand why certain individuals tend not to react strongly to a particular risk that might be present in everyday life, while 'over-reacting' to risks that are statistically highly unlikely. This includes the role of affect in linking risk to emotions like fear.

One of the key developers in this area is Paul Slovic who noted that risk perception is both analytical and affective, which offers an explanation of why the public's fears sometimes do not seem to correlate with the facts.[76] Analytical perception is when individuals make judgements about a risk by analysing the available information (logical and reasoned assessments and the scientific aspects of hazard management). Affective perception is when the individuals' perception of danger is an initial, fast, intuitive reaction. Individuals use affect to see risk as feelings: the goodness or badness of risk posed by undertaking a certain activity.[77] Individuals tend to base their risk judgements on the feelings created in response to the risk, meaning that the majority of risk evaluations are formed rapidly and automatically.[78][9] Slovic *et al.* attribute this to the role of affect, which helps to link the assessment of risk to emotions such as fear.[79] Rogers *et al.* believes that 'risk as feelings' is crucial to terrorism, as it is likely that it has the strongest influence on public perceptions to the threat of terrorism. A lay person's risk perception is comprised of a number of factors as listed below, that cause a gap between actual and perceived risk.

While the research and literature on risk perception grew outside the terrorism area, its features provide considerable value to assessing people's responses to terrorism. According to the risk analysis literature, risk perception is influenced by ten factors:

1 Control (individuals are less afraid of risks they feel they have some control over, like driving and skiing).
2 Dread (if individuals see a risk as uncontrollable, a high risk to future generations and involuntary, like terrorism).
3 Choice (if individuals can choose what activity to pursue).
4 Involvement of children.
5 The risk is new (if the risk to the populace has not been identified, or existed before hand).
6 Whether the risk is natural or human-made.
7 Whether there is prior awareness or knowledge of the risk.
8 Risk benefit trade-off (weighing the risks against the rewards).
9 Trust (the degree to which individuals trust the institution(s) or product(s) in question).
10 Proximity to the risk (fear of personally becoming or of someone you care about becoming a victim of terrorism where the terrorism threat is perceived to be directed at your own homeland rather than abroad

at 'someone else', e.g. embassy or military personnel deployed over-seas.[80]

Accumulatively these factors can lead the risk scholar to define and plot perceived hazards and risks, as defined by the public, on a grid with an x axis that goes from non-dread to dread risks and y axis from known to unknown risks.[81] Non-dread risks are those perceived to be more control-lable, low risk to future generations and not affecting themselves (for instance familiar items like using home appliances). Dread risks are those seen as uncontrollable, high risk to future generations and involuntary (like nuclear weapons). The y axis has unknown risk that is not observable, unknown to those exposed and delayed effects (e.g. nitrates or carcinogenic compounds). Known risk is observable, old risks and risks known to science (for instance driving a car). According to a study by Slovic, Fischhoff and Lichtenstein, terrorism falls into a quadrant of dread risk and known risk (leaning towards the unknown quadrant). In comparison, nuclear power is seen as both – dread risk and unknown risk.[82] It is worth noting that these studies were undertaken in the US and prior to 9/11. Consequently, the hazard of terrorism on the grid may have changed slightly in the post-9/11 environment. Figure 2.1 shows a risk matrix with terrorism capitalised. This illustrates the perceived levels of unknown and dread risk elements of various activities and hazards that influence public perceptions.

Risk perceptions are influenced by past experiences and pre-existing knowledge, and communications and messages received. This then frames individual perceptions of perceived benefit or perceived risk, and whether the benefits might be high or low. For instance, activities perceived as favourable like driving a car are likely to be seen as of low risk and high benefit as individuals feel they are more in control, while negatively per-ceived activities are likely to be seen as higher risk and lower gain, and less controllable. Terrorism is a particularly complex hazard for individuals to interpret and respond to because, as Slovic remarks, 'it comes from the intentions of other people, and those are hard to understand.'[83] Unlike the study of risks of environmental pollution, nuclear power and activities like driving and diving, the hazard of terrorism by its very nature is stochastic, being difficult to determine when, where, and what type of attack may occur. For these reasons terrorism is seen as a dread risk.

Analysing the risk perceptions of the public prior to and during terrorist attacks is complicated by the limited risk analysis literature specifically on terrorism since this type of research had only gained pace post 9/11. Lennart Sjoberg noted that although there lacks material on risk perceptions and ter-rorism prior to 9/11, the psychometric model still provides some explana-tory power for understanding terrorism.[84]

Critical to this study is that these perceptions can influence people's behaviours following a terrorist attack (e.g. avoidance reactions to perceived higher risk and lower gain activities). Viewing risk perception this way

Figure 2.1 Risk matrix that plots the level of perceived concern generated by various risks.

Note

The figure only contains 32 of the perceived hazards and risks drawn from the original diagram.

suggests that the feeling (affect) precedes risk evaluation. This is referred to as the affect heuristic, which suggests that the perception of risk can be influenced by the information provided on the perceived benefit or perceived risk.[85] This has implications for risk communication as discussed in the next section.

Given that the majority of the case studies will not have risk analysis literature to draw upon, the following pages will instead develop findings from assessing available data from other secondary sources to establish what risk perceptions might have been evident among individuals before, during and after the strategic terror event. For example, the familiarity of the risks in the populace subjected to strategic terrorism will be judged by their previous experience of the type of attacks discussed, their frequency, location, and the means that were used (e.g. conventional or non-conventional weapons). These aspects will be documented in sources that extend from mental health studies, opinion polls, media articles covering first-hand accounts and information provided by public health and government authorities. A chronology of events will also be offered. The model will also assess how risk communication before, during and after an attack may have amplified or reduced individuals' risk perceptions. This aspect will dovetail into the social amplification of risk and risk communication sections.

Despite the best endeavours to understand the likely perceived risks of the targeted populace in the case studies, the conclusions drawn here on dread and known risks will not be as robust as would be found in controlled studies and surveys that formed the psychometric paradigm framework and risk matrices. In an ideal environment studies would have been conducted at the time of the attacks. This type of risk perception study requires appropriate design of survey instruments to quantify and model the various factors and their interrelationships to capture the responses of individuals and their societies to the hazards that confront them.[86] Of the five case studies, various types of risk analysis surveys on terrorism were primarily developed following the 9/11 and anthrax attacks. It is intended that the conclusions drawn regarding dread/non-dread and known/unknown risks will serve as a guide to illustrate the possible differing risk perceptions that may well have occurred.

For the purpose of the book and to enable a realistic comparison of risk perceptions within and across the case studies, it shall be assumed that the perceived risk of terrorism will probably remain in the dread/unknown risk quadrant of the risk matrix (bottom right-hand corner). However, within this quadrant, reference will be made to how the risk may have moved along the dread/non-dread risk x axis, and the known/unknown risk y axis. For instance, how the public's perceived risk during a prolonged terrorist campaign could become more of a known risk and less of a dread risk through their greater familiarity and adaptation to the threat. With the aforementioned considerations, reasonable assumptions can be drawn in the absence of rigorous data to provide a good indication of the likely risk perceptions of the public before, during and after a strategic terror event.

Risk communication

Risk communication can be an essential tool to reduce the adverse changes in behaviours and attitudes by individuals following a terrorist strike. Risk communication stemmed from the area of risk perception informed by work on natural hazards by Gilbert White, and that of Baruch Fischoff, Paul Slovic and others on technological hazards in the 1970s.[87] The risk literature suggests that risk communication should be a two-way interchange between source organisations and those, including the public and its representatives, who are the intended recipients of risk messages.[88] According to the US National Research Council risk communication is defined as an 'interactive process of exchange of information and opinion among individuals, groups and institutions.'[89] However, this definition lacks sufficient context in risk to fit with risk perception and risk management. The definition of risk communication that shall be used here is Baruch Fischhoff's. This is 'creating two-way channels, in which recipients are treated like partners, shaping how risks are managed and sharing what is learned about them'.[90] Ragnar Lofstedt noted that at its best, 'risk communication is not a top-down communication from expert to the lay public, but rather a constructive dialogue between all those involved in a particular debate about risk'.[91] Risk communication research has been used in various areas covering mainly natural and technological hazards including food safety, regulation, environmental policy and nuclear power.[92]

Following a terrorist attack it is essential that authorities take immediate steps to reduce fear and anxiety through sound risk communication. The longer the delay, the more fear can grow.[93] Government leaders and spokespersons need to have an understanding of at least the fundamentals of risk communication. Incorporating the findings of risk communication in to terrorism research can provide a guide to which issues will get out of hand or escape attention, in the absence of deliberate competent communication.[94]

While the vast majority of the risk communication literature has been developed outside the terrorism area, a leading writer on this subject matter, Baruch Fischhoff, has adapted the research to terrorism. Fischhoff noted that as terror caused by terrorism is a continuous 'mind game', punctuated by events with horrific consequences, counter-terrorism involves a battle of wits, for the hearts and minds of civilian populations.[95] Incompetent risk communication can further terrorists' short- and long-term goals, therefore communicating effectively about risks is one element of that battle. Fischhoff outlines three principles for effective risk communication.

> First, manage risk well – so as to have a credible message to communicate. If terror seems to be managed poorly in other ways (messages being 'spun' or inconsistent policies like alert levels and advisories), then the credibility of communications will suffer and their messages may prompt further scepticism. Second, create appropriate communication

channels. Having appropriate channels should increase public confidence by demonstrating that a common framework underlies preparation, alert, crisis, and recovery plans. Third, deliver decision-relevant information, concisely and comprehensibly. This entails a study of what the public already knows, and then the design (and evaluation) of communications bridging critical gaps. How people will evacuate, respond, seek medical treatment or change their daily lives to mitigate the threat of strategic terrorism is shaped by risk communication.[96]

Maintaining the credibility of communications and ensuring the public has trust in those delivering the messages is essential for effective risk communication. Brooke Rogers noted that 'trust is believed to reduce social uncertainty and complexity, and influence risk perceptions and acceptance of risks'.[97] Trust has been examined extensively in risk analysis and is seen as essential to risk communication.[98] The lack of trust can cause individuals to view certain risks as greater than they are, or to lose confidence in those leading and developing policy. This process is often referred to as the social amplification of risk which is discussed in a later section. For terrorism, the public's lack of trust and confidence in their government and authorities can exacerbate the 'disorientation' effect of terrorist attacks. This can lead to the public not supporting government counterterrorism measures or stance through to it failing to adhere to health and security advice during or after a terrorist attack.

Research on the affect heuristic in risk perception has provided additional attributes to consider when conducting risk communication. Slovic *et al.* observe that 'if the general affective view guides perceptions of risk and benefit, providing information about benefit should change perception of risk and vice versa'.[99] Therefore information stating that benefit would be high for a particular type of technology or activity would lead to more positive overall affect that would, in turn, decrease perceived risk. Slovic used the affect heuristic to explain why people are sensitive to different forms of risk communication. Studies have shown that risk communication formats that produce more affect-laden imagery (caused by information presented using scenarios and anecdotes) induces a higher level of perceived risk than risk communication that evokes no affect.[100] Carmen Keller *et al.* suggest that as feelings and affect are important factors that increase or decrease perceived risks, affect, therefore, should be taken into account for successful risk communication.[101] The manner in which risks are presented can either decrease or increase the levels of perceived risk and subsequently influence the behaviours and attitudes of individuals. There are two types of risk message to consider that provide a more detailed background to risk communication: informing and influencing.

Informing and influencing

The goals of risk communication and risk messages are either to inform the public (informed consent, or decision support) or influence the target audience (such as public health advocacy).[102] There are ethical issues, however, with regard to the appropriateness of employing influencing risk messages. For instance, is it right that public agencies disseminate messages aimed at changing the public's behaviour? Persuasive messages are deemed acceptable when, for example, they are constructed by public health communicators as they are rarely controversial. Their values are fundamental to society (live long and healthy lives) and often advocate individual rather than societal action.[103] Informed consent/decision support is to inform about decision risks without advocating a specific position or action.[104] The recipient is only likely to listen and take on board the message if they have the desire to do so (because they are facing a threat), the message is suitably designed for them, and their environment and context do not contradict or negate the message (no barriers). When it comes to informing choices, a risk message cannot be regarded as successful by whether it influenced an individual to change their behaviour. An individual informed of the risks, may continue to choose to engage in hazardous behaviour such as smoking, or driving without using a seatbelt.[105] Messages are more effective in achieving a behaviour change when, in addition to producing understanding, they are specific about any desired response and proximate in time and place to that response.[106] These attributes could be essential for risk communication when responding to a terrorism threat where variations in responses could be sought on depending when and where people reside in proximity to the threat.

Risk communication can entail both informing and persuading risk messages depending on the stage of the terrorism incident (prior, during or after an attack). Informing could include providing the public with information regarding the threat level in certain geographical areas, the type of threat a country could face and actions they could take to reduce the risk of an attack. The latter would include reporting suspicious packages, or the avoidance of certain travel destinations, or possible self-protection measures people could embark on following a large-scale conventional or chemical, biological, radiological (CBR) attack. It is important that the risk communicator does not attempt to disguise the message as information on a person's choices when actually its target is to change behaviour.[107] To do so would undermine the trust and credibility of the risk communicator. Behavioural changes (or fair participation), rely on a minimum of trust among the communicators in order to be effective.[108] The communicator therefore needs to ensure that informing messages are not interpreted as messages of persuasion.

Risk messages for persuasion could include preparations for a possible attack (for instance Israelis being instructed to prepare a sealed room prior to Iraqi Scud missile strikes in 1991) and measures the public needs to take to safeguard themselves and others around them following a conventional or CBR attack. These could include vaccination strategies, the distribution of antibiotics, decontamination measures, emergency response centres and evacuation plans. In such cases it would be imperative for the risk messages to effectively influence people's behaviour and attitude where their health and the health of others are at risk. This would fall under what Ann Bostrom refers to as public health advocacy where the priority of the risk communication is to influence the behaviour of the target audience to reduce health risks and persuade people to take actions that improve their well-being.[109] When the threat to the public's health subsides (e.g. those exposed to a CBR attack have been treated and no further contamination/exposure is likely to occur or an area that has been bombed is declared safe to return to), the risk messages could then revert to informing. This could include information on which areas are safe to return to after a CBR event, encouraging the public to re-use transport means previously targeted by terrorists (e.g. airlines) and addressing public concerns that a decontaminated area is safe. In all these cases the authorities would not look to influence the public's behaviour but to inform people adequately of the debate so that they make their own choices, to encourage appropriate risk framing. This does not require individuals knowing everything about an issue but just enough to be able to make appropriate choices.[110]

A point to consider is that communication using fear arousal does not increase the effectiveness of the risk messages, but actually interferes with their overall success. According to a study by Irving Janis and Seymour Feshbach, when a mass communication is designed to influence an audience to adopt specific ways and means of averting a threat, the use of a strong fear appeal, as against a milder one, increases the likelihood that the audience will be left in a state of emotional tension which is not fully relieved by rehearsing the reassuring recommendations contained in the communication.[111] In addition, when fear is strongly aroused but is not fully relieved by the reassurances contained in a mass communication, the audience will become motivated to ignore or to minimise the importance of the threat.[112] These findings suggest that risk communication messages to counter the terror of terrorism need to ensure that they aim for a relatively low degree of fear arousal as that is likely to be the optimal level, and not play up ominous threats, alarming contingencies, or signs of impending danger.[113] Combined with excessive precautionary measures, this can create further anxiety and avoidant behaviour.[114]

Examples of inadequate risk communication

To illustrate the key elements of risk communication in terrorism, the material below considers two incidences where poor risk communication by authorities led to adverse reactions from the public. These are the Swedish Acrylamide alarm in 2002 and the BSE beef scare in Britain during the early to mid-1990s. In the first example, in April 2002 the Swedish National Food Administration (SNFA) and researchers at Stockholm University (SU) announced in a press release 20 hours ahead of a press conference that their research revealed fried and baked foods such as potatoes and bread contained more than 500 times the permitted amount of Acrylamide, a known cause of cancer. The gap between the press release invitation and the actual press conference led the media to speculate, develop myths and worry leading to alarmist headlines in the following morning's newspapers. Three days after the press conference sales of chips fell by 30–50 per cent, and 40 per cent two weeks later despite no SNFA consumer advice to withdraw the products.[115] From a risk communication point of view, Ragnar Lofstedt concludes that the SNFA and SU press release was poorly worded and ideally the initial announcement of their findings should have been made at the press conference to reassure the public as was originally planned, rather than causing some public concern.

The second example is the Bovine Spongiform Encephalopathy (BSE) disease in British cattle. The British government from the mid-1980s through to the 1990s sought to reassure the public about the safety of British beef by maintaining a 'no risk' message that beef was perfectly safe. By doing this they underestimated the public's ability to deal with risk and created an information vacuum. According to Douglas Powell and William Leiss who examined the BSE episode, the BSE risk messages from industry and government never included timely references to the latest scientific developments and they consistently failed to acknowledge both the content and context of the evolving public concerns about BSE risks.[116] Consequently, despite continued reassurances, the public lost trust in the government and the food industry leading to a dramatic drop in beef consumption. This culminated in late 1995 when beef consumption dropped by 20 per cent, the equivalent of 1.4 million households no longer buying beef, and thousands of schools taking beef off the menu.[117]

It is worth noting that employing the principles of risk communication to terror situations does have limitations. Unlike the non-terror environment of BSE or the Measles, Mumps and Rubella (MMR) vaccine public scare in relation to autism in the UK, risk communication in the context of terrorism needs to consider that providing information on the nature of the threat could in turn cause the source of the risk to alter behaviour (i.e the terrorist group). Lawrence Freedman notes that risk communication needs to consider a number of factors, observing:

> The inherent uncertainty in the information, the ability of the attackers to adjust their behaviour on the basis of what the defenders have revealed about their state of preparedness, and the fact that warnings have political, economic and social effects even when no attack materializes, must affect the calculations which lead to warning events.[118]

However, risk communication is more than alerting the public to threats and attacks: it is also concerned with informing the public of preparations, crisis and recovery plans, and how they could engage with authorities including the emergency services and public health bodies. Effective risk communication in recovery plans is particularly needed where issues of short- and long-term contamination are involved or when many people deliberately avoid previously targeted transport systems.

Risk characterisation

Effective communication requires successful risk characterisation that identifies the risk and frames the means of communicating with the public. Risk characterisation is designed to improve the understanding of risk among public officials and interested and affected parties (including the public) in a way that leads to better and more widely accepted risk decisions.

According to the US National Research Council, there are seven principles for implementing the process of risk characterisation as listed below. Risk characterisation should be a decision-driven activity, directed toward informing choices and solving problems. This entails describing the potentially hazardous situation accurately, and addressing the significant concerns of the interested and affected parties. The information provided should be understandable and accessible to all those involved in the process from, for instance, authorities, the public, and interest groups including industry, lobbying groups, and the media. The extract below lists the seven key characteristics of risk characterisation.[119]

> A risk characterisation is part of a process that begins with the formulation of a problem (the likelihood of harm) and ends with a decision.
>
> Second, coping with risk situations requires a broad understanding of the relevant losses, or consequences to the interested and affected parties.
>
> Third, it is the outcome of an analytic–deliberative process that depends on systematic analysis that is appropriate to the problem, responds to the needs of the interested and affected parties, and treats uncertainties of importance to the decision problem in a comprehensible way.
>
> Fourth, this early inclusion and representation of interested and affected parties is imperative.
>
> Fifth, deliberation (that frames analysis) and analysis (that informs deliberation) are complementary and must be integrated throughout.
>
> Sixth, those responsible for risk characterisation should develop a diagnosis of the decision situation so they can customise the needs of the decision, particularly in terms of level and intensity of effort and representation of parties.
>
> Last, from an organisational perspective, each organization responsible for making risk decisions should work to build a capability to

conform to the principles of sound risk characterisation (staff training, organisational structure).

The study notes, for example, that not addressing the decision-relevant questions, using reasonable assumptions and meaningfully including the key affected parties can lead to considerable expense and delays and jeopardise the quality of understanding and the acceptability of the final decision.[120]

There are also three considerations for the formulation of risk problems: fairness, prevention and rights.[121] Fairness includes moral responsibility and distributional equity. Prevention concerns more the environmental aspect in preventing pollution, but in strategic terrorism this could extend to adequate civil defence preparations to reduce the impact of an attack. Last, it is essential to recognise that individuals or groups have the right to control their own lives. Even a communication policy that seeks to influence people's behaviours and attitudes needs to respect that ultimately it is up to individuals to choose whether they follow advice. Exceptions would be in situations where strict quarantine, vaccination or decontamination procedures need to be enforced to control, for instance, the release of a CBR agent, or when evacuation or curfew are needed or there are threats to public order caused by a conventional or non conventional attack.

Coupled with the above are two variables that can influence the gathering and interpretation of information, and effect the success of a risk characterisation: choosing a risk measure and making simplifying assumptions. An example of different ways to assess risk is measuring death (e.g. per million of people or within x miles of the source). The measure chosen can make a great difference when one risk is compared against another, or whether it is seen by the recipient as informative and legitimate. Simplifying assumptions are often needed when information is incomplete or too complex to gather by regular methods. These can include not factoring in local conditions when conducting a risk analysis, misrepresenting local habits or customs, and/or failing to recognise that individuals may be unable or unwilling to follow instructions either because they do not understand them, do not have the motivation to comply, or are unable to make sense of the language of risk estimation. The latter could include Israelis during the 1991 Gulf War who wore their gas masks on with the air-tight sealed cap on, causing them to suffocate, and others who needlessly injected themselves with atropine, a cardiac stimulant with a wide range of medical applications including as an anti-nerve-gas agent, incorrectly believing there had been a chemical missile strike near by. Fischhoff noted that 'peoples' current beliefs shape their future understanding and knowing these details is essential for effective communication. If we do not know where people are coming from, it is very difficult to get them to another place.'[122] Therefore seeking partnership and understanding the public is essential.

Social amplification of risk

While risk perception can lead to avoidance behaviour, the public's risk perceptions can be amplified by experts failing to take the social context of risk into account when making decisions and conveying information to the public.[123] This exacerbation of perceived risk is often referred to as the social amplification of risk. This approach provides a framework that recognises how social institutions and structures process a risk to shape its effects upon society, and the responses of management institutions and people.[124] Nick Pidgeon noted that the perceiver of risk is rarely an isolated individual, but a 'social being' who operates within networks of information and formal relationships with others.[125]

Social amplification or attenuation may occur in several ways. It can begin with a risk event such as an industrial accident, the release of a government report on a risk, or a public interest group highlighting a new health threat. In the context of this book, the risk event could be a terrorist attack, a failed attack, or a terrorism alert advisory, with the perceived risk amplified or attenuated through nodes that include risk communicators such as the mass media and government, social institutions and organisations, that collectively conceptualise, identify and manage the risks. These serve to amplify or attenuate the signals society receives about the risk. In addition, the informal personal networks of friends and neighbours on whom individuals continually rely as reference points then validate perceptions and contextualise risk.[126] Collectively these transmit signals to society about the seriousness of a risk. The concept behind the social amplification of risk model will be used extensively here for guiding the thinking of how responses from government authorities through to the media may influence the terror of terrorism.

Following a risk event, Kasperson's model includes five 'stations' that influence risk perception. They are sources of information (personal, direct and indirect communication); information channels (individual senses, informal social networks, professional information brokers); social stations (opinion leaders, governments agencies NGOs), individual stations (evaluation, cognition in social context, intuitive heuristics); and institutional group and individual behaviour (attitude, political and social action, behaviour and organisational responses, and social protest and disorder). Collectively these transmit signals to society about the seriousness of a risk. The ingredients for social amplification include public perceptions of great risk, intense media coverage of even the most minor incidents or failures, social group mobilisation and opposition, conflicts over value issues and disappointments with failed promises or lack of trust.[127]

Importantly Kasperson noted that the degree of amplification or attenuation will effect the extent to which risk ripple effects accompany the risk or risk event. Slovic noted with reference to terrorism, that social amplification of risk which introduced the concept of 'accidents as signals' helps to explain why some events have enormous 'ripple effects', extending beyond the immediate direct damage to encompass many other victims (e.g. economy, companies, industries, agencies etc.). The events of 9/11 caused, according to Slovic, 'not just ripple effects but cascading waves of impacts, likely to batter us for much of this century'.[128] These ripple effects can lead to actions by individuals to reduce the perceived risk of terrorism but in some cases to cause harm to themselves (e.g. Americans driving rather than flying after 9/11), or seeking medical attention placing pressure on limited resources as in the case of the sarin and anthrax attacks. However, Nick Pidgeon cautioned that the social amplification of risk may be too general to subject to direct empirical testing and may overly simplify the concept of a one-way process from risk events through transmitters (to amplify or attenuate perceived risk) to the receiver.[129] It may instead be more complex with more interactions between the source and receiver of the message.

An example of risk amplification and ripple effects that Kasperson points to is the case of Goiânia, Brazil where in 1987 scrapyard employees opened up a cylinder containing cesium 137 from a cancer therapy machine, leading to ripple effects beyond the immediate health consequences to the locals exposed to the radiation. Seeing the cesium as glistening, family members and friends of the scrapyard workers passed it around describing it as 'carnival glitter', and nearby children played in the yard spreading the material on their hands and bodies.[130] This caused 250 to be contaminated and four to die in the months after the event. Although there were physical and health consequences, the publicising of the event led to severe economic decline for the region, mainly triggered by a sensational and lengthy São Paulo television broadcast a month later that was then followed by an intense period of dramatic and often exaggerated media coverage. This led to the wholesale value of agriculture in the Goiânia state declining by 40 per cent due to consumer concerns over possible contamination, even though no contamination was ever found in the products.[131] Property prices in the immediate vicinity of the contamination plummeted, and hotel vacancy rates were 40 per cent in the six weeks after the event. It also extended to hotels in other parts of Brazil refusing to allow Goiânian residents to stay, airline pilots refusing to fly Goiânian residents, cars with Goiânian number plates being stoned, and anti-nuclear movements capitalising on the event.[132]

Based on the social amplification of risk model, this book will explore to what degree the effects of strategic terrorism are amplified or attenuated by the targeted society, and how these effects can influence the political system through exacerbating the terror to further change people's behaviours and attitudes, and erode the public's trust and confidence in political authorities due to poor risk characterisation and risk communication. The effect on the public's trust of authorities could be influenced not just directly by the terrorist attack(s) but by the government's subsequent handling of and response to the event through risk characterisation. As Fischhoff noted, public misunderstanding of the risks through poor risk communication can intensify the attendant pain and regret. This could then 'transcend into a public's dissatisfaction extending to the political leaders and officials who seemingly failed to meet their information needs'.[133] The general issue of how the erosion of trust can affect political systems is beyond the scope of this book, but the risk analysis field contains a valuable discourse in this area in general terms of trust.[134] While trust in authorities plays a central role in the risk perception of hazards, the following pages will focus on the pre-existing understandings and information provided to the public in shaping their risk perceptions, and ultimately any changes in their behaviours and attitudes following strategic terrorism.

In the context of this book, the main risk event will be regarded as the terrorist attack. In the 1991 Gulf War chapter, this will include Israeli preparations and Iraqi threats of attacks prior to the start of the conflict (Desert Storm). This book will then examine how Kasperson's five 'stations' that influence risk perception may amplify or attenuate the risk. The five stations will include issues of how the government's risk communication, the mass media, public health responses and social interactions can then serve to amplify or attenuate the public's risk perception of terrorism through, for instance, risk communication, social interactions, the mass media and the strategy of first responders.

As the degree of amplification or attenuation will affect the extent to which risk ripple effects accompany the risk or risk event, the case studies will identify how accidents as signals might then have longer-term consequences beyond the original risk event. For instance, how subsequent terrorism alert advisories and public health strategies are conveyed to influence the behaviours and attitudes of individuals.

Means of evaluating risk communication

The following outlines the criteria that will be used for measuring whether good practice was followed and the success of the risk communication employed in the case studies. The good practice criteria will be measured against Baruch Fischhoff's guidelines, and the effectiveness of the risk communication against the National Research Council 1989 guidelines. The principles from Fischhoff relating to terrorism in 2005 were written in response to 9/11 and draw upon lessons from the existing risk analysis literature.

Baruch Fischhoff's good practice guidelines are:

1 Manage risk well – so as to have a credible message to communicate. If terror seems to be managed poorly in other ways (messages being 'spun' or inconsistent policies, connected with alert levels and advisories), then the credibility of communications will suffer and their messages may prompt further scepticism.

2 Create appropriate communication channels. Having appropriate

channels should increase public confidence by demonstrating that a common framework underlies preparation, alert, crisis and recovery plans.

3 Deliver decision-relevant information, concisely and comprehensibly. This entails a study of what the public already know, and then the design (and evaluation) of communications bridging critical gaps. How people will evacuate, respond, seek medical treatment or change their daily lives to mitigate the threat of strategic terror is shaped by risk communication.[135]

To define whether risk communication was successful in the case studies, this book shall use the NRC's criteria whose three points are as follows:

1 Success is defined in terms of the information available to the decision-makers rather than in terms of the quality of the decisions that ensue. Risk communication does not lead to better decisions because risk communication is just one part of risk management (risk characterisation). It is still possible for the recipients to make a poor choice even when they have been presented with all the information.

2 Successful risk communication need not result in consensus about controversial issues or in uniform personal behaviour as not everyone shares common interests or values.

3 The recipient must be able to achieve as complete an understanding of the information as he or she desires. The communication process is therefore not just the level of knowledge in the messages, but also the level of knowledge on which the decision-makers act.[136]

Although the National Research Council's 1989 publication does not look at terrorism, it does offer useful guidance on measuring successful communication following a terrible event to a public with little prior understanding of its possibility. It sets out four key elements:

1 Emphasise information relevant to any practical actions that individuals can take.

2 Be couched in clear and plain language.

3 Respect the audience and its concerns.

4 Seek strictly to inform the recipient, unless conditions clearly warrant the use of influencing techniques.[137]

Where there is a foreseeable potential for emergency, this book will use the NRC's suggestions that advance plans for communication are drafted and should be developed with the intended audiences (e.g. emergency services and local communities). These should provide information that is relevant to people's risk-averting actions and should specify actions that may be taken.[138] It will also be assessed, where possible, whether there was co-ordinating information among the various authorities involved, and a single place where the public and the media could get hold of information.

As this could be particularly pertinent for cases involving chemical, biological and radiological (CBR) weapons, these aspects will be closely assessed in the Gulf War chapter where there was the real perceived threat of chemical weapons being used, the sarin attack and the anthrax case studies.

In these case studies an assessment will consider how long it took for the full scale of the lethality and extent of contamination to be known, and whether authorities provided accurate and timely information. Other questions asked include whether the risk messages were explicit about the limits of knowledge of the risk and the existence of disagreement among experts or others. Furthermore, where there was ambiguity in the evidence available to government and public health responders on the nature and lethality of a major attack, whether this was conveyed sufficiently in risk communication to avoid the public perception of incompetence or poor preparation by the authorities.

3 Methodological approach

The choice of case studies

The five case studies were selected first for the extent of available behavioural science (psychiatry and psychology) literature, and second, the accessibility of public opinion polls and print media information from the respective countries. The case studies will incorporate literature based on the psychiatry diagnostic tool, the Diagnostic and Statistical Manual of Disorders third edition (DSM-III) and fourth edition text revision (DSM-IV-TR) developed by the American Psychiatric Association. DSM-III was released in 1980, DSM-IV in 1994, and DSM-IV-TR released in 2000. As mentioned in Chapter 2, DSM is a categorical classification system developed for use in clinical, educational and research settings that divides mental disorders into types based on criteria sets with defining features. The mental disorders section of the International Statistical Classification of Diseases and Related Health Problems (ICD) is another commonly used guide and the two classifications use the same diagnostic codes. These quantitative approaches allow for direct cross-comparison of data across the various available studies within and across the case studies.

This book also draws upon an area of psychology looking at risk perception and risk communication. The book will not critique the extensive body of literature in the behavioural sciences but incorporate key findings pertaining to the chosen case studies to further the understanding of the terror of terrorism.

The limited availability of relevant DSM data limits the number of case studies. This is not to say that DSM literature does not exist on other strategic terror events. Potentially the book could have examined events like the 1995 Oklahoma bombing, and the IRA and ETA terrorist campaigns. However compared to the five studies chosen, an assessment of the available literature and data revealed that these cases lacked sufficient and accessible information on both risk communication and risk perception, and public opinion polls were not available to acquire the holistic overview required for the thesis.[1]

Two case studies on Israel were chosen because public and private behavioural science institutions that evaluate strategic terror on its society have generated valuable, publicly available literature to assess the effect of the 1991 Gulf War and the Second Intifada. The prominence of 9/11 and the anthrax attacks has led to numerous research papers and books. There is far more behavioural science literature on 9/11 than on any other of the case studies. There is also public opinion poll evidence on how September 11 might have influenced the behaviours of the US public to protect itself from terrorism.

The anthrax attacks case study, while having the least available DSM data, does offer valuable sources pertaining to changing behaviours and attitudes particularly among those suspected of having been exposed to anthrax. In addition, there lies considerable information on risk communication and risk perception enabling one to understand how information given to the public by politicians and public health organisations may have amplified or reduced the terror generated by the attacks.

Case study structure

Each case study will first have an introduction to include a brief chronology of the event including casualties, an analysis of the known strategic and political objectives of the perpetrator(s), and whether there is evidence to suggest the behavioural effects translated into the intended political effects. Out of this will come the key questions to be assessed. Each study will consider the key findings from psychiatry (DSM-based literature) and from psychology (risk communication and risk perception). Consideration will also be given to how a government's and a public health official's risk communication strategy may have amplified or reduced the levels of fear and anxiety, and to the public's perception of strategic terror according to the risk literature. Non-behavioural science sources will also be examined, including public opinion polls, media and other publications that may shed further light on the public's perceptions and changes in behaviours and attitudes. Attention will be paid to the public's proximity to the incident and the time lapsing from the attack(s) (time and space), to gain an insight into the terror generated in both the short and long term. Each case study then concludes with a consideration of the lessons learnt and what patterns, if any, can be discerned.

The reasoning behind the time and space categorisation is that according to the Diagnostic and Statistical Manual, geographic proximity to bombings and time lapse is significantly related to the prevalence of psychological and behavioural symptoms.[2] Since a large part of this study will examine DSM-III and IV literature, it will follow a similar structure.

Broadly speaking the proximity categories used here are:

1 Those who are immediately exposed to the attack.
2 Those in close proximity.
3 The rest of the country in which the attack took place.

As a guide the time-lapse categories are:

1   The period immediately after the attack (hours to the first week).
2   Mid-term response (one–six months).
3   Long-term response (one year plus).

Given that the literature discussed in the case studies is not all written with a uniform time and space classification, a degree of flexibility to what is regarded as close proximity and time lapse has to be incorporated. This is especially so where a series of strategic terror attacks may have taken place, for instance, Iraqi missile strikes during the 1991 Gulf War and the Second Intifada. To ensure there are not too many variables when examining population responses and to sufficiently compare the diverse studies, this book will focus on the general responses of the adult population rather than dividing them into subgroups, for instance, by sex, age (children/adults), and ethnicity. Nor will it examine the terror effects on the emergency services personnel and first responders.

In addition to incorporating material on psychiatry (DSM) and psychology (risk communication and risk perception), are other sources that include public opinion polls and first-hand accounts. There are DSM-based papers for all but the anthrax case study, and far more DSM studies on September 11 and the 1991 Gulf War than for the other studies. Not only does DSM research provide quantitative assessments of the effects of terrorism but also DSM-IV has been developed to account for ethnic and cultural considerations, thus enhancing its cross-cultural applicability. This enables comparison of the key findings of the surveys undertaken in different countries to draw key lessons from the diverse case studies.

Public opinion polls provide useful quantitative material that shed further light on the changes in behaviour and threat perceptions of individuals. With the exception of the sarin case study, there is extensive data to draw upon for all the case studies. While public opinion poll data provide a valuable source in the assessment of peoples' perceptions and changes in attitudes to the terrorist attacks, there are limitations to the uses of this information. Lennart Sjoberg, for instance, criticised the methods of polling firms in studying risk perception, for being diverse, seldom comparable and apparently unaware of developments in research on risk perception.[3] To illustrate this criticism, Sjoberg referred to the methods used by Gallup in a series of polls after 9/11 which asked about 'worry' about being a victim of terrorism and the 'likelihood' of 'acts of terrorism' on one's community and the nation as a whole.[4] Sjoberg makes four criticisms of the Gallup poll: First, no questions about risk were explicitly posed. Second, the questions of 'worry' and 'likelihood' (one for personal risk and the other for societal risk) are not comparable, since the personal risk question was phrased in terms of worry, not likelihood as the societal risk question. Third, the societal question asks about acts and the personal question asks about a consequence: acts are activities, while becoming a victim is a consequence. Fourth, Sjoberg criticises Gallup for failing to define what 'an act of terrorism' is as it could be interpreted by the interviewee to mean a failed attempt, a successful strike or something in between.[5] As the respondents cited societal risk to be greater than personal risk, then this suggests that people believe they can protect themselves from the risk, and general risk is more important than personal risk for policy attitudes, therefore the consequences are more important than the acts. Nonetheless, Sjoberg does make reference to Gallup polls to support his hypothesis on risk perceptions and behavioural patterns, and suggests that the lessons from risk perception research should be useful to those who study public opinion for the purpose of informing the media and politicians about the current beliefs and attitudes of people.[6]

Assumptions investigated

Throughout the book, five key assumptions will be evaluated to improve our understanding of the terror of terrorism. These are based on evidence contained in the mental health, international relations and risk analysis literature outside the five main case studies. This also serves as a useful background to previous work undertaken on the key themes explored here.

First, people change their behaviours and attitudes to minimise the perceived risk of strategic terrorism to them, but they do not panic. Studies on bombing raids on Britain, Germany and Japan in the Second World War, terrorism and civilian disasters present little evidence of a panic-prone public.[7] Disorganised flight in the presence of a real or perceived danger (e.g. mass panic) is rare whereas outbreaks of multiple unexplained symptoms (OMUS) like mass psychogenic illness may be more common, in particular following an attack involving a non-conventional weapon.[8] In the Second World War, civilians proved to be more resilient than had been predicted despite expectations of mass panic and air-raid neurosis, largely because, according to Edgar Jones *et al.*, civil defence planners had 'underestimated their adaptability and resourcefulness, and because the lengthy conflict had involved so many in constructive participating roles.'[9] Even the atomic attacks on Hiroshima and Nagasaki did not cause panic or large-scale unrest, with survivors instead engaging in efforts to cope and work together to recover.[10] However, the survivors of Hiroshima and Nagasaki would not have been aware of the dread risk and public health threat posed by the radiological fallout that ensued given the lack of public awareness in 1945 of the true devastation nuclear weapons caused.

Disaster management research also suggests that panic is rare in major fires and all too often people's behaviours have been misperceived as irrational. Although a number of major fires have been reported as causing panic including the Cocoanut Grove Nightclub fire in 1943 in which 488 people died, the Beverly Hill Supper Club fire and the Summerland Fire in the Isle of Man in 1973 in which 50 people died, subsequent analysis suggests this was unlikely. Jonathan Sime believes that many of the assumptions made about people panicking in a fire are questionable, noting, 'contradictory arguments and invalid assumptions exist in references to panic in the newspapers, building regulations and academic literature. It has been argued that an important reason for this is the lack of consideration of the way in which the concept of panic in fires is used.'[11] Helsloot and Ruitenberg state that, while contrary to popular belief, most citizens react in a rational way to disaster situations; in rare instances panic can occur when there is the perception of no rational escape.[12] This can stem from four conditions: a perception of immediate and serious danger; the perception that there are only a few escape routes; perception that the escape routes are closing; and lack of communication about the situation. Sime also adds that flight behaviour with people rushing to the exits (e.g. pushing and shoving) can be misperceived by observers as irrational behaviour and panic.[13]

While the vast majority of the studies suggest panic is extremely rare, there are instances of this occurring on a widespread scale. This includes the gas attacks against German and Allied forces during the First World War. According to Carol Fullerton *et al.* and Tim Cook, the use of gas led to panic, dread, and significant fear, and anxiety.[14] Helsloot and Ruitenberg noted that, despite their conclusion that panic is rare, their assumptions are based on surveying literature and analysing instances in Western society where crisis situations and cases of strategic terrorism in non-Western cultures may produce a different response from the populace. This supposition is supported by Harshit Sinha who explored how panic may have been evident in a developing country following the outbreak of the Plague in 1994 in the Indian town of Surat City, Gujarat. Although only 53 died, the Plague led to a mass exodus of people including medical staff and the elite leading to the collapse of the local administration.[15]

Evidence to set up the assumption that individuals change their behaviours and attitudes to reduce the perceived risk includes the radiological contamination incident in Goiânia, Brazil in 1987, and earlier studies on the victims of terrorism. Heightened concern by those residing near the contaminated area in Goiânia led 125,800 people to undergo screening that they were contaminated, but only 249 actually were.[16] In addition, the Goiânia state was treated by many Brazilians as a no-go area as far for as visiting or consuming produce from there were concerned. This led to a decline in wholesale agriculture in the state, a large drop in property prices in the immediate vicinity of the contamination, hotel vacancy rates at 40 per cent in the six weeks after the event, and airline pilots refusing to fly Goiânia residents.[17] Studies to support the hypothesis of avoidance behaviour from terrorism can also be found in earlier mental health terrorism cases that use DSM diagnostic tool, including those in Northern Ireland, Spain, Israel and the Oklahoma bombing.[18] There is also evidence outside the DSM-based terrorism literature of individuals undertaking avoidance behaviour following trauma, for instance, after road traffic accidents.[19]

Second, the degree of behavioural change is influenced not just by the strategic terrorism event itself but also by the adequacy of the risk characterisation and risk communication by local and national authorities, politicians and the emergency services. Although there is little literature to demonstrate how risk communication can influence the public's responses following a terrorist attack, there are examples from risk analysis and crisis management literature to set up this assumption. This includes risk analysis studies on the Swedish Acrylamide alarm in 2002 and the BSE scare in Britain during the early to mid-1990s which suggest poor risk characterisation and risk communication leads to adverse reactions by individuals.

There is also evidence from the Second World War that levels of fear and anxiety are influenced by the quality of the authorities' emergency response following strategic bombing raids on cities. Irving Janis concludes that from analysing the British and German civilians air-raid experiences, the ability to 'minimise the fear-arousing effects of air-raids [was] dependent largely upon the availability and efficiency of rescue organisations, medical facilities, and social-service welfare organisations'.[20]

The final example is Harshit Sinha's account of the Plague in Sirat City, Gujarat. Sinha noted that despite killing only 53 people, a number of risk characterisation and risk communication failures exacerbated the public's response. Poor risk characterisation included the absence of an epidemiologist and entomologist in the survey team, which led to unanswered questions about the origin, transmission and nature of the disease. Authorities failed to educate victims about the significance of pathological examinations meaning many refused them, complicating further scientific assessments of the Plague. Furthermore authorities held off in providing definitive statements on the Plague, causing confusion and chaos among the populace. Exaggerated reports by the media heightened the fear and they failed to disseminate correct information. Collectively this led to 'various ill-notions, psycho fear and panic gripped the minds of people.'[21]

Third, the psychometric paradigm provides a valuable framework for understanding the public's risk perceptions to strategic terrorism. The psychometric model that emphasises dread and new risk as primary dimensions (Fischhoff, Slovic, Lichtenstein *et al.*) has formed the basis of much work on risk perception. Although the literature has been developed outside international relations, incorporating this model provides a significant contribution to understanding the terror of terrorism.

The psychometric paradigm shows that certain attributes of hazards, such as the potential to harm large numbers of people at once, personnel uncontrollability, dreaded effects and perceived involuntariness, makes those hazards more serious to the public than hazards that lack those attributes.[22] The book will seek to examine to what degree this framework can be applied to the five case studies and what insights this might provide. It is hypothesised that the psychometric paradigm can be a valuable tool to provide a

greater understanding of the terror of terrorism and the public's risk perceptions and behavioural responses.

This approach will have the added challenge of transferring the concepts
developed in rigorous studies by Paul Slovic and Baruch Fischhoff among
others to case studies where the researcher may need to rely heavily on what
observations can be captured from the secondary literature.

*Fourth, the extent of mental health and behavioural effects declines with the time
lapsing after and proximity to a terrorist attack.* This hypothesis derives mainly
from the mental health literature on the effects of time and proximity. In
particular this includes studies based on the various versions of the DSM.
DSM-IV-TR suggests that time elapsed from an attack does lead to a
gradual reduction in PTSD and related symptoms among those initially
diagnosed with these symptoms.

Evidence on time outside the five main case studies examined in this
book includes the impact of terrorist attacks in Northern Ireland, the US
(1995 Oklahoma) and France. A study on the 1987 Enniskillen bombing in
Northern Ireland that killed and injured 60 showed that over the subsequent 12 months, PTSD reduced among the victims during this period,
but there were a small number of instances of PTSD remerging 12 months
later or only manifesting after 12 months.[23] Research on the Oklahoma
bombing showed that those with PTSD symptoms declined by 10 per cent
six months after the attacks.[24] The reduction of PTSD over time is consistent
with a wider review of individuals with PTSD caused by many types of traumatic instances. According to research led by Sara Freedman and Dalia
Brandes of 256 PTSD cases admitted to an Israeli hospital shortly after a
single traumatic event during the late 1990s, most individuals recovered
within one year of their traumatic experiences.[25] The same study found that
those who remained ill for one year rarely recovered.

The hypothesis that a population adapts to an ongoing threat of attacks
can also be found in literature on air raids during the Second World War.
Irving Janis's RAND study concluded that during the Blitz in Britain, there
was a 'definite decline in overt fear reactions as the air blitz continued, even
though the raids became heavier and heavier.'[26] As the attacks intensified the
population displayed more indifference towards the air raids and air-raid
sirens tended to be disregarded unless attacking planes were overhead.[27] This
trend of 'emotional adaptation', as Janis calls it, was also found among
German civilians interviewed after the war. Janis concludes therefore that a
'sizeable proportion of the civilian population exposed to successive air
attacks during World War Two displayed a gradual decline in fear
reactions'.[28]

Evidence to set up the proximity component of this assumption includes
Enrique Baca *et al.*'s study on the Spanish victims of terrorism from
1997–2001 which found a much higher prevalence of psychiatric symptoms
(mainly of anxiety or psychosomatic) among the victims than in the general
populace.[29] Similarly, proximity also determined the psychological effects of

terrorist attacks in Northern Ireland during the Troubles and France in 1995–1996 with those closer to bombings having a higher degree of PTSD than those further away from the attack and less injured.[30] Proximity was also found to be a determinant among populations exposed to strategic bombing during the Second World War. Those who experienced a 'near miss' expressed higher rates of fear than those who were not directly involved in danger but exposed to extremely heavy attacks.[31]

While some mental health disorders like PTSD can only be classified as so six months after the event, the literature can still provide a detailed insight into the change, if any, in the following months. This proposition will also encapsulate evidence of behavioural effects from various sources including public opinion polls, hotline surveys and DSM papers to assess this assumption.

Fifth, due to the limited terror of strategic terrorism, the effects on the political system are slight. As noted in Chapter 2, Lawrence Freedman argues that strategic terror is a two-stage process: first, there are independent, deliberate acts of violence, or threats of violence against a populace, intended to produce a particular psychological effect – terror – on the assumption that, second, these will influence the target's whole political system by altering its attitude and behaviour. As the terror is limited, the direct effect on the political system is marginal.

The concept of using terror for political ends is raised in the literature on aerial bombardment and terrorism in political science and international relations. Paul Wilkinson noted that 'far from leading to a climate of collapse in which the primary target is prepared to surrender to the terrorist's demands, terrorism may lead to mobilisation and hardening of resolve to resist demands and eliminate terrorism'.[32] Therefore terrorism is not an effective weapon in the achievement of political change. In his view, the few cases where terrorism has played a major part in bringing sweeping political changes have arisen in certain colonial struggles against foreign rule.[33]

Similarly, Walter Laqueur believes that terrorism has only succeeded in very specific circumstances. This includes terrorism mounted by groups with narrow, clearly defined aims; by those seeking to keep a particular issue alive in the public's mind, for instance, Palestinian Arab groups conducting terrorist attacks to publicise their cause; and finally, by terrorist groups facing imperial powers who themselves are no longer able or willing to hold onto their colonies or protectorates.[34]

From a psychiatry perspective, on the other hand, David Alexander and Susan Klein believe that historically 'terror has proved to be an effective instrument of coercion and intimidation' whether by state organisations or terrorist groups. Alexander and Klein suggest that in the short term, terror can be effective.[35] This book will, therefore, assess the amount of terror generated by terrorism and the coercive effect terrorism can have on political systems.

4 Israel and the Scud missile attacks during the 1991 Gulf War

Introduction

Israel's experience of Iraqi Scud attacks in January to February 1991, and the associated threats of chemical or biological (CB) warfare, provide an insight into the effect limited, conventionally armed missile strikes and threats of non-conventional warfare, can have on a population's sense of security. In turn, this further informs our understanding of a population's resilience to strategic terror in the context of terrorism. This chapter explores to what extent the fear of the unknown persisted in shaping Israeli perception throughout the conflict. Since Israel's forces were not directly participating in the conflict in Iraq, this case study provides the closest thing possible to a set of 'control' data on which to study the social-psychological effect of missile attacks and missile defences, without the influence of how a war on the front line could be effecting perceptions and morale in the home country. While it is important to take into account the social and cultural aspects of Israel when transposing lessons learnt to other countries, the unique situation Israel experienced offers a valuable case study to assess the effect of limited missile strikes and threats of non-conventional weapons on population centres. Conventional warheads contain high explosives while non-conventional warheads are those that contain a chemical, biological or nuclear device. Uzi Rubin, a former member of Israel's National Security Council, summarised the Gulf War experience as, 'a searing, traumatic experience for Israel's people and leadership, prompting considerable soul searching'.[1] The plethora of medical papers on the Gulf War measuring the psychological and physiological conditions captures the degree of terror caused by the attacks. Zahava Solomon, one of the key Israeli psychologists to conduct research during this period, gave the following assessment of the Gulf War:

> In retrospect, the Gulf War, so termed by Israel was a misnomer. Israel was not engaged in the fighting and as wars go suffered comparatively little damage. Yet this war or storm, however one wishes to describe it, was a highly, stressful, fearful and embarrassing experience for Israelis.[2]

This chapter is divided as follows:

- Background and overview
- Strategic and political objectives
- Political effects
- Effects of proximity and time
- Changes in behaviours and attitudes
- Risk communication
- Risk perception
- Risk amplification.

As the war progressed, the Israelis became accustomed to the missile threat and fear of the threat diminished. This adaptability was assisted by the near predictability of when (after dark) and where (metropolitan areas) the missiles would fall, and the type of warhead the missiles carried (conventional rather than non-conventional). The perceived dread risk and elements of unknown risk may have therefore become less of a dread risk and more of a known risk as a pattern emerged, enabling Israelis to change their behaviours and attitudes to reduce the perceived risk posed by the Scuds. There is mixed evidence to suggest that proximity influenced fear and anxiety. The most profound evidence though can be found among those who were close to the missile-impact zones, in particular those who had buildings damaged or destroyed and were subsequently evacuated to hotels. The levels of uncertainty that Israelis encountered at the outset of hostilities did contribute to higher levels of cardiac deaths and misuse of gas masks and atropine injections in the early days of the war. The incorrect use of protective equipment may have been partly due to inadequate risk communication from the authorities and their understanding on how the information given on using gas masks and atropine would be interpreted. In addition the public's fears and anxieties may have been exacerbated by the plethora of mental health professionals legitimising or even encouraging these responses. The political effects were limited, despite the initial shock of the attacks within the political establishment. The terror generated failed to trigger an Israeli retaliation and bring it into the war as intended by Iraq. But this was largely due to US pressure for Israel to stay passive, together with the fact that Iraq did not use chemical warheads, and the deployment of the Patriot missile defence system that led to the perception that Israel could defend itself even though the system only had a limited success in intercepting the Scuds.

Background and overview

This section provides a background to the events of the war, including a broad overview of the physical and psychological victims, prior to examining in detail the terror caused. On 2 August 1990 Iraq invaded Kuwait. Besides the complications in removing Iraq's forces from Kuwait, there were concerns within the region of the possibility that Iraq could launch ballistic missiles to attack states who sided with the US-led coalition.

At 2:00am on 17 January, the day after the UN deadline for Iraqi forces to withdraw and when Desert Storm began, Iraq launched the first of 39 ballistic missiles to be fired in 18 different attacks against Israel – an average of one attack every two and half days. Of the 40 missiles that reached Israel, 26 landed in the Tel Aviv area, six in Haifa, five in the West Bank and three in the south of the country. In two-thirds of the attacks (12 of 18), a single missile arrived; in the other six incidents, six Scuds landed.[3] The largest attack comprised of eight Scud missiles arriving simultaneously.[4] In one attack six missiles were fired towards a single area. Despite the initial fears that Saddam Hussein would launch missiles armed with a chemical or biological warhead, all 39 missiles were conventionally armed causing limited physical destruction on the ground and few deaths as a direct result of the attacks.

The casualties

Assessing the casualty statistics of the war reveals the extent to which the fear of missile strikes took hold of the population, as compared to the relatively low number of serious casualties caused directly by the attacks. Around three-quarters of the casualties caused by the missile strikes themselves were acute psychological reactions, and fewer than one-quarter of casualties were physical injuries. Out of 1,059 war-related hospital emergency room admissions, only 234 were for injuries sustained from the direct outcome of the missile strikes. Only two died of their wounds, 221 suffered mild injuries and ten were classified as having moderate wounds. One person succumbed to severe wounds.[5] Almost all the missiles landed on residential areas. The low number of casualties caused by the missile attacks themselves is all the more remarkable considering that the sealed rooms that the Israelis took to during the attacks offered virtually no protection against flying shrapnel from the missiles.

The 825 indirect casualties (including those arriving at hospital emergency rooms after five false alarms) included 11 people who died. Of these, four died from heart attacks, six from suffocation caused by wearing their gas mask incorrectly through not removing the air-tight protective cap before use. A further 40 casualties injured themselves while rushing to safety when the air-raid sirens sounded, 230 needlessly injected themselves with atropine and 544 were admitted to hospital for acute psychological distress.[6]

These figures show that over four times more people died from the indirect rather than the direct effects of the missile attacks. More people died of fear than from the actual missile strikes. Furthermore 66 per cent of indirect casualties were acute psychological cases (70 per cent of those who needlessly injected themselves with atropine are included). These figures suggest that, with over two thirds of casualties being psychological cases, the use of the ballistic missile in the Gulf War caused sustained unease and fear among a segment of the population leading to many succumbing to a psychological disorder – but few to direct physical harm caused by an attack. While the population responded to the war in a well-disciplined, self-controlled manner, most people kept their anxieties under control, followed the emergency instructions and maintained their sense of mastery under attack.[7] Those who found it difficult to cope with the attacks adapted their behaviours by leaving the high-risk zone.[8]

Although the casualty rate from the missile strikes was low, physical damage to property was high. While property damage was not reported in ten of the 18 attacks, the cost of property damage as a whole ran into several hundred million US dollars. In Tel Aviv 3,991 apartments sustained damage, of which 87 were destroyed and 869 were badly damaged. A total of 1,647 people was evacuated to hotels. The damage in the Ramat Gan suburb was 3,742 apartments hit, of which 105 destroyed and 600 badly damaged. 1,047 Ramat Gan residents were evacuated to hotels and their accommodation paid for by the government.[9]

Strategic and political objectives

In the months leading up to Iraq's invasion of Kuwait tensions had been steadily increasing between the two nations through disputes on borders, debt and oil. Iraq was in debt to Kuwait by US$14 billion, a debt incurred during the 1980–1988 Iran–Iraq war when Kuwait was allied to Baghdad. Iraq hoped to solve its debts through a combination of raising the price of oil through OPEC oil-production cuts and calling on Kuwait to either re-negotiate or cancel its debts. Kuwait however increased oil production and lowered prices in an attempt to leverage a better resolution of their border dispute. In addition Iraq considered Kuwait's slant drilling into the bordering Rumelia oil fields illegal. Saddam Hussein decided that to resolve the issue he would invade the country. On 2 August 1990 Iraq's forces invaded Kuwait with the equivalent of three divisions. Ideologically, Iraq justified the invasion through calls to Arab nationalism and Kuwait was described as a natural part of Iraq separated by British imperialism, the war wad portrayed as a way towards a greater Arab Union and the restoration of the empire of Babylon. The international community responded by condemning the invasion and the UN passed Resolution 678 on 28 November 1990, giving Baghdad a withdrawal deadline of 15 January 1991 and authorising 'all necessary means to uphold and implement Resolution 660 that demanded Iraq withdraw immediately and unconditionally its forces from Kuwait.

The prime objective of Iraq's ballistic missiles strikes against Israel during the 1991 Gulf War was to force the nation to respond militarily against Iraq and thus put severe pressure on the Arab allies in the American-led coalition to withdraw their support and forces. Saddam Hussein believed that through missile threats and attacks, Israel would be forced to retaliate against Iraq by conducting air strikes thus pulling the nation into the war. Hussein calculated that with Israel in the war, the Arab forces would not be willing to fight if a coalition with Israel was involved and this would improve Iraq's prospects in the conflict.

Political effects

While the missile attacks prompted the Israeli populace to develop an emergency routine as will be detailed in the changes to behaviours and attitudes section, Iraq failed to bring Israel into the war and thus threaten the stability of the coalition. Despite the failure to bring Israel into the war, the attacks did to some degree surprise the government. Uzi Rubin believed that the first attacks 'shocked Israel's government and its military High Command to its core'.[10] Rubin commented that there had been a belief that Iraq would not dare launch missiles against Israel for fear of a devastating retaliation. As the allied coalition efforts to halt Iraqi missile strikes failed, Israeli military leaders prepared plans to attack and destroy Iraqi missile launchers.

Despite these difficulties, the Patriot PAC-2 missile defence system was crucial in reducing the pressure on the government for Israel to retaliate against Iraq, with all the problems that would have presented to the Arab members of the coalition. The operational presence of the Patriot with its visually spectacular 'intercepts' gave the impression that something was being done to prevent unimpeded missile strikes. Politically this may have been significant as if showed the Israeli public that their nation was not defenceless and was taking measures to protect itself. The Iraqi Scud strikes might have brought Israel into the war if it had not been for the fact that the coalition immediately responded by launching a massive 'Scud hunt' in the form of strike aircraft and special forces operating on the ground.[11] Furthermore, the coalition's air and special forces strikes against Iraqi launch sites reduced the pressure on any Israeli participation that might have threatened the coalition's political cohesion.

It is doubtful that Patriot would have retained its value in the event of a non-conventional attack. The confirmation of just one missile armed with a chemical or biological warhead unleashing its payload onto Israeli territory would have significantly undermined people's sense of security and created considerable political pressure to retaliate. Nevertheless, in the face of conventional bombardment Patriot diminished the public's anxiety. With the conventionally armed Scud missiles not causing extensive physical damage or casualties prior to Patriot's deployment, and the missile defence system having a low intercept success following its deployment, just the mere operational presence of Patriot may have alleviated the pressure on the country to become militarily involved in the Iraqi theatre of operations. While the Patriot served as a valuable tool of reassurance, the terror of the Scud missiles was not ultimately sufficient enough to force the Israeli government to respond. The Israelis adapted well to the missile campaign. Had chemical weapons been used, the outcome may have been very different.

Effects of proximity and time

Proximity

The majority of the documentation on the 1991 Gulf War suggests proximity to the missile impact areas influenced behavioural and psychological reactions, although there is some material that questions this assumption. A comparison of hospital admissions located in regions struck by missiles with the rest of the country suggests that proximity influenced anxiety. A study of patients admitted to hospital following missile strikes on Tel Aviv (one of the main targeted areas) showed that 28 per cent were admitted for atropine poisoning and severe anxiety compared to 21 per cent in the rest of the country.[12] Up to 80 per cent of those located near the impact zone are thought to have suffered from extreme emotional distress.[13] Most of this group was displaced due to damage to their homes. Many of those who lost their homes in the attacks and had to stay in hotels refused to leave their rooms or the hotel in the first few days after the blast because of stress-related anxiety, fear, and phobias.[14] In an initial medical assessment of the evacuees carried out in the first 48 hours, the majority were found to be suffering from acute stress. The evacuees were treated for acute PTSD by a municipal healthcare team. By the end of the war, 1,700 people from the Tel Aviv area had been temporarily relocated to hotels.

A survey on the psychological state of those displaced by a missile attack provides a more detailed insight into the terror effects of Iraq's Scud campaign. An assessment of 240 evacuees at one hotel showed that the displaced population exhibited emotional reactions in four overlapping stages – with 20 per cent requiring individual attention from mental health professionals.[15] The first reaction was shock occurring in the first 48 hours after the destruction of their home and relocation. The second, lasting three days, involved intense generalised anxiety accompanied by insomnia, fainting, vomiting and headaches. The third was the onset of trauma at the end of the first week, continuing into the second. This consisted mainly of signs of depression and mourning. The final stage was characterised by signs of adaptation and the symptoms subsiding.[16] Although the emotional condition of the evacuees gradually improved, the refusal of many to leave their hotels was surprisingly persistent throughout the first three stages. There remained much anxiety about what might happen with regard to the war and their personal circumstances.

Further evidence on the effect of proximity can be gauged from the geographic locations of the increased cardiac deaths attributed to the missile strikes. The increased mortality was limited largely to regions struck by missiles, where the force of the impact and explosions was widely felt, and where the fear of chemical attack was probably also greatest.[17] In Tel Aviv and Haifa cardiac deaths increased by 78 per cent on the first day, compared to an 18 per cent increase in the rest of the country.[18] The initial increase in mortality may have been caused by emotional stress and breathing difficulties, the latter exacerbated by using gas masks and staying in sealed rooms for an extended period resulting in hypoxia.

Another insight into the effect of the missile strikes on Israelis can be captured from a survey that analysed sleep patterns during the Gulf War, keeping in mind that 38 of the 39 missiles that struck Israel were launched during the hours of dark. During the third week of the war a telephone survey of 200 adults recorded that 28 per cent complained of sleep problems (10 per cent complained of mid-sleep awakenings, 4.5 per cent on difficulties falling asleep and 13.5 per cent of a combination of the two).[19] Those residing in the Tel Aviv and Haifa areas reported significantly more sleep disturbances than the rest of the country with around 37 per cent believing they had sleep problems. Around 17–20 per cent of this group also reported the combination of sleep awakenings and difficulties falling asleep, compared to 3 per cent recorded in 1981. Although the warning time from the alarm sirens increased from 60–90 seconds to five minutes later in the war, Israelis had to don gas masks, place infants in sealed cradles and seek shelter in prepared sealed rooms. It is thought that people were afraid of not being woken by the sirens or of being given sufficient time to respond – rational fears, given the brief warning time and the nature of the threat. Despite the rate of subjective complaints about insomnia, objective research on sleep patterns revealed that the overall quality of sleep was in reality minimally effected.[20] Therefore responders thought they were sleeping worse than they actually were.

While the majority of the literature provides evidence showing that proximity did influence the terror of the missile strikes, a small number of studies question this assumption. An assessment of 60 patients and staff attending primary care clinics around Israel showed that proximity to the geographic area where Scud missiles fell did not appear to be a significant factor in the self-reporting of health side-effects from the missile strikes.[21] Seventy per cent of the patients reported health effects related to the missile attacks or civil defence measures. However the survey noted that the lack of random sampling, the relatively small number of patient encounters and the focus on only three clinics may have limited the strength of the findings.

A separate study undertaken over a four-week period also showed that proximity to the attacks was not related to reported anxiety and symptoms when data from Haifa were compared to the northern low-risk areas.[22] It was thought this may have been due to two factors. First, the whole nation was alerted during the missile warnings. Second, being a small country with strong social and community relations, people outside the high-risk areas probably exercised empathy and communal behaviour, and felt similar levels of concern, tension and anxiety. The relatively small size of Israel may well have reduced the effect of proximity. Israelis living in low-risk areas would not have been too far from the impact zones.

An additional means of measuring proximity was assessing the levels of morale using data from the pre-war period against changes in morale during Desert Storm.[23] Measuring the level of morale in Israel's major cities, namely Jerusalem, Tel Aviv and Haifa, indicated that the missile attacks had only a small adverse effect on morale. People living in areas with a high risk of a missile attack like Tel Aviv did not experience a greater decline in morale than residents of low-risk communities.[24]

Time

As the missile campaign progressed, the psychological reactions declined. This conclusion derives from data derived from national surveys like the Israel Defence Force (IDF) Department of Behavioural Sciences (DBS), observations noted in medical journals on hospital admissions on the misuse of atropine injections and gas masks, together with deaths indirectly caused by the attacks.

A study undertaken by the IDF's DBS of 8,000 Israelis over the duration of Desert Shield and Desert Storm provided a detailed insight into the changing perceptions of Israelis. The DBS survey is arguably one of most comprehensive studies undertaken during the Gulf War. The survey showed that from the second week of the conflict (24–25 January) there was a marked decline in expectations of conventional and chemical attack among respondents from 92 per cent and 54 per cent down to 69 per cent and 27 per cent respectively by 1 February. The DBS survey also asked respondents whether they 'panicked' without defining what this term meant. While not defining this, levels of worry and panic too declined from 71 per cent and 41 per cent on 25–26 January to 46 per cent and 32 per cent respectively on 1 February. The same survey also showed that from 1 February the expectation level of a chemical attack flattened out from 26 per cent, peaking at 33 per cent on 6 February and declining to 26 per cent at the war's end on 24 February. This was in marked contrast to the first two weeks of the war when fear of a chemical attack reached 46 per cent at the outbreak of hostilities with the launch of Desert Storm, to then dip to 21 per cent three days later, only to rise again to a peak of 54 per cent on 27 February. The expectation of a conventional attack reached its peak on 27 January at 92 per cent.[25]

Four national surveys of Israelis conducted during the first 12 days of the war showed that the percentage of subjects reporting anxiety-related somatic symptoms declined from 38 per cent after the first missile attack to 20 per cent 12 days later.[26] Furthermore, the proportion of the somatic reactions decreased as the populace grew used to its predicament. Although anxiety declined, the expectation of a CW attack did not wane, but actually reached its peak at the end of the survey.

An assessment on the increase in cardiovascular deaths which was attributed to the stress of the Iraqi missile strikes suggests that the first few days of the war were the most pressurised causing the highest increase in the number of deaths compared to the year before.[27] During the 24 hours of 18 January when the first attack took place, cardiac deaths increased from an average of 92 to 147.[28] There might have been, however, some explanation for the absence of a substantial increase in mortality during the rest of the conflict. First, those most susceptible to fatal cardiac arrests died in the first attack. Second, reduced efficiency of the ambulance service during the initial missile attacks may have played a role. Third, individuals adapted rapidly to the new situation. Overall, the parts of the Israeli populace directly exposed to the attacks were regarded to have shown a quick recovery with most people recovering quickly from the initial shock. They were able to care for themselves, search for missing relatives, take care of their property, collect information and help others.[29]

A good source on the psychological reactions of Israelis over time can be gained from looking at hospital admission records and deaths caused by the misuse of gas masks. A study led by Avi Bleich identified that the highest number arriving at hospital were those who experienced some form of stress reaction or who had atropine during the first two attacks.[30] In addition four of the six deaths from the misuse of gas masks occurred during the first attack. By the fifth day of the missile campaign, the total number of those admitted with stress and atropine poisoning had declined from 343 in the first attack to 23 in the third. This represented a drop from 93 per cent to 21 per cent of the total hospital admissions. In Tel Aviv, one of the major cities to be targeted, a third of the 70 casualties admitted to the emergency department for acute psychological stress and unnecessary injections occurred in the first few days.[31] Clearly the terror generated by the attacks significantly declined in the first few days of the war as the populace adapted and became accustomed to the security predicament.

A separate study revealed that the number of psychological casualties was not related to the number of physical casualties. While the stress reactions and unjustified injections declined dramatically after the first attack, the physical casualties were at their highest in the second, third and fifth attacks. For the rest of the war, physical casualties comprised the vast majority of hospital admissions. The large numbers of psychological casualties at the beginning of the war probably coincided with high levels of fear caused by the threat of chemical weapons combined with a sense of passivity and helplessness.[32] The number of injections was highest during the first two attacks when the population was not sure if a chemical attack had actually taken place.[33] When this is combined with the DBS national survey data, somatic reactions, and reports from the missile impact site this strongly infers that Israelis became accustomed to the attacks and, as a result, the terror caused by the missiles decreased. However, the degree of adaptation could have been assisted by the pattern that emerged in the timing and location of the attacks as will be discussed in the risk perception section. This most probably assisted Israelis in adapting their lives to the missile attacks as the perceived risk became less of a dread risk and more of a known risk.

Changes in behaviours and attitudes

At the outset of the conflict many Israelis knew they were likely to face attacks from a weapon system, of which many Israelis had no prior experience and which might be armed with chemical weapons. The uncertainty over Saddam Hussein's true intentions and actual capabilities, which had served to fuel anxiety, would soon be clarified. As risk research shows, uncertainty and the inability to control an external threat contributes to a dread risk perception. This section outlines the risk and threat perceptions during the war which changed from a high degree of uncertainty at the outset of the conflict to a greater degree of predictability as Israelis became accustomed to the threat.

It soon became clear to the Israelis that a constant pattern was emerging from the missile attacks. They all occurred at night and were conventionally armed. The predictability of the timing enabled Israelis to adapt their lives to this as part of what became to be the emergency routine. This sense of predictability encouraged Israelis to return to work and led to the gradual reopening of some schools, though places of entertainment remained closed and meeting in large groups was forbidden.[34] A new lifestyle developed. In the morning Israelis went about life as normal. From the early afternoon, there began a large exodus from the central region of population centres to outlying areas. By 4:00pm the streets in Tel Aviv emptied.[35] Across Israel people would return to their homes in the evening to be close to their sealed rooms and gas masks, and to prepare themselves for the night of attacks. A large proportion of the population, by their own admission, adjusted well to the war stresses, although this is not independently validated.[36] Empirical evidence on the habituation of the population from the second week of the war (24–25 January) included a drop in the use of the telephone hotlines and a reduction in the number of emergency admissions to hospitals of people needlessly injecting themselves with atropine or people suffering from adverse stress reactions.[37]

The pattern of night attacks and of missiles armed with conventional warheads was supplemented by an emerging pattern on targeted areas. After the first series of attacks, it became evident that the Scuds were aimed at certain population centres, particularly the metropolitan centres of Tel Aviv and Haifa. Consequently, the defence authorities divided the country into 'high-risk' and 'low-risk' zones, and issued 'missile forecasts' and related guidance in accordance with the risk levels of the various zones.[38] As the war progressed, Israelis were therefore able to anticipate and prepare themselves for the attacks. The fact that authorities provided missile forecasts reflects how an increased sense of predictability took hold of Israel as the war progressed. Adaptation was also facilitated by the decreased frequency and destructiveness of the attacks. In the last three weeks of February there were only seven strikes, and after the middle of the month none of them did any damage.[39] This may partly have been due to the deployment of the Patriot PAC-2 missile defence system.

Evidence to support the view that people were getting used to the missile campaign comes from a survey by the Israeli Institute for Military Studies. The study showed that, four days into the war, those who reported to feel 'not so terrible' during the attacks increased from 44.2 per cent to 52.2 per cent. The first survey was undertaken over 19–20 January and the second four days later on 22–23 January. While adaptation did eventually occur, the perceived risk posed by the missiles was so great for some that after the first attacks there was a spontaneous evacuation from the Tel Aviv and Ramat Gan regions of 100,000 inhabitants to areas less likely to be targeted, for instance resort cities.[40] The exodus was facilitated by the government's decision to close schools for the first three weeks of the war, and parts of the economy like shops in the first few days of the war.[41] One Israeli who fled a metropolitan area for the coast stated, 'I feel better about being here (in a town on the Red Sea) because you don't hear the Scuds hit ... not everyone is ready to be a hero'.[42] About half of these people returned after the public schools re-opened on 2 February, but as many as one-third remained away until 25 February when hostilities ceased in Iraq.[43] One survey found that less than one in five reported that they fled at least occasionally high-risk areas at some point in the war because of the attacks.[44]

The increasing predictability of the timing and location of missile strikes and the adaptation to the emergency routine (donning of gas masks and returning from work early) may have reduced the levels of uncertainty that initially surrounded Saddam Hussein's intentions and capabilities, but throughout the war around half of the population continued to fear a non-conventional attack. The DBS survey revealed that Israelis consistently expressed higher expectations of conventional than chemical attack from just days after the Iraqi invasion of Kuwait through to the end of the Gulf War in late February. The proportion of those surveyed expecting a chemical attack during Desert Shield and Desert Storm ranged from 20–40 per cent less than those expecting a conventional attack. At the start of Desert Storm, when one might have expected uncertainty over the type of warheads to have been at its highest, only 46 per cent expected a chemical attack compared to 79 per cent expecting a conventionally armed strike. The 23 per cent lower rating at the start of Desert Storm is all the more remarkable considering the heightened preparations in Israel for the possibility of chemical attack, the escalating war of words with Iraq whose leader threatened Israel with destruction and the continuing publicity about Iraq's use of chemical weapons during the 1980s. The concern about CW was so great for some that 18 per cent of the population in targeted urban areas mistakenly reported that they had smelled gas during the attacks.[45]

As the war progressed the threat perception among Israelis changed, with a decreased expectation of both conventional and chemical missile attacks. Researchers also noted a downward trend in people reporting strong fear during the attacks, and during the interval between them. In February fewer people felt greater apprehension about the consequences of a possible conventional attack than in January.[46] Israelis' anxiety when in the sealed rooms during the attacks also declined in intensity reflecting a process of adaptation.[47] Although Israelis came to believe as the war went on that the possibility of a non-conventionally armed missile attack was slim, the order to wear gas masks and remain in sealed rooms stayed in effect throughout the war. This was a reminder that the risk of a chemical or biological attack was not discounted.[48]

Risk communication

Making a detailed assessment of the risk communication strategy and its effectiveness is complicated by the lack of information available. Despite the lack of risk communication material written on the 1991 Gulf War, there is evidence elsewhere that provides some insight into the effectiveness of the Israeli government's risk communication strategy.

During the first four days of Desert Storm, Israelis were instructed to remain at home, within reach of their gas masks and their sealed rooms. Initially the warning time of attack was 90 seconds – providing very little time for civilians to don their gas masks and move into their sealed rooms. The warning time was later extended to five minutes when the Israeli warning sirens were linked to the US ballistic missile early warning network (which comprised of the Defence Support Programme satellites designed to detect the hot plume of ballistic missile launches). The Israeli Army appointed Brigadier General Nachman Shai as the official radio spokesman for the duration of the war whose duty it was to inform the Israeli population of a missile attack and give instructions as to when people could remove their masks and leave the sealed rooms.[49] The announcement of an impending missile strike came with a warning over a dedicated radio station that only broke its silence when an attack had been identified with the code words *Nachash Zepha* meaning 'poisonous viper', followed by the message below:

> Due to a missile attack on Israel, a real alert has been sounded. All residents must immediately put on their gas masks and close themselves off in their sealed rooms. After the family has entered the room, the doorway should be sealed with masking tape. The air-conditioning must be turned off immediately. You must check to see that your children have put their gas masks on properly. Stay tuned to the radio for further announcements.[50]

To assist in informing the populace of which areas of the country were attacked and which remained at risk while checks were carried out to see if a chemical weapon had been released, and in enabling the all clear to be given quickly to those who could remove their masks and leave the sealed rooms, the army divided the country into six regions, each represented by a different letter.[51]

One factor enabling successful risk communication is whether adequate risk characterisation has been conducted to understand the perceptions, knowledge and behaviours of the target audience. For effective risk communication, this entails a two-way dialogue. Some mental health papers question whether Israelis were adequately informed and whether it was properly understood by government how they would interpret and understand its advice on civil defence preparations and the use of protective equipment prior to the onset of hostilities. Several medical journals believe that the widespread state of anxiety and the mistakenly injected atropine could be in part due to the process of preparing the population for possible CW armed missile strikes.[52] Every attack or false alarm was followed by a number of admissions to emergency departments of patients suffering from acute psychological distress, with anxiety as a major component. As noted earlier, around three-quarters of those who arrived at hospitals after an attack came for psychological symptoms. As the conflict proceeded and as the public's practical knowledge of the various aspects of the problem increased, there was a considerable reduction in the level of anxiety, as well as in the number of unnecessary injections.[53] Israel's experience does raise questions concerning the methods used to disseminate adequate information about CW protection among a civilian population.[54]

While the lack of effective information on the use of protective equipment could have contributed to its misuse, the government did provide a reassuring message to its populace that it was still in control despite the apparent vulnerability and restraint it showed by not retaliating against Iraq. The Israeli government went to great lengths to emphasise that the refusal not to respond militarily was an act of control.[55] The government emphasised in frequent television and radio broadcasts that they had the power to respond forcefully and decisively at any time, and that they were choosing for the time being to delay a response.[56] Use of the term 'delay' gave the impression that a response was possible. This strategy may have enabled Israelis to feel a large measure of control even in inaction.[57] This was an effective tool of risk communication because, while providing reassurance that Israel's predicament was involuntary, it did not convey that it was powerless to exert force to improve its security.

Risk perception

This section is divided into two sections. First, the response of the nation to violence followed by the probable risk perceptions of Iraq's missile threat and capability in the lead-up to the 1991 Gulf War. Second, how these perceptions evolved during the conflict.

Prelude to war

Familiarity with conflict

Since the state of Israel was created in 1948, the nation has endured years of violence through conflict and tension with its neighbours through the three Arab–Israeli wars and more recently the First Intifada. Applying lessons learnt from how the Israelis coped during the 1991 Gulf War has to take into account the pre-existing threshold the population had for enduring violence. Although Israelis had long been used to violence in their country, the threats posed by the missile strikes presented a new threat which past experiences provided little support to draw upon.[58] Nevertheless these past experiences arguably provided some coping mechanisms. It is possible that the Israeli public, with its history of intermittent wars and almost constant exposure to external danger and violence, may had become to some extent psychologically immunised against the danger associated with a war situation, including the severity of imminent missile attacks.[59] How significant these past experiences may have been is hard to ascertain, but nevertheless this factor should not be omitted.

Perceptions of Iraq's missile threat

As the 15 January UN deadline approached for Iraq to withdraw from Kuwait, the Israelis' risk perception of the threat posed to themselves by Baghdad's missile capability was framed by two key themes. First, the information available to Israelis concerning Iraq's capability and the likelihood of this being used against their state. Second, their perception of Israel's limited military capability to defend itself against missiles strikes.

Israeli perceptions of Iraq's capability can be divided into three factors. First, it was recognised during Desert Shield (from Iraq's invasion of Kuwait until the UN January deadline passed) that Iraq possessed non-conventional warheads for its missiles (primarily chemical). It was not reliably known prior to Desert Storm if the Iraqis had successfully developed a chemical warhead for their missiles, but what was sure was that if they had, their extended range missiles would only carry a small quantity of chemical agent and would be very inaccurate.[60] Second, Iraq had missiles capable of striking Israel. The range of the Al-Hussein missile had clearly been demonstrated a few years earlier during the Iran–Iraq War of the Cities where this weapon system proved that it had a range of 500 km when it impacted on Tehran. Last, Iraq's chemical weapons attacks against Iranian forces during the war, and against Kurds in Halabja in north-eastern Iraq in March 1988, proved Saddam Hussein's willingness to use such weapons. Pictures shown by the

Israeli media in the lead-up to hostilities of nerve gas used by Iraq in the war with Iran and the attacks against Kurdish villagers made the threat all the more terrifying and believable.[61] A survey of the secondary literature reveals that Israelis were not fully informed of the CB threat they could face – it might entail potential long-term injury, prolonged death through disease or chemical poisoning, genetic deformities passed down through generations. Zahava Solomon remarked that, 'the ordinary person, even the generally well educated, had little idea of the nature and scope of the power of these weapons: exactly what the weapons could do to them, what distances their effect might spread, how long their poison might linger on in the environment'. Solomon adds, 'Where the facts were sparse, imagination filled in with a vengeance'.[62]

The threat of a chemical or biological attack on Israel was reinforced by the Israeli government's decision in October 1990 to distribute gas masks to the entire population and recommend the creation of a sealed room in each home. This policy implied an admission on the part of the government and the IDF that the threat of chemical warfare was real.[63] The distribution of gas masks was accompanied with the provision of atropine, an anti-nerve-gas injection. Despite the availability of gas masks and atropine, a segment of the population believed that the missile attacks would never come and some did not claim their gas masks until days before the 15 January UN deadline for Iraqi forces to withdraw from Kuwait. Consequently as the deadline grew nearer, there was a last-minute rush and the public were instructed to prepare a sealed room in which civilians were to reside in the event of chemical attack. These sealed rooms were a crude attempt at increasing protection for Israelis in the event of a chemical or biological attack.

Contributing to Israel's own perceptions of the Iraqi missile threat was the realisation that the state did not have the ability to defend itself by either intercepting the missiles or launching a pre-emptive strike (given Israel's non-war stance). The US pressured Tel Aviv not to pursue offensive military operations against Iraq. Israel's sophisticated and advanced air-defence network, tailored to counter attack from fighters and bombers, offered no defence against ballistic missiles – and the Israelis knew this. The general population of Israel were unaware of the possible deployment of the Patriot missile defence system in the conflict. Those who were aware, knew that the Patriot's PAC-2 capability to intercept missiles remained as yet unproven in battle conditions. This situation was remarkably different to that of previous conflicts Israel had fought with its neighbours. For instance during the 1967 Six Day War, Israel successfully destroyed Egypt's airforce before it took to the air. In the early 1980s Israel destroyed Iraq's nuclear reactor out of concern that this facility was being used to develop the country's nuclear capability. In the lead-up to Desert Storm, the only defence Israel could rely on was the coalition's ability to seek and destroy the Al-Hussein missiles and their Transport Erector Launchers (TEL) before they were used: a daunting task and one that left Israelis helpless.

Generally the situation in Israel was one of anxiety and apprehension, but not of panic as the 15 January deadline approached. There were more questions than answers over 'if' and 'when' Iraq might launch Scud missiles, the payload they would carry and the intensity of the attacks should they come. For all concerned the lead-up to the deadline was a new and uncertain period. The most visible demonstration of unease among the population was the thousands of civilians fleeing towns out of fear of what could become of them if they stayed. First tourists and then Israelis took flights out of the country culminating with an estimated 14,000 departing in the days prior to the deadline.[64] In addition a number of Israelis left the metropolitan areas of Tel Aviv and Ramat Gan, regarded as potential targets, for areas they considered to be safer, like the coastline.

Consequently the missile threat may have been viewed as very much a dread risk with uncertainty as to what the missiles would be armed with, when and how many would be fired over what time period and the casualties they would cause. Their targets were generally believed to be the main metropolitan areas. It was a known and dread risk that Iraq had the capability and intent of launching conventionally armed missiles against Israel as demonstrated by the War of the Cities of the 1980s. nevertheless the threat of conventionally armed missiles were an unfamiliar risk to Israelis who had then no prior experience of missile attacks on the homeland. More alarming for Israelis was Iraq's potential and history of launching chemical weapons. But whether Iraq would do this against Israel or had the capability of successfully executing a chemical warhead on a Scud missile was unknown. Therefore the initial uncertainty and apprehension over what warheads would be employed meant this threat had a higher dread risk combined with the uncertainty of how the conventional missile strikes would affect Israel.

Risk perceptions during the conflict

As the war evolved, the risk perceptions of Israelis to the Iraqi missile threat may have altered from dread risk to known risk as familiarity with the threat developed and the destruction, casualties and deaths were fairly low. This included awareness that the missiles were likely to be armed with conventional rather than non-conventional warheads as previously feared, together with the sense of predictability over the timing and targets of the strikes. This enabled Israelis to adapt to the threat and consequently the risks became more known and of less dread.

Attack timings

Learning that the missile attacks only took place at night, Israelis were able to adapt their lives to fit what became known as the emergency routine. Once the instructions to Israelis to stay at home during the first four days of

Desert Storm were lifted, the country could go about its business with relative ease. Importantly this meant that Israel's economy was not as adversely affected as it could have been, with the workforce returning to near pre-war levels. The Gulf War did have a major impact on Israel's tourism costing the nation an estimated US$2 billion indicating that many potential overseas visitors chose to stay away from Israel.[65] Iraq could have caused considerable disruption to Israel and mounted more pressure on the nation to retaliate had some of the attacks taken place during the day making them less predictable. After the first few attacks, Israelis gradually became accustomed to what they should expect.

Specific targets

With the missile attacks concentrated in the cities of Israel's coastal plain, most of the population was out of their trajectory; within the target areas, only a small minority was actually exposed to a direct or a close hit.[66] Although Israelis had no idea prior to and during the first few days of the missile strikes whether they would concentrate on specific areas, the targeting pattern that emerged arguably added to the predictability and aided adaptation to the conflict and accuracy of missile forecasts. Despite this sense of predictability, the possibility of Iraq changing its targeting practices could not be ruled out for the duration of Desert Storm.

Warheads

While there was initial concern that Iraq might use chemical weapons against Israel, the threat of which was taken seriously enough for the Israeli government to issue protective equipment and advise its populace to have access to a sealed room, no chemical weapons were fired during the conflict. Despite the absence of chemical weapons being employed, the fear of a CW attack persisted.

Minimal casualties and fatalities

As the missile strikes progressed numbers of fatalities and casualties from the attacks were fairly minimal. As outlined in the summary of the 42-day war, out of 1,059 war-related hospital emergency room admissions, only 234 were for injuries sustained from the direct outcome of the missile strikes. Only two of these casualties died of their wounds, 221 suffered mild injuries and ten were classified as moderate wounds. One person succumbed to severe wounds.[67] Four times more people died from the indirect effects of the attacks: four from heart attacks, six from suffocation caused by wearing gas masks with their air-tight caps on.

Risk amplification

Five actions undertaken by Israel may have amplified or reduced the public's perceived risk of Iraqi missile threats and attacks. These are:

1   The civil defence preparations prior to Desert Storm.
2   Use of the sealed room and restrictions on civilian movements during missile alerts.
3   The use of telephone hotlines to seek support and advice.
4   The deployment of the Patriot missile defence system.
5   The advice from mental health community.

Unfortunately there is limited quantitative evidence to suggest how these actions may have influenced the public's risk perceptions and their levels of fear and anxiety.

Civil defence preparations

The distribution of gas masks and nerve-gas antidotes may have heightened levels of fear and anxiety among the population during the lead-up to war, but it also may have enhanced Israelis' sense of security knowing that they had some form of protection against a chemical or biological attack. The studies do not reveal whether the levels and extent of habituation would have been less had gas masks and atropine not been distributed. Lack of protection might have led to increased levels of fear and unease among Israelis. Israel benefited from the knowledge that if war did come, it would probably not occur until after 15 January, the UN deadline for Iraq to withdraw its forces from Kuwait. As Israel has only a small population, the authorities had time to distribute gas masks and atropine to all residences. Unfortunately there is no data to show how civil defence preparations might have effected the perceived risk, fear and anxiety.

The sealed room and restrictions on civilian movements

The curtailing of school, work, community activities and sports events and travel decreased contact among Israelis leaving them in their houses in preparation for missile strikes. While these actions and restrictions were probably necessary, they may have served to reinforce and amplify the seriousness of the threat. Israelis were unsure whether Saddam Hussein would attempt to implement his threat to incinerate half of Israel – the threatened use of chemical or biological weapons making the first missile strike particularly difficult to endure. For people in the sealed rooms during a missile alert, the main lines of contact outside those they shared living space with were the television, radio and telephone.[68] During the missile attack alerts, the imposed isolation may have been reduced by people's sense of connection, that they were all in the same situation, donning their gas masks and entering the sealed rooms whenever the missile alerts were sounded. The sense of connection was increased by the universally received messages of warning and calm from chief Israeli spokesman, Nachman Shai, which were broadcasted on radio and television during and after attacks.[69] Despite this, the perceived threat remained strong. Prior to the deployment of Patriot, one family living in Tel Aviv at the time of the first missile strike commented, 'We were very scared that night, with the helpless feeling of knowing that we were not protected'.[70] The reality of the threat was brought home daily by on-the-spot television coverage of damaged or destroyed buildings and interviews with the survivors who had lost their homes and all their possessions.[71]

Research by Klingman and Kupermintz suggests that being in a sealed room served to amplify the perceived risk of the missile threat. The predominant behaviours Israelis reported when they were in the sealed room were monitoring and communicating activities with significantly fewer reporting negative reactions. In their survey of 93 university students in Haifa and Tel Aviv, 93 per cent noted 'I listened to the radio or watched television', 'I talked to the others in the sealed room' (78 per cent), 'I listened to noises coming from the outside' (76 per cent), 'I constantly checked to see if everyone was OK' (73 per cent). Negative emotional responses were 'I was angry at myself for being afraid', (4 per cent), 'I thought I was going crazy' (4 per cent), 'I cried' (6 per cent); 'I had headaches' (6 per cent), 'I had stomach aches' (7 per cent) and 'I sweated' (8 per cent).[72]

Telephone hotlines

During the war, telephone hotlines were set up to supplement an existing service to cater for the expected demand of Israelis seeking advice and an outlet for their experiences. Hotlines were originally established in the 1970s to offer anonymous emotional support. Although designed to prevent suicide, callers requested help on issues like parental, marital, family, personal and psychological problems. During the Gulf War each hotline service was tailored to provide advice to specific segments of the population that deemed to have special needs. These included the elderly, students, children, new immigrants and Holocaust survivors. These hotlines were seen as providing an important public service, as meeting specific needs of the people who turned to them, and as not having much, if any, negative overflow. The hotlines had to strike a balance between legitimising an individual's fears and anxieties, on the one hand, and providing information, advice and support that would bolster coping and control.[73]

A study of the of 3,215 calls to seven hotline centres compared with non-war calls revealed that 70 per cent were new callers and one-third of the calls were for 'environmental pressures', as compared to a non-war rate of zero.[74] The high percentage of new callers suggests that Israelis felt the need to consult the hotlines because of the pressures exerted by the conflict.

Furthermore in 98 per cent of the cases callers expressed variations of anxiety directly related to the stressful situation of the war. The nature of the calls included those seeking an outlet to discuss their fears and anxieties and those wanting practical advice on civil defence preparations.[75] It is possible that Israelis' exposure to psychologists openly talking about the fears and anxieties in the media and providing instructions on how to behave increased the legitimisation of seeking psychological help. It is also possible that psychologists explicitly told people to call crisis lines.[76] The uncoordinated plethora of public health professionals offering different types of advice may have legitimised, spread, augmented or even created the public's anxiety.[77] While the hotline-usage data point to a significant number turning to hotlines during the Gulf War, it is not clear what proportion was directly caused by the missile threats or the ongoing health professionals advice in the media, or to what degree the hotlines decreased or increased the public's fears and anxieties.

The deployment of the Patriot missile defence system

While surveys used various methodologies to examine the overall trends in the changes in behaviours and attitudes as a result of the missile strikes, an area not covered in any detail is the effect the deployment of the Patriot PAC-2 missile defence system had on the risk perception of Israelis.

The operational use of the Patriot PAC-2 missile defence system marked the first time missile defences were used in conflict. The fact Israel did not directly participate in the conflict provided the researcher with the closest thing possible to a set of 'control' data; the 1991 Gulf War provided the first opportunity to measure the effect missile defence can have on a population's levels of fear and anxiety. To provide protection against missile attacks, US-manned Patriot batteries were flown into Israel to reinforce those already supplied to the IDF within days of Desert Storm breaking out. Israel requested the immediate deployment of Patriot following extensive television coverage of the Scud 'intercepts' in Dharan, Saudi Arabia. The US responded by rushing 32 of the missiles to Israel in 17 hours[78] with the first Patriot battery becoming operational around 20 January. The Dutch government also supplied a Patriot unit. Originally designed as an anti-aircraft missile, its software had been significantly upgraded and its fusing mechanism modified to give Patriot some anti-missile capability.[79]

The PAC-2 Patriots deployed during the Gulf War played a tremendous role in reducing the anxiety created by Iraq's Scud attacks against Israel and Saudi Arabia. The deployment of Patriot was greeted with relief and appreciation by the Israeli public[80] and released pressure that had been building on the Israeli government to order the IDF to launch attacks against Iraq.

The DBS survey suggests that the deployment of Patriot on 20 January led to a decline in the levels of fear and anxiety and expectations of a missile attack among the Israelis. Apprehension over the results of a chemical attack declined from 55 per cent on the 18 January to 40 per cent on 20–21 January. Similarly panic levels (and panic was not defined) decreased from 32 per cent on 19 January to 25 per cent on 20 January. Expectations of a chemical and conventional attack too declined from 18–20 January from 46 per cent to 21 per cent (chemical) and 79 per cent to 55 per cent (conventional).[81] The expectation level of a chemical attack reached its lowest point on 20 January. Following these dips, all levels were to increase gradually peaking on 27 January only then to gradually decline. This peak may have been attributed to seven missiles strikes recorded on 25 January – six of which came in one attack against Tel Aviv and a further six missiles on the following day: three against Haifa and three landing in central Israel. From the third week of the conflict (1 February), the levels of worry flattened and did not exceed those measured during the first two weeks.

While public anxiety did not disappear, the knowledge that something was being done combined with the displays of spectacular Patriot 'intercepts' provided at least some reassurance. Until Patriot was operational, Israeli civilians were instructed to remain near their gas masks and sealed rooms. Once incoming Scuds started to be 'intercepted' a sense of normality gradually returned. The sense of normality and adaptation is all the more remarkable considering that damage on the ground may have actually increased following the Patriot deployments, although there is no evidence to suggest that the Israeli public were aware of this.

Prior to Patriot's deployment around 20 January, 13 Scuds were fired causing damage to 2,698 apartments and wounding 115 people. Following Patriot's deployment, there were 14–17 Scuds engaged over Tel Aviv and Haifa causing damage to 7,778 apartments and wounding 168.[82] This marks a 280 per cent increase in buildings damaged during Patriot's operational period. The increase in physical damage could have occurred from either first, falling fragments of Scud and Patriot missiles following a successful interception; second, the intercepts broke the Scuds into large pieces that fell to the ground; third, the interceptor missed its target, or chased the Scud or fragments into the ground. The interceptor potentially caused more damage when it struck the ground intact than a Scud missile would as the amount of explosive and fuel payload carried would have been greater than that carried by the Scud on re-entry.[83] Estimates on misses range from 56 per cent given by then Congressman Les Aspin in May 1991 to as much as 80 per cent or more according to the Israelis.[84]

From the public's point of view, the dramatic visual impact of Patriot was enhanced by the fact that there was no other visual television news coverage of coalition military activities, apart from press conference briefings and limited footage from CNN in Baghdad. Thus, according to Theodore Postol, 'The Patriot was given centre stage on television for a significant part of the Gulf War, having a magical effect on the public's perception of events'.[85]

While it is hard to gauge to what extent the deployment of Patriot hastened the adaptability of the Israelis, evidence from surveys and first-hand accounts suggests that Patriot served to reassure the population and reduce the levels of fear and anxiety. The fact that these levels then gradually increased, peaking on 27 January, infers that Patriot did not help to maintain the low levels expressed in the DBS survey on 20 January throughout Desert Storm. It is difficult to ascertain whether this peak on 27 January and subsequent levels would have been higher had it not been for the deployment of Patriot.

The advice from the mental health community – so-called 'experts'

While fear of the unknown and anxiety among the population were key elements of the Israeli experience, so too were attempts by the Israeli government and mental health professionals to stem these fears. From the outset it became clear that the fear of the unknown was to become a major factor in the campaign equalling if not exceeding the effect of direct casualties caused by the Scud missile strikes. After all three times more people were killed by the fear of the attacks than the attacks themselves.

One of many unique variables of the war was the plethora of mental health professionals including psychiatrists, psychologists and social workers offering advice, opinions and information via the media and telephone hot-lines. In the one corner were the missile 'terror weapons' striking Israel. In the other were mental health professionals attempting to address and calm the resulting fears and anxieties. Despite the good intentions of the mental health professionals, their work lacked co-ordination and in some instances may have exacerbated pre-existing fears and anxieties.[86] The media became inundated with mental health personnel offering advice of one sort or another, some at times allowing their new-found public exposure to get the better of them.

Conclusion

Overall the Israelis responded to the war in a well-disciplined, self-controlled manner with most people keeping their anxieties under control, following the emergency instructions.[87] Moreover, anxiety levels declined and a sense of mastery increased. However, some signs of apprehension continued unabated.[88] In this context it could be concluded that it is public perceptions of whether non-conventional weapons were likely to be used that mattered, rather than the true intentions of the adversary. The latter can gain from creating the impression that such attacks may occur without ever having to take the fateful decision to actually carry them out. A pre-existing reputation for ruthlessness and/or irrational behaviour can exacerbate these risk perceptions.

Research on the 1991 Gulf War suggests that time and proximity to the missile attacks was strong determinants of the level of terror resulting. Misuse of atropine and gas masks, and the arrival of the 'worried well' at hospitals, for instance, all decreased as the attacks progressed. The effects of time could also be partly explained by the changing risk perceptions of the Iraqi missiles from an unknown intent of when, where and what they might be armed with prior to Desert Storm through to a greater sense of certainty of the timing (after dark), targets (metropolitan areas like Tel Aviv and Haifa), and nature of the attack (i.e. conventionally armed weapons). The contrast between expectations of a chemical attack and the reality that Israelis encountered is further reinforced by a survey four weeks after the war finished, establishing that 61 per cent of Israelis thought Iraq would use chemical weapons.[89] While the Israeli risk perception of the Scud threat may have developed into more of a known risk than a dread risk as people became accustomed to the missile campaign, the environment was still a dread risk (uncontrollable and involuntary). While Israelis could take protective measures themselves during missile alerts, they still had no control over the perpetrators of the missile strikes.

The reduction in atropine poisoning and deaths from wearing gas masks inappropriately could also be attributed to inadequate risk characterisation prior to hostilities. The authorities did not fully understand how their populace would interpret and understand the government's advice on civil defence preparations on the use of protective equipment, leading to misunderstandings that led to death in some cases. While the authorities' risk characterisation may have contributed to the misuse of protective equipment, the uncoordinated plethora of public health professionals offering different degrees of advice may have, in line with Roger Kasperson's ripple-effect concept, amplified levels of fear and anxiety. The Israelis' exposure to psychologists openly talking in the media about their experiences increased the legitimisation of seeking psychological help. As Solomon noted, this may have spread, augmented or even exacerbated public anxiety.[90]

The proximity effect is less defined than that of time, but still suggests that those nearest to the sites of impact suffered the most. While those who were evacuated after their property was damaged or lost encountered significant psychological problems, the literature is not conclusive on the degree to which proximity affected the terror experienced. Increased cardiac deaths were limited largely to regions struck by missiles and residents of the targeted regions reported significantly more anxiety than the rest of the country. However studies on sleep disturbance and reported anxiety and symptoms showed proximity had no effect. The small size of Israel may well have limited the effects of proximity.

Iraq's 1991 Scud attacks on Israel demonstrated how a minor missile power can compensate for its military inferiority by utilising conventionally armed missiles to wage asymmetric warfare against a technologically superior adversary. The Israeli case suggests that, coupled with threats to use chemical or biological weapons, conventionally armed attacks are able to exert unease and anxiety out of proportion to their destructive power, but the terror generated is limited and not in this case sufficient to cause a shift in the political establishment even though it was thought Iraq would be deterred by Israel's military capability. Israel did not enter the war, but this was partly helped by the predictability of when and where the missiles would strike and how they would be armed. In addition the deployment of Patriot added a sense of protection to a nation that had perceived itself to be defenceless.

Despite the often terrifying nature of the attacks and the continued uncertainty of the war, only a very small number of deaths resulted, and the physical destruction caused to buildings was concentrated to certain areas. The fact that more people died as an indirect effect of the attacks than the attacks themselves demonstrated the fact that the Scud attacks were not as lethal or destructive as was previously thought. Were there to have been major disasters caused by a missile attack, for instance, striking a large public gathering, the adaptation and habituation demonstrated by the Israelis may have occurred far more slowly and not have reached such a high level.

Clearly this study relied on a series of medical papers to draw its conclusions. Despite the plethora of research undertaken during the Gulf War there are a number of variables that could have influenced the empirical evidence and conclusions drawn. Zahava Solomon noted that 'the pressure of war made it difficult, if not impossible, to plan the studies carefully. The specified circumstances and the issues that were examined often called for improvised measures, whose reliability and validity there was no time to ascertain.'[91] Inconstancies exist in the methods used in terms of sample size and period of evaluation. Despite the difficulties in comparing studies like with like, there were consistencies in the conclusions drawn: that Israelis adapted well to the missile threat through the emergence of an 'emergency routine', while apprehension over the possibility of a non-conventional attack persisted throughout the conflict albeit at lower levels during the latter half.

The role of the mental health professionals and government information provides a good insight into how authorities could handle information in the event of a major terrorist incident possibly involving chemical, biological or radiological attack. The high demand for the hotlines indicated a need for a passive information service: one that is there if you need it. Asher Arian and Carol Gordon are arguably correct in their summary that the 'missile attacks were designed to terrorise the civilian population and to involve Israel in the war'. They add 'But the population was not terrorised. There was no collapse of civilian morale. And Israel did not get involved in the war.'[92]

The risk amplification section outlined five areas where the country's response may have altered the public's risk perceptions and fears and anxieties.

While there is limited quantitative evidence, the preparations and restrictions placed on society, together with the need to seek shelter during the attacks, including the preparation of a sealed room, may have reinforced the seriousness of the threat and belief in the possibility of a CB weapon being deployed. The deployment of Patriot provided the reassuring perception that Israel was not unprotected and could do something to actively defend itself, even though ground damage increased following its deployment.

Conventionally armed missile strikes combined with threats of non-conventional attack may cause anxiety in the early stages of a conflict, but gradually the population becomes accustomed to the new environment, with the development of an 'emergency routine' and adaptation. The speed at which adaptation occurs is dependent upon the concentration of attacks, an increased sense of predictability, timing, concentration, payload, targets and pre-existing thresholds of conflict and violence. The context of the war (whether the people supported the country's involvement) also has an effect. Fluctuations in these variables and how the country handles its public information would all influence the level of adaptation.

5 The Tokyo sarin attack

Introduction

The religious sect Aum Shinrikyo (which means Aum Supreme Cult) became the first-known non-state actor to successfully release a chemical weapon in a populated area with their sarin attacks on Matsumoto on 27 June 1994 and Tokyo's subway system on 12 March 1995. The latter injured 3,796 and killed 12 and is the focus of this chapter. Compared to the other case studies, the assessment of this event relies more on qualitative evidence from first-hand accounts and observations than on quantitative material like medical papers and opinion polls. This study provides some key findings into how a populace responds to a chemical attack in a built up area, and how the response of the emergency services and government communication strategy can exacerbate the terror caused. A particular strength is the first-hand accounts and threat perceptions captured by interviews and observations by commentators.

The chapter is divided into the following sections.

- Background
- Strategic and political objectives
- Overview of the attack
- Political effects
- Effects of proximity and time
- Changes in behaviours and attitudes
- Risk communication
- Risk perception
- Risk amplification.

To fully understand the nature of the subway attacks and their ramifications on the social and political fabric of Japan, it is first necessary to place into context the rise of the Aum Supreme Truth sect. This entails an overview of Aum's previous attempts at chemical and biological attacks that had limited success, and the failures of Japan's law enforcement community to curtail Aum's activities despite having a number of opportunities to intervene.

Background

The origins of the Aum Supreme Truth sect stemmed from the 1980s when the partially blind Shoko Asahara (born Chizuo Matsumoto) ran a series of yoga schools as part of his organisation titled the Aum Association of Mountain Wizards. Bound by the belief that he had received a message from God ordering him to lead God's army to survive the coming Armageddon then scheduled for the end of the twentieth century, Shoko Asahara turned his organisation into a religious group and renamed it the Aum Supreme Truth sect. Drawing heavily from the rituals and beliefs of Tibetan Buddhism, and the physical rigour of yoga, Asahara began developing a powerful personality cult.[1] Four factors contributed to the sect's rapid rise:

1   The popularity of new religions in Japan
2   The collapse of Japan's economy
3   Dissatisfaction among the young with Japan's rigid society
4   The government granting the sect official religious status.

Japan has historically had a turbulent past with regard to religion, in particular in the early part of the twentieth century in the way it was abused through state Shintoism before and during the Second World War. Since the Meiji Revolution in 1869 Japan has endured three successive waves of new religions (*shinshukyo*) all of which purported to provide answers for and to address the special needs of certain constituencies that felt left out or alienated from society.[2] The spiritual vacuum of the post-war years provided fertile ground for new cults and creeds – the best established being the Soka Gakkai, a sect based on Buddhism.[3] According to Daniel A. Metraux, the considerable wealth that had been achieved in the 1980s created a spiritual void that on occasion led to a fascination with mystical and occult phenomena often associated with 'New Age' practices.[4] Aum with its promises of spiritual well-being offered an avenue for the disaffected.

Aum appealed to the disaffected in society who could not conform to the values and lifestyles of modern Japan and reacted against the perceived materialism of the economy that was generating considerable wealth for many. The collapse of the Japanese economy fuelled the recruitment of new members with 7,000 joining in 1991 as the economic boom came to a sudden end. By 1995, Aum had over 10,000 members that included 1,000 'renunciates' (*shukke*) members who followed Aum's lifestyle of beliefs and practices. Aum's rise was secured not just by a huge increase in members and cash donations, but also the granting of official religious status in 1989 that provided Aum with the special tax breaks afforded to all religious organisations.

Despite its religious appeal, Aum had a more sinister side. By 1990 Aum had already committed fraud, kidnapping, imprisonment of minors against their guardians' will, murdered four people and cultured botulinus toxin, a lethal bacterium, signalling the beginning of its biological weapons pro-gramme.[5] Aum had an ambitious plan to mass-produce AK-74 rifles with the aim of manufacturing 1,000 rifles and one million rounds by 1995. Aum's representative in Russia unsuccessfully attempted to hire a Mil Mi-26 heavy-lift helicopter and purchase second-hand T-72 tanks, MiG-29s and even a nuclear warhead.

The centre for Aum's chemical weapons (CW) research and development was the Satian 7 facility at Mount Fuji. Costing around US$120 million to build, the chemical plant was completed in 1993 and began running experi-ments in September of that year. The intention was to mass-produce not only sarin, but other nerve agents. Production of sarin had commenced by November of 1993. A target of 70 tonnes of sarin had been set by Asahara, aiming for mass-production by April 1994. In order to avoid the attention of the Japanese authorities, Aum Shinrikyo had set up two chemical com-panies, Bel Epoch in Shizuoka and Hasegawa Chemical in Tokyo, for pur-chasing large quantities of various chemicals.[6] The sect used an array of front companies to purchase the necessary equipment and materials to manufac-ture chemical and biological weapons (CBW). By 1995, Aum had at its dis-posal 37 companies to assist in its CW research and development.

Strategic and political objectives

The Tokyo sarin attack had two key aims. First, to lead a *coup d'état* to follow the anticipated day of Armageddon and second, to distract the National Police Agency (NPA) from launching raids against the sect's facilities. Shoko Asahara had convinced himself and his fellow sect members that Armageddon would occur by the end of the 20th Century. Throughout the 1980s and 1990s until the arrest of Shoko Asahara, the anticipated date for Armageddon changed. In 1987 Ashara made his first major prediction that between 1999 and 2003 a major nuclear war would break out, but this could be averted if there were an Aum branch in every country. The religious sect used his apocalyptic preaching to build whole communities and raise millions of dollars.[7] Cult members believed that only loyal followers would survive. Armageddon was initially predicted to be in 2002, but was then re-scheduled for 2000, followed by 1999. In 1993 Aum had opted for 1996 as the day of reckoning, and then in the following year for 1995.

In response to their belief that Armageddon was to arrive, Aum planned a *coup d'état* called operation X-Day. The idea was to use helicopters to spray sarin over the legislature and bureaucracy, killing thousands and paralysing the state. To govern the nation, Aum established a shadow cabinet of 24 ministries that would step in to run the country. Predictions of Armageddon received an unexpected boost on 17 January 1995 when the Kobe earth-quake hit Japan. The guru claimed he had predicted the earthquake.

The final factor that drove Aum to launch its attack was the knowledge that its facilities were soon to be raided in connection with the disappearance of Kiyoshi Kariya who had been kidnapped and murdered by the sect weeks earlier. Kiyoshi Kariya's sister was a member of Aum and had donated large sums of money to the sect, but became disenchanted with the cult and fled from her Shinrikyo residence. To track down her whereabouts, Aum kidnapped Kiyoshi Kariya on 28 February 1995. After kidnapping Kiyoshi Kariya, Aum brought him to Satian 2 for questioning and administered a truth drug sodium thiopental Aum had manufactured itself. The following day Kiyoshi Kariya died because too much sodium thiopental had been administered. The kidnappers had failed to take adequate safeguards to protect their identity, having left their fingerprints on a hire van they used to take Kiyoshi Kariya to Satian 2, enabling the police to identify one perpetrator as an Aum member.

Aum's police informers had notified Asahara on 18 March 1995 that Aum Shinrikyo's facilities were to be raided within a matter of days. Asahara felt he had no option but to launch a pre-emptive strike against the police and instructed Seiichi Endo who was Aum's Chief of the Health and Welfare Ministry to manufacture sarin. Attacking the National Police Agency (NPA), it was thought, would distract the police's attention from Aum as they would be dealing with the aftermath of the chemical attack, thus averting the raid. Although Aum had destroyed sarin compounds in late 1994 in preparation for their public relations exercise in inviting the media into Satian 7, Nakagawa hid a key compound in Satian 6 that was one step away from sarin synthesis: difluoromethylphosphonate.[8] On 18 March Asahara ordered the manufacture of sarin for the subway attack. The following evening sarin was produced from the difluoro compound.

Overview of the attack

Aum's method of deploying the sarin was to have five members carrying two bags, each containing 60ml of crude sarin onto allocated trains. To release the sarin gas, the bags would be placed on the floor and punctured with an umbrella allowing the chemicals to pour onto the carriage floor and slowly evaporate into sarin gas. Seiichi Endo produced nearly two gallons of sarin for the attack, but the sarin was only 30-per-cent pure.

Shortly after 7:30am, five members of the Aum Supreme Truth cult boarded five trains at different ends of the Hibiya, Marunouchi and Chiyoda lines, knowing that by 8:15am, all five trains would converge upon Kasumigaseki, the closest station to the police headquarters. As there was sufficient sarin to fill only 11 bags, only five trains were attacked with three bags of sarin on the Hibiya line. The sarin bags were deployed on subway cars nearest to the exits used by police from the Tokyo Metropolitan Police Department (TMPD) and the NPA, and punctured a few stops before reaching the Kasumigaseki junction. Knowing that Tokyo's subway system is highly reliable, Asahara could depend on the trains converging at Kasumigaseki between 8:09 and 8:13 at the height of the rush hour. Despite using a crude delivery mechanism, there were in all 12 deaths and 3,796 injuries on the following lines.[9]

1	Hibiya line to Megro:	7 deaths; 2,475 injured
2	Hibiya line to East Zoo Park:	1 death; 532 injured
3	Marunouchi line to Ogikubo:	1 death; 358 injured
4	Chiyoda line to Yoyogi:	2 deaths; 231 injured
5	Marunouchi line to Ikebukuro:	No deaths; 200 injured.[10]

In all around 5,500 people went to 280 medical facilities in the days following the attack.[11] One thousand required hospitalisation.[12] The majority of the casualties were treated at St Luke's Hospital because of its proximity to the Kasumigaseki and Tsukiji stations. An indication of the different levels of contamination commuters were exposed to can be gained by looking at St Luke's statistics where 82 per cent (532) of patients were regarded as having mild injuries, 16 per cent (107) moderate and less than 1 per cent (5) categorised as severely injured.[13] With only 54 in total regarded as critically or severely injured, hospitals were still faced with a hundredfold increase in patients.[14]

Ambulatory (walking wounded) patients were given showers, non-ambulatory patients were decontaminated by means of bed baths and a change of bedclothes.[15] Two died from their injuries. Within four days, 95 per cent of those who had been admitted were discharged. Of the victims who survived the attack, 43 per cent were on the platform at the time of the incident, while 31 per cent were on the train and 15 per cent somewhere else in the station. Nine per cent were in other places, suggesting that sarin can spread some distance from its origin.[16]

Political effects

The sarin attack had two objectives. The first was to attack the NPA to distract the police's attention from proceeding with the raid on the sect's facilities. The second was to initiate the process of Armageddon and a *coup d'état* to take over Japan. The raids still proceeded against Aum and the attacks failed to precipitate a *coup d'état*. While the attacks failed to cause the desired effect, it is important to investigate what political effects, if any, Aum had on Japan.

The political establishment chose to implement measured steps to clamp down on Aum rather than impose draconian laws. Despite the widespread dispersal of the sarin attack on Tokyo and the clear intent to launch further strikes in the following weeks with, for example the attempted release of sodium cyanide on 5 May at Shinjuku subway station, there was no heavy-handed clamp-down on the sect nor instigation of widescale security measures to constrain civil liberties. Arguably the terror generated did not prompt the political establishment to take swift action to deal with Aum.

Despite being bankrupted by the end of 1995, initial legislation failed to cause Aum to collapse completely as the Liberal Democrat Party (LDP) government had sought to achieve through its strategy of implementing legislation that would be just enough to ensure that Aum did not pose a threat to society. As will be discussed below, it took four years for sufficient legislation to be passed and the deficiencies of earlier statutes to be addressed before Aum posed no threat.

Despite the large number of casualties, the fatalities were low and Tokyo's infrastructure was only mildly affected. The potential ripple effects directly caused by the release of sarin were limited by the subways reopening so soon after the attacks. Although Aum attempted to cause maximum chaos, the subway system was back in operation the day after the attacks. Decontaminating the effected carriages and infrastructure was not complex as sarin can be rapidly degraded to a harmless substance by applying sodium hydroxide, an effective and inexpensive detoxifying agent. Sodium hydroxide is available commercially and can be used to counter many nerve agents and other poisonous, organic gases.[17] The decontamination process was carried out by Japan's Self Defence Force's CW unit who were on the scene the afternoon of the attack.

Raids

Although the attacks aimed to halt the police raids against Aum, no police were among the dead and the raids proceeded on 22 March, ten days after the subways were struck. The casualties and disruption caused were not sufficient to halt operations. Prior to the raid, on 20 March Aum hid sarin and intermediate compounds under the floor of its hospital. Many documents related to the production of sarin were burnt. Aum was aware of the impending police operation and as soon as the police left their Tokyo headquarters on 22 March to raid Kamikuishiki, Aum Shinrikyo sent a coded radio message warning its sect of the imminent raid. The largest of the raids was carried out at Kamikuishiki.

In the raids, the police confiscated large quantities of chemicals, including 50 tons of phosphorus trichloride, the starting materials to produce sarin. In addition 1.5 tons of nitric acid and 60 tons of glycerol used in the manufacture of explosives were discovered.[18] The police also discovered US$7million in cash and 22lbs of unassayed gold bars.[19] There were also 50 followers that had been fasting, some unconscious on the floor. The only arrests made were of three doctors on the premises and a cult official on suspicion of unlawful confinement.[20]

The political response

Despite the unprecedented nature of the attack and the revelations surrounding the sect's activities, Japan's political system responded in a measured manner by enacting three sets of laws. These were: tightening the Religious Corporations Law that provided tax incentives; legislating to tighten up controls on the manufacture of sarin; and the ruling LDP government implementing legislation that gradually increased the pressure on Aum to make the group impotent.[21]

Japan resisted the temptation to dramatically curtail the rights of religious groups and undermine civil liberties. A controversial act Japan could have used against Aum to assure it posed no further threat to Japanese society was the 1952 Anti-Subversive Activities Law to disband the organisation. This legislation was originally designed to counter the potential threat posed by subversive groups during the Cold War, for instance, communists. However, on 31 January 1997 the Public Security Commission (PSC) declared that there was insufficient evidence that Aum posed any future danger. The main impact on the political and social landscape was, according to Mark Mullins, the recognition that, 'the time had come to be more concerned for the protection of the public from dangerous and abusive religious groups rather than be overly concerned about the protection of religious freedom'.[22] The new social climate enabled politicians to argue successfully to tighten regulations concerning religious groups.

In December 1995 the ruling LDP passed legislation to amend the 1951 Religious Corporations Law to tighten the overseeing of religious groups.[23] The key amendments required religious corporations to submit to the Ministry of Education an annual report providing details of their finances, constitution and list of officers. Second, groups operating in more than one prefecture were required to register with the Ministry of Education, as opposed to their local authority.

The Tokyo Public Prosecutor revoked the sect's religious status on 30 October 1995 as Aum was deemed as working against the good of society through its criminal activities. The sect was still allowed to continue running their businesses and membership of the group was still legal. However without special tax concessions and with mounting claims brought against the sect by victims of their activities and local government authorities, Aum was declared bankrupt and all assets were frozen on 14 December 1995. It seemed to observers that the financial crisis and notoriety of the sect would bring about its end.

In spite of its financial crisis, the arrest of its key leaders, declining membership and the confiscation of its properties and assets, the sect still existed in 1999. It was hoped that Aum would be unable to survive under this pressure. Faced with its continued existence, the LDP introduced two laws that while not directly mentioning Aum, were designed with the sect in mind. The first law, the Group Regulation Act, allowed any sect that has carried out mass murder in the last ten years to be placed under the surveillance of the Public Security Investigation Agency for a period of three years. Should a group be shown to have committed violent acts or illegal activities, the Public Security Examination Committee is authorised to prohibit the use of its facilities for a period of up to six months. The second bill grants a court-appointed trustee to seek information from the Public Security Investigation Agency regarding the targeted group's assets so that these can be seized and used to compensate victims.[24] The two laws were a halfway point between the implementation of the Anti-Subversive Law and the reliance on existing legislation that had in the past proved insufficient to deal with Aum.

From the political account above, Aum clearly failed to achieve its political objectives. First, it failed to achieve its long-term ambition of taking over Japan, or avert the raids against its facilities. Second, the political effects were marginal. The LDP moved carefully and probably too slowly to curtail the activities of Aum to ensure it did not pose a continuing threat to society by putting in place tight controls and oversight systems to evaluate its practices.

Effects of proximity and time

Proximity

The majority of the evidence available on proximity focuses on those using the metro system on the day of the attack, and much of this is from personal testimonies or publications summarising first-hand accounts rather than quantitative evidence like medical papers or opinion polls. An example of this is David Kaplan's *The Cult at the End of the World* (1996) that suggested there was extreme anxiety among those in the carriages when the attack occurred although he does not define he means by some of his terms. According to David Kaplan, when a Hibiya line train was leaving its next stop following the release of sarin, 'Growing panic in car number three reached critical mass. Passengers gagging, vomiting, handkerchiefs across the face. Confusion and hysteria swept across the train.'[25] However, 'despite the strange odours and the sudden and visible onset of illness among so many passengers, there was no panicky stampede'.[26] This observation is similar to that of David Brackett (1996) who noted that despite the popular image of a nerve-gas attack causing mass panic and hysteria, there was in the first few minutes 'little if any panic'.[27] However neither Kaplan nor Brackett actually define what they mean by panic, and their evidence is very much based on their own observations during their research. Consequently these conclusions need to be verified by other sources to examine their robustness. A more credible qualitative source is Haruki Murakami's work, *Underground: The Tokyo Gas Attack and the Japanese Psyche* (2001).

During 1996 Murakami interviewed 60 victims of the subway attack including a few relatives of the deceased.[28] The personal accounts of those in the contaminated carriages suggest there was no real sense of panic. Again Murakami does not define panic, but his assessment does provide first-hand evidence about whether there was calm on the trains and in the stations. Individuals responded in an orderly fashion as they were evacuated from the affected areas. Marunouchi-line commuter Ikuko Nakayama, when asked by the police if people panicked, recalled, 'Everyone was so silent. No one uttered a word.' She added, 'Oddly enough, I was extremely calm. I knew it was sarin (from having read before the symptoms of the victims from the sarin attack in Matsumoto in June 1994 reporting pupil contractions).' Similarly a passenger on the Hibiya line remarked that as he walked through the station with collapsed people lying who may or may not have been alive, 'I still didn't sense any danger. I don't know why. In retrospect that seems odd – why wasn't I afraid? – but then neither was anyone else.' Furthermore, when the public address system announced that poison gas had been detected and passengers were advised to head for safety above ground, 'The passengers stood up and got off the train, but still there wasn't any panic. They walked a little faster than normal, but there was no pushing or anything. Some put handkerchiefs to their mouths or were coughing, but that's all.'[29]

However, the station attendants were said to be 'all in a panic'. Murakami unfortunately does not examine why the attendants were 'panicking'. Another passenger on the Hibiya line reported that when someone came walking from the next carriage where the gas had been released shouting 'sarin sarin', those around him stood up but did not run to escape.

Despite these first-hand accounts, there is little material about the perception of Tokyo's populace not in the subway system in the hours after the attack. One could assume, based on the proximity evidence in the other case studies that those not near the subway system would have experienced considerably less fear and anxiety – and would have been, for the most part, unaware of the incident until they saw the media reports.

Time

To assess how the passage of time affected the terror generated by the attack, this section examines the effects over the first few days, the weeks after and then the subsequent years. In total over 75 per cent of those who arrived at hospital suffered from psychosomatic symptoms – also referred to as the 'worried well'. This high figure is derived from examining those who sought medical attention. In all around 5,500 people went to 280 medical facilities in the days following the attack. The total number of poisoned victims, as summed up in the police record, came to 3,795 of which 1,046 required hospitalisation – some for no more than a few hours, some for many days.[30] There were 12 deaths. This left over 1,705 (22 per cent) who arrived at medical facilities believing they had been exposed to sarin, but who did not require physiological treatment, and 2,749 (50 per cent of the total) categorised as 'poisoned' by the police but not requiring hospitalisation, although this did not specify whether medical treatment was provided to the latter in the subsequent days and weeks. Therefore around three-quarters of those attending medical establishments did not require medical treatment. David Alexander and Susan Klein believed that the reported ratio of those who sought medical help to those who required immediate medical care was approximately 450:1.[31] This underlined the pressure the medical facilities were under to provide care to those most in need while being inundated with less urgent cases or those that did not need treatment. There was also a significant proportion among those requiring medical attention that exhibited psychological problems. Of the 111 victims 33 per cent were regarded as having mild or serious injuries from the subway attack and showed signs or symptoms of agitation and other psychological symptoms.[32]

In the weeks after the attack, a survey of 610 victims at the Department of Psychiatry at St Luke's International Hospital revealed that psychological reactions were still prevalent with 60 per cent of the 475 respondents reporting symptoms of PTSD.[33] Symptoms included nightmares and numerous flashbacks that included unusual odours, coughing of neighbours, subways, ambulance sirens, depictions of the attack on television, and news of other terrorist attacks.[34] Hundreds of people came to hospitals in the following weeks believing they had been poisoned, but only had psychosomatic symptoms.[35]

Supplementing the evidence from the medical literature is Murakami's work that reveals the individual psychological problems victims experienced in the months after the attack. An analysis of interviews with survivors reveals a number who complained of nightmares, insomnia, mood swings, tiredness and trying to avoid news reports of the attacks in view of the fear these rekindled. Several mentioned becoming apprehensive about taking the subway. For some just walking outdoors caused fear and anxiety. Some of those who did seek advice from mental health professionals were told they had PTSD. One commuter on the Marunouchi line at the time of the attack noted:

> I was afraid to commute again. I'd board the train and see the door slide shut before my eyes, and in that very instant my head would seethe with pain. If I talk for more than one hour my head would be killing me. One day in August it took me three hours to get to work. I had to stop along the route and rest until the pain subsided.[36]

While there is evidence of psychological effects persisting for some weeks after the attack, it is hard to discern to what degree they declined or fluctuated in the absence of material that provides a more detailed breakdown.

In the weeks and months that followed the subway attack, Japanese society focused its attention not so much on the fact that a chemical weapon had been unleashed on the subway system, but on how it had produced a sect as violent as Aum. Searching questions were asked of why and how a segment of their populace could turn against its fellow citizens in such a brutal fashion and how much a sect had obvious wide appeal evidenced by the large number of members and assets it had built up. One Japanese person summed up this perception noting,

> Well-educated young Japanese, some of the country's best minds had, in the name of religion, betrayed the country, its culture, and the Japanese people. Aum was a home-grown terrorist organisation, a pure product of the proud culture in which it took root and thrived to maturation and ultimate evil. Aum was uniquely a Japanese problem.[37]

The shooting of Police Chief Takaji Kunimatsu ten days after the subway attack served to fuel the unease in Japan that its society was ill prepared to respond to Aum's violent activities. Shortly after the shooting, anonymous callers telephoned television stations warning of further attacks on police officials if the investigation into Aum was not stopped. That evening's edition of the *Yomiuri Shimbun* led with the large headline 'WHAT HAPPENED TO OUR SAFE SOCIETY?'.[38] *Time* magazine summed up the psychological impact of the attack, noting:

> The terror has triggered an unprecedented psychological shock wave. While Kobe's earthquake two months ago knitted Japan together in a spontaneous effort to help the stricken, the subway killings and the police shooting have had the opposite effect, straining the ties of courtesy and trust that are so tightly woven into the fabric of society. It seems that the *antei na kuni*, or 'safe society' on which the Japanese have long prided themselves, can no longer be taken for granted.[39]

Members of the sect were also attacked. On 23 April Aum's chief scientist Hideo Murai was stabbed and killed during a press conference he was giving outside Aum's headquarters. The Japanese coined a new word to capture the pervasive mood of apprehension and unending saga: 'sarinoia'.[40] Not since the Japanese Red Army conducted its campaign against the Japanese system had there been a violent and concerted challenge to the status quo.

To exacerbate the feelings of insecurity, Aum planned further CW strikes to disrupt the investigation into the subway incident which itself was conceived to disrupt the police's impending raids on the sect following the disappearance of Kiyoshi Kariya. First, it attempted to release sodium cyanide at Shinjuku subway station on 5 May 1995, Japan's largest and busiest station. Although the bags containing the weapon had set themselves on fire as planned, the bags containing the chemicals had not ruptured to cause a chemical reaction that could potentially have killed thousands. While the device failed to detonate as planned, the attempt clearly revealed that Aum remained intent on launching further attacks.

While further incidents perpetrated by Aum fuelled anxiety, the Japanese greeted the arrest of Shoko Asahara with relief. However, the relief was marred by a parcel bomb that was sent to newly elected Tokyo Governor

Yokio Aoshima who had announced he was considering disbanding Aum. Hours after Asahara's arrest on 15 May, the Governor's secretary opened the package, but survived.

The shock to the nation in the weeks after the subway attack is summarised by Kanzo Nakano, then director of the Kudan Nakano Clinic for neurology and internal diseases, who believed the attack, 'suddenly destroyed our trust in the fundamental humanitarianism of Japanese relationships and challenged our values and belief in the safety of our society'.[41] While society asked searching questions and for a time the populace was concerned over what Aum might unleash next, the Japanese culture may well have exacerbated the fear and anxieties that followed. This is covered in the risk amplification section.

In the longer term, mental health problems are believed to have persisted among the victims for some years after the attack. In 1998 the Tokyo Metropolitan Police Department (TMPD) contacted 5,300 people who had reported being affected, of which 1,247 agreed to be interviewed. More than 70 per cent of the respondents said they still suffered from some psychological after-effects, including PTSD and increased use of alcohol or sleeping pills.[42] In the multiple-choice survey, 56.7 per cent cited some sort of psychological problems. In addition 18.4 per cent said they were paranoid they might some day experience a similar incident, 17.5 per cent reported sudden flashbacks of the scene of the crime and 7.4 per cent complained of recurring nightmares.

A survey that followed the progress of 582 patients admitted to St Luke's following the subway attack found that somatic and psychological symptoms remained five years on.[43] Some continued reporting unexplained physical symptoms in the five years after the attack, suggesting they could be part of PTSD. Of the psychological symptoms, only levels of depression reduced significantly during this period. PTSD levels using the DSM-IV criteria produced less than 3 per cent each year among the victims. However this increased to 9.7 per cent (1998) and 14.1 per cent (2000) when including physical symptoms in the PTSD diagnosis, suggesting that PTSD rates may have actually increased among a segment of survivors. In contrast to the assumption in the Introduction that psychological symptoms would decline over time, this study suggests the opposite. Unfortunately there are no additional surveys to verify these findings.

Changes in behaviours and attitudes

Interviews with survivors prove a good means of evaluating the behavioural changes. These provide a mixed picture with some commuters noting they chose to avoid the subway while others returned to using this transport system without much difficulty. Comments include, 'I was afraid to commute again.'[44] Another survivor noted trying to avoid news of the attack, adding. 'Even now when a [news] report touches on the gas attack, something tightens in my chest. I have not travelled on that route since.'[45] Another commuter observed:

> When in a confined space I'll just stop, especially underground – in the subway or an underground entrance to a department store. I'll start to get on a train and my feet won't move. No one can really understand what it's like, this fear.[46]

Evidence of survivors who did not change their routines included a station assistant who reported, 'the attack didn't upset me to the point where I thought "I can't take it, I have to change jobs." Not at all.' A commuter noted 'Afterwards, I was not scared to travel on the subway.'[47] Another survivor responded, 'Of course, when I first went back to work I was scared the same thing may happen again. It takes positive thinking to overcome fear, otherwise you'll carry around this victim mentality for ever.'

While some people may have expressed initial fear and anxiety about returning to the subway, there is some evidence to suggest that they did return to their regular daily lives. One person who was hospitalised recalled that he found sleeping in the hospital frightening, particularly when left alone and touching something cold like a bed frame, but also observed how he eventually overcame his fears of travelling on the subway.[48] He noted:

> Back at home it was the same. Whenever I touched anything cold, those fears resurfaced. Even when I took a bath by myself. I could not do it alone, I was too scared. Some of the victims are afraid of taking the subway, even now. I was scared at first, too. The day I returned to work I took exactly the same route as I did before the attacks. I even made sure I sat in the same carriage – the same seat. I felt a bit queasy when passing Kamiyacho (where everyone piled out sick) where the attack happened, but having got over it, my spirits lifted. That wiped the slate clean of any anxieties.[49]

While the general populace of Tokyo returned to using the subway system, there was a notable edginess among commuters when they encountered noxious smells on the subway system. In the widespread coverage of the attacks, many survivors recalled a strong pungent odour caused by the impurities in the sarin and this became a sign to look out for in a sarin attack. On the day of the attack when the subway returned to service, one subway line was stopped while a foul-smelling package was investigated. It was later found to contain fish.[50] In the days and weeks that followed, commuters encountered similar but harmless strong odours, at times believing another attack may have been launched. This included a strong smell from a homeless person causing the evacuation of a subway train. The widespread fears about further gas attacks were heightened by a spate of reports of odours from noxious substances stemming from a mixture of copycat exercises and a few that may have been perpetrated by Aum to exacerbate the unease in Tokyo.[51] The fear of another gas release in Tokyo led, on 19 April, to 600 commuters being hospitalised with sore throats and eyes from a youth spraying mace at Yokohama station. On 21 April, another mysterious gas emission in Yokohama sent 24 shoppers to hospital.[52]

The return to normality was assisted by the subway system resuming in the late afternoon of the attacks. Passenger volume dipped slightly but returned to normal soon after the system went back on line.[53] Taxi drivers reported a surge in business as people avoided the subways suggesting a proportion felt the risk was too great. For most there was no real alternative to commuting on the subway although they had a heightened awareness and anxiety when doing so. Some were reported to sniff the subway carriages before boarding and fewer people dozed in their seats out of concern there might be another chemical attack.[54]

The fear of further attacks by the religious sect led to further changes in behaviour when Asahara warned in early April that on 15 April, something terrible would happen to Tokyo worse than the Kobe earthquake. After the Tokyo and Matsumoto sarin attacks, the public took the threat seriously and rumours spread that Aum intended to poison the water supply, prompting residents to store water in their bathtubs. In addition, it was rumoured that Asahara intended to release sarin in a crowded shopping district of Shinjuku, leading stores to increase security or close completely on 15 April.[55] Nothing happened on 15 April. As with the subway-passenger volume evidence, there is again little quantitative material to assess to what extent the Japanese populace changed their behaviours and attitudes in response to the terrorism.

Risk communication

Risk communication may have amplified or attenuated the strategic terror in two ways: First, by communication with those directly exposed to the sarin, and second, by how the government responded and informed the public in the days and weeks after the attack. This includes the government's handling of the Tokyo attack and of the continuing threat posed by Aum.

As noted in the proximity section, there was general calmness on the trains following the attacks. However there is some evidence to suggest that this turned into confusion and heightened fear and anxiety due to lack of information. Survivors noted they only felt considerable fear when they had difficulty in contacting the emergency services and when the emergency workers took a long time to arrive. Ikuko Nakayama, while on a Marunouchi-line platform, recalled that only when nobody answered the emergency phonecall for assistance did she then 'feel real fear', adding, 'everything I had believed up until then just crumbled. From that moment on it was total chaos'.[56]

On the rest of the subway system, the information given to the public and other transit workers was confusing. Transit workers operating the Hibiya line first announced to passengers on the train and in the stations that they had a sick passenger, then later announced that an explosion had occurred at Tsukiji, followed by an announcement to evacuate the train. Despite these reports the Hibiya train continued to operate departing from Tsukiji and heading for Kasumegaseki. The confusion was possibly the same across the subway system given that the operators had no measures in place to centrally collate the information around the network to ascertain whether this was a co-ordinated attack. Each station initially believed they had isolated sick passengers. Although the NPA suspected at around 8:45 that it was a sarin attack when it dispatched the CW unit, it was 45 minutes later before the subway system was shut down.

According to Robyn Pangi, there was no public affairs strategy in place to cope and co-ordinate a response to a mass-casualty attack, concluding:

> The first confusing messages were transmitted to the public by the transit department. False announcements on trains added to the confusion among victims and responders. Further messages were transmitted by the media. The images portrayed on the 9:00am news, which may have exacerbated the nervous frustration of victims and concerned parties, were of confusion and chaos: victims were shown becoming ill and staggering around the city, and searching for answers.[57]

Not only was there confusing information about what was going on, but there was a lack of information for those commuters who had potentially been exposed to sarin about what signs to look out for to indicate poisoning and what protective measures they should take. Several commuters were initially unaware that they had been contaminated and carried on with their daily routine. Some survivors reported afterwards that they first they realised something was wrong with them when everything looked dark – caused by the contraction of the pupils. Only when these people heard from media reports or from colleagues that these were the symptoms of sarin poisoning did they seek medical attention.[58] No government authority used the media to provide health advice on what symptoms to look for in sarin poisoning or what the general populace should do (i.e. when they should seek medical attention).

This lack of official information continued in the days after the attack. In contrast to the cult's position of innocence, Japanese authorities seemed intent on keeping the public in the dark.[59] The day after the attack the police held a meeting with news media officials to inform them that the sarin used was produced in the same manner as that released in Matsumoto in 1994, but they did not hold a press conference to air their suspicions that Aum was behind the attack.[60] Even when 2,000 police officers in nuclear, chemical, biological (NBC) protective equipment raided Aum's facilities days later, the police refused to publicly acknowledge any link between the sarin attack and the cult.[61] However, the raids strongly suggested to the Japanese that Aum was considered to be the prime suspect.

Aum, by comparison, launched an effective public relations exercise insisting the attack had been carried out by US and Japanese forces. Aum's lawyer Yoshinobu Aoyama denied the sect's involvement, blaming the Japanese government, and Asahara released two videos shortly after the initial series of police raids. In the first video he answered a series of questions posed by the NHK television network denying involvement or any connection with the kidnapping of Kiyoshi Karya and the seized chemicals. Asahara asserted he did not understand why these incidents had happened or why the chemicals seized were said to be for the production of sarin. In the second video, Asahara claimed the perpetrator of the sarin attack was 'unmistakably' the US.[62]

The authorities' lack of openness caused what Robyn Pangi observed as the perpetration of 'general fear within the population and among victims, who only knew that the perpetrators were at large and thus could launch a follow-up attack'.[63] Aum's claims of innocence extended to their charismatic 'Information Minister' Fumihiro Joyu whose public profile grew to almost celebrity status.[64] Joyu denied Aum's involvement, launching an aggressive campaign to persuade the Japanese of its innocence. Television networks, recognising their ratings increased when they had Aum members on their show, were agreeing to preconditions established by the sect for appearances of its members.[65] These series of events suggests that the perpetrators sought to use the media to convey their innocence by appealing to their own popularity. Rather than being broadly despised by the general populace, Joyu's treatment by the media suggest he was welcomed by their audiences.

With little information from the government and the emergency services, the media turned to what information sources they could get hold of. Drawing comparisons with the then-US President Bill Clinton's handling of the Oklahoma bombing that occurred shortly after the Tokyo subway attack, Kanzo Nakano of St Luke's International Hospital criticised the Japanese government for the lack of leadership it showed in the immediate aftermath of the attack observing,

> President Clinton stood beside the victims and gave a clear and quick message that he would never forgive the terrorists. This seemed to help the American people recover their trust in their society and leaders, and order and justice was reasserted. But in Tokyo, on the contrary, our leaders and the police kept silent during the initial hours when the whole public was in shock. Ironically the spokesman for the cult seemed to be on television constantly, lying to the public through the media. This fact not only made victims feel deserted, but also pushed the general public into further anxiety.[66]

Based on the available evidence, the Japanese authorities did not implement an effective risk communication strategy immediately following and in the weeks after the attack. Those exposed to the sarin had to acquire information from news reports about what symptoms to look out for etc. As Louise Lemyre observed, 'the lack of a proactive public communications strategy by public authorities while media images portrayed suffering at the scene of the attack, coupled with the lack of follow-up care and support, had a significant influence on the public response to this incident'.[67]

This lack of information and advice meant that hospitals were inundated with thousands of people who incorrectly believed they required urgent medical treatment. In the following weeks, Aum launched an effective public relations campaign while the Japanese government was not highly visible, with no leading figure to take Japan through this period. Leaders and the police kept silent during the initial hours when the whole public was in shock. There is little evidence to show that the authorities had carried out work and were sufficiently prepared to develop an effective risk communication strategy in response to a CW attack. Based on the apparent absence of such a strategy, it could be suggested that there had been very little if any prior work on how they would engage with the public. If there was a strategy, it was not implemented. The slow response by the emergency responders also exacerbated the psychological conditions of the victims as will be shown next. Overall it could be suggested that the authorities did not expect this type of attack, did not know how the population might respond or what risk communication to employ and when.

Risk perception

The risk perception of the Japanese and Tokyo citizens prior to the attack centres on two key themes. First, the limited experience of conventional and non-conventional terrorist attacks on its territory in recent times, and second, the public's awareness of Aum's intention and capability to launch indiscriminate CB attacks.

Japan's only experience with terrorism prior to 1995 had been the Japan Red Army (JRA). With six core active members plus sympathisers, they sought to overthrow the Japanese government and monarchy and to help foment world revolution.[68] However their attacks had mainly occurred outside Japan. During the 1970s, the JRA carried out a series of attacks around the world, including the massacre in 1972 at Lod Airport in Israel, two Japanese airliner hijackings and an attempted takeover of the US embassy in Kuala Lumpur. Mainland Japan though had not experienced a bombing campaign since 1945. The only non-conventional attack Japan had encountered was Aum's release of sarin in Matsumoto in 1994 that killed seven. But at the time the police wrongly blamed a local inhabitant and took seven days to identify it was sarin. Unlike for instance Israel, Britain or Spain who experienced terrorist attacks on their homeland by Palestinian militants, the IRA and ETA respectively, the people of Japan had not been exposed to this type of risk in their everyday lives so were not accustomed to this type of threat.

To the Japanese terrorism was something that happened abroad, such as in the Middle East or in parts of Europe. Limited violence from organised crime gangs had been the most Japanese society had experienced. Consequently the perception of mass-casualty attacks or bombings is likely to have been deemed a low risk and one that did not pose a threat to general society. This risk perception was reinforced by the public's lack of awareness of Aum's true capabilities and intentions beyond reports of alleged kidnappings and fraudulent activities.

Prior to the subway attack, the Japanese public had limited awareness of Aum's capability and intentions to manufacture and release chemical weapons in population centres. This was despite the fact that Aum had already released various types of CW with varying degrees of success, including the release of anthrax in Tokyo in 1993; that attack led only to a foul smell and the death of small birds. Partly because no one noticed the anthrax attempt, Aum was not blamed for it until after the Tokyo attack. One event that did capture the public's attention because of Aum's greater success occurred nine months before the Tokyo attack when Aum released sarin in Matsumoto on 27 June 1994.

This was aimed at forcibly deferring a land dispute ruling to be given by three judges in the city of Matsumoto. In 1991, a food firm bought a plot of land in Matsumoto. Ostensibly it was meant to be a production plant but turned out to be a temple for Aum's new branch. As Aum had falsified their documents, not revealing the true purpose of the land purchase – illegal under Japanese law – the original owner filed a civil law suit to invalidate the sale. Aum responded with a harassment campaign against locals that included threatening calls. Aum's lawyers recognised that they looked set to lose the court battle that would end in May 1994. As a result Aum decided to launch a sarin attack, in an attempt to poison the judges thereby delaying the ruling due that summer. Although the judges survived the attack, seven nearby residents were killed, 264 admitted to nearby hospitals and the total poisoning casualties were estimated to be about 500. The attack was a success: the judges postponed their ruling indefinitely.

As the police did not identify Aum as the perpetrator, the incident did not inform the public of the dangers posed by Aum. The police mistakenly arrested and charged a resident of Matsumoto believing he had accidentally produced sarin while mixing garden herbicidal chemicals together. However, there were some accusations that Aum was behind it, with a number of anonymous letters sent to the media and government offices describing the attack in detail, noting Aum's links to violence and warning that sarin attacks could occur on Tokyo's subway and in concert halls.

In the five years, up to the subway attack, the police had a number of leads pointing to the cult. However for some years they ignored the threat from Aum partly because of a belief that religious groups had to be treated with special care to guarantee their freedom in post-Second World War Japan.

A rare occasion where the public did become suspicious of Aum producing lethal chemicals for potentially sinister uses came in November 1994 when soil samples taken by the police outside Satian 7 were found to have traces of methylphosphine acid monoisopropyl, a residue left when sarin decomposes.[69] The police had been alerted after residents living near Satian 7 began complaining of a noxious odour coming from Aum's compound. By this time Aum had infiltrated the police with its own informers.

Weeks after the police took their covert sample, Aum's police informers notified Asahara of the evidence taken. With this knowledge, Aum embarked on a public relations exercise by inviting the media into Satian 7 for a press conference on 4 January 1995. Having converted the CW facility into a shrine after destroying or moving out related production equipment and chemicals, Aum announced at this press conference that Satian 7 was used for meditation and holding treasures. The police and the public at large did, however, not have much time to assess Aum's attempts to cover up its CW programme as the nation's attentions were temporarily diverted to dealing with the Kobe earthquake that struck on 17 January.

Prior to the subway sarin release, the public had only a limited awareness of the threat Aum posed, of the protective measures required in the event of a sarin attack and hardly any experience of previous terrorism on Japanese territory. Consequently the populace had barely any experience or awareness to fall back on when responding to the attack or preparing for such a situation. With no prosecutions brought by the police, no publicity was generated that could have raised the public awareness of Aum or suggested that the public could be exposed to a CW attack. For the vast majority, the subway attack was a new and unfamiliar risk.

Risk amplification

Discussion on how the response measures may have actually exacerbated rather than contained or controlled the fear and anxiety has been partly touched on in the risk communication section. The perception of the way the emergency responders reacted to the incident may have contributed to the overall terror the targeted populace encountered. As mentioned earlier, one passenger noted that only when nobody answered the emergency phone to call for assistance did she then 'feel real fear', adding, 'Everything I had believed up until then just crumbled. From that moment on it was total chaos.'[70]

While there is limited information about the extent to which the emergency response may have exacerbated the perception of fear and anxiety, there is considerable evidence to demonstrate that the emergency responders were clearly overstretched, possibly leaving many at the affected stations to feel vulnerable. If the delay of first responders left most of those in need of attention feeling increasingly fearful and anxious as it did for the passenger noted above, then there may have been many others whose fears and anxieties were amplified by the slow response.

Evidence of the lack of emergency responders across the subway system can be demonstrated by the fact that 541 arrived at St Luke's Hospital with the assistance of non-medical motorists, while only 64 arrived by ambulance and 35 in minivans operated by the Fire Defence Agency.[71] The scale of these is reinforced by casualties at Kodemmacho station having to wait for around half an hour for the first ambulance to arrive as all the others were at Tsukiji station. A commuter on the Hibiya line recalled that, after the attack, survivors at Kodemmacho who were not seriously injured had to flag down cars to get those seriously hurt to hospital. Even the police at Kodemmacho station, when asked which hospital the injured should be taken to, took several minutes talking on their radios before being able to advise.[72] At the hospitals, the extent of fear and anxiety was reduced by the fact that the medical authorities knew this was another sarin attack. Clearly the emergency services were overwhelmed by the volume and scale of the attack.

The fear and anxiety of those who had sarin poisoning may have been reduced by the Tokyo hospital staff having at hand an incident report from the Matsumoto attack that detailed how to treat exposure to sarin. The report's author, Dr Nobu Yanagisawa of Shinshu University, on the morning of the attack, coincidently had available an incident report from Matsumoto that he had just completed. On learning of the subway attack he faxed copies of the report to Tokyo's hospitals. Yanagisawa recalled afterwards that 'The most important thing in a mass disaster is triage. If you don't have a good grasp on the situation and people come in screaming "I can't see" the whole scene can easily descend into a state of panic.'[73] Yanagisawa, who treated the victims of Aum's June 1994 sarin attack in Matsumoto, realised on seeing the television reports that sarin may be the causative agent.

While the emergency service response at the stations may have exacerbated the terror among those waiting to be attended to, the nature of Japanese society itself may have negatively contributed to long-term after-effects in those in need of psychological care.

In Japan an intense stigma is attached to those who seek mental health treatment. Therefore, many victims of PTSD, particularly those most in need of treatment, were forced to endure their problems without proper psychological care. Japanese society provided an unwelcoming environment for victims coming to terms with the mental scars. Victims received little support or empathy at work despite compassion being a highly valued trait among the Japanese.[74] Several survivors complained that the government had little interest in addressing their mental health problems, with no accurate assessment made of the needs or treatment policy established.[75]

There is a belief among many in Japanese society that a psychological illness is contagious. The subway victims were treated very differently to those caught up in the Kobe earthquake. Victims of this natural disaster could share their pain and grief with their neighbours who had shared a common experience. These factors probably increased the prevalence of PTSD in those caught up in the sarin attack.[76] The failure of government to provide adequate mental health support probably exacerbated the isolation and stigmatisation of the victims.[77] The fact that little information was given to the victims about the possible long-term side-effects of sarin exposure and the fact that the cult remained active and potentially able to launch further attacks served to exacerbate these psychosomatic symptoms.[78] Only five years after the attack did the Japanese government officially respond to the mental health of the victims. The first time the group of government-led mental health specialists offered psychiatric intervention for the victims, 84 turned up to the first day of the clinic.[79]

Conclusion

Evidence from the Tokyo subway attack reveals that overall most people responded calmly and there was little panic among those actually caught up in the incident with many recounting an almost surreal sense of calm as they were evacuated from the contaminated areas. Despite the general calm response, a proportion expressed strong fear and anxiety. The nature of the attack means that those on the trains and in the stations may well have perceived the attack with a high degree of dread risk and unknown risk not knowing what they had been exposed to, and the realisation of the potential threat this posed to their health. While the event would have been uncontrollable to those on board and difficult to flee from while the trains were moving, some may well have believed their lives were at risk when they observed passengers collapsing and suffering from severe reactions to a substance they could not see but which had a pungent smell, and after the announcement on some lines that it was poison gas or a bomb.

Given the potential that this was a high dread risk, the reports of calmness are all the more significant suggesting that in this case the commuters were not prone to panic but were able to respond in a measured way which even surprised some individuals. In the following days and weeks the uncertainty surrounding what Aum might try to do next, together with the murders, postal bombing, Aum's threat to cause greater destruction on 15 April than the Kobe earthquake and the attempted release of sodium cyanide on Shinjuku station, all served to provide a sense of unease among the citizens of Tokyo. Unfortunately there is no quantitative evidence to demonstrate the extent to which the Japanese risk perceptions, concerns, behaviours and attitudes changed.

The continuing dread risk perception of the potential threat Aum posed led some to change their behaviours and attitudes. This included those in the attack as well as those in the rest of the city. As discussed, many survivors remarked how they initially avoided travelling on the subway, and some of those who did found it very difficult. Meanwhile there were also some survivors interviewed afterwards who returned to the subway without much difficulty. The observation that taxi drivers reported a surge in business as people avoided the subways suggests a number felt the risk was too great. However, for most there was no real alternative to commuting on the subway, although they had a heightened awareness and anxiety when doing so. This led to false alerts as benign odours were interpreted as possible chemical attacks, some commuters sniffing the subway carriages before boarding and fewer people sleeping in their seats for concern there might be another chemical attack.

Arguably the overwhelmed and under-prepared emergency services at the attacked stations and the government's insufficient risk communication immediately following and in the days and weeks after the attack, may well have compounded the general sense of unease and concern. There are observations that there was no public affairs strategy in place to cope and co-ordinate a response at the time of the sarin attack leading to confusion and uncertainty as victims sought answers, through to criticism of the Japanese government for a lack of leadership as compared to, for instance, Bill Clinton's handling of the Oklahoma bombing. As with the behaviour, there is not enough statistical evidence to investigate the extent of these perceptions. However, comparing the government's responses against risk communication best practice strongly suggests that the messages and engagement the populace received from its leaders was insufficient and may have exacerbated the fear and anxiety as to what Aum could do next, and the threat to the populace, amplifying the perceived risk of the situation.

In terms of emergency risk communication, the public's main source was advice from the media, from colleagues and from hospital statements. Beyond that there were no co-ordinated government pronouncements on what the Tokyo populace should do and what symptoms people should be wary of. The lack of information continued in the period after the attack with an absence of government communication on the attack and the remaining threat. Meanwhile, the religious sect conducted an effective public relations campaign.

One area where there is reasonable quantitative evidence is that of the mental health studies examining the psychological effects of the attacks. These provide evidence of proximity and time on those directly affected by the attacks. Higher levels of fear and anxiety were reported among those who had difficulty in contacting or receiving assistance from the emergency services. Overall over three-quarters of those who attended medical facilities on the day and in the period after the attack did not need to do so as they did not require treatment. With only 54 critically or severely injured, there was a near hundredfold increase in the numbers of patients hospitals had to examine and treat. Further, a study revealed that 33 per cent of the 111 victims (at St Luke's), regarded as having mild or serious injuries showed signs or symptoms of agitation and other psychological symptoms. In the weeks after the attack, a survey of 610 victims revealed that psychological reactions were still prevalent with 60 per cent of the 475 respondents reporting symptoms of PTSD. While there is variation between the two studies, it does suggest that a significant proportion of victims did go on to develop PTSD-related symptoms.

Separate surveys suggest that mental health problems persisted among the victims for some years after the attack. The TMPD survey in 1998 of 1,247 people who had reported being affected revealed that more than 70 per cent of said they still suffered from some psychological after-effects, including PTSD and increased use of alcohol or sleeping pills, suggesting they had to resort to substances to overcome the psychological effects. A study of 582 people admitted to St Luke's following the subway attack continued reporting unexplained physical symptoms in the five years after the attack, suggesting they could be suffering from PTSD. When including the physical symptoms in the PTSD diagnosis, the rate of PTSD was identified to be 9.7 per cent in 1998 and 14.1 per cent in 2000. This demonstrates that a number of victims continued to show PTSD and related symptoms for at least five years after the attack. Ideally there could have been general population surveys of Tokyo's citizens to reveal how the attacks, if at all, had affected the mental health of those not on the subway on the day of the attack, but who were within the city.

A unique factor to come out of the Tokyo case is the way in which their society and government handled those suffering from psychosomatic symptoms. The stigma surrounding mental illness in Japanese society, together with the reluctance of the Japanese government to respond to these needs, may well have exacerbated these problems and hindered individuals' recoveries. In addition some qualitative evidence suggests a reluctance or difficulty among commuters about returning to the subway system.

On the political strategic angle, the attack had no definite political impact. The government gradually implemented legislation to considerably tighten control of Aum Shinrikyo, but did not take immediate repressive measures or implement the draconian laws it had at its disposal. The prime strategic objectives of Aum of preventing further investigations into its activities and replacing the Japanese government with its own cabinet-in-waiting were not realised.

6   September 11 attacks

Introduction

The September 11 attacks on the World Trade Center (WTC) and the Pentagon provide a unique opportunity to assess the social-political and psychological consequences of a mass-casualty, conventional terrorist incident on a nation. In all 2,819 lives were lost in the WTC, 125 in the Pentagon and 246 on the four hijacked airliners.[1] The attacks of September 11 (9/11) marked a watershed in terrorism. They formed arguably the most dramatic attack ever undertaken. To America, September 11 was comparable to Pearl Harbor in 1941. A significant amount of literature exists on this episode, including on the short- and long-term psychological effects. As most of the studies on 9/11 have focused on the attacks on New York rather than the Pentagon, this chapter will primarily explore the New York component with emphasis on New York City (NYC).[2] Risk analysis has covered 9/11 in some detail from the handling of risk communication by the former mayor, Rudy Giuliani, with respect to those in NYC, and more broadly through President George W. Bush's response. This chapter is divided into the following sections:

- Background
- Strategic and political objectives
- Overview of the attacks
- Political effects
- Effects of proximity and time
- Changes in behaviour and attitude
- Risk communication
- Risk perception
- Risk amplification.

Background

As the son of a Saudi construction businessman, Osama Bin Laden became interested in religious studies and was inspired by religious tape recordings of sermons by Abdullah Azzam, a Palestinian of Jordanian origin and the historical leader of Hamas. Having become deeply religious, Bin Laden moved to Afghanistan in 1980, which had been invaded by the Soviets a year earlier, leading to a decade of conflict, and providing Islamic extremists with a rallying point. Bin Laden's grievances with the US may have began as a reaction to specific US policies, but they became deeper as the belief grew that the US should abandon the Middle East, convert to Islam and end what he saw as the immorality and godlessness of its society and culture.[3] In 1988 when Moscow announced it was to pull its forces out of Afghanistan, Bin Laden and Azzam, who had established a recruiting network to distribute arms and train anti-Soviet fighters, agreed that they should not disband this system but form a foundation or base (Al Qaeda) as a potential general head-quarters for the future of jihad.[4] Benefiting from pan-Islamic, as opposed to pan-Arab ideology, Al Qaeda drew from the vast financial resources and technical expertise mobilised during the decade-long anti-Soviet campaign.[5]

In 1989, Bin Laden was persuaded to move his base to Sudan by the Sudanese political leader, Hassan al Turabi. In 1991 he established a network of businesses and terrorist enterprises in Sudan. His time in Sudan allowed him to strengthen the international network and develop formal and informal alliances with Islamic extremist organisations in other regions. In parallel, Al Qaeda issued a fatwa on Western 'occupation' of Islamic lands, and specifically blaming the US for 'occupying' these areas.

Although he built up his network in Sudan, Bin Laden was forced to leave in 1996 through a combination of changing political circumstances in the country that made Khartoum less welcoming to the exiled Saudi. Sudan had agreed with Libya to stop providing sanctuary to its enemies. Bin Laden was also facing financial problems. He returned to Afghanistan where he gradually developed links with the ruling Taliban through his relationship with their leader Mullah Omar and acquired far greater freedom than he encountered in Sudan. Al Qaeda members could travel freely within the country, enter and exit with no immigration controls, purchase and import vehicles and weapons, develop a sanctuary to train and indoctrinate fighters and terrorists, forge closer ties with Islamic militant groups, and plan terror-ist operations.[6] Between 1996 and 9/11, it is estimated that between 10,000–20,000 Bin Laden supporters went through his training camps, some of whom were hand-picked to be part of Al Qaeda.

The base in Afghanistan allowed Al Qaeda to develop from an organisa-tion providing training, funding and logistical support for allied groups into one conducting terrorist attacks itself. The landlocked country provided Al Qaeda with a political, security and geographic shield. Sanctions imposed on Afghanistan by the international community were strengthened and human intelligence gathering became severely limited.[7] Al Qaeda's first major attack was the 1998 bombings of the US embassies in Tanzania and Kenya. These were planned, directed and executed by Al Qaeda and supervised by Bin Laden and his deputies. This was followed by an attack on the US navy's

USS Cole in 2000 that killed 17 and injured 40. This attack demonstrated that Al Qaeda was a credible threat against US assets both internationally and domestically. Despite Al Qaeda's international reach, its *modus operandi*, financing and resources were already widely recognised, and planning had already begun for 9/11 unknown to the US.[8] A key 9/11 planner was Khalid Sheikh Mohammed who first presented the 9/11 proposal to Bin Laden in 1996 and was given the go-ahead in 1998 or 1999.[9] Over the next three years, Bin Laden provided the logistical support and nominated several of the 9/11 hijackers. By mid-2000 Al Qaeda had the resources in place to run the operation. By May that year, two of the Al Qaeda operatives who would be on one of the hijacked aircraft were already in the US and three of the four from the Hamburg cell were soon to join them.[10]

Strategic and political objectives

Although in the days and months after 9/11 Al Qaeda did not claim responsibility for the attacks, the 1998 fatwa issued by Al Qaeda that called for the killing of Americans provided an insight into the organisation's objectives. The fatwa issued against the US in the name of the World Islamic Front and signed by Osama Bin Laden, read:

> The ruling to kill the Americans and their allies – civilians and military – is an individual duty for every Muslim who can do it in any country in which it is possible to do it, in order to liberate the al-Aqsa Mosque and the holy mosque [Mecca] from their grip, and in order for their armies to move out of all the lands of Islam, defeated and unable to threaten any Muslim.[11]

The 1998 fatwa and the subsequent attacks on American interests including 9/11 suggest Al Qaeda sought to coerce the US to withdraw its military bases in the Arabian peninsula and reduce its support for pro-western Middle East governments. With no group or country claiming immediate responsibility, government officials, media and the public were left to speculate over who the perpetrators were. Within the first hour of the aircraft striking the World Trade Centre, a Palestinian organisation had reportedly contacted the media claiming they had masterminded 9/11, but this was later discounted as a hoax.[12] America compared 9/11 to Pearl Harbor in 1941, but September 11 was very different: within minutes of Pearl Harbor it was evident from their markings that the aircraft were Japanese, instead of airline names on their fuselages as was the case in 9/11. As one US reporter put it, 'This was Pearl Harbor redux without the face of an enemy.'[13] With no one claiming responsibility let alone releasing a manifesto of demands, the US was presented with a war on terrorism that looked to have an unidentified opposition. Confusion and ambiguity reigned over who the perpetrators were and what their agenda was. On September 11 ambiguity gave way to speculation that Osama Bin Laden's Al Qaeda network was behind the attacks after US intelligence reportedly had information from associates of the group discussing the day's events.[14] The gravity of 9/11 was as much about the symbolism of the WTC attacks as the casualties caused. Stephen Evans noted that 'There was no bigger symbol of America.' The towers were 'immense global icons of the American way: an assertion to the world of can-do confidence and defiant grandeur'.[15] Although Bin Laden did not publicly admit to masterminding the attacks, he expressed his support for 9/11 and the reasoning behind them in a television statement released on 7 October 2001.

> Here is America struck by God Almighty in one of its vital organs, so that its greatest buildings are destroyed. Grace and gratitude to God. America has been filled with horror from North to South and East to West, and thanks to God what America is tasting now is only a copy of what we have tasted. Our Islamic nation has been tasting the same for more than 80 years, of humiliation and disgrace, its sons killed and their blood spilled, its sanctities desecrated.[16]

Fred Halliday observed that Bin Laden's statement did not explicitly note what marked the beginning of the '80 years' time frame; possibly it was the collapse of the Ottoman Empire or the British takeover of Palestine?[17] Steven Simon summarised Al Qaeda's aims as seeking to 'purge' the Middle East of American political, economic and military influence as part of a wider 'defensive jihad' agenda 'to defeat a rival system portrayed as an existential threat to Islam'.[18] A further insight into the rationale behind the attacks came from an interview with one of the alleged architects of 9/11, Khalid Sheikh Mohammed who noted that the attacks were designed to 'cause as many deaths as possible and to be a big slap for America on American soil'.[19] 'The head of the snake' as Bin Laden had called the US in often repeated lectures in the mid-1990s, had been struck.

Overview of the attack

At 08:02 Eastern Time American Airlines Flight 11 from Boston to Los Angeles, departed from Boston's Logan airport. Just before 8:30am four hijackers armed with knives hijacked Flight 11. The Federal Aviation Administration (FAA) alerted North American Air Defense Command (NORAD) at 8:40am that Flight 11 had been hijacked. Three minutes later, the FAA informed NORAD that a second aircraft, United Airlines Flight 175 had been hijacked. At 8:46am, Flight 11 (a Boeing 767) with 92 people on board, including nine crew and two pilots crashed into the north tower of the WTC between the 94th and 98th floor at 470mph. Eighteen minutes later United Airlines Flight 175 from Boston to Los Angeles carrying 65 people, including seven crew and two pilots, crashed into the south tower (at 550mph) at approximately the 80th floor. Minutes later at 9:40am American Airlines Flight 77 from Dulles to Los Angeles with 58 passengers, four crew and two pilots, flew into the west side of the Pentagon. A fourth hijacked aircraft, United Airlines Flight 93 from Newark to San Francisco carrying 45 people including five crew and two pilots crashed into Stony Creek, Pittsburgh after passengers and crew struggled unsuccessfully with the hijackers to regain control of the aircraft. Flight 93 was believed to be bound for the US Capitol building in Washington, DC.[20] Fearing there could be more hijacked aircraft approaching the states, US air traffic control received an order at 9:44am to close US airspace to all private and commercial aircraft. It took three hours to empty their skies of 4,836 aircraft.[21] US-bound international flights were ordered either to turn back or land in Canada.[22]

Thousands of WTC workers were already at their desks in both towers at the time of the attacks. Many working on the floors struck by the aircraft were killed instantly. The majority of those on the floors above were trapped, their escape routes cut off by fire. Of those trapped in the building, many jumped because of conditions inside. In a collection of 20 videotapes shot by amateurs and professionals from nearby streets and buildings, at least 37, and probably well over 50, can be seen jumping or falling from the north tower, while no one visibly fell from the south tower.[23] Close examination of the fate of the towers suggests that 1,100 or more people in or above the impact zones survived the initial crashes, roughly 300 in the south tower and 800 in the north.[24] Many of those lived until their building collapsed. In all, about 600 civilians died in the south tower at or above the impact zone. In the north tower, every person believed to be above the 91st floor ultimately died: 1,344.[25] In the Pentagon 125 were killed.

Opened in 1973, the twin towers were originally designed to withstand the impact of a Boeing 707, the largest aircraft at the time of their construction, but not a fire following impact. According to Wilfred D. Iwan of the California Institute of Technology, the lateral impact alone of the 767 crashing into the towers could not have caused the collapse. The impact force only equalled 9 per cent of the pressure the towers were designed to take.[26] However, the fire from the aircraft was fed by more than 91,000 litres of jet fuel in each tower. The explosion from the fireball erupting from the 767s was equivalent to 400 tons of TNT. As jet fuel burns at 1,700°C, steel loses its strength at 800°C and melts at around 1,500°C, a severe and rapid reduction in the load-carrying capacity of the steel beams occurred once the intense heat reached critical conditions.[27] The concrete cladding on the cores could only keep the heat at bay for a short time before the steel frame melted and collapsed on one floor, inflicting massive pressure on the already weakened floor below. Even the steel structure at the lower end of the tower that remained at normal temperature gave way under the enormous weight of around 100,000 tons. The collapse of just one level meant the structure had to withstand 50 times its intended load. The cumulative effect of this process led to 'pancaking' as one floor collapsed onto the one below.

To a worldwide audience of millions, the south tower collapsed at 10:02am causing huge clouds of dust and debris to envelop the streets of Manhattan and pedestrians to flee from the dust. At Ground Zero hundreds of firemen and rescue workers were killed as they attempted to rescue those trapped in the towers. Half an hour later the second tower collapsed. WTC7, severely damaged from the collapse of WTC 1 and 2 collapsed at 17:21. In the immediate aftermath of the attacks New York authorities feared that up to 10,000 could have perished. The WTC complex had a capacity of 50,000.[28] In all 2,819 lives were lost in the World Trade Center, 125 in the Pentagon, and over 246 on the four hijacked airliners.[29] It is estimated that the emergency services assisted with saving the lives of 5,000 people from the WTC before the towers collapsed.[30]

Political effects

With no political agenda released by the perpetrators after 9/11, it is not possible to state whether the attacks themselves resulted in the desired political change. It was believed that the attacks were primarily for retribution against American foreign policy and followed through on the 1998 fatwa issued by Al Qaeda. US forces did not pull out of the Middle East. They were actually increased and invaded Iraq and Afghanistan – Al Qaeda's base. Washington did not reduce its support for Middle East governments. While there is no evidence to support that foreign policy changed in line with what Al Qaeda wanted (and foreign policy is beyond the scope of this book), there were; however, some significant domestic responses including the ratification of a series of counter-terrorism measures. These included an Executive Order mandating the use of closed military tribunals for foreign terrorists (which do not presume the accused are innocent nor allow defendants to choose their own legal counsel) and several extra-judicial initiatives instituted under the auspices of the uniting and strengthening America through the Providing Appropriate Tools Required to Intercept and Obstruct Terrorism (PATRIOT) Act passed in October 2001. Collectively, these measures provided:

- New powers of detention and surveillance to the Executive branch of government and law enforcement agencies; and reducing the courts' judicial oversight of law enforcement powers;
- A broad new crime of 'domestic terrorism' as is defined in Section 802 of the Patriot Act as 'activities that (A) involve acts dangerous to human life that are in violation of the criminal laws of the US; (B) appear to be intended (i) to intimidate or coerce a civilian population; (ii) to influence the policy of government by intimidation or coercion; or (iii) to affect the conduct of a government by mass destruction, assassination or kidnapping';
- A decreased distinction between intelligence collecting and gathering

evidence for a criminal proceeding expanded the ability of the government to spy through wiretaps, computer surveillance, access to medical, financial, business and educational records and covert searches of homes and offices;

- The indefinite detention of non-citizens even if they had never been convicted of a crime; and[31]
- The tripling of the number of border patrol, customs service inspectors and Immigration and Naturalisation Service inspectors at the northern border of the United States, and US$100 million to improve technology and equipment on the US border with Canada.

While 9/11 had a profound impact on the US domestic and foreign policy, there is no evidence to support that the attacks achieved their goals beyond attacking America's political, financial and military symbols of power. The attacks did not initiate the process of converting the US to Islam or instigating a jihad revolution to end the so-called 'immorality and godlessness of its society' as it was portrayed by Al Qaeda. The attacks may have led to the infringement of civil liberties with extensive internal surveillance programmes, immigration controls and security around key buildings and landmarks reducing freedom of movement. But these were not part of the terrorists' goals. Other terrorist groups have sought to undermine the legitimacy and integrity of the entire political system by encouraging indiscriminate repression, abuse of the legal process, coercing policies of appeasement and forcing 'deals' with the aim of turning an opponent's strength against him. As Grant Wardlaw points out, to 'disorient the population by showing that the government is unable to fulfil primary security functions for its subjects: that is the provision of safety and order'.[32] There is no evidence to support that this has been a tactic of Al Qaeda, although the attacks have to some degree resulted in these outcomes.

Effects of proximity and time

Proximity

Proximity was a major determinant of the psychological problems that ensued. The few studies that provide an insight into the effect of proximity vary from solely covering New York City to national surveys. Within New York City, proximity to the WTC influenced the levels of PTSD. The prevalence of probable PTSD among the survivors who were in the towers that day is estimated to be 37 per cent.[33] Of those who saw the attacks in person 12.5 per cent were thought to have PTSD, while for those who lived in Manhattan south of 110th Street but who did not witness the attacks, it was 7.4 per cent. The prevalence of symptoms was consistently higher among persons who were directly affected by the attacks than among those who were not directly affected.[34]

A valuable means of identifying the effect of proximity is to compare the impact of 9/11 on individuals' mental health in New York City boroughs with those in the surrounding regions of New Jersey and Connecticut, and the average for New York State. After 9/11 (October–November 2001), the prevalence of probable PTSD was higher in the NYC boroughs of the Bronx, Brooklyn, Staten Island and Manhattan (9 per cent for the Bronx and Brooklyn, 8.5 per cent for Staten Island, 7.7 per cent in Manhattan), than the average for New York State (4.6 per cent), New Jersey (5.3 per cent) and Connecticut (1.1 per cent).[35] Six months after 9/11, the probable PTSD rates were lower across the board but still higher in the NYC boroughs than in New Jersey, Connecticut and the average for New York State.

Surveys that compared the psychological impact of 9/11 on New York City and Washington, DC also found that proximity was a determining factor in the consequences of the terror attack. A study led by William Schlenger examined trauma symptoms among residents in New York City and Washington, DC with other major US towns one to two months after 9/11 and concluded that 'probable PTSD' was associated with direct exposure to the terrorist attacks among adults.[36] The prevalence of PTSD in the New York City metropolitan area was substantially higher (11.2 per cent) than in Washington, DC (2.7 per cent), and the other major cities of Chicago, Los Angeles and Houston (3.6 per cent), and elsewhere in the country (4 per cent). The figures for elsewhere in the country and other major metropolitan areas were, according to the study, within the expected range of a community sample.[37] The survey concluded that geographic proximity to the WTC crash site was significantly related to the prevalence of PTSD. Despite the initial increase in PTSD levels found among residents of the New York metro area, the study noted that the prevalence rate had to be adjusted to control for already existing factors of increasing PTSD rates down to 5.1 per cent. Residents of the New York metro area were 2.9 times more likely to experience PTSD than those not living in the New York metro area and the national average due to the socio-demographic differences of race/ethnicity, age, sex and education characteristics that made those living in the New York metro areas more prone to PTSD.[38] However, after controlling for these factors, it was found that individuals who were in the WTC or surrounding buildings at the time of the attacks were more likely to experience PTSD than those who were not. Even when taking into account that residents of New York were more likely to experience PTSD, the data showed being in the WTC or surrounding buildings at the time of the attacks led to higher rates of PTSD.[39]

William Schlenger's research team also identified a proximity effect through measuring the amount of clinically significant distress in New York, Washington, DC, and the rest of the US, concluding that the distress levels were far higher in the cities attacked on 9/11. During the surveyed period of early October to early November, distress was recorded at 16.6 per cent for New York, 14.9 per cent for Washington, DC, and approximately

12 per cent for other major metropolitan areas and the remainder of the US.[40] The figure for national stress is in line with a separate survey conducted by Silver *et al.* who recorded stress nationally at 17 per cent two months after the attacks.[41]

Despite the shock of 9/11 to those residing thousands of miles from the attack, many of those who did not live within 50 miles of the disaster sites and/or did not lose a loved one, adapted quickly and returned to their regular work schedules and routines.[42] Evidence to support this assessment can be found in a Pew public opinion survey that was conducted one year after 9/11. Pew noted that in New York and Washington, DC many more residents struggled with the emotional consequences than individuals in other cities.[43] While only 34 per cent of the nation in the Pew survey reported two or more emotional consequences (sad, depressed, angry or recollection of the attacks), this rose to 48 per cent in New York, but only 35 per cent in Washington, DC. In addition, 69 per cent of DC residents believed they worked or lived in a probable terrorist target area compared to 42 per cent of New Yorkers and 32 per cent in the rest of the nation. While New Yorkers encountered the most emotional consequences and DC residents and workers expressed the greatest concern of further attacks in their area, both New Yorkers and Washingtonians (57 per cent and 52 per cent, respectively) were worried that that they or their families might be victims of a future attack, compared to 40 per cent for the rest of the nation. The perception of heightened risk in the two attacked cities is shown by the fact that 60 per cent of both population centres took one or more preventative measures to reduce their personal risk of terrorism. This included avoiding public events, handling mail differently and travelling by air less often. These reactions are discussed in more detail in the risk analysis section.

The effect of proximity is further underscored by a study of risk perceptions led by Baruch Fischhoff. The November 2001 study examined the probability judgement for terror risks 100 miles within and outside the WTC area. The survey showed that 44 per cent of respondents within the 100 miles believed there was a 50 per cent probability of being hurt in a terrorist attack compared to 20 per cent among those residing more than 100 miles from the WTC.[44] In addition, 18 per cent were travelling less often within the 100 miles compared to 10 per cent outside. While perceptions differed, symptoms including having trouble sleeping within and outside the 100-mile zone were similar at 8.8 per cent and 8.45 per cent respectfully. The survey suggests that respondents outside the immediate attack area saw less personal risk from terror than those nearby.[45]

Time

There is much more evidence assessing the effect of time that of proximity. However, the studies conducted do not have a consistent structure to effectively compare and contrast the regions and time periods covered. The surveys available can be divided into those that examine mental health effects like PTSD for the New York City area and surrounding region, and those for a national level. Despite the mixed data, an analysis of the available information provides insight into the consequences of a mass-casualty, conventional attack.

First, this section will examine how Americans reacted on the day of the attacks, then in the following weeks and months and finally one year and three years on. From one month onwards a number of empirical sources from scientific studies and opinion polls capture the effects. For the day of the attacks, the research relies on first-hand media reporting.

A review of first-hand accounts and documentary evidence show there was no overt panic in the evacuation of the WTC. When the building was on fire before the arrival of the emergency services, there was an orderly evacuation.[46] Pre-existing social networks (people knowing each other before hand) may have aided the calmness of the evacuation.[47] A succinct insight into the behaviours inside the towers prior to their collapse can be gained from a *New York Times* special report that studied 102 minutes of phone conversations, email and voice messages from those trapped above the impact zone. The *New York Times* summed up the conversations as 'bravery, decency and grace'. The *Times* interviewed family members, friends and colleagues of those who died, obtained times of calls from mobile-phone bills and 911 records, analysed 20 videotapes and listened to 15 hours of police and fire service radio tapes. Overall the assessment provides a picture of colleagues cooperating with each other, and listening and following instructions broadcast over the intercom system. Very few of those trapped above the impact zone, knowing it was unlikely that they could get out of the WTC, exhibited panic.[48]

Further support for this finding can be found in a report by the National Research Council of Canada which analysed 324 first-hand accounts from survivors of the WTC attack. Although 83 per cent recognised the situation was very serious in the first few minutes, seeing flames, smoke or falling paper, only 55 per cent of the survivors evacuated immediately, 13 per cent stopped to retrieve their belongings, and 20 per cent secured files and searched floors before evacuating.[49] Initially 8 per cent decided to stay but changed their minds, and 4 per cent were trapped due to collapsing ceilings and walls, but then managed to escape.[50] Many commented how calm and helpful the occupants were during the evacuation. The study did not suggest individuals were panicking in the WTC.[51] However, neither the *New York Times* or the NRC studies defined what they meant by panic.

In the hours after the attack, Manhattan witnessed an orderly mass exodus of survivors leaving the area via bridges that stretched across the East River, the only way out of Manhattan.[52] According to a *New York Times* reporter, 'Many walked in bewilderment and fear, some doused in ash from head to toe, some wearing surgical masks, some holding a handkerchief or a washcloth over their mouths. Some walked, others ran.'[53] Approximately

5,000 people were evacuated to New Jersey and Staten Island by the Port Authority, and 600 of the more seriously injured were taken to hospitals, 150 in a critical condition.[54] While order and calm remained, there was uncertainty over whether other attacks would follow. The day after the attacks the *New York Times* summed up the atmosphere on 9/11 stating:

> Every sound was cause for alarm. A plane appeared overhead. Was another one coming? No, it was a fighter jet. But was it friendly or enemy? People scrambled for their lives, but they didn't know where to go. Should they go north, south, east, west? Stay indoors? People hid beneath cars and each other. Some contemplated jumping into the river. For those trying to flee the very epicentre of the collapsing World Trade Center towers, the most horrid thought of all dawned on them: nowhere was safe. For panic-stricken hours yesterday morning, people in Lower Manhattan witnessed the inexpressible, the incomprehensible, the unthinkable.[55]

In the days after the attack, there were no signs of mass panic or social disorder in the New York community but a broad range of positive, public responses. These included rescue work, volunteering, providing resources and donating blood.[56]

There are a number of PTSD statistics from various studies undertaken following 9/11. However, there are great variations in these figures. This is due to variability in the quality and methodology of the studies and the fact that most relied on self-reporting. Unlike diseases, there are no pathognomic signs of PTSD which complicates the ability to reach a definitive diagnosis. Furthermore, the surveys were conducted in the field (e.g. telephone interviews) rather than in a controlled clinical setting.

One of the early quantitative studies on New York City was led by Sandro Galea conducting a survey of Manhattan residents five to eight weeks after the WTC attacks. The study revealed an increase in depression and PTSD. Of the 1,008 adults interviewed by phone, 7.5 per cent reported symptoms consistent with a diagnosis of PTSD and 9.7 per cent expressed symptoms of depression.[57] Overall 13.6 per cent reported symptoms that met the criteria for either PTSD or depression and 3.7 per cent reported symptoms that met the criteria for both.[58] Based on the number of individuals residing within seven miles of the WTC, it is estimated that 67,000 persons had PTSD and 87,000 depression.

As a baseline for the increase, the survey authors noted that a national US survey undertaken before September 11 revealed that only 3.6 per cent of the population were believed to have PTSD, and depression within 30 days of the survey was 4.9 per cent.[59] The attacks therefore led to a two-fold increase in PTSD rates in the Manhattan area.[60]

The development of PTSD was not unexpected given the scale of the event. A study by Sandro Galea *et al.* noted that severe, lasting psychological effects are generally seen after disasters that caused extensive loss of life, property damage and widespread financial strain, and after disasters caused intentionally. According to the report's authors, 'These elements were all present in the September 11 attacks, suggesting that the psychological sequelæ in New York City are substantial and will be long lasting.'[61] It had been estimated that there may be hundreds of thousands of new cases of PTSD alone in New York with up to one-third of those closely involved in the World Trade Center attacks including rescue workers, victims and witnesses ultimately suffering PTSD.[62]

In addition to surveys suggesting an increase in PTSD and stress in the weeks after 9/11, there is also evidence to suggest that there was an increase in substance abuse in an attempt to escape from these memories and threats from future terrorism. The use of cigarettes, alcohol and marijuana among Manhattan residents was found to have increased five to eight weeks after the attacks by 28.8 per cent (9.7 per cent increase in smoking, 24.6 per cent in alcohol consumption and 3.2 per cent increase in marijuana use).[63] It was thought that those who increased smoking cigarettes and marijuana were more likely to experience PTSD than those who did not.[64] An additional means of escapism New Yorkers pursued in the weeks following 9/11 can be found in the 20 per cent increase in the number of births in New York hospitals nine months on from the attacks.[65]

Another indicator of the psychological disposition caused by 9/11 is the number and type of calls a New York-based support line, Lifenet Hotline Network, received. In January 2002, Lifenet Hotline received 6,600 calls, up from a monthly average of 3,000 calls before 9/11, and 5,300 in December 2001.[66] In addition the type of calls changed. Before 9/11, only 1 per cent of those who contacted Lifenet reported symptoms of trauma, such as anxiety. In January 2002, 21 per cent of callers reported anxiety or symptoms of PTSD, with many experiencing sleeping and eating problems, depression and resorting to substance abuse. Similarly employee-assistance programmes and managed-care companies quickly found their existing panels and personnel were inadequate to meet the need and recruited additional mental health professionals throughout the northeast US.[67]

Over the next six months, presented levels of PTSD and stress proved to be less than expected despite expectations that around one third of those who experienced the disaster would develop PTSD. The actual levels of PTSD were less than expected and declined considerably over the months. Galea *et al.* calculated that the prevalence of PTSD related to 9/11 in those living south of 110th street in Manhattan declined from 7.5 per cent one month after, to 1.7 per cent at four months and then 0.6 per cent six months after the event.[68] Subsyndromal PTSD declined even more from 17.4 per cent one month after 9/11 to 4.7 per cent six months after. In the rest of New York City, PTSD was even lower, recorded at 2.3 per cent and 1.5 per cent after four and six months respectively. The study concludes that the there was a rapid resolution of most of the probable PTSD symptoms in the general New York City population. Six months after 9/11, other clinicians also found that Manhattan residents and workers with severe symptoms were far fewer than expected.[69]

Further indication of the lower-than-expected mental health effects can be found in the relatively small numbers who sought counselling. Soon after the attacks New York City established a programme called Project Liberty to provide free counselling for New Yorkers. With a budget of $154 million and 3,000 hired therapists, it was expected that one in four citizens would need therapy for emotional problems resulting from the attacks. By March 2003, only 643,710 people had sought help through Project Liberty, whereas officials had expected 2.5 million.[70] It was suggested the lower numbers were because those who were directly affected by the attacks (lost loved ones or their jobs when the towers collapsed) were often too busy putting their lives back together or when they did seek support, it was often for practical matters (e.g. getting death certificates for insurance purposes).[71] A survey of Manhattan residents and workers three to six months after 9/11 also found lower than expected numbers seeking help with only 11 per cent receiving any psychiatric support or taking medications for anxiety, depression or psychotic conditions despite the city-wide escalation in psychiatric services.[72] This finding is reinforced by an analysis of those who sought mental health services in New York City one year after 9/11 that showed that the percentage of New Yorkers who used mental health services in the community one year prior to and post 9/11 showed a smaller-than-expected increase from 16.8 to 20 per cent.[73] While there was a slight increase in the volume of visits to mental health services, there was a surge in visits of existing patients of 8.5 per cent.[74] The lower-than-expected increase by those who had not previously used mental health services suggested the psychological resilience of many New Yorkers may have been higher than expected.[75] Collectively these figures illustrate a lower-than-expected number who felt it was necessary to seek counselling or acquire medications to cope with the aftermath of 9/11, and the greater-than-expected resilience of those living in New York City.

On the national level Americans believed that ordinary citizens behaved responsibly rather than panicked on 9/11.[76] Early quantitative evidence to examining the terror generated across the US within the first few weeks after September 11 includes a study conducted by Mark Schuster at the RAND Corporation. In the two months following September 11, Schuster implemented two surveys to assess the immediate and mid-term effects of the attacks; one on 14–16 September 2001 and a second on 9–28 November 2001. In the initial survey, 44 per cent of respondents reported they had experienced at least one of five substantial stress symptoms since the attack (including insomnia and being upset) and 90 per cent reported low levels of stress symptoms.[77] In November this declined to one in five adults expressing substantial stress symptoms and one in six with persistent stress. The survey revealed a correlation between the amount of time individuals watched television and stress. Of those who watched 13 or more hours of television 58 per cent reported stress.[78]

Over the longer term, a series of national surveys from September 2001 to September 2004 provides a good snapshot of the longer-term psychological effects on the US population by measuring post-traumatic stress. Table 6.1 shows that post-traumatic stress peaked in November 2001 at 17 per cent then to decline to just under 6 per cent in March 2002 when it steadily fluctuated and declined to 4 per cent by September 2004.[79]

While 9/11 had an initial psychological impact nationally, a segment of the populace continued to exhibit post-traumatic stress symptoms in the following years.

While mental health surveys suggest that problems of PTSD and stress from 9/11 remained in subsequent years, there are surveys that question their accuracy suggesting that after a year the effects were a lot fewer than expected. For example, Mark Schuster's study was criticised for including as one of its five symptoms for being 'substantially stressed', if respondents expressed 'quite a bit' of anger at Osama Bin Laden.[80] Galea *et al.*'s study was criticised for concluding that 7.5 per cent of individuals living south of 110th Street weeks after 9/11 had symptoms of PTSD as this may have 'reflected temporary distress rather than mental illness'.[81] Surveys can classify normal, expected emotional reactions as symptoms of mental disorder. For instance, a resident of New York City who was working in Manhattan and later reported difficulty in falling asleep and concentrating, and irritability could have been diagnosed as having 'symptoms of PTSD' although each symptom may have arisen from reasons unrelated to the attacks.[82]

While the studies covering the effect of time showed that 9/11 caused mental health effects including substance abuse, this steadily declined over a period of 18 months. However, the initial surveys may have overestimated the mental health effects of 9/11 on the population of New York City as demonstrated by Project Liberty and other surveys which demonstrated less demand for counselling and support than was expected. The major increase in those attending mental health care came primarily from existing patients. Despite the difficulties in comparing and contrasting different studies to establish the true effects of time, it is evident that there was a significant

Table 6.1 National PTSD rates following 9/11 in the US 2001–2004 (percentage)

Wave 1: September 2001	11.7
Wave 2: November 2001	17
Wave 3: March 2002	5.8
Wave 4: September 2002	5.2
Wave 5: March 2003	3.3
Wave 6: September 2003	4.4
Wave 7: September 2004	4.5

decline in the mental health effects over time and the people were more resilient than had been expected.

Changes in behaviours and attitudes

While 9/11 caused some PTSD and related symptoms among New Yorkers, the attacks also had a significant impact on a proportion of the population's perceived risk of terrorism, leading many to alter their daily lives. Evidence includes changes in travel plans and use of transport, phobias and heightened sensitivity to everyday innocuous events. A useful insight can be gained from surveys that examined travel patterns in the weeks and months after 9/11, demonstrating that the fear of flying becoming the predominant effect of 9/11. In New York there were reports of people who developed fears of crossing bridges, riding the subway or entering tall buildings. The sounds of aircraft or the smell of gas burning aroused heightened vigilance and in some instances led to flashbacks.[83]

The impact of 9/11 on those in New York is illustrated by a survey of three counties in New York (covering Long Island and Queens) from 20 October–11 November which revealed that large numbers changed their everyday lives after 9/11:

- 26 per cent had delayed or cancelled plans to travel by air.
- 7 per cent had changed their upcoming holiday plans.
- 18.5 per cent drove into Manhattan less often.
- 17 per cent used mass transportation into Manhattan less often.[84]

A year after the attacks, only a small fraction of New Yorkers continued to practise risk-averse behaviour. A survey conducted by the *New York Daily News* in August 2002 provides a snapshot of the continuing effects. It concluded that 'there were plenty of signs that the shock of 9/11 on New Yorkers has subsided'. Eighty-nine per cent went about their business without making an effort to avoid potential terror targets, such as subways, tourist sights (77 per cent) or tall buildings (80 per cent).[85] In addition, while 42 per cent of respondents said they never experienced signs of psychological distress – depression, nightmares or anxieties – after the terrorist attacks, 35 per cent who initially experienced such symptoms said they had vanished, but 21 per cent note they continued to have problems.[86] Therefore a large majority of New Yorkers did not avoid certain buildings and regions a year after 9/11.

The greatest impact of 9/11 was found to be on domestic airline passenger numbers. Following the re-opening of US airspace, domestic passenger traffic was down by almost 40 per cent on the same period the year before, gradually recovering to 19.8 per cent in November and then 14 per cent in January 2002.[87] By January 2002, 13–14 per cent of Americans had altered their travel plans, 5–7 per cent had reported stopping flying altogether and

45 per cent of leisure travellers believed it was not safe to fly.[88] The fear of flying post-9/11 had almost become contagious and more socially acceptable, and thus less aberrant. Dr Michael Liebowitz, director of an anxiety disorders clinic at New York State Psychiatric Institute, noted that, 'Before, you looked silly if you didn't fly and everybody was embarrassed about it. Now there's much more social support for it because so many people were affected.'[89] The spread of fear of flying could be classified as mass sociogenic illness, which can include an overexaggerated response to a real or perceived terrorist threat. Symptoms of mass sociogenic illness include the presence of extraordinary anxiety, symptoms being spread via sight, sound or oral communication.[90] Robert E. Bartholomew and Simon Wessely state that: 'No one is immune from mass sociogenic illness because humans continually construct reality and the perceived danger needs only to be plausible in order to gain acceptance within a particular group and generate anxiety.'[91]

The reduction in air travel was accompanied by an increase in the number who drove. In May 2002 the Massachusetts Turnpike, for example, saw a traffic increase of 4.3 per cent, higher than in May 2001.[92] There is also evidence to suggest that the increased traffic on rural interstate highways after 9/11 led to a higher number of road fatalities. A comprehensive insight can be found in Gerd Gigerenzer's paper in *Risk Analysis* that compared the number of road deaths in the months prior to 9/11 to the subsequent 18 months.[93] By taking into account the normal annual expected increase in road traffic of 0.9 per cent, Gigerenzer was able to identify the percentage of Americans who turned to the roads in abnormally high numbers. As expected, in the eight months before 9/11, the road travel mileage of Americans had risen by an average of 0.9 per cent –as it had for the previous five years. However in the three months after 9/11, miles on rural interstate highways (where much of the long-distance driving occurs) increased by 5.2 per cent, and in the first three months of 2002 by 3.7 per cent and then 2.2 per cent in the subsequent six months (April–September 2002). It then declined to –0.2 per cent in October 2002 to March 2003. Urban road travel rose by 1 per cent during this period – in line with annual growth.

As passenger miles increased, so did road fatalities. Taking into account the annual expected increase in road traffic, Gigerenzer estimates that the number of Americans who lost their lives on the road trying to avoid the higher perceived risk of flying was 1,595. Gigerenzer postulates that the reason for the rise is that the Americans perceived to dread risk of flying was greater than driving, despite the actual risk being the opposite. This caused a mediated secondary death toll from 9/11. It is quite possible that the change of risk appraisal could have been due to the fear of the terrorism threat to the aviation sector, together with the perception that driving provided individuals with a sense of greater control rather than handing control of their journey to someone else: a pilot in an aircraft that could be hijacked and destroyed.

The underlying reasons behind these behavioural responses can be partly explained by surveying the public's threat perceptions of terrorism after 9/11. Two months after the attacks nearly two-thirds (64 per cent) of the nation reported fears of future terrorism at least sometimes and 59 per cent reported fear of harm to a family member as a result of terrorism.[94] Six months after 9/11 these levels declined to 37 per cent and 40 per cent respectively.[95] A separate national survey conducted in October 2001–March 2002 found that 50 per cent of Americans were very concerned that there would be another attack on US soil in the near future and 11 per cent not very or not at all concerned, while 31 per cent were very concerned about becoming a victim of terrorism and 31 per cent not very or not at all concerned. This suggests that Americans believed the risk of further attacks against the nation was greater than being personally threatened by terrorism.[96] In addition, only 18 per cent believed the attacks had shaken their sense of personal safety and security a great deal while 47 per cent thought the attacks had little or no effect on their sense of safety and security. Therefore, the perceived risk of further terrorism was far more widespread than the emotional responses of fear and anxiety.[97]

As could be expected, the levels of risk appraisal of further attacks were higher among those residing around New York. Six weeks after the attacks 82 per cent of respondents in three New York counties reported they were very or somewhat concerned about another major terrorist attack in the future, and 81 per cent concerned about a chemical or biological attack.[98] On average during the first year after the attack, 31 per cent of Americans were 'very worried' and 42 per cent 'somewhat worried' about terrorism indicating that terrorism remained a major concern for a large section of the populace.[99] Over the five years following 9/11, the level of belief that Americans had that they or someone in their family would become a victim of terrorism fluctuated from 58 per cent after 9/11 to 30 per cent (see Figure 6.1). From June 2005 to August 2006 this remained around the 40-per-cent mark.[100] It needs to be considered to what extent military operations in Afghanistan and Iraq might have influenced these perceptions. For instance, levels of the expectation of terrorist attacks might have been influenced by the lead-up to and after the 2003 invasion of Iraq. Figure 6.1 shows these trends.

An assessment of the longer-term behavioural effects of 9/11 can be made by examining a series of Gallup polls taken after 9/11. These revealed a significant proportion of individuals who continued to alter their lives. Around one in five Americans said they had permanently changed the way they lived as a result of 9/11, and a little more than half (53 per cent) believed most Americans had changed their lifestyles.[101] See Figure 6.2 for a representation of those who had altered their lives since 9/11. The percentages have not varied greatly.

To ascertain the nature of these behavioural changes Gallup asked respondents over five years about their travel patterns and whether they go into

How worried are you that you or someone in your family will become a
victim of terrorism –very worried, somewhat worried, not too worried,
or not worried at all?

Numbers shown in percentages

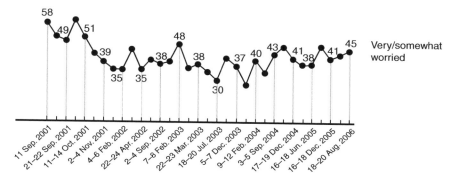

Figure 6.1 Percentage of individuals and family's concern of terrorism
2001–2006.[102]

Percentage of Americans saying that they personally have
permanently changed the way they live because of 9/11

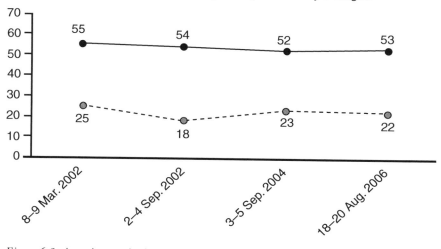

Figure 6.2 Americans who have altered their lives since 9/11.[103]

skyscrapers or attend events with large crowds. Americans were less willing to travel overseas (48 per cent in 2001 to 47 per cent in 2006), and less willing to fly (43 per cent in 2001 and 30 per cent in 2006). See Figure 6.3 for details. Somewhat fewer said they were less willing to go into skyscrapers (35 per cent in 2001 and 22 per cent in 2006) or go to events attended by thousands of people (30 per cent in 2001 and 23 per cent in 2006).[104]

Overall the Gallup surveys infer that 9/11 has had a long-term effect (over five years) on changing Americans' behaviours to minimise their perceived risk of terrorism to themselves. These trends suggest these effects could continue for several more years with individuals exhibiting avoidance behaviour in relation to certain means of travel and destinations.

Risk communication

The risk communication section is divided into two parts. The first details the communication strategies employed on the day of the 9/11 and during the subsequent weeks by the Mayor of New York, Rudolph Giuliani, and President George W. Bush. The second covers the messages in the two to three years that followed, included those from the federal government. While other government figures who took roles at the federal and state level, Giuliani and Bush were the two most prominent. Overall Giuliani's

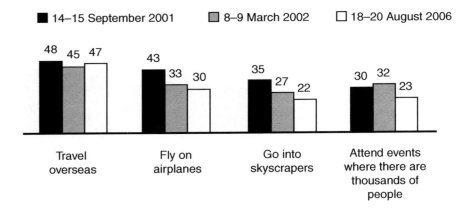

As a result of the events that occurred on September 11th, would you say that you are less willing to –[RANDOM ORDER], or not? Percentage 'less willing'

■ 14–15 September 2001   ▨ 8–9 March 2002   ☐ 18–20 August 2006

Travel overseas	Fly on airplanes	Go into skyscrapers	Attend events where there are thousands of people
48 45 47	43 33 30	35 27 22	30 32 23

Figure 6.3 Behavioural changes 2001–2006.[105]

performance proved to be effective, while Bush was initially charged with being uncommunicative with his populace before finally connecting with Americans.

Rudolph Giuliani

Prior to 9/11 Giuliani was seen as an ineffective and scandal-ridden mayor. To some commentators, Giuliani 'seemed all but finished, a lame duck', required by term-limit laws to leave office at the end of 2001 and a figure whose personal life had been 'racked' by cancer and a bitter divorce.[106] Critics found him 'pompous and dogmatic, a person who divided people'.[107] As one US editorial put it, 'his legendary marital problems were threatening to turn the final months of his term into a farce'.[108]

Prior to 9/11 Giuliani and his staff practised various emergency scenarios and potential responses to reporters' questions on a monthly basis in case of a disaster. One such scenario was the WTC collapsing. Despite these exercises, Giuliani quickly recognised on September 11 when he personally saw people jumping from the building that he was in 'uncharted waters' and would have to 'make up' the 'response'.[109] Although New York's emergency planning gained momentum after the 1993 WTC attack, emergency and city officials admitted after 9/11 that none of their scenarios had envisioned an attack of this scale and none had projected the potential to cause so many casualties among the first responders.[110]

Giuliani's handling of the day of 9/11 and the subsequent weeks met many of the criteria for effective risk communication. By evaluating what happened on the ground and recognising the need to provide clear and effective information to the public, the mayor allowed for a two-way interchange between himself and the intended recipients of the risk messages. The so-called 'Giuliani Model' as it became known entailed an open exchange in a common undertaking, not a series of canned briefings, and discussions were not restricted to technical and 'non-emotional' issues. On the day of the attacks Giuliani sought to develop messages to influence the public's behaviour so instructing those in Manhattan what to do, and to informing on events providing reassurance that the governance body of New York City was still functioning. Early on he sought to develop a sustained interchange with the media to convey his messages, most notably the walking press conference while he was being evacuated to a temporary command centre.

A valuable account of Giuliani's strategy and movements on 9/11 can be gained from his publication, *Leadership*. Although it may be influenced by his personal interpretation of events, it does offer a helpful insight. Giuliani felt the need to get information to the public. Within an hour of the attack, communicating with the people to provide calm and contribute to a safe and orderly evacuation was one of his two priorities. Giuliani's other priority was to establish a command post (after his original command centre at WTC7 had to be evacuated when the towers were attacked).[111] As reported by Giuliani's communication director, Sunny Mill soon after the attacks, the mayor kept saying 'We have to talk to the people. We have to communicate. Get a press conference.'[112] Regular briefings were important because there were rumours of further attacks. The CNN and CBS television networks reported that a second plane was heading to the Pentagon; Fox News reported that the State Department building was on fire;[113] and other news agencies reported fires on the Mall and attacks on the Capitol building – all of which were untrue.[114]

Giuliani placed great importance on personally seeing the WTC and took advice from the emergency services on the safety measures to take.[115] To convey this advice to the public he requested a fire commissioner at the command post to accompany him to a press conference so he could inform people in the WTC and Manhattan how to evacuate. Having been forced to evacuate the first temporary command post, Giuliani writes that as he was walking along the street he was greeted by reporters and gave his first press conference that day while walking, determined to tell the public they should walk north away from the WTC. The press conference was able to demonstrate that the leaders of the city were alive and in control. To ensure that the 'walking press conference' reached the widest audience, Giuliani instructed that all footage be declared 'pool' so all networks could share what they had. Just before 11am Giuliani held an official press conference, this time on the phone to a local television station and asked 'everyone to remain calm and do what they could to evacuate Lower Manhattan'.

In line with risk communication best practice, Giuliani conveyed, directly and clearly to the widest possible audience any practical actions New Yorkers should take (e.g. walk north away from the WTC area). Not only did Giuliani hold regular press conferences, but he went to the towers to see the devastation for himself. Live television pictures of the walking press conference as Giuliani and his entourage were fleeing the collapsing towers may have reinforced his bond with the public. One New Yorker commented, 'people were amazed he was down at the site and part of the masses and had to run for his life. It made us feel we're all in it together.'[116] Another newspaper commented that these television images 'showed the mayor standing with the city's firefighters, police and citizenry as a man in control'.[117]

Giuliani came over as having respect for the audience and its concerns. While providing accurate and up-to-date information is a good practice in risk communication, on the first day there was considerable uncertainty over how many had been killed. Faced with reporters asking for an official estimate, Giuliani's staff suggested that if they did not provide one the press might say they did not know enough about the situation. Not wanting to play the guessing game, Giluani stated in the press conference 'when we get the final numbers, it will be more than we can bear'. Through this he displayed empathy with New Yorkers and respected the audience and its concerns while at the same time admitting there remained considerable uncertainty over the casualty numbers.[118] Giluani's awareness of the audience needs can be seen from how he dealt with the city in the following weeks.

Giuliani wanted to show that life should go on, why this was important, what was at stake, what had been lost and why New York had been attacked. For instance, Giuliani told New York traders that they need to continue their work as their role was important for US growth and that the economic system was just as important as the ability of Americans to make choices about their lives.[119] In the weeks after 9/11, the mayor held daily or twice-daily press conferences following closed-door meetings with key players in the recovery effort. The mayor's approach became referred to in some quarters as the 'Giuliani Model' and as a template for crisis communication.[120] When flanked by other officials, the mayor displayed empathy and mastery over information. When he asked a different official to report, he implicitly asked the public to imbue his team with their trust.[121] This process provided reassurance to the public.

If newspaper editorials could be regarded as a weathervane to the public's perception of Giuliani's performance, it appeared his actions were well received. According to the *Boston Globe*, Giuliani's greatest benefit came not just from the speeches he made, but from his impromptu remarks to boost morale 'delivered with calm authority to inform and inspire the citizenry' which encouraged New Yorkers to get back to normal life as much as possible.[122] By the second week the *New York Times* editorial page, normally hostile to Giuliani, called him 'the mayor of the moment'.[123] The *Chicago Tribune* noted that during press conferences Giuliani was 'crystal clear in his answers and responded to the answers so appropriately, showing concern on the one hand and passing on real information at a time when people needed it'.[124] By December the *New York Times* observed that,

> For weeks afterwards, Mr Giuliani was more than just a mayor. Day after day, his calm explanation of complicated, awful news helped to reassure a traumatised city that it would pull through, and that someone was in charge. The man who seemed to have finished just a few weeks earlier was now being greeted with cheers wherever he went: Rudy! Rudy! Rudy![125]

By the end of the year, *Newsweek* declared Giuliani as 'the mayor of America'[126] and *Time* magazine named Giuliani in December 2001 as 'man of the year', commenting that every time he spoke, 'millions of people felt a little better' and that 'his words were full of grief and iron, inspiring New York to inspire a nation'.[127]

While praise from even his harshest critics could have been a result of the patriotism that flooded the US after 9/11, according to risk communication analyst Vincent Covello, Giuliani's strategy followed a model similar to that which Winston Churchill followed in the Second World War of compassion, conviction and optimism.[128] David Ropeik believed Giuliani was good at expressing empathy and acknowledging fear and uncertainty. This helped establish a connection and made it easier for audiences to hear difficult information. Ropeik points to Giuliani's speech on 9/11 as 'Whatever it [the loss of lives] is, it will be more than we can bear....'[129] Giuliani's performance was in stark contrast to Bush and Vice President Cheney who were not around for much of the time.

While Giuliani came over as providing truthful facts in a timely manner, he hired three publicists to deal with his newfound fame that led him to land spots on *The Late Show with David Letterman* and *Good Morning America*.[130] Arguably hiring publicists provided Giuliani with the resources to 'spin' the event to meet his goals of communicating effectively with the American public.

Giuliani was a strong united voice to Americans, providing them with credible information and updates when possible. This was required to dismiss potential myths and rumours that circulated in the aftermath of a disaster.

George W. Bush

Initially Bush did not perform adequate risk communication on 9/11. First, he kept a low profile moving between airforce base shelters or in flight on Air Force One for most of September 11. Second, his speeches did not adequately meet the needs of the country. It was not until his speeches at the National Cathedral of Washington and Ground Zero on 14 September that he started to meet the nation's needs according to risk communication criteria. On September 11, the speeches Bush made, combined with his lack of visibility, did not provide, according to risk communication principles, the American public with the leadership and support it required. Before analysing this proposition, an overview of the day's events is necessary to put Bush's performance into context.

At the time of the attacks, President Bush was visiting an elementary school in Florida. Before walking into a classroom, Bush was informed in a telephone conversation with US National Security Advisor Condoleezza Rice that a passenger aircraft had hit the WTC. At this time White House officials knew only that it was a single aircraft and not that it was a terrorist attack. At 9:07am Andrew H. Card Jr, Chief of Staff entered the classroom in front of the attending media and whispered into Bush's ear that a second plane had struck the WTC and that the US was under attack.[131] After a brief news conference at 9:30am, Bush then spent the rest of the day at airforce base underground shelters or aboard Air Force One.

While Bush had intended to return to Washington, DC once Air Force One was airborne at just before 10am, the Secret Service and Vice President Cheney strongly advised the President against it. Bush accepted the advice and the aircraft changed course to head west. Until his televised address to the nation from the White House that evening, Bush was taken by Air Force One to military bases in Louisiana and Nebraska as a precautionary measure to protect the US Commander-in-Chief. To some this appeared as a lack of leadership. The president's political aides had to face a central question: how could Bush appear in control, and calm the nation, from a bunker in Nebraska?[132] Bush had to overrule his aides to give his speech at the White House, who were insisting he should not return to Washington.[133] Bush's tour of airforce bases was criticised by the media the following day, with the *New York Times* noting that 'at the height of the Cuban missile crisis, when the sense of danger was just as palpable, John F. Kennedy stayed in Washington'.[134] To his critics, Bush appeared to send the message that if it was not safe for him to be out of a shelter or an aircraft, then how could it be safe for the rest of America?

When Bush did address the nation, risk communication practices suggest his comments may not have been adequate. The President's first statement on the attacks came at a news conference at 9:30am on September 11, where he gave a brief address, starting with, 'Today we have a national tragedy' and concluded with the remark that the US would 'hunt down those folks'.[135] Calling the perpetrators of the worst act of terrorism on American soil 'folks' seemed inappropriate, leading to criticism of his choice of words. After landing at Barskdale airforce base, Bush gave his next televised speech of the day but it was recorded rather than live for security reasons. Until his address to the nation from the White House at 8.30pm that evening, Bush only gave intermittent television addresses at various airforce base bunkers to update Americans on the situation. This was in contrast to Giuliani who seemed to be everywhere at once providing information and reassurance on 9/11, while President Bush was seen according to the *New York Times* as 'wooden and distant'.[136]

With the help of speech writers, President Bush referred to the 9/11 perpetrators that evening as 'evil' rather than 'folks', but still fell short of starting the healing process, unlike Giuliani who managed to connect with New Yorkers from the beginning.[137] The challenge facing Bush was immense and aptly outlined by a *New York Times* reporter, who noted on 12 September:

> Will he prove to be a Jimmy Carter, whose presidency was poisoned by his inability to resolve the Iranian hostage crisis? Or will he enhance his reputation, as Ronald Reagan did after the explosion of the space shuttle Challenger and as Bill Clinton did after the Oklahoma bombing?[138]

Risk communication researcher Paul F Deisler noted that statements by federal officials were slow to come on 9/11 and it was not until four hours after the south tower of the WTC was hit that President Bush gave his initial message of 'assurance to the public, a statement that by its very existence, gave assurance that he, the President, was safe and actively on the job'.[139] Earlier statements made by Bush failed to provide this needed 'assurance'. In the days following, federal officials gave mixed and circumspect messages and overall little was said at first to help the average citizen know what, if anything, he or she could personally do.[140]

Arguably the White House failed to communicate effectively to the public the reasons behind Bush visiting isolated air bases: the lack of information left room for miscommunication and misinterpretation. The *Boston Herald* remarked this strategy 'sent a message of weakness'.[141] Another US newspaper reported that initially 'it appeared Bush was running away from the trouble'.

Despite the initial challenge there was a noticeable improvement in Bush's ability to communicate evidenced by a speech he gave at the national cathedral on 14 September when he acknowledged the suffering, noting, 'we are in the middle hour of our grief'. Arguably there were two occasions in the weeks after 9/11 where Bush communicated effectively in response to the attacks. The first was Bush's visit to Ground Zero just hours after his national cathedral speech. Giuliani's *Leadership* suggests the initiative for Bush's visit partly came from the Mayor. Giuliani believed Bush's Ground Zero visit was 'vitally important' and recognised that he is at his best among regular Americans, who 'intuitively sense his sincerity'.[142] Amid the rubble and with one arm around the shoulder of a firefighter, Bush shouted through a megaphone 'I hear you and the people who knocked these buildings down will hear all of us soon.' One US newspaper commented that the President's visit to Ground Zero 'showed promising signs of opening up more'.[143]

The *Washington Post* and the *New York Times*, America's liberal newspapers that are traditionally critical of Republican presidents, praised the President. Mary McGrory of the *Washington Post* wrote: 'If Bush lacked eloquence on Tuesday [11 September], he more that made up for it with his fine speech at Friday's National Cathedral service.'[144] Similarly the *New York Times* commented that Bush had 'managed to reach out in ways both symbolic and practical', 'rose to the occasion' and 'After a shaky start, his speech on Friday at the National Cathedral struck the note of sombre confidence that the nation was looking for.' The article added that in his trip to Manhattan he 'succeeded in bonding with New York'.[145]

The second occasion where Bush proved effective was his address to a joint session of Congress on 20 September when he displayed a confidence and passion not shown before.[146] The vivid speech, carefully drafted and written by the President's leading speechwriter Michael Gerson, received praise from the US media that was 'effusive'.[147] A highlight of the address included the following:

> Whether we bring our enemies to justice, or justice to our enemies, justice will be done. ... The Taliban must act and act immediately. They will hand over the terrorists or they will share their fate. ... Either

you are with us or your are with the terrorists. ... We will not tire, we will not falter, we will not fail.[148]

The speech demonstrated compassion, resolution included and a demand to the Taliban to hand over suspected Al Qaeda leaders in Afghanistan. Importantly Bush also provided a lead on how Americans should respond to the attacks, stating:

> I know many citizens have fears tonight, and I ask you to be calm and resolute, even in the face of continuing threat. ... No one should be singled out for unfair treatment or unkind words because of their ethnic background or religious faith. ... It is my hope that in the months and years ahead, life will return almost to normal. We'll go back to our lives and routines, and that is good. Even grief recedes with time and grace.[149]

Despite criticisms of Bush's use of language in the days after 9/11, some commentators had argued that his Texan phraseology resonated well with Americans. His description of Osama Bin Laden as 'wanted dead or alive', and his promise to 'smoke out' his followers, was seen as 'good old-fashioned plain speaking'.[150]

A key question is whether Bush's political management affected America's domestic recovery from the attacks. The nature of the attacks meant that America could continue to function. There were, for instance, no chemical, biological or radiological agents involved for survivors and the population at large to be concerned with. Had the attacks occurred on America's nuclear power installations, as initially considered by the perpetrators of, the resulting radioactive fall-out and the need for the population to receive potentially life-saving advice would have been critical. As it was, just getting away from the WTC and the Pentagon, arguably a natural survival instinct, was sufficient. At most, had Bush handled 9/11 poorly throughout, it could have cost him his chances of re-election and may have even damaged the Republicans' prospects at the 2002 mid-term elections. As it was, the Republicans' gained control of both houses in the mid-terms. Bush's speeches at Ground Zero, the Washington National Cathedral memorial service, and the address to Congress assisted the emotional recovery of Americans, but even without these speeches, America would still have functioned effectively. Unlike in New York where Giuliani provided information that may have saved lives (informing and influencing), there was no need for the rest of the country to receive accurate information to reduce loss of life. No mass evacuation or vaccination or decontamination strategy was required, for instance.

Terrorism alert advisories post-9/11

In the months and years following 9/11 the federal government had to demonstrate the best means to communicate and convey terror alerts to the US public from intelligence that was fragmented and ambiguous while not compromising security or intelligence sources. At the same time the alert messages had to be clear, consistent and accurate together, including information about areas at heightened risk, time frames and precautionary measures the public should take. Therefore an understanding of how the public would interpret and implement the risk messages was essential. An assessment of the alert advisories suggest that they often failed to follow risk communication practices, leading to contradictory and ambiguous information that threatened to undermine the credibility of the system in the public's eyes. In addition there was a risk that the public would embark on actions that could be detrimental to their own security and well-being and that of others. Discussion on this latter point is contained in the risk amplification section while this section focuses on how the terror alerts fared in regard to risk communication best practice.

From March to November 2002, the Attorney General was directed by President Bush to administer and make public announcements regarding threats to the nation. After the Homeland Security Department was created in November 2002, a Homeland Security Advisory System (HSAS) was implemented under the control of the Office of Homeland Security's Secretary, at that time Tom Ridge. The colour-coded HSAS was comprised of five alert stages: low (green), guarded (blue), elevated (yellow), high (orange) and severe (red). The intention was to notify federal, state and local government agencies, private industry and the general public of the terrorist threat and thus what measures they should undertake. The risks included the probability of an attack occurring and its potential gravity. When the alert level changes, the Department of Homeland Security (DHS) typically provided information on why the national threat level changed but often failed to address locations or time frames.[151] In addition, many of the alerts were accompanied with contradictory and uncoordinated messages from various parts of the federal government.

The orange alerts of 16 March–16 April 2003 and 20–30 May 2003 are examples of this. When Secretary Ridge raised the alert to orange on 16 March, he did so believing the invasion of Iraq could lead to reprisal attacks against the US by Al Qaeda or its sympathisers. There was no intelligence to suggest an attack was to occur.[152] In the alert of 20–30 May 2003, the Homeland Security Secretary stated that Al Qaeda had entered an operational period following the bombings in Saudi Arabia and Morocco, which could include attacks against the US. However the day after the alert was raised FBI Director Mueller stated there was no specific information regarding potential targets of the timing of an attack.[153]

An example where the threat time frame and location were included is the orange alert of 21 December 2003–9 January 2004. This specified a heightened alert for the use of aircraft for potential strikes and several locations were also reported to be at particularly high risk. When the general orange alert was lowered to yellow on 9 January, some sectors, like the aviation industry, were advised to continue on orange alert. This marked the first time that the DHS had lowered the national alert but retained a higher alert status for a specific sector or location – thus implementing better risk communication practices through providing clearer information on what areas the threat pertained to and thus what actions those sectors should undertake.

There were also occasions when leading figures outside the DHS made statements to the public, suggesting there was a heightened risk of attack but the DHS did not to raise their alert status. For example, on 26 May 2004 Attorney General Ashcroft announced at a press conference with the Director of the FBI that there was credible intelligence to suggest Al Qaeda was to attack the US 'hard' in the next few months. Later that day Secretary Ridge publicly contradicted Ashcroft's security assessment by responding 'there is nothing specific enough (to raise the alert level)'.[154]

This failure to follow effective risk communication practices led to a report by the Congressional Research Service, a research arm of the Library of Congress, to criticise the DHS threat advisory system. It noted there was a:

A perceived lack of coordination in the federal government's warning notification process and inconsistent messages regarding threats to the homeland have led to an erosion of confidence in the information conveyed to the nation. The information conveyed to the public often has been inconsistent regarding the threat or the timing of a suspected attack. This lack of coordination and unity in message has led to a dilution in the American public's belief in the pronouncements and a questioning of the utility of the Homeland Security Advisory System (HSAS).[155]

In particular the report noted that the threat level was raised based on speculation that an attack may occur soon rather than upon receipt of any specific new information; at times warnings had been issued without changing the HSAS; and third on many occasions the messages were contradictory.[156]

A report by the General Accounting Office released in March 2004 similarly criticised the risk communication practices of the HSAS. The report noted that threat advisories should include where possible the nature of the threat, when and where it is likely to occur, over what time period and guidance on actions to be taken. In addition the messages lacked consistency, accuracy and clarity.[157]

In parallel to the HSAS, the US public were advised to prepare for a potential terrorist attack (conventional or CBR). When the DHS increased its threat assessment to orange in February 2003 the Federal Emergency Management Agency (FEMA) issued a nine-page, step-by-step, civil defence document urging Americans to build a 'disaster supply kit' to prepare for a biological, chemical or nuclear attack.[158] The guide, *Are You Ready? A Guide to Citizen Preparedness* advised Americans to review their preparedness measures (evacuation and shelter) for a potential conventional or CBR attack and warned them to avoid high-profile or symbolic locations and exercise caution when travelling.[159] At the same time the DHS also launched the website 'Ready.gov' containing this information. These advisories came in the backdrop of another statement purporting to be from Bin Laden issuing further threats to the West. The net result was Americans purchasing duct tape and other products as advised by FEMA in what many felt were preparations for a near-term attack.

While the HSAS had to be mindful of not revealing information on threat time frames and locations that could be used to the advantage of terrorists, allowing them to adjust their plans accordingly, the alert advisories clearly lacked essential elements of risk communication practice. While the fragmentation and ambiguity of intelligence makes providing time frames and locations of threat alerts challenging, consistency and clarity are important. In addition the public needed to be told why alert levels had been raised, about the challenge of false positives and what actions were needed. There were times when raising the alert to orange led the public to question what they should do differently on an 'orange day' to a 'yellow day'. As Baruch Fischhoff noted, the public needs to be educated regarding the philosophy underlying each threat level to help the public understand why false alarms are inevitable, thus minimising cumulative apathy.[160]

Despite all the terrorism alerts, there were no further successful Al Qaeda attacks against the US. While a number were allegedly intercepted during the planning phase, no one was caught in the closing stages of a strike, suggesting, that for many of the alerts at least, there was possibly no threat. Meanwhile, the public could have taken precautionary measures that were harmful to themselves and, in the case of avoiding flying in preference for driving, this led to an increase in the number of road deaths (equivalent to six times more than the 256 who died in the hijacked aircraft on 9/11 as will be discussed below).

Risk perception

Prior to 9/11, America's main experience of terrorism consisted of overseas attacks on military or diplomatic facilities. This included the bombing of the US embassies in Tanzania and Kenya in 1998 and the bombing of USS Cole in October 2000. There had been some attempts with varying degrees of success to conduct attacks on mainland soil. The most noticeable was Al Qaeda's first attempt on the WTC in February 1993 through detonating a bomb in the parking area with the intention of weakening the support structures to cause the collapse of the towers. Although the bomb detonated, no severe structural damage was done to the towers. The second main attack was the 1995 Oklahoma bombing that killed 168 and injured hundreds. Unlike the 1993 WTC bombing, this was perpetrated by a home-grown terrorist, Timothy McVeigh, who sought to attack the US government for becoming 'increasingly hostile' in its assault on the Waco building in 1993 and in the siege shootout the year before. A reminder of the threat came later in 1993 when the FBI reportedly uncovered several other planned attacks, including one on the UN building in New York. During the period after the Oklahoma bombing through to April 2000, Gallup surveys revealed that immediately after the bombing, 42 per cent of Americans said they were very or somewhat worried that they or someone in their families would become victims of similar attacks.[161] One year later, 35 per cent said they were worried and, five years after the bombing, in April 2000, just 24 per cent said they were worried. As for expectations of an attack, nearly nine in ten Americans said it was very (47 per cent) or somewhat (42 per cent) likely that bombings or similar acts of violence would occur elsewhere in the United States in the near future.[162] Only 8 per cent thought this was not likely to occur. Therefore prior to 9/11 a quarter believed they or a family member could become a victim of a terrorist attack – a significant proportion in view of the rarity of attacks on the US mainland.

With the absence of any Al Qaeda attacks or attempts in the US prior to 9/11, the public's main awareness of the group's potential threat to their homeland probably stemmed from their targeting of US interests abroad and the reporting of the 1993 trial bombing. In May 1994, four men – Mohammed Salameh, Nidal Ayyad, Mahmud Abouhalima and Ahmad Ajaj – were sentenced to life for the bombing of the World Trade Center, which killed six people and injured 100.

Additional evidence to show the degree to which Americans believed their nation was at risk of a terrorist attack prior to 9/11 can be captured from a Pew opinion poll conducted in May 2001. As part of larger poll that also covered views on missile defence and China, 64 per cent of respondents believed international terrorism was a major threat to the well-being of the US.[163] With the National Missile Defence programme a major public issue prior to 9/11 to defend the US against a limited missile strike, 77 per cent believed terrorists posed a greater threat to the US than missile strikes by so-called 'rogue nations' like North Korea. Fifty-five per cent believed that countries such as North Korea, Iraq and Iran could launch missile attacks on the United States. While the Pew research looked at the threat of terrorism to the nation, it did not investigate to what degree respondents felt they were personally threatened by an act of terrorism or how seriously they took this issue. Pew suggested that terrorism was seen as a higher priority threat to the US in the months before 9/11 than the threat of a missile strike.

Prior to 9/11 the US public was aware of the potential threat that terrorism and Al Qaeda posed to the US. However, the nation had not encountered a sustained bombing campaign or other direct attack on its homeland by an overseas organisation with the exception of the 1993 WTC incident so had not become accustomed to this type of risk. The vast majority of Americans had few experiences of terrorism, unlike, for example, Israelis who prior to the Second Intifada, experienced terrorism and violence as a part of everyday life. Therefore if prior experience of terrorism can assist a populace's ability to adapt and respond, then the lack of experience might have reduced Americans' coping mechanisms to respond and adapt proportionately without adverse changes in their behaviours and attitudes to reduce the perceived risk to themselves.

Risk amplification

There are two main areas for consideration. First, risk amplification on 9/11 and the subsequent days. Second, how the terror alerts may have changed people's behaviours and attitudes.

9/11

As 9/11 was a mass-casualty conventional attack where the threat lasted for one day (as opposed to say a series of missile strike attacks, suicide bombings or the release of anthrax where a threat could persist for a period of time), it is hard to establish whether the public's behaviours or attitudes were amplified or attenuated by the performance of the risk communicators on September 11 and the following days. The first area to consider is to what degree Giuliani's response reduced or amplified level of fears and anxiety. The main evidence comes from newspaper accounts which reported that Giuliani successfully encouraged New Yorkers to get back to normal life, and assisted in the healing of the city after the attacks. However, had Giuliani not been perceived as effectively communicating with New Yorkers, to what degree could New York have recovered as it did? A survey of the literature does not provide evidence to support whether the actions by Giuliani and Bush amplified or attenuated people's behaviours and attitudes (beside patriotic support). Americans may have felt their actions had a positive effect as discussed in the previous section. Despite the positive reception Giuliani received in connecting with New Yorkers, empathising with their predicament, and calling for them to return to their daily routines, it may well be that individuals were resilient enough to have taken these actions on their own. With no direct lingering threat (e.g. from a radiological device or a biological attack), it was safe for New Yorkers and other Americans to return to their daily routines. It was not until the anthrax attacks started that this changed.

Terror alerts

The risk communication section discussed the shortfall of the terror alerts in integrating risk communication practices over the three years after 9/11, concluding that there were many occasions where best practices were not employed. The heightened level of alerts and how they were handled by the populace may have had a detrimental effect on their behaviours and attitudes, for instance, encouraging road travel at the expense of air travel leading to an increase in road traffic fatalities.

It could be hypothesised that choosing to drive rather than fly was exacerbated by the terror alerts. Could the threat advisories unintentionally have led the public to decide that the perceived risk of flying was too high given the warnings of further Al Qaeda strikes in the US? While there are no studies that specifically examine the link of terror alerts and driving behaviour, Gigerenzer's timeline graph (shown in Figure 6.4) of the peaks in road travel and related deaths provides some means of matching this with alerts over terrorist attacks or an announcement that a significant arrest had been made, for instance, the arrest in June 2002 of the alleged 'dirty bomber'. In the graph there are peaks in November 2001, January, March, June and September 2002, and March 2003. An assessment of terrorism alerts by Washington coincided with these peaks during or in the following month as listed in Table 6.2.

It could be argued that many Americans interpreted the terror alerts to mean it was better where possible when travelling long distances to go by car rather than by air. However, this then led to more road fatalities. While

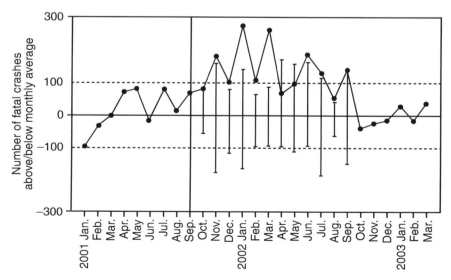

Figure 6.4 Number of fatal traffic accidents before and after 9/11 (see page xiv for author's note).[164]

Table 6.2 A comparison of alert advisories and traffic fatalities

Alert advisory	Traffic fatalities
30 October 2001 Attorney General Ashcroft warned of further attacks.	Fatal crashes peaked in November.
3 December 2001 (reissued on 20 December) Alert ran through to 2 January. Secretary Ridge gave a national warning about possible terrorist attacks. On 20 December, a spokesman for DHS stated that with the 'confluence of holidays this time of year, including Ramadan, Hanukkah, Christmas and New Year's, we want to make sure everyone stays vigilant'.[1]	Fatal crashes reached their highest level in January.
12 February 2002 Ashcroft called on 'all Americans to be on the highest state of alert' after an FBI warning of a possible imminent terrorist attack.[2]	Fatal crashes rose sharply again in March.
24 May 2002 Railway and other transit systems across the country received a Transportation Department warning based on 'an unconfirmed, uncorroborated report', to 'remain in a heightened state of alert'. A few days earlier, the government issued warnings about the Statue of Liberty and the Brooklyn Bridge, leading to tightened security at and around those New York City locations.[3]	Fatal crashes peaked in June.
10 June 2002 Attorney General Ashcroft announced that the US government had arrested a 'dirty bomber' – radiological dispersal device. He incorrectly described the RDD as a weapon of mass destruction. According to George Gray and David Ropeik, risk perception research suggests this announcement would have alarmed people by raising awareness of a risk with a lot of uncertainty, a risk that is new and catastrophic, which the populace would have no control over.[4]	Fatal crashes peaked in June.

10–24 September 2002

The Attorney General elevated the terror alert based on a review of intelligence and an assessment of threats by the intelligence community, as well as the passing of the anniversary of the September 11 terrorist attacks.

Fatal crashes spiked again in September, to then dramatically decline in October to seasonal average.

9 February 2003

Citing credible threats that Al Qaeda might be planning attacks on American targets, the US government raised the national color-coded threat level to orange.[5]

Fatal crashes increased gradually in March.

17 March 2003

DHS Ridge reported 'terrorists will attempt multiple attacks against US and Coalition targets worldwide in the event of a US-led military campaign against Saddam Hussein.'[6]

Fatal crashes increased gradually in March.

Notes

1 'Terror Alert to be Extended through Jan 2', *CNN*, 20 December 2001. Online, available at http://edition.cnn.com/2001/US/12/20/ret.alert.extended/index.html (accessed 1 October 2006).

2 'Ashcroft calls for "highest state of alert"', *CNN*, 12 February 2002. Online, available at http://edition.cnn.com/2002/US/02/12/terror.warning (accessed 1 October 2006).

3 'Terror Alerts on Small Planes, Scuba Divers', *CNN*, 24 May 2002. Online, available at http://edition.cnn.com/2002/US/05/24/terror.threats (accessed 1 October 2006).

4 George M. Gray and David M. Ropeik, 'Dealing with the Dangers of Fear: The Role of Risk Communication', *Politics and Public Health*, November/December 2002, p. 113.

5 'Official: Credible Threats Pushed Terror Alert Higher', *CNN*, 9 February 2003. Online, available at http://edition.cnn.com/2003/US/02/07/threat.level/ (accessed 1 October 2006).

6 'National Threat Level Raised', statement by Homeland Security Secretary Tom Ridge, 17 March 2003. Online, available at http://www.whitehouse.gov/news/releases/2003/03/20030317–8.html (accessed 1 October 2006).

this may have been a coincidence, there is a strong correlation between the two in terms of timings. To assess how seriously Americans may have taken the security alerts and terrorism threats issued by their government, a Gallup poll in 2006 found that only 13 per cent thought the US government exaggerated the threat to US citizens. The majority, 54 per cent, said the government did a good job in describing the threat, while 30 per cent said it did not go far enough.[165] This suggests that approximately half of the populace believed the terror alerts of possible attacks had to be taken seriously (with an attack possibly following). For some this may have led them to avoid the perceived risk of flying.

From the outset the colour-coded system failed to address what it was set out to do and may have exacerbated Americans' risk perception of terrorism. George Gray and David Ropeik remarked that while Ridge announced the HSAS 'empowers government and citizens to take actions to address the threat', the system made no suggestion on what citizens should do to reduce their risks at any particular stage of alert.[166] General safety advice was lacking for each threat level which could have given Americans a sense that they could do something to reduce their risk – a sense of control – reducing the perception that the risk was personal.[167] This in turn could have reduced the outcome of Americans undertaking adverse behavioural reactions, because they believed the risk was personal to themselves.

To analyse the effect of an orange alert on the US public, a Gallup poll taken after the 9 February 2003 elevation to orange, found that many Americans believed there would shortly be an attack on their soil and that they would become victims of terrorism. Around two-thirds reported further acts of terrorism were at least somewhat likely in the US over the next few weeks, including 16 per cent who said they were very possible. In addition, 48 per cent said they were either very (13 per cent) or somewhat (35 per cent) worried that they would become a victim of terrorism.[168] This was a large increase from two weeks earlier, when a January poll showed that 39 per cent were worried (including 8 per cent who were very worried).

The degree to which this may have led to changes in Americans' lives was discussed in the behavioural changes section with Gallup polls showing that over the five years since 9/11 many have changed their lives ranging from altered travel behaviours (flying or going abroad) to no longer attending major events with large crowds. Collectively these surveys strongly suggest that first many Americans believed the threat advisories would be shortly followed by an attack, and second, a significant proportion changed their behaviours and attitudes as a result. Further research would need to be undertaken to establish whether other factors were evident and to what extent, if any, there was a correlation between the terror warnings and driving/travel behaviour. The raising of the terrorism alerts appeared to have a strong influence on the public's behaviour, leading to them to undertake activities detrimental to their own well-being. It appeared that these aspects may not have been fully considered by the DHS and others in Washington, DC when developing the HSAS and related advisories.

Conclusion

In all, four aircraft were lost (two Boeing 767s and two 757s), the twin towers destroyed, the western part of the Pentagon destroyed, 3,209 lives lost and varying degrees of fear and anxiety led to some Americans experiencing long-term psychological problems. The adjusted figure of probable PTSD from 11.3 per cent to 5.1 per cent of those in New York City when taking into account the social demographics infers that when civilians are faced with a mass-casualty conventional terrorist attack they are not greatly affected psychologically to the extent that they encounter large-scale significant mental health problems.

Although proximity was a determinant in the mental health consequences of the attacks, the fact that Washington, DC had a lower rate of PTSD than US cities not struck showed that proximity did not have a uniform effect. Nevertheless, those in the immediate area of the attacked zone (e.g. those in Manhattan and the rest of New York City) had a far higher rate of adverse reactions than those outside. One of the main pieces of evidence on proximity is the 37-per-cent prevalence of probable PTSD among the survivors who were in the WTC on September 11, in those who saw the attacks in person it was 12.5 per cent and among those who lived in Manhattan south of 110th street but did not witness the attacks, it was 7.4 per cent. The rates of probable PTSD and related symptoms declined the further away from New York City the citizens were. However, the second attacked city of Washington, DC had a PTSD rate of 2.7 per cent – lower than Chicago, Houston and Los Angeles of 3.6 per cent and the national average of 4 per cent. Another study by Galea and Ahern just weeks after 9/11 and six months later showed higher rates of probable PTSD in the NYC metropolitan area than in the average for New York State and surrounding regions (New Jersey and Connecticut).

The extent to which probable PTSD was found across the board is questioned by evidence that discussed the effect of time on the terror of terrorism. For instance, studies by Mark Schuster and Sandro Galea are questioned for overexaggerating the PTSD rate by using a methodology that could be overly sensitive. The number and type of visits to New York's counsellors after 9/11 were lower and of a different population type than predicted. Those who had already sought counselling increased their visits, but as Project Liberty showed, the numbers of the general populace were significantly lower than anticipated. While there is debate over the accuracy of PTSD figures, the sharp decline in the rates among those in Manhattan living south of 110th Street from 7.5 per cent one month after, to 1.7 per cent four months and then 0.6 per cent six months after the event clearly showed that any PTSD there might have been fell significantly.

While time did lead to a reduction in levels of post-traumatic stress from 2001–2004, after the peak of November 2001 (17 per cent), levels remained around the same rate (3–6 per cent) from March 2002 to September 2004. The plateau from March 2002 to September 2004 is similar to those of the Gallup surveys that showed 18–25 per cent of Americans consistently reported that they have permanently changed the way they live because of 9/11. The two sets of data suggest that while the initial effects of 9/11 declined, there remained a continued effect on the targeted populace.

The section on time suggests Americans reacted in a calm manner after the attacks from those caught up in the WTC through to the wider population of the US. When the WTC was on fire before the arrival of emergency services, there was an orderly evacuation. Similarly in the rest of Manhattan in the hours after the attack there was an orderly mass exodus of survivors via bridges that stretched across the East River, the only way out of Manhattan. While probable PTSD declined over time, literature showed that there was an increase in substance abuse that included smoking, drinking and marijuana use.

What is most striking about this case study is how these reactions manifested themselves into risk averse reactions (perceived dread risk of certain activities) by Americans to minimise the risk of being personally exposed to a terrorist attack. Up to a quarter of the populace near New York City reduced their air travel and used Manhattan public transport less frequently. But the fear of flying may have become acceptable – leading to what Simon Wessely called sociogenic illness that can include overexaggerated responses to a real or perceived terrorist threat. These underlying threat perceptions were given clarity in a study that found that two months after the attacks nearly two-thirds (64 per cent) of the national populace reported an occasional fear of future terrorism and 59 per cent reported fear of harm to family members as a result of terrorism. Six months after 9/11 these levels declined to 37 per cent and 40 per cent, respectively. As the US had rarely experienced terrorism on its homeland, Americans were less accustomed to the daily threat and returning to normal daily routines. As mentioned, around one-quarter noted they had permanently changed their lives in response to terrorism. Gallup's national survey from September 2001 to August 2006 showed how Americans had changed their lives, with just under a half not travelling overseas, 43 per cent (declining to 30 per cent) not flying, 35 per cent (declining to 22 per cent) not going into skyscrapers and 30 per cent (declining to 23 per cent) not attending events where there are thousands of people. Such was the effect that secondary consequences occurred from 9/11 with the distortion of many Americans' risk perceptions believing driving long distances was safer than flying, leading to an increase in road fatalities in the months after 9/11. The surveys and data like that on the road fatalities illustrate the occurrence and consequence of the perceived dread risk of certain activities being disproportionate to the actual risk. Arguably the terror caused by 9/11 and the casualties that ensued stretched beyond September 11 and the ripple effects went beyond the regions attacked.

The section on risk communication showed two quite different approaches in how the main leaders handled events on and after 9/11. While Bush dramatically improved his response at his speech at the National Cathedral in Washington and the visit to Ground Zero, on the day of the attacks he was not in the public eye, or did he communicate a great deal with the public – spending much of the time being sent from one air force base to another.

Giuliani, in contrast, exhibited effective risk communication, recognising the need to influence and inform the public in the first few critical hours after the attacks. The urgency to communicate with the public led to impromptu press conferences when being evacuated from the first temporary command post. Overall Giuliani succeeded in communicating effectively with a public that had little prior understanding or expectation of such a terrible event. The gravity of 9/11 and the importance of minimising casualties meant that persuasion techniques had to be employed on the day. In the weeks after the attacks, Giuliani used these techniques by asking New Yorkers to return to work and their daily lives as soon as possible to enable the US to continue functioning effectively.

Despite the loss of life, one needs to question whether a different risk communication strategy implemented by Rudy Giuliani and Bush would have had different long-term benefits for the nation. Politically, would a lacklustre strategy and response have affected America's overall social, political and economic recovery post-September 11? Americans (particularly New Yorkers) appreciated the strong leadership that Giuliani showed and Bush received praise for some of his addresses. Based on the evidence in this chapter, a poorly thought-out or contradictory risk communication response may have only had a marginal effect on the social-economic recovery. The rationale behind this judgement is that the attacks themselves were at a single point in time, lasting one hour and 45 minutes from when the first plane struck the south tower to the crash of the fourth hijacked aircraft into a Pittsburgh field. Although observers at the time were unaware whether Flight 93 would be the last manned cruise missile of September 11, it became clear as the day drew on and all remaining domestic flights and those en route to America were accounted for that the air attacks were over. In the months that followed, the inadequately framed and delivered terrorism risk communication advisories may have contributed to distorting the public's risk perceptions, although more research would need to be conducted to evaluate if there is a correlation between these messages and the tendency of Americans to drive rather than fly long distances.

While concern over further Al Qaeda attacks persisted, for the American public the process of recovery began after 9/11 and importantly there were no further health risks from the attacks themselves (e.g. there were no credible assessments that CBRN agents were used). The one exception is found in reports by emergency responders at Ground Zero who complained in the following years that extensive dust from the site led to breathing complications. However, this book is not examining the effects of terrorism on emergency and first responders.

Assessing whether the attacks had the desired political outcome is complicated by the lack of demands or an agenda from Al Qaeda. The main aims can be derived from the 1998 fatwa issued against the US by Al Qaeda. With broad demands, including the US withdrawing forces from the Middle East and removing its support for regimes in the region, the attacks themselves were unlikely to lead the US to fulfil these demands. If the aims were purely symbolic, to strike at America's financial, political and defence centres of power, then arguably these were partially fulfilled. But, still, this left the lack of an end objective fulfilled or followed through. Instead, the domestic response was to significantly heighten security even at the expense of civil liberties.

September 11 forced the US to adopt numerous counter-terrorism measures, from establishing the DHS to better prepare the US for coping with an attack, hardening the security of vulnerable assets (transport and key facilities) and improving intelligence gathering. Faced with the challenge of balancing civil liberties and protecting the nation against terrorism, the US has assisted with maintaining the fear and anxiety that stemmed from 9/11 through advisories issued at the federal and state level. A conclusion from the research is that the populace proved resilient. While there was an element of increased fear and anxiety as a result of the attacks, together with a marginal increase in PTSD, the majority of society continued to function at a near-normal state. However, a significant proportion changed their behaviours and attitudes in accordance with their perceived dread risks leading to further casualties.

7 2001 anthrax attacks

Introduction

The anthrax sent by post to attack US media and government institutions killing five people in October–November 2001, exposed America to a type of threat for which it was not fully prepared. At first the authorities believed the attacks were part of a second wave of Al Qaeda attacks (which had been predicted) or a diversion to disguise an attack of far greater magnitude. The attacks were not the first time Americans encountered anthrax. During the 1990s there had been a number of anthrax hoaxes, over 30 in February 1999 alone. These generally took the form of letters with warnings of anthrax attached, sent to newspapers and abortion clinics.[1]

Analysing the social-political consequences of the attacks is complicated by a lack of extensive research by mental health and political science, unlike for the case studies. Nevertheless, it is still possible to provide an assessment of the short- and long-term implications these events had on America's society. The extensive media coverage, together with public health accounts, provides a valuable case study to understand the impact a limited bioterrorism incident can have on a society. This chapter does not intend to provide an exhaustive account of all the anthrax incidents at various buildings and of the people contaminated, but instead focuses on selected events: the management of the anthrax outbreak at the Brentwood postal-sorting facility in Washington, DC and the Hart Senate building. These cases provide a detailed understanding of the difficulty of characterising the lethality of anthrax and the poor internal and external communication that was involved. From these events, one can then map how the risk communication may have influenced public perceptions, and ultimately the level of terror the bioterrorism incident caused. The following sections are:

- Background and overview
- Strategic and political objectives
- Political effects
- Effects of proximity and time
- Changes in behaviours and attitudes

- Risk communication
- Risk perception
- Risk amplification.

Background and overview

The first confirmed victim of the attacks was an employee from American Media Inc (AMI) in Florida who initially sought medical care at a local hospital on 2 October. The victim was gravely ill, but was not diagnosed with anthrax until 4 October, less than 24 hours before he died. On 4 October 2001, just over three weeks after 9/11, the Florida Department of Health and the Center for Disease Control and Prevention (CDC) confirmed the first case of inhalational anthrax in the US in more than 25 years. By 6 October, a team of federal, state, and local public health and local law enforcement investigators identified an inhalational *Bacillus (B.) anthracis* spore contamination at the patient's workplace. Authorities believe that anthrax could have been picked up in North Carolina where the worker had travelled for three days on a driving holiday before the onset of illness. Based on the patient's travel route, surveillance was undertaken in all 15 intensive care units in five North Carolina counties. On 4 October, concurrent investigations were initiated in Florida and North Carolina to identify whether the anthrax was naturally occurring or an act of bioterrorism. Between 7–12 October investigators isolated *B. anthracis* from the patient's place of employment in Florida.

In all there were 11 inhalation cases and 11 cutaneous of anthrax (seven confirmed and four suspected). With five deaths, the mortality rate was 45 per cent compared to 90 per cent in previous recorded cases.[2] All the attacks were on America's citadels of political power or on its means of communication – broadcast news and newspapers.[3] Twelve cases (eight with inhalational and four with cutaneous anthrax) were mail handlers, including US Postal Service employees (nine cases), government mail-processing staff (one case), and media company mailroom workers (two cases). Six patients (one inhalational and five cutaneous) were media company employees working at sites where powder-containing mail was received: AMI, one case; CBS, one case; NBC, two cases; and the *New York Post*, two cases. Four (two inhalational and two cutaneous) were classified as 'other', including a seven-month-old visitor to ABC, a 61-year-old Manhattan hospital supply-room worker, a 51-year-old book-keeper from New Jersey, and a 94-year-old Connecticut resident. Of the 22, 20 either handled mail potentially contaminated with *B. anthracis* spores or were exposed to worksites where anthrax-contaminated mail was processed or received.

In all four envelopes anthrax spores were recovered and the path of the envelopes through the mail systems was traced. Two of the four letters, one addressed to NBC news presenter Tom Brokaw and the other to the editor of the *New York Post*, both in New York City, were mailed from the vicinity of

Trenton, NJ and were post-marked 18 September 2001. Both envelopes contained a letter stating, '09–11–01 … This is next … Take penacilin [sic] now.' These two contaminated letters passed through various mail facilities causing secondary contamination. Once processed at Trenton, they were sent onto the Morgan Central Postal Facility in New York City, where they were sorted and delivered. Cross-contamination of envelopes at the Morgan facility meant five other sorting facilities in New Jersey tested positive for *B. anthracis*.

The letters mailed to Senator Patrick Leahy and Senator Tom Daschle, both in Washington, DC, were mailed from Trenton and post-marked 9 October 2001. The last two letters contained a letter with the phrase, '09–11–01 … You can not stop us. We have this anthrax. You die now.' These letters were processed at the Hamilton, NJ facility, and transported to the US Postal Service Brentwood Processing and Distribution Center in Washington, DC. At both facilities the mail was processed with high-speed sorters, allowing for the possibility of aerosolised *B. anthracis* spores. Consequently, these envelopes together with other contaminated mail were transported to various government mail facilities. This led to at least 25 other government, postal or mail-receiving facilities affiliated with Brentwood testing positive for anthrax. Environmental sampling showed that both the Hart building and the Brentwood facility were heavily contaminated with spores.

Strategic and political objectives

One of the most mysterious elements of the anthrax attacks is that the perpetrator, whether an individual or a group, remains unknown. No one claimed responsibility. At the outset it was suspected that this could be a second wave of Al Qaeda attacks following 9/11 or attacks by another external terrorist group. For example, when Vice President Dick Cheney was asked if the anthrax mailings were linked to 9/11 he replied 'Are they related? We don't know. We don't have enough evidence to pin down that kind of connection. But … we have to be suspicious.'[4] Written in crude handwriting, the letters to NBC and the *New York Post* did not reveal who was behind the attacks. The letters read:

> This is next
> Take Penacilin [*sic*] Now
> Death to America
> Death to Israel
> Allah is Great

The Daschle letter was worded differently and read:

> You can not stop us
> We have this anthrax

You die now
Are you afraid?
Death to America

By 25 October 2001, George Tenet, Director of the CIA, and Robert Mueller, FBI Director, informed Senators they were not ruling out any possibilities, but an Iraqi connection seemed unlikely.[5] Days later attention had become domestic in the search for the perpetrator with investigators interviewing laboratory researchers in the Trenton and Princeton area, from where the anthrax letters were mailed. The public was asked to be on the look-out for a 'loner scientist with a grudge', familiar with the Trenton, NJ area. Investigation as to who the perpetrator could be focused primarily on analysing the anthrax used in the mailings and whether this matched those used by a biologist. Beyond these suppositions, the identity of the attackers and importantly the rationale behind the attacks, remained unknown.

Political effects

As the perpetrators did not declare their aims or objectives beyond the letters enclosed with the anthrax-laced envelopes, it is hard to establish what the perpetrator(s) were looking to achieve and therefore whether they met their objectives. There remains ambiguity over why the attacks were carried out. Although the letters contained messages that included 'death to America', 'Allah is great', 'death to Israel', these may have masked the true intentions of the perpetrator. Suppositions include a disgruntled government employee with access to anthrax who wanted to send a message regarding the vulnerability of America's infrastructure, but was unaware that the anthrax could leak out of the envelopes at mail-sorting offices. The intention may have been to cause fear and anxiety in the populace and put pressure on the US, or the perpetrator(s) may have sought to raise awareness of America's vulnerability to bioterrorism. While the anthrax attacks were initially seen as a second possible wave of Al Qaeda attacks further testing America's resolve following September 11, neither the regions directly affected exhibited evidence of significant fear or anxiety beyond some changes in behaviour and routines. With this in mind, it is extremely difficult to make a valid judgement as to what degree the attacks fulfilled their objectives.

Effects of proximity and time

Proximity

The main source for assessing the effects of proximity is the research done by the Harvard School of Public Health, led by Robert Blendon who tracked the behavioural reactions nationally and in three regions directly affected by the anthrax.[6] Behavioural responses included individuals taking precautions when opening mail, wearing gloves or completely avoiding opening their mail. The three areas were Washington, DC, Trenton/Princeton, NJ and Boca Rato, FL. The survey established that more Americans in the three areas were taking precautions when opening mail compared to the national total. However, while the national average was 32 per cent, in Boca Raton and Washington, DC, the figure was only marginally higher at 37 per cent. In Trenton/Princeton, 54 per cent took mail precautions – significantly more than the other regions. A more detailed analysis of Washington, DC respondents revealed that 47 per cent in the areas where anthrax was found were more careful in opening mail compared to 37 per cent in unaffected DC areas.

In the same survey, proximity also influenced the risk perception of contracting anthrax. Of Washington, DC residents whose workplaces had been closed, 26 per cent believed it was likely they would contract the disease, compared to 15 per cent of area residents without any direct experience of the threat, and 9 per cent of the general US population.[7] In addition 12 per cent of Washington DC area residents said that they or someone in their household had acquired a prescription for or purchased antibiotics because of reports of bioterrorism (compared with 3 per cent of those not affected and 4 per cent of all adults nationally). Robert Blendon noted that it was expected a higher proportion of people would report being affected by the anthrax incidents in metropolitan areas where those incidents took place than in the nation as a whole.[8] In addition, within those metropolitan areas, one would expect those located in the vicinity of reported anthrax cases and contaminated mailing facilities to report taking more precautions than those who were not within these areas.[9]

Time

The two main sources examining the effect of time on American's fears and anxieties caused by the anthrax attacks are opinion polls by Gallup running from July–November 2001 and Pew research. An analysis of a series of Gallup polls taken from July–November 2001 tracking the perceived personal risk from terrorism enables the impact the anthrax attacks had on Americans' concerns about terrorism to be assessed. Gallup asked respondents whether they were worried that they, or a family member, would become a victim of terrorism. During the period 5–6 October when the first anthrax death was announced, concerns jumped from 49 per cent to 59 per cent, equalling the level recorded just after 9/11.[10] What is quite striking is that despite three more anthrax deaths in early November, two Department of Justice threat advisory warnings of further terrorist attacks in October and November, the initiation of hostilities against Afghanistan and a fifth anthrax death in late November, the percentage of Americans worried about becoming a victim of terrorism steadily declined to 35 per cent by late

November. The lack of impact the three early November deaths had on the perceived threat of anthrax to Americans is underscored by a separate Gallup survey from mid-October to late November. This survey tracked, through three opinion polls, the percentage of Americans worried that they, or a family member, would be exposed to anthrax. The first two recorded 34 per cent and the final one 33 per cent. Both Gallup surveys clearly suggest that after an initial jump after the first confirmed anthrax death, the anxiety among Americans that they or a family member might become a victim of terrorism (or specifically anthrax) was unaffected by further anthrax deaths and warnings of further terrorist attacks.

A survey by Pew similarly concluded that the ongoing anthrax attacks had little effect on the public's fears and anxieties. In a poll conducted 10–14 October (just after the first death on 5 October), reports of new anthrax cases in New York and elsewhere were not raising public anxiety nor further demoralising Americans. Depression, sleeplessness and concern over renewed terrorism did not increase following news on 12 October of an NBC employee found to have anthrax. About 30 per cent of respondents said they were feeling depressed, compared to 33 per cent who made such reports a few days earlier and 42 per cent who said they had felt depressed in early October.[11] The number who experienced insomnia also declined from 18 per cent in early October to 12 per cent by the weekend of 13–14 October. Pew concluded that while the anthrax attacks at the early stage did not demoralise or increase fear and anxiety among the public, fears over terrorism remained high. 69 per cent had some concern there would be new attacks and 52 per cent were somewhat worried that they or their families could become victims of terrorism.[12]

Despite these concerns, a separate survey found that only a small proportion of Americans in late October 2001 considered they were at risk of being exposed to anthrax with only 14 per cent believing that they or a member of their family would be exposed to anthrax in the next 12 months.[13] To put this perceived risk into context, respondents believed that they or someone in their immediate family were five times more likely to get flu and just under four times more likely to be injured in a car accident.[14] The perceived risk of being exposed to anthrax was just higher than of contracting small-pox at 9 per cent.

Changes in behaviours and attitudes

Research indicates that there was a small but significant proportion of the US populace who changed their behaviours and attitudes in response to the anthrax attacks and some of the resulting actions could have been considered detrimental to public health. While there was no panic, fear proliferated, with people focusing their attention on the outcome of possibly getting anthrax rather than the low probability of the harm.[15]

A common perception of America's reaction to the anthrax attacks is that a large number acquired a prescription for antibiotics. The CDC recommended three antibiotic drugs that could treat anthrax: ciprofloxacin, doxycycline and amoxicillin. In all, the CDC advised 10,000 people who were potentially exposed to anthrax in Connecticut, Florida, New Jersey, New York City and Washington, DC to take the 60-day treatment.

A comparison of the national prescription levels of these drugs in October–November 2001 with the same period in 2000 demonstrates that only a small number of the public purchased these drugs when compared to the size of the US populace. Compared to 2000 levels, ciprofloxacin prescriptions were 40 per cent higher in October 2001, doxycycline increased by 30 per cent during October–November. This corresponded to an increase of 160,000 prescriptions for ciprofloxacin in October and 216,000 for doxycycline during October–November.[16] Overall this represented a total of 376,000 extra prescriptions during October–November 2001 over the year before – representing only 0.13 per cent of America's population of 290 million. These figures do not include the 10,000 prescriptions prescribed by the CDC which came from the National Pharmaceutical Stockpile.

Ciprofloxacin and doxycycline are not available over the counter but only through a prescription and consent from a medical practitioner. Therefore while these figures showed only a marginal increase in these prescriptions, there may have been a number who sought these strong antibiotics but were refused a prescription by their doctor. Evidence that provides what proportion this might have been can be found in a series of Gallup polls taken in mid-October 2001 that revealed 70 per cent of respondents did not consider purchasing an antibiotic.[17] However 3 per cent had tried to acquire a prescription for the antibiotics and 6 per cent were seriously considering it. Twenty per cent were not seriously considering this action.

After the death of two postal workers this desire increased to 5 per cent reporting having obtained the drug according to the Robert Blendon survey.[18] Although 5 per cent reported having obtained antibiotics, only 1 per cent reported taking the medication. However this percentage is higher than the figures indicated by the national prescription levels suggesting the real figure was considerably lower. While a considerable number of Americans were troubled by the anthrax attacks, only a small proportion felt sufficiently concerned to request the medication despite the known side-effects. Nevertheless, according to Congressional testimony by Kenneth Shine, president of the Institute of Medicine, the proportion who did seek ciprofloxacin led to some stores of the drug being exhausted.[19] Whatever the actual true figures might have been, there was a small proportion who unnecessarily sought a prescription for one of these antibiotics, placing pressure on limited stockpiles and exposing individuals to possible side-effects of the strong drug.

Besides acquiring a prescription to antibiotics, a Gallup poll conducted in 19–21 October found that:

- 9 per cent seriously considered purchasing a weapon and 8 per cent had already done so.
- 6 per cent seriously considered purchasing a gas mask and 2 per cent had already done so.
- 12 per cent seriously considered stockpiling food or water and 9 per cent had already done so.
- 11 per cent seriously considered avoiding public events and 8 per cent were already doing so.
- 30 per cent seriously considered using more caution when opening mail and 23 per cent were already doing so.[20]

Despite these findings, 89 per cent of respondents said they were going about their lives as usual, while 11 per cent said they were not.

Further evidence to support these type of behavioural responses can be found in the Robert Blendon study in October that showed 57 per cent of respondents had taken one or more precautions in response to the anthrax attacks. When opening the mail, 37 per cent took precautions, 25 per cent maintained emergency supplies of food, water or clothing, and 3 per cent bought a gun.[21] Background checks for handguns had increased by 39 per cent in October 2001.[22]

In addition, 12 per cent avoided public events and, when opening mail, 30 per cent washed their hands afterward and six per cent wore gloves.[23] Blendon concludes that as only 13 per cent were taking three or more of the 12 precautions listed and 43 per cent reported taking none of them, Americans were not 'panicking'. The latter figure is arguably the more revealing since it suggests the ambiguity over how the attacks would evolve and the lack of effective risk communication led a proportion to take various precautions.

The study authors suggested that the low level of precautions might be due to most Americans' belief that anthrax was not generally fatal with appropriate medical treatment. Among those surveyed, 91 per cent believed they would be very or somewhat likely to survive with medical treatment after skin anthrax and 78 per cent after pulmonary (inhaled) anthrax. Although the survey did not specifically ask respondents for their levels of fear and anxiety, the conclusion that these levels were probably low is in line with the findings of other surveys that specifically investigated these issues.

Medical anthropologist Monica Schoch-Spana believed the figures on behavioural response showed a measured response in the public's reactions and perceptions. She noted that even though Americans were confronted with bioterrorism soon after 9/11, most remained calm and resolute although concerned about personal safety – contrary to some public officials' expectations of panic. But Schoch-Spana did not define what she meant by panic. Schoch-Spana also pointed to a large-scale public health campaign that was orderly, with hundreds and sometimes thousands of people waiting in line for long periods to be swabbed and evaluated for possible anthrax exposure.[24] In addition, Schoch-Spana believed that the public phoning pubic health advice lines for information demonstrated a 'rational' response and not one of panic.[25] Although individuals with direct experience of the anthrax threat had elevated concerns over possible exposure, this fear apparently did not contribute to erratic or unruly behaviour.[26]

There is evidence, though, to suggest that a small proportion of Americans changed their behaviours and attitudes. While handling mail with more caution could be regarded as a normal response in light of the perceived dread risk and ambiguity over the extent of anthrax-contaminated letters, there a number of actions taken were not directly relevant to the situation, for instance, purchasing a gas mask or other protective clothing and a weapon. With 8 per cent reporting having taken one or both of these actions in the Gallup polls, this suggests a total of 23 million individuals. As Cass Sunstein noted in the *Journal of Risk and Uncertainty*, 'it is hard to deny that the public fear was disproportionate to its cause, and that the level of response was disproportionate too. The extraordinary ripple effects attest to the intensity of that fear.'[27] While a significant majority did not undertake any of these actions, suggesting a calm and measured response, a substantial minority of the populace felt sufficiently concerned to proceed with one of these actions despite the probability of exposure being extraordinarily low.

Risk communication

The literature on risk communication for the anthrax attacks is the most extensive of that for all the case studies. The nature of the event lends itself to effective examination: an ongoing bioterrorism event with uncertainty surrounding the agent's lethality, uncertainty on how the public should be informed and what strategies should be implemented to ensure the public conforms to the desired behaviours to limit pressure on the public health system. Further, extensive literature is available to examine the process of risk characterisation from the CDC's publicly available literature and detailed coverage in publications that carry risk analysis. There are two main avenues to analyse the risk communication performance. First, public health officials, notably the CDC. Second, government officials like the then-Secretary of the Department of Health and Human Services (HHS) Tommy Thompson and members of Congress. The ability of the CDC and other authorities to conduct effective risk communication was hampered by poor risk characterisation (assessment) because they could not predict the lethality and behaviour of the anthrax spores in an urban environment.

Hazards that are intentionally deployed, such as mailing anthrax, produce risk perception levels that are extremely high.[28] Effective risk communication during the anthrax attacks was essential to provide the public with the knowledge, information and skills they needed to ameliorate or diminish the likely effects of the hazard. However, the discussion below implies that these attributes were lacking at times.

The CDC

The risk communication employed by the CDC during the anthrax attacks was, according to a study led by John Hobbs, hindered by three factors:[29]

1   Problems related to the limited availability of epidemiological evidence.
2   Limited knowledge regarding the treatment and transmission of anthrax.
3   Poor integration between the work of public health officials and the media. The first two points are discussed in the following section and the third in the subsequent part.

The CDC – knowledge of anthrax

For any risk communication strategy, effective risk characterisation is essential. Not fully understanding the health risks can undermine the accuracy of advice given to the public. In CDC's case, it lacked sufficient knowledge of how anthrax could spread and the number of spores required for a fatal dose, operating initially on the assumption that the inhaled form of anthrax could not be contracted through sealed letters and the risk of secondary re-aerosolisation was low. This was partly based on the belief that the New York and Florida cases of those who handled contaminated letters caught anthrax through the skin but not the more lethal pulmonary version.[30] Consequently the CDC was caught by the fast changing situation where some assumptions proven valid in the past turned out to be incorrect. Three key assumptions were undermined:

1   Contrary to earlier understandings, the anthrax spores were capable of leaking from the envelopes.
2   The number of viable spores needed to cause anthrax was lower than originally believed.
3   The health risk posed by secondary aerosolisation was far greater than previous studies had suggested.

Although research conducted by the US military showed that *Bacillus subtilis* spores, used as a surrogate for *B. anthracis*, can re-aerosolise with external factors in outdoor environments, no published data were available concerning secondary aerosolisation of *B. anthracis* spores indoors, until late 2002 with a study published in *JAMA* on anthrax in the Hart building.[31] Prior to the anthrax attacks, consensus recommendations from the US Working Group on Civilian Biodefense suggested only a slight risk of acquiring inhalational anthrax by secondary aerosolisation from heavily contaminated surfaces. These recommendations were based on an incident involving accidental release of *B. anthracis* in Sverdlovsk, Russia, occupational studies of workers in goat-hair processing mills and modelling analyses by the US army.[32] These recommendations were pursued by the CDC, but later proved to be inaccurate. Based on the existing material from previous patterns of natural outbreaks, the standard point of reference, the CDC found it very difficult to answer questions from the media such as 'How much is the public at risk?'.[33] The difficulties the public health community faced in understanding the lethality of the spores is aptly described in a joint article by CDC personnel published in *Emerging Infectious Diseases* in October 2002 where they noted the following.

> Many unknowns confronted the public-health response team during the anthrax investigation. The basics about exposure to *B. anthracis* – contaminated envelopes specifically sent to media outlets and government leaders were understood quickly given events in Florida, New York, and then Washington, DC. Difficulties arose in characterising anthrax risk to individuals and groups with suspected or confirmed exposure to *B. anthracis*-contaminated envelopes or environments. Challenges also arose in the evaluation of *B. anthracis* – containing powders, epidemiologic investigation, environmental assessment and remediation, surveillance, diagnosis, treatment, and post-exposure prophylaxis.[34]

The report continues to state that while data from goat hair in textile mills more than 40 years ago provided some information about the risk of *B. anthracis* spore-containing particles, the data suggested that relatively high levels of *B. anthracis* spores were 'not necessarily or consistently dangerous' in this setting. In addition biological warfare experts considered it unlikely that terrorists could produce a *B. anthracis* spore powder for use in an envelope that would be capable of generating substantial primary (or secondary) aerosol threats for human infection or widespread contamination of environments. These assumptions were shown to be inaccurate when the anthrax letter opened in Senator Daschle's office caused spores to enter a person's nasal mucosa almost immediately. Re-aerosolisation (secondary aerosol) was also present at the high-speed mailing sorter in the Brentwood Mail Processing and Distribution Center.

To compound the CDC's difficulties in adequately characterising the risk anthrax posed, the anthrax found in Florida and New York and identified as a low risk of secondary aerosolisation may have been different to that sent to the Senate. According to the CDC's publication *Emerging Infectious Diseases*, the *B. anthracis* spore preparation in the 9 October Senate envelopes may have had a higher potential for aerosolisation than the preparation in the 18 September envelopes or the two mailings were made under or exposed to different environmental conditions (e.g. amount of moisture) that created a different potential for aerosolisation.[35] In a naturally occurring disease, once a risk is understood, it generally remains constant. However, in intentional contamination, risk may be altered by the perpetrator(s). This then further complicates risk characterisation and thus risk communication.

Alongside the lack of knowledge concerning the lethality of anthrax was the CDCs limited bioterrorism-related material ready to distribute to the public. According to Christine Prue of the CDC's Office of Communications, the organisation had few ready-made messages/materials for use with non-scientific audiences. More importantly for developing effective risk communication, no audience research existed to indicate what members of the public would need or want to know about terrorism, bioterrorism or anthrax specifically.[36] Once the anthrax attacks occurred, audience research and message pre-testing were not possible in the midst of rapidly evolving events.[37] Interviews with CDC employees who led the response to the anthrax attacks showed that while the organisation had some basic information on anthrax for use with professional and lay audiences, few, if any, existing pieces explained anthrax within the context of bioterrorism.[38] The materials that were available pertained to cutaneous anthrax (rarely found outside the rural environment) rather than inhalation anthrax resulting from criminal activity. When data did become available from the crime scenes, the severe compression of time dictated by events truncated the CDC's regular science-making and policy-making steps for adequate risk characterisation and risk communication. The process of scientific discovery (science-making), the generation of recommendations to the public resulting from those discoveries (policy-making) and news-making would normally take months.[39]

The view that the CDC did not implement effective risk communication (and risk characterisation as a prerequisite) is further supported by Christine Prue who noted that the organisation was 'not using risk communication techniques to deliver messages in a way that would build the agency's credibility with the public – particularly with those groups directly affected by the events'.[40] Consequently, the CDC hired a risk communication consultant to advise the agency in basic risk communication techniques to help the public understand complex and changing messages, and communicate scientific uncertainty with empathy.

An indication that the risk communication was not as effective as intended is the low compliance rate of those completing their 60-day course of antibiotics. A CDC telephone survey of 10,000 people found that of those who were considered at risk and prescribed antibiotics, only 44 per cent completed their 60 days.[41] With 57 per cent of respondents reporting some side-effects, the concern that they might experience side effects is thought to have significantly influenced the poor compliance rate.[42] This questions whether the CDC adequately took into account and addressed the public's concern of side-effects in its initial advice. According to risk communication guidelines, for the public to be able to achieve a complete understanding of the information, it is essential to have a good awareness of the public's perceptions and understandings. In the bioterrorism context, this also extends to understanding and addressing concerns surrounding the drugs the public may be advised to take as a preventative measure.

While the CDC coordinated the national response to the anthrax threat, in Washington, DC where a large part of the public health response was focused, Ivan Walks, the director of the DC Department of Public Health, had much of the responsibility in communicating with the public and media around the nation's capital. Ivan Walks was aware of and sought to implement core risk communication principles. He recognised that despite the difficulty of communicating scientific uncertainty, it was essential to tell the public what was known, not known and when more would be known.[43] Ivan Walks saw that credibility of the communication was essential. This required credible leaders to give a clear message and a response, to be 'honest to people'.[44]

Brentwood case study

A good example of the consequences of inadequate risk characterisation and communication is the CDC's handling of anthrax at the Brentwood postal sorting facility. Lack of knowledge about the lethality of the anthrax spores increased the danger to the employees and possibly contributed to the deaths of two postal workers. Unknown to the United States Postal Service (USPS) and the CDC, Brentwood became contaminated after processing an envelope addressed to Senator Daschle on 12 October before it was passed onto the Capitol's mailing systems. Although the authorities were aware that the Daschle letter opened on 15 October had passed through Brentwood, the CDC took the decision not to swab Brentwood employees for anthrax, despite testing all personnel in the vicinity of the Daschle letter and placing them on a course of antimicrobial drugs as a precautionary measure. The basis of this assumption was that there were no reported cases of anthrax among postal workers at facilities that processed the earlier New York and Florida letters and thus the threat to postal workers was regarded as negligible. In Florida and New York only one case occurred with a postal worker being infected, one of the millions living in the Trenton delivery area. Despite the nine-day period before the facility at Trenton was closed, two million letters went through the same machine that processed the anthrax-laced letters, and an estimated 18 million pieces of mail were processed.[45] The threat of cross-contamination to USPS workers and the general public was thus regarded as extremely low.

Upon learning on 17 October that staffers at the Capitol Hill Hart building had tested positive for anthrax exposure, Postmaster General John Potter contacted the CDC to determine whether similar measures were necessary for employees of Brentwood. John Potter was advised and reported that, 'because the Senate letter was well sealed, our employees were not at risk and no action was necessary'.[46] The following day John Potter gave a press conference at Brentwood with the facility's employees present to announce that the Daschle letter posed no threat to the postal workers there. That same day a New Jersey postal carrier tested positive for skin anthrax on 18 October.[47] Despite Potter insisting that Brentwood employees were not at risk, poor employee relations with the USPS senior management due to a long-running labour dispute did not provide a strong basis of trust among employees, leading them to wonder whether their welfare was being fully addressed.[48]

Despite the CDC's assurances, John Potter arranged independent testing at the facility. Initial field test results were negative, but laboratory test results received on 22 October showed that areas of the building were contaminated with anthrax. In advance of the test results, Brentwood was closed on 21 October following two facility employees being diagnosed with inhalation anthrax. The CDC's environmental tests, which began on 22 October, later confirmed the contamination. Despite these measures, on 21 and 22 October two employees died. During the nine-day period following the processing of the Daschle letter, over 2,000 employees processed more than 60 million pieces of mail that may have exposed workers continually to anthrax spores during the period.[49]

While poor risk characterisation made it difficult for the CDC to provide effective advice, its lack of risk communication awareness at times became a major public relations challenge that could have been avoided. Based on the CDC's scientific evidence of treating Americans suspected of being exposed to anthrax, the CDC used their Health Alert Network (HAN) to inform postal workers that they should switch from using ciprofloxacin to doxycycline. Medical evidence strongly suggested doxycycline had the same efficacy as ciprofloxacin on the strain of anthrax released but had fewer side-effects and was in greater supply. Executives at the television station NBC and legislators in the Senate Hart building had received ciprofloxacin. Postal workers expressed concerns that they were being treated as second-class citizens because they were not receiving what they believed to be the most effective medication for financial reasons while senators were receiving the more expensive ciprofloxacin. The CDC failed to take into account the risk communication practice of understanding the current perceptions of its audience, in this case the postal workers.

In the words of Marsha L. Vanderford who cowrote the message for the HAN, the CDC 'forgot to ask how postal workers might interpret the message on a relational level. Why had CDC recommended ciprofloxacin to television executives, but a less expensive drug to postal workers?'.[50] With hindsight Marsha Vanderford admits that the HAN communication should have anticipated these questions and that this might have prevented feelings of resentment by postal workers, rather than writing the communiqué in isolation from the current perceptions and beliefs, framed by existing information provided to the public.[51] Ivan Walks also faced the challenge to convey to the Washington, DC area why doxycycline became the preferred drug, having first told the media that ciprofloxacin was the most effective antibiotic. Ivan Walks had to respond to the media questions of whether doxycycline was cheaper and whether this influenced the new strategy, while trying to convey what was the most appropriate public health response in light of new scientific evidence on what worked best to counter anthrax.[52]

Political front

This section focuses on the performance of risk communication by key politicians from government departments to Congress and how this contributed to the wider public's perceptions of anthrax and the measures taken to combat it. Two main political decisions are examined: first is the response of the Health and Human Services Secretary Tommy Thompson; second is how Congress handled the identification of anthrax at its offices.

Tommy Thompson, Health and Human Services Secretary

Tommy Thompson became the first public face in early October to announce the anthrax attacks and provided an over-optimistic picture of the case. In a press conference, Thompson stated, '...the first inhalation case was an isolated case. Anthrax happens naturally and there is no evidence of terrorism.'[53] Monica Schoch-Spana believed that Tommy Thompson's reassurance that the first inhalation anthrax case in Florida was an isolated incident and was possibly a natural occurrence suggested that the 'government was employing a strategy to avert perceived public panic by portraying events in the most positive light, potentially undermining public confidence'.[54] When the intentional release of anthrax was confirmed, the government attempted to downplay the health risks of a bioterrorist attack using anthrax.[55]

Anthrax at Congress

The events that took place following the discovery of an anthrax-laced envelope addressed to Senator Daschle on 15 October provides an additional insight into the conflicting messages and confusion the public received in the handling of the attacks. At 9:45am on 15 October, an aide to Daschle opened a letter containing an unidentified powdery substance. Coming after the widely reported anthrax cases in Florida and New York, the staff member who opened the letter immediately notified the US Capitol Police. Officers arrived within five minutes and tested the powder twice for *B. anthracis*, using commercial rapid tests. The results (obtained within 15 minutes) suggested the powder contained anthrax spores. The United States Army Medical Research Institute for Infectious Disease (USAMRID) later confirmed these preliminary tests. The letter contained two grammes of powder, with each gramme reported to contain between 100 billion to one trillion spores.[56] The ventilation system was shut off at 10:30am. The letter mailed on 8 October was similar to that mailed to NBC, post marked Trenton and with similar handwriting in the address. The following day a team from the CDC arrived to begin their epidemiologic investigation to identify who was exposed and the extent of the exposure. A course of antibiotics was given to 600 people to prevent inhalational anthrax at the Hart Senate complex.[57]

While the bioterrorism events in Florida, New York and Brentwood came to the attention of the public health authorities only when persons were diagnosed with anthrax, the event on Capitol Hill was different. The presence of B. *anthracis* spores was suspected immediately, allowing an appropriate response and prompt distribution of the appropriate medication. A known source of exposure allowed a rapid epidemiologic investigation, using nasal swab cultures for B. *anthracis*, environmental sampling, serologic testing and preventing an anthrax outbreak.[58] Those deemed at risk of developing anthrax were regarded to be persons in the exposed area during or after the time the contaminated envelope was processed or opened.[59] Nasal swabs were taken from all 71 persons in the immediate exposure area.

The same day anthrax was identified in the offices, some Congressional staffers tested positive for anthrax exposure following precautionary nasal swabs. By the evening of the 16 October, 1,400 Senate staff members were swabbed by scientists from Fort Detrick, MD. In all at least 28 people including staffers of Senator Daschle and Feingold, tested positive for anthrax and were prescribed antibiotics. Fort Detrick also warned Daschle that tests revealed the anthrax powder was so fine that it could have entered the building's ventilation system and contaminated other areas.

The confusion that followed was played out in front of the media. Questions existed regarding the lethality of the spores, how they were transmitted, what sections of the Capitol should be closed and for how long, and who should be given antibiotics. Congressional leaders gave a series of press conferences that entailed conflicting accounts of the severity of the threat and how to cope with it. Daschle, in particular, provided mixed messages and attempted to provide a scientific assessment of the lethality and transmission of anthrax without accurate information. When discussing the health risk posed by the anthrax spores in the Hart building's circulation system, the Senator first stated that even if there were some traces of anthrax found in the Hart air ducts, 'it would not be of sufficient force or strength to be of health risk to those who are exposed', but then added, 'we were told it was a very strong form of anthrax, a very potent form of anthrax that clearly was produced by somebody who knew what he or she was doing'.[60] Daschle again publicly contradicted himself and demonstrated a lack of knowledge when reporters asked him on 17 October how anthrax had spread to 22 of his aides. He replied 'It has to be in the air in some way', then added that anthrax 'was affixed to the clothing' of an aide and that it may have been spread 'when staffers were hugging each other'.[61] Transmission through hugging had not been a factor in the contamination. Later Daschle was reported to have said 'As I understand it now, hugging doesn't really transfer spores. You can do that all day long and stay spore-free.'[62]

Adding to Daschle's mixed messages were contradictory statements by the newly appointed Homeland Security Chief Tom Ridge and House Minority Leader Richard Gephardt. Ridge asserted it was no more dangerous than the bacteria sent to news media offices and dismissed the term 'weaponised' as medically meaningless.[63] Gephardt countered this remark stating that the anthrax found on Capitol Hill was highly sophisticated and 'weapons grade' and implied that Ridge was understating the problem by saying that the Capitol Hill anthrax variant was no more lethal than what had been sent earlier to news organisations.[64] Besides contradictory statements over the lethality of anthrax and response measures, the Speaker of the House, Dennis Hastert, used incorrect terminology to describe the anthrax outbreak. Dennis Hastert described those who had come into contact with the anthrax as being 'infected' rather than 'exposed'.[65]

The inaccurate statements by the politicians were exacerbated by their actions. Although the anthrax was found in the Senate offices, the House of Representatives closed on 18 October, but the Senate remained open. The Senate offices are in a separate complex to that housing the two legislative chambers. According to Senators and their staffers, the Senate Majority and Minority leaders did not agree to recess the Senate on 17 October and instead decided to present the idea to all 100 Senators.[66] In addition, although Senator Daschle's offices were closed, the Capitol building was left open to tourists despite the confirmation of anthrax a short distance away.[67]

The closure of the House of Representatives sent mixed messages about the risk of anthrax and, to some, demonstrated weakness by the legislators. Postal workers at anthrax-contaminated facilities complained they were being treated differently. On NBC's *The David Letterman Show*, Senator John McCain openly criticised the House of Representatives' stance in closing their chamber. In response to David Letterman's comment, 'Your counterpart down in Washington, the House of Representatives, they're taking a nice, long break, a nice, long weekend break.' McCain replied 'Another chapter in "Profiles in Courage".'[68] Similarly the front page of the *New York Post* on 18 October carried a picture of the House leaders Dick Gephardt and Dennis Hastert with the headline: 'Wimps – The leaders who ran away from anthrax'.[69] According to Paul Deisler writing in *Risk Analysis*, the divergent behaviour of the two Houses of Congress served to 'confuse the message further: stay and keep on working in the face of terror or decamp as quickly as possible, bringing your work to a halt'.[70] There is some evidence in the literature that implies some postal workers whose facilities remained open despite the detection of anthrax believed they were receiving substandard treatment. An example of the frustration felt by postal workers can be demonstrated by a son of an employee who wrote in a publication called the *Amerasia Journal*:

It seems virtually no one, not even the Postmaster General John E. Potter, seems to care. Because if he did, he would have done the same thing that Senator Daschle did – shut down. Why are Capitol staffers and postal workers treated differently? Both sets of people are federal employees, right? They both get their paychecks from Uncle Sam, don't they? So where's the difference?[71]

Summary of risk communication

The anthrax episode provided many examples of mixed messages both from public health officials, politicians and the media. The variability in health-care recommendations and mixed messages led to a *caveat emptor* mentality perhaps most famously proclaimed by NBC's evening newsreader Tom Brokaw, 'In cipro we trust'.[72] It also led to a detrimental effect on the per-ception of the competence of public health agencies.[73] The extent of this can be captured in the Harvard School of Public Health study led by Robert Blendon during the first weeks of the anthrax attacks that examined which six public officials the public trusted to provide correct information about how to protect themselves and their families. Forty-two per cent said a senior scientist from the CDC, while more than 16 per cent chose no other official.[74] The other choices were the heads of Homeland Security (4 per cent), the Department of Homeland Security (16 per cent), the FBI (3 per cent), the US Surgeon General (13 per cent) and the respondent's city or state health commissioner (9 per cent).[75] This suggests that the public had considerably low trust in these government officials' ability to provide credi-ble information and with it in the perceived reliability of what they were saying and advice provided. Monica Schoch-Spana believed that although the public exhibited a strong appetite for candid and personally relevant information, the political and public health officials conducted conservative communication strategies to avoid what they saw was the risk of causing panic, with the result of the unintended consequence of diminishing the credibility of some officials.[76] Baruch Fischhoff concluded that as a result of confused expert roles, experts were disparaging the public, reflecting the limits of their own psychology.[77]

The lack of understanding of how the populace would interpret and respond to the risk communication messages contributed adverse behaviour by the public detrimental to the nation's public health. This included putting pressure on essential ciprofloxacin supplies by those who didn't need the drug, an estimated 20 per cent of whom went on to experience side-effects, and possibly changing the bacteriological environment from the widespread use of the antibiotics rendering some organisms resistant to the antibiotics employed.[78] Furthermore, only 44 per cent of those who should have taken an antibiotic because of possible exposure to anthrax completed the treatment for the required 60 days. Collectively these aspects posed public health concerns that could have been significantly reduced or avoided had effective risk communication been implemented. According to Kenneth Shine of the Institute of Medicine at a Congressional hearing, the risk communication strategies employed did not successfully convey the message that individuals should not take ciprofloxacin unless they were a member of a specifically defined high-risk group, (e.g. postal workers or those on Capitol Hill).[79]

While there is criticism of the CDC's and other public officials' risk communication practices, at least one region appeared to have implemented effective risk communication from the outset. According to Sandra Mullin, associate commissioner, director of communications of New York City's Department of Health and Mental Hygiene, the city applied risk communication measures based on a proactive model they called the 'Giuliani Press Conference Model' that originated from 9/11 and experience with the West Nile virus of 1999. When the police and health commissioners stood shoulder to shoulder, they sent the message that law enforcement and public health officials were co-operating and vigilantly working together.[80] During the anthrax attacks, Giuliani continued to hold twice-daily press conferences that followed closed door meetings with key individuals in the recovery effort. Besides maintaining the communication routine established after 9/11, the NYC Department of Health had learnt from their handling of the West Nile virus that first appeared in the US in 1999 that when they were unsure on the appropriate risk communication strategy, it was a mistake to 'dismiss people's fears as illegitimate' and that 'reciting data should have been sufficient to convince the worried of how wrong they were'.[81] A key lesson from the anthrax attacks was that admitting 'we don't know' and acknowledging uncertainty are often the best ways to earn long-term public confidence and acceptance of the eventual recommendations.[82]

Risk perception

Prior to the anthrax attacks, America was still coming to terms with the destructive 9/11 attacks and the possibility that there could be a second wave of Al Qaeda strikes. In the period leading up to the first confirmed anthrax attack, the federal authorities warned the US populace of the risk of further terrorist strikes by Al Qaeda. While Americans were advised to be vigilant, they were also advised to carry on with their lives as much as possible. In a speech at Chicago O'Hare airport on 27 September, Bush advised the public 'do your business around the country. Fly and enjoy America's great destination spots.' But the problem was how to strike a balance between watching for future attacks and getting on with normal life. Bush's administration officials had been telling members of Congress, police chiefs and reporters in the weeks following 9/11 that further attacks by Al Qaeda were virtually certain.[83] This included the US Attorney General's warning that 'we don't believe that we have curtailed the threat. We've got to be vigilant.'[84] Bin Laden's videotaped messages, like that of 7 October 2001, were interpreted by some as containing coded messages for a second strike on the US.

The lack of specific intelligence of further attacks fuelled the fear of the unknown. Concern of further attacks led to the US administration, the media and the public at large to red-team (identify) their society's vulnerabilities and potential targets. Concerns entailed detailed accounts of how a CBR attack could occur, its possible effects at sporting events, shopping malls, residential areas and ports. The means of delivery included crop sprayers for chemical or biological agents, 'truck bombs' containing high explosives akin to the Tanzania and Kenya embassy bombings in 1998 or the hijacking of tankers carrying highly toxic or inflammable cargo that could be detonated at symbolic or densely populated targets. The media with the assistance of experts, provided detailed accounts of how such attacks could occur and there was speculation that the next attack could be of greater magnitude than that of September 11. The knowledge that one of the hijackers Mohammed Atta enquired about crop dusters before 9/11 served to compound concern that bioterrorism could be one means through which another attack could occur.

An insight into the public's perception of terrorism in the period leading up to the anthrax attacks and the impact of 9/11 can be gained from returning to the Gallup polls. The surveys show that the fear and anxiety among Americans of becoming a victim of terrorism persisted at a high level in late September at 49 per cent (down from 58 per cent just after 9/11) just before the first confirmed anthrax death in early October. This pre-attack level contrasts with the 24 per cent prior to 9/11.[85] *Time*/CNN captured the perception of fear of terrorism in a poll conducted in early October 2001 just before the anthrax attacks were reported. In it 38 per cent of Americans believed everyday life had not returned to normal. More striking was that 40 per cent believed the chance of another terrorist attack occurring in the US in the next 12 months was 'very likely' and 41 per cent 'somewhat likely'. In addition 76 per cent of those surveyed believed the next attack in the US was likely to be a car or truck bomb, 53 per cent using a chemical or biological weapon and 19 per cent a nuclear device.[86] Based on the above evidence, the perceived risk of terrorism by the American public prior to the anthrax attacks may have increasingly been viewed as a dread risk and uncontrollable – not knowing when or where or in what form another attack may take place. The uncertainty over what type of weapon could be used in a second-wave terrorist attack that Americans were warned could occur may have positioned the terrorism risk more as an unknown risk as the perpetrators of 9/11 demonstrated the willingness to cause maximum destruction and disruption. The anthrax attacks became another episode after 9/11 that led terrorism to remain prominent in the public's imagination.

Risk amplification

Three elements are explored in this section. First, the CDC's delays in processing information created an information void leading to the media seeking less robust information sources. Second, how the media amplified the public's fear and anxiety through misrepresenting or not covering key public health messages. Third, what evidence there is to show for changes in behaviours and attitudes caused by risk amplification.

The initial lack of regular reports for the public, such as through the CDC's *Mortality, Morbidity Weekly Report* (MMWR) or the news media, created a significant information void, which may have increased the public's fear and concern. Consequently the void made it necessary for the news media to seek information from public officials and private citizens who were not health professionals and/or not adequately informed, resulting in misinformation and vagueness in newspaper, television and radio reports.[87] In addition there was no one authoritative leader nor one authoritative person with knowledge on the studies, results and recommendations, to deal with the media.[88] The amount of information that could have been released was partly exacerbated by the FBI withholding information that formed part of their criminal investigation.

Coupled with this were delays in the CDC's processing of information which meant missed opportunities to control what was being said by reporters who, in the absence of answers from CDC, would approach sources less inclined to scientific accuracy.[89] One example was speculation by some sources that the anthrax used was weapons grade. This led to a deluge of questions from the media to the CDC seeking verification. To exacerbate the lack of information, the way journalists reported on anthrax may have heightened the public's concern and increased demand for antibiotics that some experts viewed as unnecessary and perhaps detrimental.[90]

Overall the media coverage was not sensationalist and the national papers such as the *New York Times* and *Washington Post* were responsible in their reporting. However, the media may have contributed to the public's misperceptions and consequently fuelled anxieties by the way they carried scientific messages provided by the CDC. Segments of the media incorrectly reported that anthrax was a virus, rather than a bacterium. This could have undermined a journalist's credibility for those who knew the difference. In addition some television stations aired file footage from the 1995 sarin gas subway attack in Tokyo when reporting about local anthrax scares – potentially over dramatising the anthrax attacks.[91] According to Pew, 42 per cent of the public thought the media exaggerated the dangers of anthrax.[92] More seriously the media at times offered conflicting and often confusing accounts of what was happening, as well as varying degrees of advice on the dangers of anthrax and how to protect oneself.[93] In the context of the heightened anxiety following 9/11 about further attacks, the media at times presented rumour and fact together.[94]

A comparison of how public health messages were reported by the media with that of the CDC output showed that the media failed or inaccurately portrayed critical information pertaining to the lethality and the CDC's understanding of anthrax. According to one study:

- 17 per cent of the CDC items emphasised that anthrax cannot be transmitted person to person, while only 2 per cent of news items contained this message.
- Ciprofloxacin was portrayed by the media as the preferred or superior drug and framed the government's recommendation to use doxycycline as a cost-saving measure or a decision based on class or race.
- Virtually no articles covered CDC recommendations for antibiotic use and adherence.
- No media articles explained the role of nasal swabs, and only 2 per cent of the CDC material discussed this. Consequently segments of the media wrongly stated nasal swabs were a test for anthrax exposure and suggested they were only available for Congressional personnel and New York media celebrities, not postal workers.
- 10 per cent of the CDC literature and only 1 per cent of news reports mentioned that uncertainty of anthrax-related science and at times missed critical messages. For example, three of the eight CDC tele-briefings from late October to early November mentioned there was a lack of data to determine the number of spores required for exposure to develop anthrax, but this aspect of uncertainty was not reported in the news sample.[95]

It was essential for the risk communication to have conveyed the uncertainty in the data to maintain trust. As the New York City's Department of Health and Mental Hygiene recognised, acknowledging uncertainty is often the best way to earn long-term public confidence. Arguably the media's portrayal of doxycycline as a cost-saving and inferior drug to ciprofloxacin led postal workers to believe, according to Ivan Walks, that there were 'two tiers of treatment – one for the wealthy and influential, and another for the working class'.[96]

The key question is to what degree the misperceptions lead to a change in behaviours and attitudes. As outlined in the proximity and time sections, a number of Americans exhibited behavioural changes such as taking precautions when opening their mail, avoiding public events, purchasing antibiotics and gas masks. But to what extent were these behavioural changes due to the authorities' responses? While it is difficult to ascertain whether their actions and risk communication increased or reduced the behavioural changes in the absence of a controlled study to examine how alternative messages might have influenced behaviour, demands were being placed on the public health system that could have otherwise been prevented or curtailed. The demands included a number of people seeking a prescription to one of the antibiotics; 6 per cent talking to their physician about bioterrorism; 5 per cent obtaining a prescription for antibiotics; and 4 per cent called a health professional to get information on anthrax.[97] A main concern was that some people took matters into their own hands despite the Surgeon General's announcement that such behaviour was ineffective and possibly harmful, as in the case of preventative antibiotic use.[98] Widespread antibiotic use may have alleviated psychological stress for some people, but its unwarranted use could have led to antibiotic resistance together with the health system having to deal with adverse reactions to medications that should not have been taken – a public health concern.[99]

The fear and anxieties of the postal workers may have been exacerbated by several factors: the CDC's difficulty in explaining why postal workers were being administered doxycycline in preference to ciprofloxin; the closure of some Congressional buildings following the detection of anthrax while many of the contaminated US postal facilities remained open; and segments of the media misrepresenting the reasons behind the use of doxycycline. Consequently many US postal workers believed they were not receiving the same medical care and attention as those in Congress and media outlets that were possibly exposed to anthrax. Effective risk communication by the CDC, a more accurate media coverage and improved handling by Congress of their incident could have reduced many misconceptions and probably some of the adverse behavioural responses. Unfortunately there is no quantitative evidence examining to what degree the handling of the antibiotics and the closure of Congress had on the fear and anxiety of others exposed to anthrax.

Conclusion

The anthrax attacks provided a valuable insight into the challenges of risk characterisation and risk communication following a non-conventional attack. The proportion of Americans worried about themselves or a family member becoming a victim of terrorism or anthrax declined steadily over the course of the attacks after the initial jump following the first confirmed anthrax death. This was despite three more anthrax deaths in early November, two Department of Justice threat advisory warnings of further terrorist attacks in October and November, the initiation of hostilities against Afghanistan, and a fifth anthrax death in late November. Similarly while the anthrax attacks at the early stage did not demoralise or increase fear and anxiety among the public, fears over terrorism remained high.

Evidence for proximity showed that this variable was a determinant in the effect of the attacks on the populace. For instance, proximity influenced the risk perception of contracting anthrax with 26 per cent of Washington, DC residents whose workplaces had been closed believing it was likely they would contract the disease, compared to 15 per cent of residents without any direct experience of the threat and 9 per cent of the general US population. Unfortunately a large part of this data stemmed from one source, the

Harvard School of Public Health surveys. While the surveys are extensive and provide some good quantitative evidence, there are few similar studies to further validate or assess the impact of this variable.

Material on the changes in behaviours and attitudes is more extensive and provides data on how many Americans acquired a prescription for antibiotics. A survey of the national prescription levels revealed that only an extra 0.13 per cent (376,000) acquired these drugs during this period. However, this figure is in contrast to a Harvard School of Public Health survey that concluded that 5 per cent obtained the drug. This was either regionally specific or the result did not reflect the true levels of the national prescription levels. Even with this rather high figure, the Harvard survey did conclude that collectively there was a low level of precautions undertaken by the respondents and therefore Americans were not panicking.

What proves particularly valuable is the insight into how the key risk communicators (the CDC and the Postal Service) assessed the anthrax risk and the precautions they implemented and advised upon. The risk characterisation proved difficult because there data on the lethality of anthrax in an urban environment (for instance secondary aerosolisation) and the type of anthrax that was used in the attacks. The possibility that the anthrax spores in the second attack were prepared and behaved differently to those in the first batch of letters made the risk characterisation even more complex. Inadequate risk characterisation proved to be a major issue with the postal workers where, at the Brentwood facility in particular, did not recognise the risk of secondary aerosolisation and the ability of the spores to leak out of the envelopes led to contamination of facilities and personnel. As a consequence, two Brentwood postal employees died.

When it came to implementing risk communication, the CDC admitted that they did not adhere to good practices and had to hire risk communication consultants. For instance, the CDC admitted they failed to place context on why postal workers were being administered the cheaper doxycycline drug while members of Congress and media personnel were prescribed the more expensive ciprofloxacin. From the postal workers' perspective, they were not being treated or handled with the full care and attention that others were perceived to have received. While the CDC recognised their risk communication shortcomings, legislative and executive authorities too provided mixed messages and exacerbated the response. Besides Tommy Thompson's attempts to play down the anthrax events even when it was confirmed anthrax had intentionally been released, Congress's response was particularly confusing. Leaders of both houses gave different accounts and advice. In many cases, as Daschle demonstrated, those who spoke to the media were not provided with an adequate briefing on the lethality of the anthrax.

To some degree the risk amplification was covered in the risk communication section where inadequate processes for various reasons possibly led to heighten risk perceptions of anthrax. The initial absence of regular accurate reports created a significant information void, which may have increased public fear and concern. The CDC's delays in processing information meant missed opportunities to control what was being said by reporters who, in the absence of answers from the CDC, approached sources less inclined to scientific accuracy. The lack of effective risk communication led to public health concerns with some Americans deciding the perceived risk of anthrax meant they should acquire a prescription for ciprofloxacin even if they were not advised to do so by the public authorities. Their actions reduced essential stockpiles of ciprofloxacin, potentially caused antibiotic resistance in the environment through their widespread use, and led many to experience side-effects and possible complications at the expense of the nation's health. In the absence of data from a controlled study examining how influential risk communication was in shaping the public's behavioural responses, it is difficult to ascertain to what extent inadequate risk communication increased or reduced the public's dread risk perceptions and determined their subsequent responses.

With no person or group claiming responsibility for the attacks, it is hard to gauge what the aims were. If they were designed to cause terror among Americans capitalising on the pre-existing concerns from 9/11, this only had a limited effect. If the aim of the anthrax attacks was to destabilise America's war effort by turning public opinion against it, that did not succeed. By the CDC's own admission, the anthrax attacks were limited in scope in the virulence of the agent used and the targets chosen. The directors of the CDC and the National Center for Infectious Diseases (NCID) in a co-authored article observed:

> The anthrax attack was relatively small and did not involve the use of multiple agents, multiple nodes of transmission, a drug resistant organism, transmission to animals, or global spread. The surge capacity of the health-care delivery system was not challenged. In addition, unlike some of the other threat agents, the causative organism was easily isolated in clinical laboratories; there was no risk of person-to-person transmission and no risk of vector-borne transmission.[100]

These factors arguably reduced the levels of fear and anxiety that might have otherwise occurred had the attacks entailed a more virulent agent. A few months after the anthrax attacks took place, the US came under a far more severe biological threat from a naturally occurring West Nile virus with 1,700 cases in 2002, including 80 across effecting 40 states. But this did not cause the same level of fear and anxiety as the anthrax attacks.[101]

8 Israel and the Second Intifada

Introduction

The Second Intifada exposed Israel to an intensive period of indiscriminate attacks of suicide bombings, shootings, and Katusha rocket attacks from late 2000 through to mid-2004. Although there was not an official ending to the Second Intifada, the violence declined considerably in 2004 which is the period this study will go to. Unlike the violence of other periods of terrorism like the First Intifada that predominantly centred on the West Bank and Gaza areas, the Second Intifada struck at the heart of Israel, targeting buses, shops, cafes, beaches, universities and shopping centres. While only conventional munitions (high explosives) were used, the continuous terror caused was immense and at times unrelenting. This case study provides a valuable insight into the effects of a prolonged terrorist campaign against a civilian population of indiscriminate bombings and shootings.

Since this case study is not looking at one single event but a series of attacks, the proximity, time and behavioural sections will look at responses over the course of the Intifada and after an attack. This will provide an insight into the cumulative effects of the terror of terrorism. The risk perception section will assess the perspectives both before and during the Intifada (i.e. the perceived risk of an attack during the campaign). The chapter is divided into the following sections:

- Background
- Strategic and political objectives
- Overview of the attacks
- Political effects
- Effects of proximity and time
- Changes in behaviours and attitudes
- Risk communication
- Risk perception
- Risk amplification.

Background

The Second Intifada was the culmination of several factors that included Palestinian dissatisfaction with the 1993 Oslo Accords, the lack of an improvement of quality of life for Palestinians, Ariel Sharon's visit to the Haram al-Sharif/Temple Mount in September 2000 and the lack of commitment by either Israelis or the Palestinian Authority (PA) to restrain the violence from escalating once it started.

There are differing interpretations from Palestinians and Israelis as to why the Second Intifada started and peace talks broke down between the then-Israeli Prime Minister Ehud Barak and Yasser Arafat at Camp David in July 2000. Israelis believed that Barak made a generous offer to Arafat at Camp David by offering a Palestinian state in the Gaza strip, more than 90 per cent of the West Bank, a Palestinian capital in East Jerusalem and a commitment to withdraw from many of the settlements. However, this was rejected by Arafat who demanded the return of all refugees to Israel, which would have led to a minority Jewish population in Israel and the launch of a terrorist campaign to destroy Israel. The Palestinian perspective is that the Camp David offer retained much of the Israeli occupation in terms of land, security, settlements and Jerusalem. While the Palestinian Authority did themselves contribute to the start of the Intifada, it was also instigated by the response to Ariel Sharon's visit to Temple Mount/Noble Sanctuary on 28 September 2000 and Israel's overwhelming military response to the subsequent Palestinian protests.

While Israel made an unprecedented offer to Arafat, it did not enable a viable Palestinian state because it failed to ensure contiguity of a Palestinian state and the West Bank, full sovereignty in Arab parts of East Jerusalem and a compromise resolution on the return of Palestinian refugees.[1] Barak's plan would have preserved 90.6 per cent of the settlements in the West Bank and was intended to provide encirclement of 'independent' Palestinian areas.[2] These would have been connected by tunnels or bridges, surrounded by barriers and checkpoints. Settlers, meanwhile, would be linked by bypass roads directly to Israel. In addition the Palestinian negotiators and much of the nationalist movement favoured a two-state solution instead of the destruction of Israel through an Intifada or the right to return all the refugees to Israel. While according to Jeremy Pressman the Palestinian explanation was 'accurate in part', it omitted the role of the Palestinian militants in escalating the conflict and the Palestinian Authority's unwillingness to restrain their actions which had catastrophic consequences.[3]

The visit by Ariel Sharon, the then leader of the opposition Likud Party, served as a catalyst to the start of the uprising, and was partly designed for the domestic audience to undermine Barak's position and possible compromise on sensitive issues like Jerusalem and Temple Mount. Sharon called for the crushing of the Palestinians without restraint while the Israeli military responded by undermining opportunities for reconciliation or a ceasefire.[4]

While the First Intifada began as a spontaneous outburst in response to the long-term frustration of the Palestinians' predicament, a situation imposed by the Israelis, the Second Intifada was directed at Arafat and the PA, as well as the Israelis.

Strategic and political objectives

The strategic and political aims of the Intifada varied according to the factions taking part, their political and ideological motives, and Palestinian public opinion. Force was seen by some Palestinian groups as a way to bring about a two-state objective which had failed to materialise through the negotiations at Camp David. Some parties sought the destruction of Israel. As the Intifada was spontaneous with various groups involved, there was no unifying agenda. The bombings initially appeared to stem in part from Israeli policies toward Palestinian areas, blind acts of revenge at the circumstances in which Palestinians found themselves − harassed or beaten at the numerous checkpoints or occasionally killed in 'ambiguous circumstances'.[5] While the various Palestinian factions had different goals, they pursued a minimum set of strategic objectives that included: a Palestinian state with standing in the international community; satisfaction of the claims of Palestinian refugees who left their homes during the 1948 and 1967 wars between Israel and the neighbouring states; and a general improvement in personal security and economic opportunity for the population of a Palestinian state.[6]

While most of the Palestinian Liberation Organisation (PLO) factions looked for a two-state solution (West Bank and Gaza), Hamas, which during the Intifada exerted considerable political power in Gaza, sought a one-state solution of an Islamic Palestinian state in Israel as well as Gaza and the West Bank. Some organisations like Hamas had official and operational goals. While destroying Israel was Hamas's prime goal, during the Intifada the operational objective was to derail the peace process, enhance its prestige among other Palestinian groups like the PA, increase its appearance as legitimate opposition, promote ties with the Islamic world and defy Israel's military might.[7] On the individual level of those who undertook suicide bombing missions, their motivations included feelings of humiliation from the way Palestinians had been treated and the belief in a national jihad: a struggle that served to strengthen a Palestinian national entity and form a national heritage. Suicide attacks were seen to serve two tactical roles: a highly effective means of asymmetric warfare and a form of psychological warfare to wear down Israel while the Palestinian nation was strengthened.[8]

As with the First Intifada that began in December 1987 through to 1993, the initial violence was spontaneous in response to the political, social and economic conditions Palestinians had to endure. However, the First Intifada's strategy was one of civil disobedience, restricting itself to stone-throwing, demonstrations and protests. It was aimed at showing the injustice of life under military occupation.[9] The area of operation was principally the territories. The Second Intifada, however, broke through these boundaries. Suicide bombings and attacks were frequent and took place in pre-1967 Israel (main areas like Tel Aviv). Most of Israel was regarded as a possible target.

An insight into what Palestinians believed they were fighting for was captured in a December 2001 public opinion poll that showed support for the destruction of Israel coexisted with support for a two-state solution. Of Palestinians, 44 per cent, in December 2001, saw the aim of the Second Intifada as the liberation of Palestine, including pre-1967 Israeli; and in another poll, 73 per cent supported Israeli–Palestinian reconciliation based on a Palestinian state recognised by Israel. However support for a two-state solution declined in September 2002 to 44 per cent – but was still more than those who wanted either a single, bi-national state in Israel, the West Bank and Gaza.[10]

Several Palestinian leaders like Marwan Barghoutti, the leader of the Fatah paramilitary organisation in the West Bank, thought that the threat and use of force would push Israel to accept a generous two-state solution – a position that Arafat sided with and thought he could use to gain political advantage.[11] Along with other loosely organised local militias, militants like the Tanzim and the al-Aqsa brigades associated with Fatah, Sharon's visit provided an opportunity to pressure Israel through violence. Arafat may well have also thought that the Intifada would buy time while improving his position at future talks, perhaps even internationalising the peace process by bringing in other Arab states, the EU and the UN.[12] This viewpoint may have contributed to the PA's lack of action in reigning in the militants.

The belief that force could achieve a favourable political outcome was reinforced by the experience of Israel in southern Lebanon. According to Andrew Kydd and Barbara Walter, Israel's precipitous withdrawal from southern Lebanon in May 2000 convinced Hamas that the Israeli leadership's resolve was weakening and encouraged Hamas leaders to initiate the Second Intifada in September 2000.[13] The tactics of the two Intifadas were a reflection of the effects previous attacks had on Israel; the costs had to be raised. In a letter written in the early 1990s to the leadership of Hamas, the organisation's master bomb-maker, Yahya Ayyash, said, 'We paid a high price when we used only sling-shots and stones. We need to exert more pressure, make the cost of the occupation that much more expensive in human lives, that much more unbearable.'[14]

Israeli tactics were planned to deter the Palestinian terror and guerrilla attacks but had the limited goal of reducing the level of violence and maintaining a status quo.[15] This also left an intolerable environment for the Palestinian population in the territories with social and economic consequences for Israel as the Palestinians sought to change the status quo through violent means.

Overview of the attacks

The uprising began from the Palestinian side with rocks and tyre burnings protesting at Sharon's visit to Temple Mount on 28 September 2000. However, the large-scale Israeli response the following day using live rounds led to 13 deaths. From 28 September until the year's end, 325 Palestinians and 36 Israelis were killed. As the Intifada went on, the use of suicide bombings became a frequent tactic of the various militant groups. The use of suicide bombings expanded from Islamic groups, like Hamas and Islamic Jihad, to secular organisations such as Tanzim, which had split from Fatah; the Popular Front for the Liberation of Palestine (PFLP); the Popular Democratic Front for the Liberation of Palestine (PDFLP); and the al-Aqsa martyrs' brigade, an off-shoot of Fatah. By 2002, women had become suicide bombers as well.

Between the period of September 2000 and August 2002, less than 1 per cent of the attacks were from suicide bombers, but 44 per cent of all Israeli casualties were caused by suicide attacks.[16] By June 2004, 2,400 Palestinians and 800 Israelis had been killed and 50,000 Palestinians and 7,000 Israelis injured.[17] While the Israeli Defence Force (IDF) was able to adapt its tactics to Palestinian terror and urban guerrilla warfare in order to reduce the level of Palestinian violence, the IDF was unable to achieve a battlefield victory.[18] This was due to the conflict requiring a political rather than a military solution. The terrorists attacked many towns and cities but they concentrated their strikes on the metropolitan areas of Jerusalem, Tel Aviv and Haifa, and three smaller cities adjacent to the Palestinian–Israeli border Green Line (the unofficial border) – Hadera, Netanya and Afula.

In the first year of the Intifada nearly 140 Israelis were killed in terrorist attacks. This increased in the second year to 390 to then drop in the third year to 293 deaths. Finally, in the 11-month period between August 2003 and July 2004, only 25 Israelis lost their lives in terrorist attacks.[19] This totalled 848 lives lost. For Israelis, they had been living in a state of 'emergency routine' since September 2000, constantly aware that suicide bomb attacks, knife and bomb attacks could occur any where. The basic beliefs in the existence of a safe place were shaken.[20]

Political effects

The initiation of violence was shortly followed by Israel reclaiming re-occupied lands that had been handed over to the PA in 1995. Once Sharon was elected as prime minister, the violence allowed the Israeli leader to destroy the PA as a governing structure and to occupy the West Bank.[21] Sharon's administration ordered the West Bank to be divided into 64 isolated sectors and Gaza into four, using trenches. There were approximately 450 checkpoints in place by the end of 2002. Also in 2002 Sharon began constructing a barrier 8–20 feet high along the full length of the West Bank.

Pressman noted that while Arafat believed the use of force could bring about a two-state solution and there was significant support for confronting Israel, it is doubtful that Arafat expected the Intifada to last for years and result in a significant weakening of his international standing.[22] By June 2004, 2,400 Palestinians had been killed and 50,000 injured.[23] Instead of furthering the Palestinian cause, the suicide bombings in pre-1967 Israel (as opposed to the territories) helped Sharon to justify the full military response. For the vast majority of Israelis, the suicide bombings and their psychological and personal toll meant there was no alternative but Sharon's promise of security through military action.[24] Israel succeeded in portraying the suicide attacks as terrorism and in doing so pulled the Israeli and American public's attention away from repressive measures in the occupied territories.[25] Bombing the Israelis failed to produce a solution. The Intifada was, according to Bob Zelnick, a strategic blunder for the Palestinians, concluding that 'not only did Israel's response make the lives of Palestinians nearly unbearable, but changes in the Israeli strategic and political outlook made it very difficult for negotiations to resume'.[26]

When the Intifada attacks tailed off in mid-2004 and early 2005, the Palestinians were no closer to a two-state solution or a resolution to their predicament. Despite this, Hamas believed they had achieved part of their strategic objectives. A Hamas leader interviewed in October 2005 declared,

> When we took up arms and launched [the Second Intifada], we succeeded in less than five years to force the Israelis to withdraw from the Gaza Strip. This fulfilled everyone's dream. I think we have benefited from this experience by applying it accordingly to the West Bank and other occupied areas.[27]

President Bush re-engaged in the peace process in June 2002 through a Rose Garden address publicly endorsing a sovereign Palestinian state. Bush made it clear that a new Palestinian Authority leader was required: Arafat was no longer welcome. This was followed in April by the US, EU, Russia, UN, 'Quartet' three-point plan with the aim of a permanent status agreement and end of conflict by 2005 but no solution has yet been agreed upon by all parties.

Effects of proximity and time

Proximity

Evidence on proximity is broken down into two broad categories. First, those immediately exposed to an attack and its effects in the following hours. Second, studies examining the longer term effects of proximity over a period of time from months to years.

As could be expected, those directly exposed to an attack expressed higher rates of PTSD than those in the rest of the nation. According to Arieh Y. Shalev and Sara Freedman, the prevalence of PTSD among survivors four months after being caught up in terrorist attacks that occurred over the period October 2000 to March 2002 was 38 per cent.[28] A study led by Shaul Schreiber and Ornah Dolberg suggests that PTSD and related symptoms among survivors may be lower. Their survey examined 129 injured survivors from nine suicide-bombing attacks in the Tel Aviv metropolitan area who were treated in emergency rooms between September 2000 and September 2002. 20 survivors (15.5 per cent) met PTSD criteria according to DSM-IV, 54 survivors (42 per cent) had partial symptoms (subclinical PTSD) and 55 survivors (42.5 per cent) showed no long-term effects.[29] The authors concluded that full PTSD as a result of exposure to the suicide bombings was less than expected in a proportion of survivors. However, a substantial number of survivors had partial symptoms. Another study by the same authors showed that three months after the victims experienced a terrorist attack, only 13 per cent met the criteria for sufferers of PTSD, while 43.5 per cent showed no long-term psychological effects.[30] While there is variation in the PTSD figures among survivors in the Schreiber and Dolberg studies, and Shalev and Freedman studies, they are still higher than the national PTSD average of 9.4 per cent as identified by Bleich and Gelkopf's team. This infers that PTSD was slightly higher among survivors of attacks than the rest of the nation.[31]

While there are limited studies on the psychological affects of terrorism on survivors from the Second Intifada, evidence from the First Intifada supports the notion of a higher PTSD rate among survivors. An investigation of survivors from an attacked bus in 1992 found that 33 per cent had PTSD – not too dissimilar from the 38 per cent noted in Shalev and Freedman's investigation.[32] The extent to which survivors experienced a high degree of psychological effects was reinforced by the larger number of psychological casualties admitted to emergency rooms in the Second Intifada as compared to physical casualties. In Hadassah University Hospital, which treated more terror-related victims than any hospital in Israel, 60 per cent of admissions were psychological during the first 24 hours.[33]

As this case study is looking into the effects of a series of attacks during the Intifada rather than one attack, it is valuable to investigate whether there was a proximal effect for those residing/working in frequently attacked towns and cities compared to those in areas that did not directly experience violence. The studies that surveyed adults suggest proximity did not influence the level of PTSD and associated symptoms. This may be due to a combination of factors. These include a 'ceiling effect' whereby at a certain level of exposure the effects of terror plateau, and the relatively small size of Israel meaning that most Israelis irrespective of geographical location equally felt the repercussions of the ongoing terror. This may have been exacerbated by the amount of news individuals listened to, enhancing the perception that terror is not geographically contained to certain areas, reducing the perception of safety for those not nearby an attack.

There are four studies that discuss proximity. These studies are by Irwin Mansdorf and Jacob Weinberg, Arieh Shalev and Rivka Tuval *et al.*, Yori Gidron and Yosi Kaplan *et al.*, and Eli Somer and Ayalla Ruvio *et al.* All examined two separate sets of population centres: one that was frequently exposed to terrorist attacks and the one that had not experienced any local attacks.

Irwin Mansdorf and Jacob Weinberg compared those who lived and worked in Hadera and experienced multiple attacks, with those who lived under the threat, but whose cities had not actually experienced or suffered specific attacks or casualties (Raanana and Hod HaSharon). Despite their differing proximity, both samples showed similar results for symptoms of stress with a majority of adults in both groups (55.6 per cent and 55.9 per cent) stating they were 'very upset' when something reminded them of the attacks, but only a minority of respondents in either groups showed any other notable symptoms.[34] However, there were variations in behavioural responses and coping mechanisms. Interestingly those in the attacked region showed lower rates for stocking up on supplies and cash (10.3 per cent in the Hadera sample) than those in the less attacked region (31.1 per cent). Therefore while clinical symptoms of stress varied little, a greater proportion in the less targeted areas undertook precautionary measures.

Shalev and Tuval's study collected data on terrorism against civilians in two suburbs of Jerusalem during June–August 2001; one frequently and directly exposed to terrorism and the other indirectly exposed.[35] Participants provided information about exposure to terror-related incidents, disruption of daily living, symptoms of daily PTSD and a general distress (assessed with the Brief Symptom Inventory). The two communities were Efrat, 11 miles from Jerusalem, and Bét Shemesh, 15 miles from Jerusalem. The directly exposed community (Efrat) had frequent shooting incidents, daily stonings of cars, road blocks and several residents killed and injured by snipers. Daily life was thus significantly disrupted. The Bét Shemesh community by comparison had not experienced a single attack within its boundaries.

Twenty-seven per cent of the directly exposed community and 21 per cent of the indirectly exposed community met Post-traumatic Symptom Scale criteria for PTSD, a non-significant difference according to the report's authors.[36] PTSD with significant distress was 18 per cent and 16 per cent respectfully, and PTSD with significant distress and functional impairment was 10 per cent and 9 per cent respectfully. The report therefore concluded that a 'proximity effect was not found'. Possible reasons for this were that both communities were affected by the stressfulness of living near Jerusalem (a prime target for terrorism) or resided in a nation beset by terrorism. Therefore this caused equal response in two differentially exposed communities which could have created a saturation of responses by common threat factors creating a 'ceiling effect'. Repeated exposure to sights of terror defied the perception of safety, which geographic distance would normally confer. Shalev and Tuval also suggests that the media's rapid and detailed reporting of the attacks may have accounted for a lack of differences between communities as it undermined the sense of safety among those who watched and listened to the news despite their distance from the terror attacks.

A third survey that reinforces the lack of proximal effect is a study by Yori Gidron *et al.* who examined the prevalence, correlation and moderators of PTSD-like symptoms in a sample of Israeli citizens soon after a prolonged and severe wave of terrorist attacks. Volunteers (totalling 149) from five Israeli cities with minimum, moderate and frequent exposure to attacks took part in the study that was carried out just after a series of attacks between March and April 2002. The five cities were Ashkelon, Ramat Gan, Beer Sheva, Tel Aviv and Netyana. Clinically significant PTSD symptoms were reported by 10 per cent. Of the sample, 15.4 per cent were directly exposed to a terrorist attack and 36.6 per cent knew someone close who had been exposed to an attack. These figures are very similar to the Avi Bleich *et al.* study with 16.4 per cent having been directly exposed to a terrorist attack and 37 per cent with a family member or friend who had been exposed.[37]

According to Gidron *et al.*, exposure to an attack did not significantly cause PTSD-like symptoms. The only time where exposure did significantly cause PTSD symptoms was when this variable interacted with the ability of those surveyed to estimate the duration of an attack be that days, weeks or months.[38] While the sample was not representative of the Israeli adult population, it did include individuals from cities with varying degrees of exposure to terrorist attacks. Another determining factor that the authors thought might well have led to those less exposed to attacks exhibiting the same effects as those frequently exposed was the frequency of listening to the news. Participants with clinically significant PTSD-like symptoms listened more frequently to radio and television reports.[39]

Finally, a survey led by Eli Somer and Ayalla Ruvio suggests that while there was a similar percentage who had post-traumatic symptoms in the targeted and non-targeted areas, those in the high-risk areas had a greater number of stress symptoms. The survey was undertaken at the height of the Intifada in 2001–2002 and interviewed a sample from the hardest-hit areas and compared this with the least-affected areas in the south of the country. The three major cities were Tel Aviv, Jerusalem and Haifa. The smaller cities studied were Afula, Hadera and Netanya. The data from these areas were compared with the southern resort city of Eilat that had never been attacked. Of residents, 3.7 per cent of the low-impact region had severe post-traumatic distress (PTD) versus 5.5 per cent in the high impact region. In addition 6.3 per cent of those directly exposed had severe PTD compared to 5.1 per cent of those indirectly exposed. The mean prevalence of PTD (possibly equivalent to cases of PTSD) across Israel was 5.2 per cent. The study showed that while residents of the remote southern region were not less likely to develop intrusive post-traumatic symptoms than citizens in the north, symptoms like hyperarousal and avoidance were more prevalent among residents in the hard-hit region.[40]

All four surveys demonstrate that proximity among adults had no or limited effect on PTSD and associated clinical symptoms. While this book is principally concerned with the effect of terrorism on adults as outlined in the introductory chapters, it is worth noting that proximity did have an effect on adolescents and children. This demonstrates that there was not a uniform proximal response across the whole population. A study of Hadera reported higher levels of perceived stress in their children (with 62 per cent reporting at least one symptom in their children compared to 39 per cent in Raanana–Hod).[41] This finding is reinforced by a school-based screening of 1,010 pupils in Jerusalem and nearby settlements that showed proximity did have an effect on children. Higher rates of PTSD and related symptoms were found among those adolescents who were personally or indirectly exposed to attacks compared to those who reported no exposure.[42] However, the levels of PTSD overall were lower among those who lived in the settlements despite the regions' greater exposure to terrorism than in Jerusalem (6.3 per cent compared to 2.5 per cent). Therefore all clusters of post-traumatic symptoms among adolescents in Jerusalem were more severe than those in the settlements.[43]

Time

The following is divided into three parts. First, the effect of an attack in the following hours and days. Second, how Israelis responded over the course of the Intifada. Third, to what degree the avoidance behaviour was a healthy response or a cause for concern. Given the regular terrorist attacks, it has to be considered whether existing long-term behavioural responses were conducive to Israelis coping with their security situation.

As mentioned in the proximity section, over half of Hadassah University Hospital's admissions to the emergency department were for psychological conditions. A breakdown of hospital admissions showed the number of those arriving with acute psychological stress responses far outweighed those with physical injuries (about 10:1 or even higher).[44] Survivors arriving at emergency departments turned up in three waves. The first wave arrived within minutes to a few hours brought in by civilians or ambulances after an attack. This would include those suffering from acute stress (the majority suffering from Acute Stress Reaction – ASR). Four to eight hours after an attack, a second wave of admissions arrived displaying symptoms of ASR. These individuals were not identified at the scene of an attack but had fled the area and later developed symptoms, or were identified by others as suffering from physical or psychological distress. The third wave arrived one to seven days later, having gone home unaware of any psychological reaction. These individuals may have ASR or the more severe response – Acute Stress Disorder (ASD).

Despite Ilan Kutz and Avi Bleich breaking down the reactions into the three subgroups, they unfortunately do not include statistics in their paper on the numbers in each category which would have provided a more detailed insight.

Five days after an attack, 36 per cent of the trauma survivors had clinically significant distress, and there may have been a significant proportion of psychological casualties that went undetected and might have never come to formal therapy.[45] This was based on the evidence that only 59 per cent of survivors who were brought into hospitals accepted counselling.

An innovative way of illustrating how terrorist attacks may have impacted on Israeli behaviours is examining driving patterns in the days after an attack. By comparing data of average daily traffic accidents, Guy Stecklov and Joshua Goldstein identified that fatalities often increased following attacks. The survey covered the period January 2001–June 2002, concluding that attacks produced a temporary lull in light accidents followed by a 35-per-cent spike in fatal accidents on Israeli roads three days after an attack.[46] When only including bombings that caused 10 fatalities or more, road deaths increased by 69 per cent. Over the period of each attack, this represented 28 extra deaths. The three day delay in the response is thought to reveal a more general delay in reaction to violence and stress. Of particular significance is that the traffic accident pattern over the course of the survey showed no indication that the Israeli populace were becoming more sensitive or more resistant to terrorism suggesting no evidence of adaptation.[47] Demonstrating that car accidents were proportional to the severity of the attack showed that the attacks had broad, short-term behavioural effects on the general population with a relatively rapid return to normality. In all the attacks including the large strikes, the effect dissipated within four to five days. Large attacks thus led to an immediate change in people's driving behaviour.

The same study also showed a change in traffic volume in the days after an attack, suggesting that the public were less willing to drive in the following days. Traffic declined in peak and off-peak hours, with a decline during peak hours of 4.7 per cent on day three and a decline of 2.7 per cent for off-peak hours. After a large terrorist attack (causing 10 or more fatalities), off-peak traffic volume immediately declined by 7.8 per cent on the day of the incident, 10.4 per cent two days after the incident and 8.1 per cent three days after. For smaller attacks, traffic volume remained stable on the day and the day after the attack, to then decline on the third day. The report's authors believed that the third-day spike in traffic fatalities suggested the terror attacks may have had indirect effects as well as immediate casualties and that part of the increase in fatalities could be due to 'terror-induced' covert suicides and/or increased aggression on the road due to a delayed reaction to the violence and stress.[48] An increase in suicides can occur following well-publicised murders.[49] Whether the fatalities were suicide-induced or accidental due to stress, the terrorist attacks undermined the psychological well-being of Israelis with devastating consequences.

While these studies looked at the effects days after an attack, there is also valuable research that examined the longer-term accumulative psychological consequences over the course of the Intifada. One is a survey conducted by Avi Bleich's team during April–May 2002, by which time since the start of the uprising in 2000 there had been 472 persons killed (318 civilians) and 3,846 (2,708 civilians) injured representing 0.067 per cent of Israel's population of 6.4 million.[50] The research found that 9.4 per cent had PTSD and 58.6 per cent reported feeling depressed. One-third (37.4 per cent) reported having at least one traumatic stress-related symptom for at least one month. Although those surveyed showed distress and a lowered sense of safety, they did not develop high levels of psychiatric distress, which may be related to the populace getting used to the attacks and developing effective coping mechanisms. Somer and Ruvio, by comparison, identified possible diagnosis of PTSD at 5.2 per cent.[51] While this lower figure questions the degree of PTSD identified by Bleich of 9.4 per cent, together they demonstrate that a segment of the population developed PTSD as a result of the attacks. What is striking about the Bleich study is the high level of confidence found among Israelis with 82.2 per cent expressing optimism about their personal futures and 66.8 per cent expressing optimism about the future of Israel.[52] This is despite 60.4 per cent having a low sense of personal safety and 67.9 per cent a low sense of safety for their relatives.

Further evidence of adaptation and resilience can be found in Israeli responses to Katusha rocket attacks, a new threat Israel faced during and after the Second Intifada that became at times very frequent. Over a six-year period starting in 2000 just before the Second Intifada through to the Israeli war with Lebanon in 2006, Avi Kirchenbaum led a research project that measured community disruption caused by Katusha rockets. Through measuring several key variables, including social network densities, risk perceptions and pre-paredness, pre-published findings were that the rocket attacks did not disrupt the communities.[53] There was an increase in the measures of community solidarity. The research took samples from former Gush Katif (Gaza settlements) and Sderot (just outside Gaza but frequently subjected to rocket attacks).

An insight into the longer term psychological effects of an attack on individuals can be acquired from first-hand accounts. One such case is of a 25-year-old woman who was eating lunch at a restaurant when a suicide bomber entered and detonated his bomb. Despite being slightly injured, she applied first aid to the injured. A number were killed. After the attack, even the slightest reminder of what she had seen, smelt, heard or felt in the attack caused flashbacks, avoidance or both, and controlled her life. This included an occasion at a dinner party when a guest dropped a bottle on a table that caused a loud crash. This brought back memories of the attacks. Subsequently she avoided eating with others. In addition, she avoided restaurants, supermarkets and social gatherings to avoid the sight of raw meat which triggered horrific images in her mind. The clinical symptoms included flashbacks, nightmares, sleep disturbance and hyper-arousal. In addition she practised avoidance of thoughts or activities that reminded her of the event and experienced emotional numbness, detachment and difficulty in concentrating.[54] Adverse psychological reactions for some survivors may remain with them for many years. Research into survivors of the First Intifada in the 1990s several years on provides some insight into how survivors of the Second Intifada may be affected for some years. For instance, one survivor of a suicide bus bombing recalled that 10 years on, the scene from the bombing remained vivid. She recalled that the blast can still be felt, the smell of smoke and explosives remains, and loud noises still jar her.[55]

Shalev warns that despite the evidence of PTSD caused by the attacks, under continuous threat, some symptoms that are currently subsumed as post-traumatic and therefore purposeless and somewhat exaggerated (e.g. avoiding previously dangerous places and situations, responding emotionally to threat signals, remaining vigilant and 'on guard'), may reflect anticipation and self-protection.[56] Therefore while this type of adaptation may be interpreted as a negative effect of the terrorist threat, it could be assumed in some cases as a healthy response. Consequently the percentage figures of PTSD and related symptoms where avoidance behaviour is factored in may in some cases be overstated.

Rhonda S. Adessky and Sara A. Freedman provided a good discussion of when avoidance behaviour might be regarded as a cause for concern. They argued that while avoidance is a criteria of PTSD, in situations of ongoing terrorism, avoidance may actually help maintain well-being. During the Second Intifada, avoidance of places or situations that were considered to increase the risk for direct exposure to terrorism became the norm for the general population.[57] For instance, a survivor from a bus bombing agreed to ride the bus again but disembarked before it drove down the street where the attack had taken place, and getting back on the vehicle several streets further on. According to these clinicians this type of behaviour by survivors is regarded as appropriate avoidance. However, the authors noted that should this type of behaviour continue after the Intifada, this would be regarded as an inappropriate type of response. Appropriate avoidance is therefore encouraged; whereas excessive avoidance and unrealistic and over-generalisation of danger are discouraged.[58]

While threat perception of terrorism by its very nature is less predictable and uncontrollable, healthy or rational avoidance behaviour like increased arousal, some avoidance of public places and hypervigilance could be regarded as normative responses of the general population. The following section provides a detailed discussion of the type of avoidance behaviour that Israelis undertook during the Intifada.

Changes in behaviours and attitudes

Assessing the behavioural changes in the Israeli populace reveals that a number altered their daily routines in response to the Intifada. For instance the Israeli bus system witnessed a major reduction in passengers. According to Batya Ludman, a clinical psychologist at a practice in Raanana, prior to the Intifada, the use of buses was extremely popular, but bus travel declined a great deal with the less well off and soldiers using it the most once the Intifada started.[59] The reduction in bus travel saw an increase in neighbours helping each other out in car pools.[60] Furthermore, according to Marc Gelkopf, Research director and psychologist at the Lev HaSharon Mental Health Hospital, Israelis took taxis more often to reduce their reliance on buses and people would go to restaurants less often for ordering take-aways instead.[61]

While Israelis at the initial stage of the Intifada avoided public places like shopping malls at certain times, this became less prevalent with evidence suggesting that Israelis adapted to the situation and returned to near normal lives as much as possible although families still reported of being on a rollercoaster ride of when and where not to go to public places like shopping malls, restaurants, and cinemas.[62] Many of those who did not to go public places during the early days of the uprising returned to do so, although a minority continued to avoid certain areas. In addition many large-scale public events like Independence Day celebrations and big annual parades cancelled in the early period of the Intifada were re-instated in the latter years.

Immediately after an attack, Israelis conducted a number of behavioural reactions as a means of coping, from calling friends and family to check they were safe through to getting the latest news. After every attack over three-quarters (80 per cent) of Israelis would phone to check on the whereabouts of family and friends.[63] Further support of the extensive use of telephones can be found from a social worker at a hospital who noted the following when an attack took place:

> What I remember is everybody in hysteria. I was on the ward, and I felt my own panic. ... First, I had to look for my children, [I thought] please don't let them go on a bus now. The telephone system collapsed, I couldn't get through. Everybody was on their phones not thinking about what was going on in the hospital ... and finally my mother got through ... as I heard her voice I burst into such tears that she got really scared ... then I ran to [my post at] the hospital information centre.[64]

Shalev noted that 'much of the coping consists of actively seeking relevant information (e.g. about relatives exposed, sources of the threat), better structuring the situation and thereby reducing personal distress'.[65] In addition there is the use of diverting coping strategies like humour, reframing and acceptance. Therefore in order to successfully endure continuous traumatisation one had to ignore it.

Valuable evidence of behavioural changes is from an Israeli national household survey that explored the adaptation behaviours associated with the attacks. The survey was based on a theoretical model called adaptive terror preparedness (ATP). ATP includes 49 separate terror-related behavioural changes. Eight hundred household heads were interviewed over a three-week period in late 2004. Of the respondents, 12 per cent reported that they had been personally present during a terrorist attack. After an attack, 48 per cent followed the instructions of security personnel, but 21 per cent already knew what to do while 10 per cent followed their intuition. Of those surveyed, 60 per cent knew a victim of terrorism. The survey revealed that a third of the respondents changed their behaviour. In particular around one-quarter reported avoidance behaviour related to travel patterns:

- 27 per cent kept away from buses when travelling in a car
- 27 per cent travelled less often by bus
- 25 per cent travelled abroad less often
- 23 per cent avoided peak rush hour
- 22 per cent took taxis more often.[66]

Those who did take the bus undertook precautionary behaviour that included choosing a seat on an empty bus (16 per cent), sitting near the entrance of a bus (18 per cent), sitting near the driver (15 per cent), or toward the back of the bus (13 per cent). In addition the perceived security risk of the destination influenced Israeli behaviour with 41 per cent avoiding crowded public places, 43 per cent only going where there were security guards and 14 per cent travelling more by train.[67] Instead of heading to entertainment areas with crowds like cinemas and outside activities, many Israelis chose homebound entertainment instead.[68]

The survey's team led by Alan Kirschenbaum concluded that terrorism seems to have had a marginal impact on Israelis where individuals, families and larger social groups have adapted their preparedness behaviours so as to minimise its impact: behavioural adaptation had been a prime component in the survival strategy.[69] Most felt attacks were likely to take place at centres of entertainment or on public transport, and would continue being part of daily life. The 'normal' daily routines before the Intifada therefore evolved into a 'normal' of the present and future under the threat of terrorism.

Risk communication

While there is a lack of documentation specifically addressing terrorism risk communication practices and their effects during the Second Intifada, there is evidence from areas like mental health that provides some assessment of the risk communication practices employed. This segment falls into two parts. First, the general security alert information on vigilance, reporting and preparedness. Second, information provided by authorities following an attack.

The extensive ongoing campaign and the ever-present threat that Israelis encountered during the Intifada may have only required limited risk messages warning them of future attacks. The Intifada was an extension of the terrorist threat the majority of the populace had grown up and lived with, depending on the severity of the period. With few exceptions, suicide attacks would occur with no warning and with few opportunities to intercept an attack.

Despite vigilance being a necessity, as the Intifada wore on, Israelis adapted to the situation to such an extent, through carrying on with their everyday lives, that at times they had to be reminded of the terrorist threat. For instance in April 2004 Prime Minister Ariel Sharon's counter-terrorism advisor believed Israelis were becoming too complacent. The advisor warned Israelis that their alertness had 'dwindled a bit' and advised greater vigilance.[70] External events did cause Israelis to become increasingly risk-conscious of a possible attack. For instance after the assassination of Sheik Ahmed Yassin in March 2004, the founder and spiritual leader of Hamas, Israelis expected a reprisal. Public places in Jerusalem were very quiet immediately afterwards and although 80 per cent polled believed the assassination would lead to more attacks, this did not prevent near normality returning in the days after.[71]

Following an attack the Israeli government and the media worked together to provide up-to-date information. Within minutes to hours and days, the public would be kept fully informed. Information included casualty rates, road access, sources of advice and receiving hospitals. According to Shalev this was 'extremely important psychologically since for most of the population the information provided signals the absence of proximal threat, and therefore constitutes a safety signal'.[72] This suggests that the Israeli authorities practised good, sound risk communication practices, applied early and essential to inform the public accurately of events, and what was being done following a terrorist attack. While effective risk communication was undertaken, the dread risk of terrorism remained in the public's risk perception while the threat became more familiar, more known, and understood better through either direct experience or from extensive media reporting.

Risk perception

Because of the nature of this case study, this risk perception section is divided into two. First, how the Israelis perceived the risk of terrorism prior to the Second Intifada, and second, during the uprising. This is designed to capture how the populace framed their risks before September 2000 and their perceptions during the campaign.

In the lead-up to the Second Intifada, Israelis had become all too familiar with terrorism on their soil and conflict for several decades from Arab–Israeli wars, Iraqi missile strikes, together with terrorist attacks from various

Palestinian groups. In addition security vigilance and alerts had become commonplace. Israelis became accustomed and grew up with the threat that terrorism was real and never that far away. From the early 1970s Israelis had encountered terrorism intermittently. While the 1970s included some notable attacks outside its borders against its civilians like the Berlin Olympics in 1972, there were major internal attacks like the taking and killing of 26 ninth-grade high-school students in Maalot (May 1974) and the bus hijacking and killing of 35 passengers in 1978. The First Intifada ran from 1987–1993. The terrorist bombings of Jerusalem and other regions grew in the early and late 1990s with 1997 seeing significant loss of life from terrorist activity inside Israel that included attacks on buses, cafés and shops. In the late 1990s the suicide bus bombings added to a sense of a chronic, unpredictable, uncontrollable and potentially fatal threat to Israelis.[73] Despite the threat and continuing bus bombings, Israelis continued to use public transport out of necessity though one-fifth reported relatively high levels of anxiety.

Suicide attacks were not new to Israelis in the Second Intifada. The first suicide bombing occurred in October 1978 when three members of the PLO killed 18 people in an Israeli apartment building.[74] Following the attack the terrorist operational commander Abu Jihad gave a chilling warning of what lay ahead in the following years stating that 'no Israeli bus station or market place, no tourist car or restaurant will ever be safe while their dream of belonging is obstructed'.[75] Prior to the Second Intifada, suicide bombings were likely to be viewed as a dread risk and to a small degree a known risk leaning more towards the unknown risk. The limited experience of suicide bombings was to change post-September 2000.

Despite the experiences of the First Intifada, the Second Intifada from 2000 was very different. Civilian deaths increased from 42 annually in the years 1993–2000 to an average of 190 a year from October 2000–February 2004. In 2002 297 occurred. Sixty per cent (402) of the deaths were caused by suicide bombings, followed by 30 per cent in shootings (198).[76] Suicide bombings tended to cause a larger number of psychological casualties as detailed earlier. Not only had Israelis experienced a lower level of terrorism prior to the Intifada, but terrorism in the Intifada had moved from sporadic and selective targets with activity more in the occupied territories to a fully fledged, indiscriminate campaign within Israeli towns and cities that included various random targets including shops, supermarkets, restaurants, buses, pedestrian malls, beaches and a university campus. Consequently while Israelis would have perceived the risk of terrorism on their country to be likely, previous experience would have primarily been of activity centring more on the West Bank and Gaza regions rather than random and extensive attacks in the heart of Israel. Once the Second Intifada started, understandably the risk perception of further attacks was high. The dread risk remained uncontrollable, though the risk may have become more known through greater familiarity. The threat and consequences of the attacks were all too familiar for Israelis as the Intifada progressed. Nevertheless, the unpredictability of timing and location despite the best attempts to map out the threat, meant the risk also presented an all-too-often lethal unknown element.

Alan Kirschenbaum's survey in November 2004 provides an insight into what types of attack the Israeli public expected and where they believed they were most likely to occur, with 78 per cent believing a suicide bomb attack or an explosion would occur and 66 per cent expecting a missile or rocket (Katusha). Meanwhile 67–83 per cent considered use of a chemical, biological or atomic device was low. To put this into context, respondents believed an industrial or natural disaster was more likely to occur (14 per cent and 10 per cent respectfully) than a non-conventional attack.[77] As for where an attack was likely to take place, 72 per cent and 80 per cent believed that the threat to an entertainment centre or public transport was high. One-third believed there was a medium chance of themselves or their family being directly exposed to a terrorist attack and 15 per cent thought this was a high probability. This was in contrast to 51 per cent who thought that people they did not know had a high risk of being caught in a terrorist attack.[78] Thus people tended to avoid places where terrorist acts had caused or were deemed to be likely to cause, substantial damage or loss of life.

Understanding the extensive proportion of Israelis directly affected by the Intifada through being personally caught up in an attack one way or the other demonstrates the personal reminder many encountered of the threat. Their direct experience made them aware of the actual risk the Intifada posed – providing a credible risk perception of their security situation. Somer and Ruvio showed that 10 per cent of their study's participants reported being personally exposed to terrorism (present at the scene while an attack was being perpetrated), 2 per cent physically injured, and 28 per cent believed they had narrowly escaped an attack (e.g. walked from the scene just minutes before or got off a bus a few stops before it was blown up).[79] In addition one-third of those surveyed had been exposed to a terrorism-damaged site shortly after an attack and 44 per cent reported they knew someone who was personally caught up in a terrorist strike. Marc Gelkopf provides an insight from a personal observation of what the fear of terrorist attacks meant to Israelis by commenting:

> Israelis are in this pendulum movement which is not always rational, between fear and rejecting fear, between a sense of persecution and wanting to remove this mantle of persecution, between being a cosmopolitan citizen of the world and closing in upon himself, maybe a modern version of the enlightened wandering Jew going from the village to the big city and back, and feeling nowhere really in security, but wanting constantly to throw off the mantle of insecurity and thereby endangering himself.[80]

As a result of the continuing terrorism, Israelis sought to develop their own risk perception maps by assigning degrees of threat to situations and places and organising their behaviour accordingly. This varied from not travelling to East Jerusalem, or for others like residents of Tel Aviv, not visiting Jerusalem at all, or visiting local grocery stores instead of shopping malls. Ludman remarked that from his clinical practice in Raanana he observed families including his own indulging in some superstitious behaviours, for example, Sundays and Thursdays it seemed more dangerous to venture out than on other days of the week.[81]

Shalev called this a virtual 'map of fear' that gave people an illusionary but functional control pertaining to the risk they were ready to take on as long as they proved to be stable and reliable.[82] They reduced distress and apprehension. However should an attack occur that defied one's own fear map, then distress and fear would ensue. For instance some Israelis believed that attacks would not occur on Fridays because it was a day of prayer for Islam. A café at Hebrew University that hosted Jews and Arabs in Academia would not be targeted. Attacks on these places became a great surprise. However, after a few days Israelis reconstructed their fear maps.

Even when there were lulls in the violence, the presence of the Intifada in the public's imagination was reinforced by the media who in their reporting of non-terrorism events like organised crime and drug cartels often made references and comparisons to terrorism by referring to 'criminal terrorism' and 'home-grown Hamas.' According to Gerald Cromer who conducted a survey of Israeli newspapers from September 2003 to February 2005, the references and analogies to the terrorist threat meant that readers were regularly reminded of the terrorism.[83] This may have helped to maintain in Israeli minds the security predicament posed by the terrorist situation and reduced the chance of avoiding so many reminders of the Intifada, although there is little quantitative evidence to support this supposition. For some Israelis the constant reporting of terrorism in the media was too much. Ludman commented that some friends of his decided 'not to read the paper or watch the news as they feel if they have to know something, they will be told'.[84]

Despite the widespread and indiscriminate terrorism the Second Intifada posed, there is documentary evidence that Israelis' prior experience of terrorism may have contributed to their ability to cope with the Intifada. A comparison of the distress levels and possible influence of cultural backgrounds on American and Israeli medical students studying at the same university in Israel during March 2003 showed that although there was no significant difference between the two groups in terms of their sense of safety, the American students reported a higher level of fear and changed their daily activities to a greater extent than did the Israelis.[85] In addition the Americans reported a higher level of anxiety and a poorer level of social functioning than the Israelis. In Israel terrorism had become an unavoidable part of societal life. A factor that might have assisted in the Israeli's adaptation was their social links. All those interviewed were local residents with families and support systems, spoke the local language, were familiar with local customs and most had served in the military. All those interviewed had also grown up in and were familiar with continuous security threats.[86] In comparison the Americans in Israel were apart from their families and had limited if any prior direct exposure to terrorist threats or attacks.

The importance of prior experience of terrorism for coping with attacks was underscored by research that examined the Israeli response to terrorism in the early 1980s. Also pertinent to the Second Intifada is the 1983 study by Breznitz and Eshel which noted that 'although a higher baseline of pressures and stressors is characteristic of a large part of the Israeli population, the repeated exposure to intense stress can foster adequate modes of adjustment, based on learning from these experiences and subsequent habituation'.[87] This underscores the assumption that prior to the Intifada, Israelis would have had a degree of resilience and credible understanding of the risk perception threat they faced to assist them in coping with the attacks.

While the Second Intifada was another chapter in the violence the Israeli nation has experienced since its conception in 1948, the extent and indiscrimination set a new precedent. The high death toll of an average 190 annually between October 2000–February 2004 reflected the new level of violence. The concept and experience of suicide bombings and shootings were not new and thus Israelis had a base on which they could build their own resilience and response, changing their behaviours and attitudes to adapt to the new security environment. Prior to the Intifada, terrorism had been with residents of Israel for decades, and very intensely so. Nevertheless, prior periods of continuous terrorism did not reach the intensity of which the Second Intifada.

Risk amplification

The psychological effects from an attack can be reduced by the actions taken by the authorities when dealing with the physical surroundings and psychological well-being of the Israelis exposed. The Israeli response suggests the support victims received may have assisted their psychological recovery and reduced the terror of terrorism. This included a well-rehearsed psychological intervention plan and authorities quickly removing physical reminders of attacks.

First, immediately following a bombing, the National Insurance Institute of Israel, a government agency responsible for medical and rehabilitation costs caused by terrorism, contacts casualties of major attacks and provides psychological debriefing sessions to groups of survivors.[88] A Stress Unit is established in all hospitals receiving the victims. The Stress Unit refers patients identified as high risk of developing Acute Stress Disorder to the outpatient mental health clinics for continuing treatment.[89] All patients are examined by a mental health professional before being discharged. However, there is no empirical evidence to show to what degree the Stress Unit decreased the psychological effects of terrorism.

Second, a central phone line and database are established providing the public access to all admissions to hospitals related to a terrorist event thereby negating the need for families and friends to contact each hospital separately. In addition a phone service, staffed by volunteers, operated by ERAN (Mental First Aid Association) handles calls from the public suffering from fears, anxiety and uncertainty. Under the supervision of psychological trauma experts from the mental health services, the phoneline is activated immediately after every terrorist attack and covers five languages.[90]

Third, the dead are required to be identified within 24 hours of an attack in accordance with Jewish law. In addition, authorities ensure the populace, particularly those in the immediate and surrounding vicinity of an attack, is kept abreast of developments in the following hours and days via the media. This includes information on the scale of the attack, casualties, accurate descriptions of the attacked areas and road access. This enables the public to be aware of which travel routes to take, whether relatives or friends might be exposed (reassurance) and sources of advice and help.

While the media may provide valuable information on the terrorist attack, and scenes of proximal threat and safety, they may well have exacerbated and spread the terror effect. Television, radio, internet and print media coverage of terrorist attacks was immediate, graphic and extensive, contributing to the sense of a massive shared national crisis that engulfed survivors as well as unaffected citizens and mental health workers.[91] The lack of a proximity effect may be partly due to extensive media coverage. Exposure to emotionally charged, real-life television images of death and destruction can produce symptoms of PTSD and depression in adults.[92] This phenomenon has been referred to in the trauma literature as 'vicarious traumatisation'.[93]

Another area where the Israeli response attempts to reduce the psychological effects of an attack is the immediate removal by authorities of physical reminders or scars caused by an attack. Hours after a bombing, windows and buildings are repaired, gruesome reminders removed and damaged trees replaced. Shalev believes the removal of visual evidence of an attack reduces the psychological impact and facilitates the healing of traumatised survivors by reducing their exposure to reminders of trauma.[94] For patients who have received exposure therapy, they return to the street to see no reminders of the attack and see life is back as before. The extensive clean-up and removal of reminders of an attack is reinforced by a survivor of a bus bombing during the First Intifada. On returning to the site of the attack at a roadside café several weeks after the incident, a couple who had survived the bombing found that the kiosk had been rebuilt into a 'sparkling, sleek roadside cafeteria with smiling customers going about their business, seemingly indifferent to the bombing'. The survivor noted that while she had wanted the site to reflect what had happened, she recognised that this was 'the Israeli way', adding 'They cry, mourn, and clean up the mess quickly. Life goes on, albeit in some terribly altered way. Somehow survivors brush themselves off and continue.'[95]

While there is anecdotal evidence to suggest that the above actions reduced the terror of terrorism, there are no extensive data to show to what degree these interventions helped Israelis cope with the Intifada, in particular the survivors. There is also the possible effect of the media exacerbating the terror of the Intifada.

Conclusion

For many the Second Intifada presented Israelis with a direct and continuous threat to their lives during which suicide bombings, shootings and for those in northern Israel, Katusha rockets became a regular occurrence – a threat far more endemic than any had been before. Terror became a 'way of life' in most Israeli cities, with the presence of armed guards and special police units becoming part of the routine that Israelis faced daily.[96] Coupled with the intensive media coverage, this served as a constant reminder to Israelis of the threat they faced. When there was a lull in the violence, the media would present domestic crime as internal terrorism – further reminding Israelis of the Intifada.

A striking feature of the proximity discussion is that distance from the terrorist attacks did not have a strong bearing on the terror adult Israelis expressed in the surveys. However, in one study there were heightened precautionary measures by those living in the non-targeted area. While adults immediately exposed (survivors) expressed elevated psychological effects as demonstrated by the high number admitted to emergency rooms for trauma compared to physiological conditions, those in regions (and towns) frequently attacked expressed similar responses to those in parts of Israel that encountered very few if any attacks. Possible reasons for this vary. First, there could be a 'ceiling effect' whereby exposure to a continuous terrorist campaign means that after a series of attacks the terror experienced does not increase further unless individuals are directly caught in an attack. Second, the extensive media coverage following major attacks exposed all Israelis to the horror of aftermath to which those in the vicinity (town/suburb) of the incident encountered. Consequently whether one resided in Jerusalem often attacked or a town rarely exposed to terrorism did not make that much difference. While media exposure and frequency of attacks may have been strong determinants, Israel's small size meant that there was not much distance from where attacks happened and where the rest of Israelis lived. Therefore perceived terrorism exposure did not vary significantly across the nation.

A significant factor was Israelis' means of adapting to the Intifada. While they changed their behaviours and attitudes to reduce the risk of being exposed to a terrorist attack, studies by Adessky and Freedman, and Shalev infer these could be regarded as a natural response rather than a sign of negative clinical symptoms. While a prominent proportion (80 per cent) would conduct behaviours to check on the well-being of others (phoning friends and family after an attack) as a means of coping, around one-quarter changed their travel plans (e.g. travelling less by bus, using taxis more, driving) to reduce the risk of terrorism to themselves. Shalev warns that 'some symptoms that are subsumed as posttraumatic and therefore purposeless and somewhat exaggerated (e.g. avoiding previously dangerous places and situations, responding emotionally to threat signals, remaining vigilant and "on guard") may reflect anticipation and self-protection'.[97] These reactions reflected Israelis' risk perceptions with just over three-quarters believing that the threat of further terrorist attacks was high. Behavioural adaptation became a key factor in Israelis' survival strategy.

While much of the evidence suggests that Israelis adapted to the Intifada, one study did suggest that adaptation did not occur as the rate at which road accident deaths occurred, increasing three days after major terrorist attacks remained the same throughout the study period. This suggests the Israeli populace were not becoming either more sensitive or more resistant to the attacks. However, the survey only examined the period January 2001–June 2002 therefore a reduced number of deaths may or may not have occurred in the subsequent years of the Intifada.

The combination of avoidance behaviour to reduce the possibility of being exposed to an attack and viewing the days as small steps or victories was part of a conducive adaptive strategy that many Israelis undertook to respond and carry on with their everyday lives as much as they realistically could. While these changes in behaviours and attitudes could be interpreted by the DSM-IV-TR as symptoms of PTSD, in reality they greatly assisted the ability of Israelis to adapt and cope effectively to terrorism and thus cannot always be regarded as adverse psychological symptoms. As Adessky and Freedman note the perception of the security situation meant that during the Intifada, negative appraisals by Israelis such as 'nowhere is safe' and 'the next disaster will strike soon' may actually be reality-based rather than excessive.[98]

This case study provides a valuable insight into the effects of a prolonged intensive terrorist campaign where random attacks frequently disrupt everyday lives. While each attack on its own may not be regarded as a significant event in the context of incidents like 9/11, sarin attacks or the 1998 bombing of the US embassies in Africa, cumulatively the series of attacks over a period of time combined with good documentary evidence provides a valuable assessment of the impact of a continuous terrorist campaign on a society. Despite the gravity of the Intifada, in 2002 around the height of the Intifada, 82 per cent of Israelis expressed optimism about their personal future and 6 per cent expressed optimism about the future of Israel, while 60 per cent and 67 per cent had a low sense of their personal and relatives safety respectfully. As with the driving behaviour survey, it would have been valuable to learn how these perceptions may have continued in the remainder of the Intifada. However, these surveys were conducted at the height of the Intifada – with the highest number of fatalities occurring in the period 2001 through to early 2003. While the death toll from terrorist attacks may have declined, Israelis in 2001–2003 would not have known when the number of attacks and fatalities would decline.

While there is sufficient data available on the Second Intifada to make a credible assessment of the effects the terrorism campaign had on the nation, the limited availability of continuous information tracking Israelis' responses (both clinical symptoms and behaviours and attitudes) undermines the ability to capture how the populace was affected and responded over the course of the four years. Did the resilience and adaptive behaviour remain steady throughout the Intifada? How long did it take for Israelis to adapt to the Intifada and to what extent were there changes in their response to the lessening of the attacks?

The evidence suggests that Israelis adapted to the terrorist threat in their own ways and accepted the situation as part of everyday life. As the Intifada went on some increasingly ventured out to public places as they would have done normally, while a minority had taken to avoiding certain places at certain times (fear maps). There were occasions when external events would shake the risk perception of Israelis and cause greater caution in the anticipation of further bombings, for instance following the assassination of the founder and spiritual leader of Hamas in March 2004. However, despite the ongoing terror, Israelis had to occasionally be reminded of the terror threat when they were becoming too accustomed and complacent.

9   Conclusion

The introduction to this book noted Paul Wilkinson's observation that 'quantifying the terror of terrorism is a complex issue because of its subjectivity – a possible reason to why other commentators have not focused on the fear and anxiety of terrorism'.[1] Similarly, Andrew Lambert wrote that the 'analysis of airpower as a psychological weapon is scarce, and the little data that is available shows much scatter and is sometimes contradictory'.[2] The four terrorism case studies and the missile strikes chapter collectively provide extensive quantitative evidence to demonstrate the terror of terrorism. Rather than mass fear, anxiety and panic, this study revealed the effect of strategic terrorism is more complex.

The following discusses each of the five key assumptions examined, and then presents a summary chart of the key findings across the case studies. This is followed by evidence from two recent terrorism attacks, the March 2004 Madrid bombings and the London attacks in July 2005, to further illustrate the robustness of the assumptions. Subsequent to this is an assessment of how this study advances the fields of risk analysis, psychiatry and international relations. The conclusion then provides a series of policy recommendations.

Key assumptions re-examined

The following re-visits the five assumptions laid out in Chapter 3. The case studies suggest that the assumptions were shown to be robust against the evidence contained. There were, however, some exceptions. The specifics are presented below.

First, people change their behaviours and attitudes to minimise the perceived risk of strategic terrorism to themselves, but they do not panic. The public is not prone to panic but can and frequently does engage in activities that may ultimately hinder a country's response to an incident (increase casualties). The direct terror generated by an attack is limited. Beyond those directly affected (on the bus or train when attacked, by or in the WTC on September 11 2001), the repercussions are more of disruption and adversely affect individual's risk perceptions to such a degree that they often calmly embark on activities that can be detrimental to their safety, the safety of those around them or place pressure on limited resources like public health assets. Distorted risk perceptions can cause individuals to embark on activities they believe will make them safer but actually pose a greater risk to their own well-being. Therefore, the actual risk in undertaking precautionary measures can in some instances be greater than the perceived risk.

Despite evidence to suggest that panic does not occur following terrorist attacks, it needs to be considered whether the culture and social backgrounds of the targeted populaces in the case studies may have influenced the behavioural reactions. In the sarin and 9/11 studies, those attacked were generally middle class, commuting or at the office, and likely to have been accustomed to rational, well-structured co-operation with authorities. During the anthrax attacks many of those affected were from media outlets, Congress or postal workers.

Second, the degree of behavioural change is influenced not just by the strategic terrorism event itself but also by the adequacy of the risk characterisation and risk communication by local and national authorities, politicians and the emergency services. The way behavioural reactions are manifested partly depends on risk amplification through media reporting, authorities' communication and actions by government, public health bodies and emergency services. In addition, prior experiences can influence responses, for instance, experiences of previous terrorist attacks.

While evidence on risk amplification in the case studies is less definitive, there are several factors which affect the terror of strategic terrorism. These include the effectiveness of authorities' risk communication (threat advisories and advice provided during and after an attack), and how emergency services respond (e.g. speed of response and whether they have adequate resources). These can amplify or attenuate the fear and anxiety of individuals and influence the public's risk perceptions.

One key feature of inadequate risk communication is the detrimental effect on public health. This was particularly evident in the 1991 Gulf War and anthrax chapters where the public took actions that were detrimental to the safety of themselves and those around them. Examples of effective communication included the Second Intifada and parts of 9/11 and the 1991 Gulf War.

Third, the psychometric paradigm provides a valuable framework for understanding the public's risk perceptions of strategic terrorism. Authorities and governments need to clearly understand and have a better awareness of the concepts of dread risk and unknown risk. Possessing an insight into these attributes could serve to better inform authorities (the risk communicators) and emergency planners in how to prepare, respond and recover from strategic terror threats and attacks by understanding how the public may perceive and respond to certain risks caused by an attack. Understanding how the public may respond to certain risks would enable the development of effective risk communication concerning advice on what precautionary measure the public may be asked to take following an attack. This could ensure greater compliance and adherence to public health guidance, for instance, self-triage where appropriate to assess their own exposure to a possible CBR device and the type of vaccination or antibiotics programme they may be asked to undergo.

Some forms of terrorist attacks involving substances less familiar to the public (like a radiological attack) may be perceived by the public to be more of a dread risk and unknown risk. Such instances may pose a greater probability of causing inappropriate risk framing leading to adverse changes in behaviours and attitudes. In these circumstances, it would be more critical to understand the public's risk perceptions and conduct thorough risk characterisation to understand the actual risk posed to enable the development of effective risk communication. Where an attack may be perceived a less of a dread risk and more of a known risk, like the detonation of a conventional (high explosive) bomb that is likely to be a more familiar threat, effective risk communication will be less critical to reduce casualties in the immediate aftermath (in the following hours and days) as the public is likely to have a greater understanding of and familiarity with the immediate danger. For instance, those not caught up in the blast are likely to calculate they will be physically fine even though there may be the risk of secondary devices. However, it would be important to gauge how conventional and non-conventional attacks may have distorted people's risk perceptions in the following months to ensure adequate risk framing occurs for conducting their everyday lives (e.g. travel routines).

While the psychometric paradigm provides a useful framework to understand societal risk perceptions and responses to terrorism, there are not enough studies in the strategic terrorism area to assess its true value given that it derived from research focusing more on improving the management of risks between the public, industry, government and the scientific community. The few studies that have been conducted post-9/11 suggest that the key principles are valid (e.g. Baruch Fischhoff's surveys after 9/11). Using the psychometric paradigm approach of dread risk and known risk does have its limitations to understanding the public's risk perceptions of strategic terrorism. A drawback to this study was that it drew upon assessments and conclusions from non-risk analysis literature in view of the lack of risk analysis studies undertaken on the case studies. More importantly, the psychometric paradigm can only at best provide a guide to the possible risk perceptions in the absence of robust and controlled studies undertaken before, during and after the attacks. At best the matrix can illustrate what perceptions may have been rather than what they would have been with a high degree of certainty. In addition, this approach infers the public is one uniform unit rather than many subgroups with different perceptions, interpretations and experiences. However, the psychometric paradigm is a valuable tool in understanding how a populace might frame their risk perceptions and how this might then affect their behaviours and attitudes.

Fourth, the extent of mental health and behavioural effects declines with the time lapsing after and proximity to a terrorist attack. While the effects of an attack varies, in some instances its long-term effect can persist on the populace. Greater distance and time from an attack leads, in most cases, to reduced PTSD and related symptoms, and fewer changes in behaviours and attitudes. However, this is not a uniform effect as shown by 9/11 and the Second Intifada case studies.

Evidence suggests that the smaller the country the less effect proximity has on the population's response. In these situations distance has a minimal impact among adults. Beyond those directly exposed to the attack or in the immediate area that could personally witness an event, the effect of proximity is not uniform. There may be other determining factors as to why some regions express more psychological effects that others, but this book shows that greater proximity does not automatically equate to a reduction in mental health effects and behavioural changes.

Despite the diversity of the case studies, there were some common themes on the effects of time. Primarily there was a correlation between the length of time after an attack and reduction in the effects of strategic terror. As time went on the effects declined. However, there is some evidence to suggest that after an initial drop, over the longer term (e.g. five years), the remaining effects of strategic terror, such as behavioural responses, stay at the same level, as some individuals permanently changed their lives to reduce perceived risk of becoming personally exposed to an attack. The extent of PTSD and related symptoms reduced in the years following an attack (with the exception of one study on the sarin attacks).

In prolonged terror events like the 1991 Gulf War, anthrax attacks and the Second Intifada, the populace adapted and to a certain degree became used to the ongoing attacks. Perception tracking following the anthrax attacks and the 1991 Gulf War revealed a decline in threat risk perceptions. Additional attacks did not lead to increased levels. There were insufficient data to provide comparable analysis for the Second Intifada to assess how Israelis' perceptions evolved.

In a situation of continuous terror the greater familiarity and experience (risk becomes more known and less of a dread risk) can render the populace accustomed to the threat. Fear mind maps, as Arieh Shalev referred to in the Intifada chapter, become a prime means for individuals to adapt to the threat. While research based on DSM-IV criteria and other related categorisation systems allows for direct cross-comparisons and is a useful source for capturing the effects of time and proximity, it needs to be considered whether this checklist of symptoms can tend to medicalise symptoms, rather than looking at the causes of symptoms which could be regarded as natural responses.

Fifth, due to the limited terror of strategic terrorism, the effects on the political system are slight. The case studies suggest that strategic terror does 'shift the attitudes and behaviour' of political leaders and the public, but not in line with the intended goals of the perpetrators. The shifting of behaviours, attitudes and the disorientation that occurs mainly revolve around individuals changing their daily routines to reduce the perceived risk of being exposed to a potential attack. These reactions are arguably not signs of people panicking but of them creating their own risk perceptions (or fear maps) for adjusting their daily lives. In some instances this lead to inappropriate risk framing.

These activities are often accompanied by political action to counter the terrorism threat. It could be suggested that a political response can create its own form of strategic terror by unintentionally maintaining or amplifying the public's perceived risk. The public is not seeking to change the political direction of their country (e.g. succeeding to all or part of the perpetrators' demands) but instead undertaking actions of self-protection in response to the perceived risk, even if these are sometimes disproportionate to the actual risk. In many instances these responses are counter to what the perpetrators are looking to achieve. The public is more resilient than sometimes believed by perpetrators and policy-makers. The disorientation primarily extends to distorting people's risk perceptions, rather than causing wholesale changes in the political system.

Comparison of the key assumptions across the case studies

Table 9.1 lists the key case study findings across each of the five assumptions.

Evidence from two further terrorism case studies

Two additional terror incidents have occurred since the research for this study was conducted. Highlighting these provides further evidence to the robustness of the five key assumptions tested. First, the Madrid train bombings on 11 March 2004. Second, the 7 July 2005 bombings of London's public transport network and the associated failed attack two weeks later.

March 2004 Madrid train bombings

On 11 March 2004, a series of explosions occurred on four trains close to one of Madrid's main railway stations, Atocha: 191 people were killed and around 1,800 were wounded. The attacks were undertaken by a group reported to be affiliated to Al Qaeda. This event provides further evidence of the societal consequences of an attack on a transport system.

On the trains there was a mixture of calmness and chaos as the bombs exploded. Multiple devices on several trains may have compounded the fear and anxiety during the attack. One commuter, travelling in a train about 50 metres from one of the blasts at Atocha station, reported that after the initial explosion,

Table 9.1 Comparison of the key assumptions by case study

1991 missile strikes	1995 sarin attack in Tokyo	September 11	Anthrax attacks	Second Intifada
People change their behaviours and attitudes to minimise the perceived risk of strategic terrorism to them, but they do not panic				
In the lead-up to war there was anxiety rather than panic. During the attacks very few exhibited extreme reactions. The greater predictability of the timing and location of the missile strikes enabled Israelis to adapt their lives around the attacks. This became known as the emergency routine. At the beginning of the war, there was spontaneous evacuation from the Tel Aviv and Ramat Gan regions of 100,000 inhabitants to areas less likely to be targeted.	Interviews of survivors showed that the majority of the subway passengers reacted calmly to the attacks with only a small minority expressing panic. In the following weeks, some avoided the subway. Taxis reported an increase in business. In the weeks after, there were cases of innocuous pungent odours on the subways leading to passengers mistakenly believing that there was another attack. There was a lack of quantitative evidence to make a thorough assessment.	That there was no overt panic in the self-evacuation of the WTC. Very few of those trapped above the impact zone (knowing that it was unlikely that they could get out of the WTC), exhibited panic. In the following months and years there were significant changes in behaviours and attitudes to reduce the perceived risk of terrorism. This included flying less often (5–7 per cent decrease flying in January 2002), not travelling overseas, or not going into sky scrapers. Reduction in air travel was accompanied by an increase in long-distance	The large-scale public health campaign was orderly with people queuing patiently to be swabbed. There was heightened anxiety but not panic among those who thought that they had been exposed to anthrax but received delayed treatment (e.g. postal workers). The anthrax attacks led to a small proportion undertaking measures that they thought would protect themselves. Most were for opening mail. Some 0.13 per cent of Americans sought an antibiotic prescription, 2 per cent reported purchasing gas masks, 8 per cent avoided public	Those attacked expressed heightened anxiety but very little evidence of any panic. A significant minority changed their behaviours and attitudes. A prominent proportion (80 per cent) would conduct behaviours to check on the well-being of others (phoning friends and family after an attack) as a means of coping, around a quarter changed their travel plans (e.g. travelling less by bus, using taxis more, keeping away from buses when driving a car) to reduce the risk of terrorism to themselves.

Table 9.1 Continued

1991 missile strikes	1995 sarin attack in Tokyo	September 11	Anthrax attacks	Second Intifada
		road travel leading to an extra 1,595 road traffic fatalities in the 18 months after 9/11. Between 2002–2004, 18–22 per cent of Americans reported permanently changing the way that they lived.	events, and between 23–33 per cent took precautions when opening mail. This showed a measured response in the public's reactions and perceptions to anthrax.	

The degree of behavioural change is influenced not just by the strategic terrorism event itself but also by the adequacy of the risk characterisation and risk communication by local and national authorities, politicians and the emergency services

1991 missile strikes	1995 sarin attack in Tokyo	September 11	Anthrax attacks	Second Intifada
While the missile alerts were clear, the lack of effective information on the use of protective equipment (gas masks and atropine injection) may have contributed to their misuse. Civil defence preparations heightened the risk perceptions, while the deployment of the Patriot missile	There was a lack of information for those icommuters who had potentially been exposed to sarin on what signs they should look out for to indicate poisoning and protective measures they should take. The lack of official information continued in the days after the attack releasing very little information in	On 9/11 Rudolph Giuliani demonstrated effective emergency risk communication while President Bush was distant. Bush improved markedly in the weeks that followed. A lot of the time the terrorism alert advisories post-9/11 provided mixed messages and were not clear. In response to the	There were many mixed messages, both verbal and actions undertaken, by public health officials, politicians and the media. The risk characterisation of anthrax by CDC to assess its lethality proved difficult, with a lack of available data on anthrax in an urban environment (for instance secondary aerosolisation) and the	The evidence available suggests that, following an attack, the Israeli government and the media worked effectively to provide up-to-date information. There were occasions of reduced alertness as Israelis became accustomed to the terror threat. The Israeli response suggests that support

defence provided reassurance. So-called 'mental health experts'' media commentary may have heightened concerns.

comparison to the Aum sect who launched a public relations campaign.

The limited information available in the study suggests that the lack of an effective emergency response may have exacerbated the perception of fear and anxiety, with many passengers having to rely on members of the public to ferry them to hospital.

mixed terrorism advisories in the months after 9/11, the public may have undertaken precautionary measures in response to the terror alerts that were harmful to themselves and, in the case of avoiding flying in preference to driving, led to an increase in the number of road deaths.

type of anthrax that was used in the attacks. This led to a delay in identifying the risk of anthrax spores leaking out of envelopes, causing secondary aerosolisation.

CDC admitted that it did not adhere to good practices and had to hire risk communication consultants. This included poorly conveying why postal workers were given the cheaper antibiotic drug compared to Congressional and media employees.

The initial lack of regular accurate reports for the public created a significant public information void, which may have increased the public's fear and concern. This was compounded by the CDC's inadequate risk characterisation. This may have contributed to

victims received may have assisted their psychological recovery and reduced the terror of terrorism. This included a well-rehearsed psychological intervention plan and authorities quickly removing physical reminders of attacks.

Table 9.1 Continued

1991 missile strikes	1995 sarin attack in Tokyo	September 11	Anthrax attacks	Second Intifada
			increase in demand for antibiotics, thus placing pressure on limited stockpiles and risking causing antibiotic resistance from their widespread use.	

The psychometric paradigm provides a valuable framework for understanding the public's risk perceptions of strategic terrorism

1991 missile strikes	1995 sarin attack in Tokyo	September 11	Anthrax attacks	Second Intifada
In the lead-up to war, Israelis knew Iraq had the missile range to strike Israel, and had used chemical weapons against its own people (Kurds). During the war, greater familiarity of the threat (time and location of attacks) reduced the dread and unknown risk perceptions.	Japan's citizens had limited experience of conventional and non-conventional terrorist attacks on its territory, and the public's awareness of Aum's intentions and capabilities in launching indiscriminate CB attacks. This was despite a sarin attack in 1994 in Matsumoto that was wrongly attributed to a local resident.	America had limited experience of terrorism on US soil including the 1993 WTC and 1995 Oklahoma bombings. Terrorism was seen more as an overseas problem. In May 2001 64 per cent of respondents believed international terrorism was a major threat to the well-being of the US. Despite this, the gravity of 9/11 meant Americans had no prior experience to draw upon. Risk	Prior to the anthrax attacks, America was still coming to terms with 9/11 and the possibility that there could be a second wave of Al Qaeda strikes. Officials warned of further attacks and the public and media speculated what form these might take. While the threat of terrorism was a known risk, when, where and by what means remained unknown. The risk perception of	In the lead-up to the Second Intifada, Israelis had become all too familiar with terrorism and conflict for several decades from Arab–Israeli wars to terrorist attacks. However, the Second Intifada involved extensive suicide bombings and the attacks took place within Israeli towns and cities rather than just in the occupied territories as had occurred before. The high frequency of the attacks

terrorism was greater than the actual risk.

meant that, while the dread risk of terrorism remained, Israelis became increasingly familiar with the threat, thus it became more of a known risk.

perception studies undertaken prior to 9/11 identified the US populace as viewing terrorism as a dread risk and known risk leaning more towards the unknown quadrant.

The extent of mental health and behavioural effects declines with the time lapsing after and proximity to a terrorist attack

Proximity
Majority of studies showed proximity to the missile impact areas influenced the behavioural and psychological reactions.

Proximity
Evidence from those on the subway showed that while there was anxiety on the attacked carriages, there was little evidence of any panic. The available evidence suggests that Tokyo's populace reacted calmly to the attacks. Lack of data precluded a more detailed assessment.

Proximity
Proximity was a major determinant on the psychological problems that ensued. Within New York City, proximity to the WTC influenced the levels of PTSD. Those outside New York City had lower levels of PTSD-related symptoms and lower perceived judgment for terror risks.

Proximity
Proximity affected Americans in areas where postal facilities were contaminated. They took more precautions when opening mail compared to the national total.

Proximity
Those directly exposed to an attack expressed higher rates of PTSD than those in the rest of the nation. Over the course of the Intifada proximity did not influence PTSD and associated symptoms between those living in frequently attacked and non-attacked areas. This could be due to a ceiling effect or because Israel's geographic size meant that terror affected all equally.

Table 9.1 Continued

1991 missile strikes	1995 sarin attack in Tokyo	September 11	Anthrax attacks	Second Intifada
Time	*Time*	*Time*	*Time*	*Time*
As the missile campaign progressed, the psychological reactions and expectations of missile strikes declined. Although expectations of chemical attack remained at 25 per cent at the end of the war.	Over 75 per cent of those who arrived at hospitals suffered from psychosomatic symptoms. There continued to be several hundred seeking medical attention in the following weeks, incorrectly believing that they had been contaminated. The limited evidence available showed that PTSD increased among survivors over time. PTSD was around 3 per cent among victims 1995–1997 to then increase in 1998 and 2000.	There was no overt panic in the self-evacuation of the WTC. In the hours after the attack, Manhattan witnessed an orderly mass exodus of survivors. Over the six months after 9/11, presented levels of PTSD and stress declined and were less than expected. Nationally, stress declined from 17 per cent to 4.5 per cent in 2004.	After initial heightened concerns following the first deaths, fear and anxiety declined. Despite three more anthrax deaths in early November, two Department of Justice threat advisory warnings of further terrorist attacks in October and November, the initiation of hostilities against Afghanistan, and a fifth anthrax death in late November, the percentage of Americans worried about becoming a victim of terrorism steadily declined from 59 per cent in early October to 35 per cent by late November.	There is mixed evidence. This includes evidence that suggests there was a three-day delay among Israelis reacting to the violence and stress after each bombing. Longer-term accumulative psychological surveys showed 9.4 per cent had PTSD and 58.6 per cent reported feeling depressed by April 2002. Survivors continued to encounter psychological problems for several years.

Due to the limited terror of strategic terrorism, the effects on the political system are slight

The attacks failed to coerce the Israeli government to retaliate and bring Israel into the 1991 Gulf War. This could have broken up the allied coalition.

Aum did not achieve its objectives of deterring the police raid on Aum Shinrikyo's facilities and to cause a *coup d'état* in preparation for what was believed to be impending Armageddon. Japan's government gradually introduced legislation to curtail Aum's activities, including revoking its religious status.

With no political agenda released by the perpetrators, it is not possible to state whether the attacks themselves resulted in the desired political change. 9/11 did have a significant internal effect on America leading to extensive counter-terrorism measures.

While there was no publicly announced intent by the perpetrators, in 1998 Al Qaeda issued a fatwa that called for attacks on Americans and their interests. The fatwa provides context and objectives that the organisation was trying to achieve.

With no declared aims or objectives beyond the letters enclosed with the anthrax-laced envelopes, it is hard to establish what the perpetrator(s) were looking to achieve and therefore whether these objectives were met. If they intended to create extensive fear and anxiety capitalising on 9/11, this was not achieved.

Aims varied according to the Palestinian factions' ideological and political motives. Their aims broadly encompassed seeking to gain an independent Palestine, to destroying Israel.

Israel conducted extensive military operations in the occupied territories and the Palestinians did not achieve their two-state solution. Hamas did believe that Israel leaving Gaza in 2005 was an achievement caused by the Intifada.

People got off quickly but I still feel we all kept calm. It was only one minute later that two more bombs exploded in rapid succession. People started to scream and run, some bumping into each other and as we ran there was another explosion.[3]

Another commuter noted that after the second explosion, 'It was at this point that people rushed out of the station. People crying. It was shocking.'

As with the case studies, the attacks had psychological effects on the populace. One to three months after the attacks, 2.3 per cent of Madrid residents were thought to have reported symptoms consistent with PTSD and 8 per cent of symptoms consistent with major depression. While PTSD was lower than in Manhattan after 9/11, depression was about the same.[4] After 18–25 days, probable PTSD was estimated at 1.9 per cent.[5] Factors thought to have influenced PTSD included how close respondents lived to the attacked locations and physical proximity to the bombings. However, there was only a marginal reduction in the level of PTSD among the victims in the following months. A study led by Fraquas and Teran of 56 victims found that rates of PTSD only declined from 41.1 per cent one month after the attack to 40.9 per cent six months later.[6]

As happened after 9/11 with reduced passenger numbers on airlines and on the London underground after 7/7, Spaniards avoided the dread risk by avoiding travelling by train, but unlike Americans, they did not follow this through to take to their cars instead. Research led by López-Rousseau showed that in March and April 2004 passenger numbers declined by 4 per cent and 6 per cent respectfully. However, they then increased by 3 per cent in May 2004. Furthermore, highway traffic actually decreased by 1 per cent in March and 3 per cent in April along with a reduction in road fatalities.[7] Normally, seasonal traffic would increase during this period. López-Rousseau hypothesises that there were psychological and cultural reasons as to why the Spanish reacted differently from the Americans. First, more people died in 9/11 so it had a greater psychological impact. Second, Spaniards rely on cars less than Americans. Third, Spain has frequently been exposed to terrorism (mainly by ETA). Gigerenzer concluded that the experiences of ETA may have provided the Spanish with less of a dread risk and more of a calculated risk perception.[8] Therefore, inappropriate risk framing did not take place.

It was believed that Islamic radicals with connections to Al Qaeda carried out the bombings. Their attack was in retaliation to the Spanish government sending troops to Iraq. The general elections which were held three days after the attack led to the ruling government, José María Aznar's Popular Party, being defeated by the Socialists. While it was widely seen as the influence of the bombings that increased support to pull Spanish troops out of Iraq, prior to the attacks public support for pulling the troops out was already high at 80 per cent.[9] In the days following the bombings, many Spaniards felt that Aznar's government was not providing reliable and up-to-date information about the terrorists responsible. Some saw the government incorrectly blaming ETA just hours after the bombings in an effort to change the electorate's views about the election.[10] Further research would be required to examine the correlation between the attacks to improve the incumbent's electoral prospects.

July 2005 London bombings

An overview of the literature following the 7 July bombings and the failed attempt two weeks later on the London Underground reinforces the key findings on the effects of time, proximity, behavioural effects and prior experience of terrorism.

As with the Tokyo sarin attack, evidence suggests that, while there was some panic in the trains, overall there was calmness, particularly when the evacuation took place. In the initial moments after the attack a survey of first-hand accounts of those on the bombed trains and bus suggested a mixed response. On one of the lines, the Circle line, one passenger remarked 'People started panicking, screaming and crying as smoke came into the carriage.'[11] Another reported, 'People were incredibly calm but very very scared'[12] On the Piccadilly line train, a commuter noted 'Some people were very calm and people were telling everybody not to panic.'[13] On the same line at King's Cross it was also observed that 'People were screaming and panicking. It was pitch black and then there was smoke. We thought the carriage was going to catch fire. I was sure we were all going to die down there.'[14] Another commuter on the same line reported 'A few people were panicking, but people in our carriage were very good.'[15] The high levels of fear and anxiety and reports of panic may well be because of the horrific injuries being personally experienced and the belief among some that a fire would break out causing further fatalities. Individuals may panic in the moments before death, realising they will not make it out alive. Despite these reports, extraordinary mobile-phone footage showed calmness on the trains in the partially smoke-filled carriages both before and during the evacuation along the tunnels.[16]

Two of the key mental health studies conducted since 7/7 to examine the effects of PTSD-related symptoms were undertaken by researchers at King's College, London led by James Rubin. Their first study was a telephone survey conducted 18–20 July 2005 that covered 1,010 participants in the London area, and the second six to eight months later that re-interviewed 574 respondents.[17] The two surveys demonstrated that the behavioural and psychological effects did reduce over time but there was a minority who remained affected by the attacks. Collectively the two surveys found that:

- Those reporting substantial stress in the first three weeks after the attacks through to seven months later declined from 31 per cent in 2005 to 11 per cent in 2006.

- Perceived safety concern while travelling declined from 19 per cent in 1995 to 12 per cent in 2006.
- Those that intended to travel less often declined from 30 per cent in 2005 to 19 per cent in 2006.[18]

Similar to Shalev's, and Adessky and Freedman's[19] arguments in the Second Intifada chapter, the first Rubin study found that while just over one in five were reporting substantial stress, the second survey noted, 'the perceived lack of safety, changes in behaviour and altered perceptions could all be seen as normal responses to what is perceived as an ongoing threat'.[20] While it is not clear to what degree prior experience may have assisted with Londoners' coping responses, prior experience is likely to have reduced the psychological and behavioural effects of strategic terror. Evidence of proximity having an effect on responses can be found in the first Rubin *et al.* survey that showed that levels of distress were highest among those who had direct exposure to the bombings.[21]

Further comparison of the Rubin surveys can be made with the other case studies through their use of an identical tool for measuring the presence of stress as employed by Mark Schuster's 9/11 survey.[22] The first Rubin survey concluded that 31 per cent of Londoners reported substantial stress as compared to 44 per cent of those in New York.[23] The authors suggest that the lower level of distress among Londoners in comparison to that in the 9/11 survey could be attributed to prior experience of IRA terrorism in London, with respondents who had been previously exposed to terrorism or a false alarm showing a significantly reduced short-term emotional response.[24] This supports evidence from the Second Intifada and 1991 Gulf War of prior experience assisting with the coping response. However, it also noted that these differences could also be in due part to a greater loss of life and more dramatic images from 9/11 than 7/7. Further similarities between 7/7 and the Second Intifada were found in the first Rubin survey which revealed that 55 per cent of Londoners believed their lives were in danger and 58 per cent believed their close family or friends were at risk too.[25] These figures were similar to those levels captured in the Avi Bleich survey of the Second Intifada of 60.4 per cent having a low sense of personal safety and 67.9 per cent a low sense of safety for their relatives.[26] Furthermore, the first Rubin survey showed there was a significant proportion who did not feel safe travelling on the underground (46 per cent) or in central London (33 per cent).[27]

The failed attacks on 21 July 2005 reminded Londoners of the terrorism threat. Although there is insufficient evidence to evaluate the behavioural effects of the failed attempts, it could be assumed that the attempts reinforced the perceived terrorism threat posed to London's transport system. Unfortunately, the first Rubin survey concluded the day before the 21 July attack. Therefore it does not provide an insight into these effects beyond the cumulative outcome of both the 7 and 21 July events.

To some of those who would have used the London Underground, the

21 July attempt may have reinforced or exacerbated changes in their behaviours and attitudes to avoid or reduce their use of this form of transport. This may have been compounded by the understanding that in the days after 21 July, the failed suicide bombers were still at large and could therefore launch another attack. The main effect 21 July may have had was raising the serious prospect that the 7 July bombings were the start of a wave of attacks in London. The UK faced the possibility that a bombing campaign was underway, which unlike the IRA campaign, would entail suicide bombers with no warning of nor limit on the possible destruction.

As with the case studies, 7/7 showed behavioural changes among a significant minority of the populace. The first Rubin survey showed that 32 per cent reported they would use the tubes, trains and buses or travel into central London less often. This is reinforced by London Underground statistics that showed four weeks after the 7 July bombings and the failed attacks two weeks later, there was a 10–15 per cent decrease in passenger numbers on weekdays and 20–25 per cent at weekends.[28] As London Underground noted, the lower numbers at the weekend were likely to be passengers who had a choice of whether to travel compared to weekday commuters who had to use the underground to move around London efficiently. The longer-term effect on travel behaviour in the following months is demonstrated by a London Transport report that noted tube passenger numbers in 2005 were 30 million less than that expected that year, and were five million down from the previous year.[29] Passenger numbers were expected to reach one billion in 2005. However, figures for 2006 suggest this was only a temporary lull with passenger volume in June 2006 being 77.6 million journeys made compared to 73.6 million in June 2005.[30] London Underground believe that its determination to resume services as soon as possible was a key factor in persuading people not to avoid travelling on the underground once the system recommenced. Although one of the bombs exploded on a bus, passenger numbers on buses increased after 7/7, possibly because travellers went from using the tube to the buses believing this was a safer form of transport and provided a greater chance of survival from a bombing than being trapped in a tunnel on an underground train.[31]

While underground travel reduced, data from one London regional train service operator, South Eastern, reported a surge in the number of commuters carrying bicycles on trains into London after 7/7 possibly to avoid the perceived dread risk of using the underground or buses in central London.[32] 7/7 also affected the number of visitors to London with attractions in the capital reporting a fall of 6 per cent in the rest of 2005, and tourist numbers in the capital down by about 3 per cent.[33] However, overseas visitors to the UK in 2005 were at a record high of 30 million.[34] This suggests that while visits to London attractions were down, this did not have an effect on the rest of the UK.

The above two studies validate many of the assumptions. While the London and Madrid bombings provide evidence on the psychological and behavioural consequences, further research could be conducted to evaluate risk communication, risk perception and risk amplification. The attacks led to changes in behaviours and attitudes, with the adverse behavioural effects declining in the months after the attacks. The numbers who had PTSD declined in the London studies, but remained the same in the six months after the Madrid attacks.

Contributions to the key fields

As this study took a multidisciplinary approach, it would be appropriate to investigate how this book may contribute to key areas in the fields of risk analysis, psychiatry and international relations, and what worked well and what did not.

Risk analysis and the social amplification of risk

The social amplification of risk model can be adapted as a valuable tool for international relations. As mentioned in the Introduction, the social amplification of risk model recognises how social institutions and structures examine a risk to shape its potential effects upon society, and the responses of management institutions and people.[35] There are three main areas where the social amplification of risk model can be adapted for wider applicability in political science and international relations.

First, the risk event can be the terrorist attack, or alert advisories. Second, the five stations that Roger Kasperson outlined that influence risk perception need to include additional variables to assess how a society's response to a strategic terror event influences peoples' behaviours and attitudes. This includes how the emergency and public health response can affect people's fears, anxieties and perceived risk.

In the Tokyo case study, for instance, the delay in the arrival of the emergency services after the sarin attack led to heightened fear and anxiety among those passengers on the attacked trains. During the anthrax attacks, the CDC's poor risk communication led a number of postal workers to believe they were being given a cheaper and less effective antibiotic than that given to Congressional and media workers at sites that had been exposed to anthrax, therefore heightening their anxiety. In the months following 9/11, the extensive debate in the US about possible further attacks on airlines reinforced the perception that driving long distances was safer than taking internal flights. This led to an increase in road fatalities.

The third area for adaptation is how the social amplification of risk model can be employed to further the understanding of strategic terrorism as a tool of coercion. While the perpetrator of a risk event may seek to influence the political system, the responses in the five stations of the model can amplify or attenuate the potential coercive power. This risk model therefore has considerable value for use in the political context.

While the social amplification of risk model has a number of merits, a key constraint to using this approach is the limited data available to populate the framework. Ideally the researcher would have sufficient information to populate the prime nodes (e.g. public responses, government actions and media). In reality, the researcher often has to draw upon limited evidence for specific areas. This raises the question of whether there could be inaccuracies in the conclusions drawn. Its predictive value could then be questioned. In addition, it could be questioned whether the model has sufficient variables to capture the main interactions within and between the stations, and whether these elements may be too simplified.

Although there are limitations in the use of this framework, the model aids understanding of the effects of strategic terrorism through guiding the researcher to ask a series of questions of what effect certain events may have on the public and the political response to strategic terrorism. Importantly it has the ability to be used on different levels from the macro level of assessing the potential coercive ability of attacks through to the micro level of how individuals could perceive risks and thus change their behaviours and attitudes. Through a greater understanding of the cause and effect of the variables interacting, the researcher could then use the framework as a guide to assess what actions could be taken by governments and authorities at certain points to reduce the terror and coercion generated by strategic terrorism.

Psychiatry – advancing the understanding of panic and PTSD

One of the main features in this book has been the examination of whether panic occurred following attacks and the use of the DSM of mental disorders tool to understand the terror generated. In the mental health area, this study does not necessarily add to or challenge the definition of panic. It is worth noting that the evidence in the case studies supports the mental health and crisis management assumption that panic is rare following incidents, whether they be an intentional act like terrorism or unintentional, for instance, a fire in a building. However, these were largely based on evidence drawn from first-hand accounts or observations made by others. This raises the question of whether psychiatry could provide a better interpretation of panic for use in the field outside the clinical diagnoses setting during and shortly after an attack from personal accounts and observations collated. It is uncertain whether the use and understanding of the term panic by the public in expressing their responses is strictly in line with that of Robert Campbell's definition of panic as an 'overwhelming anxiety; panic attack'. This would be an area that psychiatry might need to address with its own expertise to better equip its researchers and interpret the responses of individuals following terrorist attacks.

An area where this study could contribute to the knowledge of psychiatry is to question the most appropriate use of the DSM tool of mental disorders to evaluate whether individuals have PTSD or related symptoms. It needs to be considered whether the checklist of symptoms for PTSD can lead to medicalise symptoms (identifying adverse conditions that are not there), rather than looking at the causes of symptoms which could be regarded as natural responses. In particular criteria C that include 'effortful avoidance and numbing/dissociation' to avoid activities related to the trauma may need to be revised for use in the strategic terrorism context. This study demonstrates that there is a significant proportion of the public that changes their behaviours and attitudes to reduce the perceived risk of terrorism. As Shalev noted in the Second Intifada chapter, many of these responses could be viewed as quite normal and nothing to be concerned about.[36] Therefore it could be considered whether the DSM-IV TR checklist is too sensitive to certain changes in behaviours after a terrorist attack and whether it can appropriately take into account the fact that some responses do not warrant an assertion that someone has an adverse symptom.

Many instances where changed behaviour may be seen as 'irrational' could instead be seen as reasonable based on the situation of uncertainty an individual is faced with, and the information the individual is presented with. The latter then frames their risk perceptions and impacts their decisions. There may be instances where, if individuals were given accurate and sufficient information, this would allow them to make an *informed* decision; their response may well be different and thus not 'irrational'. In the strategic terrorism context where there are multiple channels of risk communication, psychiatry could learn from risk communication to evaluate to what degree people's responses are influenced by the information they are given. Their responses could therefore be a product of the information received that frames their risk perceptions which then affect their behaviours and attitudes. This element would also fit neatly in the social amplification of risk model. Despite these limitations, international relations and political science have a lot to gain from incorporating rigorous quantitative evidence, and the tools and techniques employed to further understand the terror effects of terror.

International relations

There are three areas where this book advances the field of terrorism studies in international relations. First, the myth of a panic-prone public should be dispelled in preference to viewing individuals as changing their behaviours and attitudes to reduce the perceived risks of terrorism to themselves and those around them. Second, the discipline can be strengthened by employing tools from risk analysis and mental health. Third, there is extensive quantitative evidence on how the public responds to strategic terrorism and from this, political ramifications can be ascertained.

The evidence challenges the common conception of a panic-prone public, held in some areas of political science, and supports those advocating resilience. As outlined in the introductory chapters and subsequently shown in the case study evidence, the concept of individuals panicking and the use of the term panic are too widely used without sufficient proof. The evidence demonstrates that the public is more resilient to extreme situations than many political science experts and policy-makers would believe. It needs to be recognised that panic rarely occurs and that an attack can cause changes in behaviours and attitudes to varying degrees which in some circumstances can cause further casualties and fatalities.

The multidisciplinary approach clearly shows that international relations can and should use the new tools developed and tested in other disciplines when discussing the terror of strategic terrorism. While terrorism has been tackled extensively by political science and international relations, they have lacked effective techniques to fully understand its effects on population centres and to make informed analyses about its social and political effects as a tool of coercion. The incorporation of key features from risk analysis (risk communication, risk perception and the social amplification of risk) and mental health goes a long way to address these deficiencies. Risk analysis provides a valuable framework to incorporate evidence drawn from a wide variety of sources while the mental health area has a robust diagnostic tool to measure the short- and long-term effects of terror.

Leading on from new tools and techniques is the plethora of quantitative evidence available from DSM-based studies through to public opinion surveys that collectively enable the researcher to quantify the effect of terror. Although the data sources vary according to the studies available, the increasing amount of terrorism studies being undertaken by risk analysis and mental health provides political science with an increasing amount of data sources to draw upon.

A key contribution in the study of terrorism is demonstrating to what degree disorientation occurs to create an effective form of strategic coercion. The disorientation that does transpire centres more on individuals changing their daily routines, sometimes undermining their safety, rather than collectively influencing the political system through causing the targeted populace to feel they are completely alienated from society and to lose all confidence in the status quo.

At most, the disorientation that occurs can hinder a state's ability to recover from an attack. Beyond those in close vicinity of the terrorist strike (on the attacked bus, train or in the building), the repercussions for the wider society are mainly disruption to the public's normal behaviours (e.g. avoiding venues with large crowds or transportation systems or locations previously attacked). In some situations, this could place extensive pressure on limited public health resources or have economic implications with segments of the public not returning to previously attacked locations or transport systems.

In more severe cases, the release of a chemical weapon that could not be easily cleaned up or a radiological weapon may cause contamination to such a degree that it prohibits the use of business districts for subsequent months or even years. Even if the area was decontaminated and declared safe by authorities, workers, customers and companies may feel the perceived risk of re-entering the area is too great despite assurances of it being safe to do so. In the case of the 1995 sarin attack, it was fortunate that Aum Shinrikyo used a chemical that was rapidly degraded to a harmless substance allowing for the attacked transport system to resume hours later.

While these responses can adversely affect individual's risk perceptions to such a degree that they calmly embark on activities that can be detrimental to the safety of themselves and those around them, or place pressure on limited resources like public health assets, these outcomes are not sufficient themselves to initiate political change in line with the perpetrators' political objectives, but possibly have economic ramifications.

Despite this conclusion, it needs to be considered to what degree the political objectives of terrorist groups examined in the case studies were attainable either due to the ambiguity over what they sought or to their demands being unrealistic. Aum Shinrikyo sought to cause a *coup d'état* in preparation for what they saw was impending Armageddon. Al Qaeda did not release a clearly defined agenda of political demands after 9/11. The rationale behind the anthrax attacks and who the perpetrators were remain unknown. With several factions involved in the Second Intifada, the political aims of the uprising varied from seeking to gain an independent Palestine to destroying Israel. The case of strategic terror where there was a clearly defined and understood objective was the 1991 Gulf War, where Iraq sought to get Israel to retaliate and thus undermine the allied coalition. A lesson the Gulf War provides for strategic terrorism is that even when the populace is subjected to extensive attacks, there is a large degree of resilience. The terror generated was insufficient to undermine the whole political system. The terror of strategic terrorism may cause individuals to change their daily routines, but collectively there is little evidence to suggest that this provides sufficient momentum to cause the disorientation and terror across the populace sought by terrorist groups to influence and coerce the political system in line with their objectives.

Policy recommendations

The shifting of attitudes and behaviour caused by strategic terrorism is a two-part process — those caused directly by an attack followed by those created by the targeted country's reaction. The latter can be further explained through the social amplification of risk framework where amplified risk can lead to behavioural changes as discussed in the earlier chapters. The public's responses can also be divided into two: primary and secondary avoidance patterns. First, the public tends to avoid or visit less frequently region/towns or facilities that are attacked to reduce the perceived probability of being exposed to a terror incident. While many undertake actions in direct response to the perceived threat, this is often accompanied by a series of secondary actions that are not directly related to the original attack or threat. The latter can be amplified or reduced by the authorities' immediate response after an attack and in the weeks and months that follow. This can affect the overall number of casualties including those that would not normally be included in the attack statistics. The human cost of a strategic terror attack does not stop with the event itself. The longer-term consequences should be taken into account when measuring the true human cost and political effects of terrorist attacks.

People react sensibly to strategic terrorism but this can be undermined by the actions of politicians and authorities. However, as the terror of strategic terrorism is limited, the potential consequence of actions by politicians and authorities is not extensive. It can be speculated that in certain scenarios the response of the targeted country could have a significant effect. If the lethality or contamination from an attack was significantly greater, like a CBR strike, how a country responds (communication and public health response) could affect the number of casualties. Fortunately, the case study evidence base for these types of incidents is limited.

Three key recommendations that could be integrated into emergency planning and policy are listed below.

1 **Preparation**

It is essential that from the outset of an attack the people trust their government including their public health authorities' advice on measures that will enhance their well-being and that of those around them. As part of advising the public to be vigilant and issuing terrorism alerts, authorities should also consider advising the public that were a major terrorist attack to occur, there may be ambiguity in the advice provided in the first few hours after an attack. In particular this could be so after a CBR event where the nature of the device may initially be unknown. As such the changing information should not be interpreted as the authorities mishandling the situation. Within the first hour of an attack authorities need to provide information to the public on what they believe may be the cause. After a severe attack like a CBR device, medical facilities may not be able to cope with the demand (either through closing because it is contaminated or overwhelmed by patients). Consequently, the public need to be aware that they may be advised to conduct self-triage to establish whether they should seek medical care. Where appropriate the public could be advised following an attack on what symptoms to look out for to ascertain to the degree of exposure or contamination. This aspect is essential to building initial trust and effective engagement with the public.

2 **Response**

In the initial period after an attack (particularly after a CBR event), medical facilities could be severely overstretched. In the case of a CBR incident, authorities need to provide messages quickly and avoid holding statements that only recognise that an incident has occurred and emergency services are on scene. The public needs to be told what is known, not known, and when more information will be provided.

The public needs to be regarded as not prone to panic but able to be effectively engaged by authorities. Accurate information should be disseminated as soon as possible to inform the public of what actions they are advised to undertake or avoid. This could reduce secondary contamination and assist hospitals receiving the injured from being overwhelmed by the 'worried well'. Advice could include suggesting those with no symptoms or very mild symptoms to go home and take a shower. At the same time, health authorities would want to avoid individuals attending medical facilities or returning home in (or passing through) contaminated areas thus risking secondary contamination. Implementing these strategies could, though, be undermined should a terrorist attack entail the detonation of multiple devices with different chemicals or include the use of a radiological dispersal device. The targeted populace and public authorities could then be faced with an array of contaminants to deal with.

One possible means to reduce the pressure on limited public health resources is to appeal to the public's altruism by conveying the message that certain actions could risk the well-being and health of others. For instance, attending medical facilities after a CBR attack if they could alternatively treat themselves could prevent those who need care from receiving it, or unnecessarily acquiring certain antibiotics could put pressure on limited supplies.

3 **Recovery**

In the following weeks and months, effective risk communication will be needed to avert inappropriate risk framing. This should be designed to:

- Prevent, as much as possible, the public undertaking adverse behaviours to avoid perceived dread risks (e.g. avoidance of certain means of transport). This could be best achieved through effective risk communication by first understanding the public's perceived risks and probable behavioural responses to various actions. This information could be used to create messages that inform the public of the actual risks associated with certain actions.

- Encourage appropriate risk framing for the public to return to decontaminated areas regarded by authorities to be safe. The challenge is to address the public's concerns the actual safety of an area that is officially declared safe and about unknown long-term health risks, for instance, from a radiological or chemical attack in a populated area. With a non-CBR attack, there may be concerns surrounding the quality of the air from collapsed buildings as occurred at Ground Zero following 9/11.

Concluding remarks

The threat of terrorism involving both conventional and non-conventional devices to cause maximum destruction and disruption is likely to persist for the foreseeable future. As such, the findings and recommendations are of considerable value and insight to those looking to understand the terror of terrorism and for policy-makers in responding to the threat.

Preparing for and responding to possible threats and attacks, entail more than just the physiological aspects of stockpiling decontamination equipment, screening bags, procuring vaccines, etc. Psychological and behavioural effects of terrorism should be addressed as well. Strategic terrorism can cause short- and long-term mental health compilations from PTSD in its severest form through to related symptoms like stress. But critical to the response in reducing the impact of strategic terrorism is engaging the public effectively through various forms of communication and preparedness. The importance of these will vary depending on the event and be influenced by the countries' prior experience of terrorism.

Fortunately terrorist groups have not successfully employed CBR weapons to cause extensive and persistent contamination. The use of such weapons would exploit the public's dread risk perceptions of seeking a risk-free environment and concerns over how safe an area that has been decontaminated actually is. A minimal or very low level of contamination that is regarded as safe may prove to be a hard sell to the public by the authorities. This has the potential to cause the most significant changes in the people's behaviours and attitudes, leading them to take actions which may be detrimental to their well-being, and the well-being of those around them; therefore undermining a society's ability to recover.

While this study cannot provide a uniformed and one-size-fits-all strategy to help countries prepare for, respond to and recover from terrorist attacks, a common theme is that the terror of strategic terrorism directly generated by an attack is limited. Terror is probably an inappropriate term to label the effects of strategic terrorism. Disruption and distorting risk perceptions are better suited.

The desired shifting of attitudes and behaviour, as defined by Lawrence Freedman's strategic terror definition as an intended consequence of threats and attacks, should be regarded as both the consequence of direct action from the perpetrators and the response of the targeted country. The latter can cause a change in behaviours and attitudes be detrimental to the well-being of the populace, in some cases causing death, that can be reduced through effective risk communication and risk characterisation. International relations requires additional tools outside its traditional area to discuss and advise on terrorism. The risk perception, risk communication and mental health effects have been well documented and discussed separately in various areas, but less so among the international relations and government policy communities where there is a tendency to believe in the existence of a panic-prone public. Integrating the findings with associated studies would provide a credible quantitative and qualitative evidence base for discussion of the actual terror of strategic terrorism, and importantly, for measures to prepare and engage with the public.

Notes

1 Introduction

1 Tara O'Toole, Michael Mair and Thomas V. Inglesby. 'Shining Light on "Dark Winter"', *Clinical Infectious Diseases*, Vol. 34, No. 7 (2002), pp. 265–274 and 'Dark Winter Exercise Findings', *University of Pittsburgh Medical Center*. Online, available at www.upmc-biosecurity.org/website/events/2001_darkwinter/findings. html (accessed 14 March 2008).
2 Christian W. Erickson and Bethany A. Barratt, 'Prudence or Panic? Preparedness Exercises, Counterterror Mobilization, and Media Coverage – Dark Winter, TOPOFF 1 and 2', *Journal of Homeland Security and Emergency Management*, Vol. 1, No. 4 (2004), p. 3.
3 Robert Pape, *Dying to Win: The Strategic Logic of Suicide Terrorism* (New York: Random House: 2005), p. 28.
4 Walter Laqueur, 'Postmodern Terrorism', *Foreign Affairs*, September–October 1996, p. 36.
5 Grant Wardlaw, *Political Terrorism: Theory, Tactics and Counter-measures* (Cambridge: Cambridge University Press, 1982), p. 34.
6 Martin Navias, 'Saddam's Scud War and Ballistic Missile Proliferation', *London Defence Studies*, No. 6 (1991), pp. 54–55.
7 Aaron Karp, *Ballistic Missile Proliferation: The Politics and Technics* (Oxford: Oxford University Press, 1995), p. 48.
8 Andrew Lambert, *The Psychology of Air Power Based on Case Studies since the 1940s* (London: RUSI, 1995), p. 29.
9 Richard J. Overy, *Air War 1939–1945* (London: Europa Publications, 1980), p. 208.
10 Irving Janis, *Air War and Emotional Stress: Psychological Studies of Bombing and Civilian Defense* (London: McGraw Hill, 1951), 1st edn.
11 Edgar Jones, Robin Woolven, Bill Durodié and Simon Wessely, 'Civilian Morale During World War Two: Responses to Air-raids Re-examined', *Social History of Medicine*, Vol. 17 (2004), pp. 463–479.
12 Eric Morris and Alan Hoe, *Terrorism: Threat and Response* (London: Macmillan, 1988), p. 44.
13 D. P. Sharma, *Victims of Terrorism* (New Delhi: A. P. H. Publishing Corporation, 2003).
14 Peter R. Neumann and M. L. R. Smith, *The Strategy of Terrorism: How It Works, and Why It Fails* (Abingdon: Routledge, 2008), pp. 59–65.
15 Lawrence Freedman, 'The Politics of Warning: Terrorism and Risk Communication', *Intelligence and National Security*, Vol. 20, No. 3 (September, 2005), pp. 379–418.

16 Jessica Stern, 'Dreaded Risks and the Control of Biological Weapons', *International Security*, Vol. 27, No. 3 (Winter 2002/03), pp. 89–123.
17 Simon Wessely and Valery Krasnov (eds), *The Psychological Responses to New Terrorism: A NATO–Russia Dialogue* (Amsterdam: IOS Press, 2005).
18 Paul Wilkinson, *Terrorism and the Liberal State* (London: Macmillan, 1977), p. 47.
19 Ibid.
20 Andrew Lambert, *The Psychology of Air Power*, p. 5.
21 Ibid., p. 8.

2 Overview of the key disciplines

 1 John Garnett, 'Strategic Studies and Its Assumptions', in John Baylis, Ken Booth, John Garnett *et al.*, *Contemporary Strategy: Theories and Policies* (London: Croom Helm, 1975), p. 3.
 2 Peter R. Neumann, *Britain's Long War: British Strategy in the Northern Ireland Conflict, 1969–98* (Basingstoke: Palgrave, 2003), p. 4.
 3 Garnett, 'Strategic Studies and Its Assumptions', p. 5.
 4 Neumann, *Britain's Long War*, p. 4.
 5 Garnett, 'Strategic Studies and Its Assumptions', p. 11.
 6 See Kenneth Waltz, 'The Emerging Structure of International Politics', *International Security*, Vol. 18, No. 2 (1993), pp. 44–79.
 7 Garnett, 'Strategic Studies and Its Assumptions', pp. 12–14 and Neumann, *Britain's Long War*, p. 5.
 8 Peter Paret, 'Clausewitz', in Peter Paret (ed.), *Makers of Modern Strategy: From Machiavelli to the Nuclear Age* (Oxford: Clarendon Press, 1986), p. 207.
 9 Ibid., p. 204.
10 Lawrence Freedman, 'Strategic Terror and Amateur Psychology', *The Political Quarterly*, Vol. 76, No. 2, April (2005), p. 162.
11 Ibid., p. 163.
12 R. D. Crenlinstein, 'Terrorism and Meaning: Terrorism as a Struggle over Access to the Communication Structure', in Paul Wilkinson and A. M. Stewart (eds), *Contemporary Research on Terrorism* (Aberdeen: Aberdeen University Press, 1987), p. 419.
13 Peter R. Neumann and M. L. R. Smith, 'Strategic Terrorism: The Framework and its Fallacies', *The Journal of Strategic Studies*, Vol. 28, No. 4 (2005), p. 577.
14 Lawrence Freedman, 'Strategic Terror and Amateur Psychology', *Political Quarterly*, Vol. 76, No. 2 (April 2005), p. 161.
15 Thomas Schelling, *The Strategy of Conflict* (Harvard, MA: Harvard University Press, 1960), p. 4.
16 Conor Gearty, *Terrorism* (Aldershot: Dartmouth, 1996), p. xi.
17 Walter Laqueur, *The Age of Terrorism* (London: Weidenfeld and Nicolson, 1987), p. 145.
18 Paul Wilkinson, 'Terrorist Targets and Tactics: New Risks to World Order', *Conflict Studies*, No. 236 (1990), p. 1.
19 Bruce Hoffman, *Inside Terrorism* (London: Victor Gollancz, 1998), p. 43.
20 Thomas Thornton, 'Terror as a Weapon of Political Agitation', in Harry Eckstein (ed.), *Internal War: Problems and Approaches* (New York: Free Press of Glencoe, 1964), p. 73.
21 Andrew Rathmell, *Covert Action and International Terrorism in Middle East Politics: Syria 1949–1961*, Doctoral thesis, King's College London, 1994, p. 5. Rathmell lists the rules and procedures that include the Geneva Conventions and various international agreements where the central element is the prohibition of attacks on non-combatants.

22 Brian Jenkins, *International Terrorism: A New Kind of Warfare* (RAND P-5326, 1974), p. 2.
23 Laqueur, *The Age of Terrorism*, p. 5.
24 Max Abrahams, 'Why Terrorism Does Not Work', *International Security*, Vol. 31, No. 2 (2006), p. 43.
25 Abrahams, 'Why Terrorism Does Not Work', p. 52. Abrahams cites Robert A. Hart, 'Democracy and the Successful Use of Economic Sanctions', *Political Research Quarterly*, Vol. 53, No. 2 (2000), p. 279.
26 Abrahams, 'Why Terrorism Does Not Work', pp. 43–44.
27 Pape, *Dying to Win* and Robert Pape, 'The Strategic Logic of Suicide Terrorism', *American Political Science Review*, Vol. 97, No. 3 (2003), pp. 1–19.
28 Pape, *Dying to Win*, p. 65.
29 Ibid., p. 75.
30 Abrahams, 'Why Terrorism Does Not Work', p. 46.
31 N. O. Berry, 'Theories on the Efficacy of Terrorism', in Wilkinson and Stewart, *Contemporary Research on Terrorism*, p. 293.
32 Ibid.
33 Neumann and Smith, 'Strategic Terrorism', p. 574.
34 Ibid.
35 Paul Wilkinson, *Terrorism Versus Democracy: The Liberal State Responses* (London: Frank Cass, 2002), p. 49.
36 Wilkinson, *Terrorism Versus Democracy*, pp. 49, 220.
37 Garnett, 'Strategic Studies and Its Assumptions', p. 3.
38 Neumann and Smith, 'Strategic Terrorism', p. 577.
39 Alex P. Schmid and Albert J. Jongman, *Political Terrorism: A New Guide to Actors, Authors, Concepts, Databases, Theories, Literature* (Oxford: Transaction Books, 1988), p. 2.
40 Neumann and Smith, 'Strategic Terrorism', p. 572.
41 Neuman and Smith, *The Strategy of Terrorism*, p. 95.
42 Wardlaw, *Political Terrorism*, p. 34.
43 Ibid.
44 Thomas Thornton, 'Terror as a Weapon of Political Agitation', in Harry Eckstein (ed.), *Internal War: Problems and Approaches* (New York: Free Press of Glencoe, 1964), p. 85.
45 Wardlaw, *Political Terrorism*, p. 182.
46 Harvey Griesman, 'Terrorism and the Closure of Society: A Social-impact Projection', *Technological Forecasting and Social Change*, Vol. 14, No. 2 (1979), pp. 135–146 cited in Wardlaw, *Political Terrorism*, p. 197.
47 Wilkinson, 'Terrorist Targets and Tactics: New Risks to World Order', p. 4.
48 Thomas Schelling, *The Strategy of Conflict*, p. 5.
49 Ibid., pp. 5–6.
50 Wardlaw, *Political Terrorism*, p. 35, and Gearty, *Terrorism*, p. 9.
51 Schelling, *The Strategy of Conflict*, p. 15.
52 Schmid and Jongman, *Political Terrorism*, p. 19.
53 Wardlaw, *Political Terrorism*, pp. 35–36, and Neumann and Smith, 'Strategic Terrorism', p. 587.
54 Charles Rycroft, *Anxiety and Neurosis* (London, Allan Lane, 1968).
55 *Stedman's Medical Dictionary*, 27th edn (New York: Lippincott, Williams and Wilkins, 2002), p. 107.
56 Ibid., p. 654.
57 Ibid., p. 1304.
58 Robert Jean Campbell, *Psychiatric Dictionary*, 7th edn (Oxford: Oxford University Press, 1996), p. 507.

59 Ibid.. p. 507.
60 Simon Wessely, 'Victimhood and Resilience: The London Attacks – Aftermath', *New England Journal of Medicine*, Vol. 353, No. 6 (2005), p. 549.
61 David Alan Alexander and Susan Klein, 'Biochemical Terrorism: Too Awful to Contemplate, Too Serious to Ignore', *British Journal of Psychiatry*, Vol. 183 (2003), p. 492.
62 Ilan Kutz and Avraham Bleich, 'Conventional, Chemical and Biological Terror of Mass Destruction: Psychological Aspects and Psychiatric Guideline', in Joshua Shemer and Y. Shoenfeld (eds), *Terror and Medicine – Medical Aspects of Biological, Chemical and Nuclear Terrorism* (Lengerich: Pabst Science Publishers, 2003), p. 495.
63 *The ICD-10 Classification of Mental and Behavioural Disorders*, 4th edn (Washington, DC: American Psychiatric Association, 1994), cited in Kutz and Bleich, 'Conventional, Chemical and Biological Terror of Mass Destruction', p. 495.
64 *Diagnostic and Statistical Manual of Mental Disorder*. 4th edn, Text Revision (DSM-IV-TR) (Washington, DC: American Psychiatric Association, 2003), p. xxix.
65 Ginny Sprang, 'The Psychological Impact of Isolated Acts of Terrorism', in Andrew Silke (ed.), *Terrorists, Victims and Society: Psychological Perspectives on Terrorism and Its Consequences* (Chichester: Wiley, 2003), p. 137 and *Diagnostic and Statistical Manual of Mental Disorders*, p. 463.
66 William E. Schlenger, Juesta M. Caddell, Lori Ebert *et al.*, 'Psychological Reactions to Terrorist Attacks: Findings from the National Study of Americans' Reactions to September 11', *Journal of American Medical Association*, Vol. 288, No. 5 (2002), p. 581.
67 Alexander and Klein, 'Biochemical Terrorism', p. 493.
68 Ibid.
69 Ross H. Pastel, Collective Behaviors: Mass Panic and Outbreaks of Multiple Unexplained Symptoms', *Military Medicine*, Vol. 166 (December 2001), pp. 44–46.
70 Ibid.
71 Naomi Breslau, Victoria C. Lucia, and Glenn C. Davis, 'Partial PTSD Versus Full PTSD: An Empirical Examination of Associated Impairment', *Psychological Medicine*, Vol. 34 (2004), pp. 1205–1214. See also Jerome. C. Wakefield and Robert. L. Spitzer, 'Lowered Estimates – but of What?', *Archives of General Psychiatry*, Vol. 59 (2002), pp. 129–130.
72 Paul Slovic, 'Perceptions of Risk', in Paul Slovic (ed.), *The Perception of Risk* (London: Earthscan Publications Ltd, 2000), p. 223.
73 See Paul Slovic, Baruch Fischhoff and Sarah Lichtenstein, 'Rating the Risks', *Environment*, Vol. 21, No. 4 (1979), pp. 14–20, 36–39; Paul Slovic, Baruch Fischhoff and Sarah Lichtenstein, 'Perceived Risk: Psychological Factors and Social Implications', Proceedings of the Royal Society of London. Series A, Mathematical and Physical Sciences, Vol. 376, No. 1764 (1981), pp. 17–34; and Frederic Bouder, Brooke Rogers, Kristian Krieger and Ragnar Lofstedt, 'Understanding and Communicating the Risks of Nuclear Waste', in Brooke Rogers, Kristian Krieger, Frederic Bouder and Ragnar Lofstedt (eds), *The Future of Nuclear Power in Europe: The Role of Public Perceptions and Risk Communication*, 2006. Unpublished report.
74 Paul Slovic, 'Perceptions of Risk', p. 223.
75 Carol S. Fullerton, Robert J. Ursano, Anne E. Norwood and Harry H. Holloway, 'Trauma, Terrorism, Disaster', in Robert J. Ursano, Carol S. Fullteron and Anne E. Norwood (eds), *Terrorism and Disaster: Individual and Community*

Mental Health Interventions (Cambridge: Cambridge University Press, 2003), pp. 1–21; and Brooke Rogers, Richard Amlot, G. James Rubin, Simon Wessely and Kristian Krieger, 'Mediating the Social and Psychological Impacts of Terrorist Attacks: The Role of Risk Perception and Risk Communication', *International Review of Psychiatry*, Vol. 19, No. 3 (2007), p. 280.

76 David Ropeik and Paul Slovic, 'Risk Communication: A Neglected Tool in Protecting Public Health', *Risk in Perspective*, Vol. 11, No. 2 (2003), p. 1.

77 Paul Slovic, Melissa L. Finucane, Ellen Peters and Donald G. MacGregor, 'Risk as Analysis and Risk as Feelings: Some Thoughts about Affect, Reason, Risk, and Rationality', *Risk Analysis*, Vol. 24, No. 2 (2004), p. 311.

78 Rogers *et al.*, 'Mediating the social and psychological impacts of terrorist attacks', pp. 279–288.

79 Slovic *et al.*, 'Risk as Analysis and Risk as Feelings', p. 311.

80 Adapted from Ropeik and Slovic, 'Risk Communication', pp. 2–3.

81 Paul Slovic, Baruch Fischhoff and Sarah Lichtenstein, 'Facts and Fears: Understanding Perceived Risk', in Slovic, *The Perception of Risk*, p. 142.

82 Ibid., p. 142.

83 Cited in Terence Monmaney, 'Response to Terror: The Psychological Toll', *Los Angeles Times*, 29 September 2001, p. A1.

84 Lennart Sjoberg, 'The Perceived Risk of Terrorism', *Risk Management: An International Journal*, Vol. 7, No. 1 (2005), pp. 43–61.

85 Rogers *et al.*, 'Mediating the Social and Psychological Impacts of Terrorist Attacks', p. 281 and Slovic *et al.*, 'Risk as Analysis and Risk as Feelings', p. 312.

86 'Introduction and Overview', in Slovic, *The Perception of Risk*, p. xxiii.

87 Gilbert F. White, *Human Adjustment to Floods: A Geographical Approach to the Flood in the United States* (Chicago, IL: University of Chicago Press, 1981), Baruch Fischoff, Sarah Lichtenstein and Paul Slovic, *Acceptable Risk* (New York: Cambridge University Press, 1981), Paul Slovic, 'Risk Perception', *Science*, Vol. 236 (April 1987), pp. 280–285, cited in Ragnar Lofstedt, 'Risk Communication: Pitfalls and Promises', *European Review*, Vol. 11, No. 3 (2003), p. 417.

88 *Improving Risk Communication*, National Research Committee on Risk Perceptions and Communication (Washington, DC: National Academy Press, 1989), p. 151.

89 *Improving Risk Communication*, p. 5.

90 Fischhoff, 'Psychological Perception of Risk'.

91 Lofstedt, 'Risk Communication', p. 417.

92 See *Improving Risk Communication*; Baruch Fischhoff, 'Risk Perception and Communication Unplugged: Twenty Years of Process', *Risk Analysis*, Vol. 15, No. 2 (1995), pp. 137–145; Lofstedt, 'Risk Communication: Pitfalls and Promises', pp. 417–435.

93 Paul F. Deisler, 'A Perspective: Risk Analysis as a Tool for Reducing the Risks of Terrorism', *Risk Analysis*, Vol. 22, No. 3 (2002), p. 408.

94 Fischhoff, 'Risk Perception and Communication Unplugged', p. 137.

95 Baruch Fischhoff, 'Psychological Perception of Risk', in David Kamien (ed.), *The McGraw-Hill Homeland Security Handbook* (New York: McGraw Hill, 2006), pp. 463–492.

96 Ibid.

97 Rogers *et al.*, 'Mediating the Social and Psychological Impacts of Terrorist Attacks', p. 284.

98 Timothy Earle, 'Thinking Aloud about Trust: A Protocol Analysis of Trust in Risk Management', *Risk Analysis*, Vol. 24, No. 1 (2004), pp. 169–183; Roger E. Kasperson, Dominic Golding and Seth Tuler, 'Societal Distrust as a Factor

in Siting Hazardous Facilities and Communicating Risks', *Journal of Social Issues*, Vol. 48, No. 4 (1992), pp. 161–187; Ragnar Lofstedt, *Risk Management in Post-Trust Societies* (Basingstoke: Palgrave Macmillan, 2005); Nick Pidgeon, 'Exploring the Dimensionality of Trust in Risk Regulation', *Risk Analysis*, Vol. 23, No. 5 (October 2003), pp. 961–972; Orwin Renn and Debra Levine, 'Credibility and Trust in Risk Communication', in Roger E. Kasperson and Pieter Jan Stallen (eds), *Communicating Risks to the Public* (Dordrecht: Kluwer Academic, 1991), pp. 175–217.

 99 Slovic *et al.*, 'Risk as Analysis and Risk as Feelings', p. 315.
100 Carmen Keller, Michael Siegrist and Heinz Gutscher, 'The Role of Affect and Availability Heuristics in Risk Communication', *Risk Analysis*, Vol. 26, No. 3 (2006), p. 633.
101 Ibid., p. 637.
102 *Improving Risk Communication*, p. 3.
103 Ann Bostrom, 'Future Risk Communication', unpublished paper, pp. 11–13. Ann Bostrom outlines a variety of social science theories and models pertaining to risk communication and how individuals respond. These include theories of reasoned action, theories of social learning, group decision-making, transtheoretical stages to changes, decision analysis, the health belief model (influential in health risk communication), prospect theory, support theory, subjective expected utility and multiattribute utility theory.
104 Bostrom, 'Future Risk Communication', unpublished paper, p. 12.
105 *Improving Risk Communication*, p. 80.
106 Ibid., p. 24. Generally single messages can be expected to have little effect on recipients' behaviour, but organised programmes or messages, in which different messages are aimed at different specific purposes, can be effective.
107 Ibid., p. 81. The document offers some guidance on what is regarded as acceptable. Generally the use of influencing techniques could compromise important values such as personal autonomy or constitutional guarantees such as freedom of speech or association, and the more closely the influence technique approaches deception, the more it needs to be legitimated in order to be acceptable. Legitimacy is what makes people consider a particular influence attempt either responsible or irresponsible and either appropriate or inappropriate for government officials.
108 Ortwin Renn and Debra Levin, 'Credibility and Trust in Risk Communication', in Kasperson, *Communicating Risks to the Public*, pp. 175–218.
109 Bostrom, 'Future Risk Communication', unpublished paper, p. 11.
110 *Improving Risk Communication*, p. 82.
111 Irving L. Janis and Seymour Feshbach, 'Effects of Fear-Arousing Communications', *Journal of Abnormal and Social Psychology*, Vol. 48, No. 1 (1953), p. 89.
112 Ibid., p. 90.
113 Ibid., p. 88. Janis and Feshbach make reference to the warnings about the danger of nuclear weapons conveyed in civil defence communications in the 1950s that was in their minds probably too alarmist.
114 Edgar Jones, Robin Woolven, William Durodié and Simon Wessely, 'Public Panic and Morale: World War Two Civilian Responses Re-examined in the Light of the Current Anti-terrorist Campaign', *Journal of Risk Research*, Vol. 9, No. 1 (2006), pp. 57–73.
115 Ragnar E. Lofstedt, 'Science Communication and the Swedish Acrylamide "Alarm"', *Journal of Health Communication*, Vol. 8 (2003), p. 414.
116 Douglas Powell and William Leiss, *Mad Cows and Mothers' Milk* (London: Queen's University Press, 1997), p. 11.
117 Ibid.

118 Freedman, 'The Politics of Warning: Terrorism and Risk Communication', p. 387.
119 Paul C. Stern and Harvey V. Fineberg (eds), *Understanding Risk: Informing Decisions in a Democratic Society* (Washington, DC: National Academy Press, 1996), p. 37.
120 Ibid., p. 10.
121 Ibid., p. 39.
122 Baruch Fischhoff, 'Assessing and Communicating the Risks of Terrorism', in Albert H. Teich, Stephen D. Nelson, Stephen J. Lita and Amanda Hunt (eds), *Science and Technology in a Vulnerable World* (Washington, DC: AAAS, 2002), p. 52.
123 Rogers *et al.*, 'Mediating the Social and Psychological Impacts of Terrorist Attacks', pp. 279–288.
124 Roger E. Kasperson and Jeanne X. Kasperson, 'The Social Amplification and Attenuation of Risk', in Howard Hunreuther and Paul Slovic (eds), 'Challenges in Risk Assessment and Risk Management', *The Annals of the American Academy*, Vol. 545 (May 1996), p. 100.
125 Royal Society, *Risk Analysis, Perception and Management: Report of a Royal Society Study Group* (London: Royal Society, 1992), p. 111.
126 Ibid.
127 Kasperson and Kasperson, 'The Social Amplification and Attenuation of Risk', p. 100.
128 Paul Slovic, 'Terrorism as Hazard: A New Species of Trouble', *Risk Analysis*, Vol. 22, No. 3 (2002), p. 426.
129 Royal Society, 'Risk Analysis, Perception and Management', p. 115.
130 John Peterson, 'Perception vs Reality of Radiological Impact: the Goiânia model' *Nuclear News*, Vol. 31, No. 14 (1988), pp. 84–90.
131 Ibid.
132 Ibid.
133 Baruch Fischhoff, Roxana M. Gonzalez, Deborah A. Small and Jennifer S. Lerner, 'Evaluating the Success of Terror Risk Communication', *Biosecurity and Bioterrorism*, Vol. 1, No. 4 (2003), p. 255.
134 See Michael Siegrist, Heinz Gutscher, and Timothy C. Earle, 'Perception of Risk: The Influence of General Trust, and General Confidence', *Journal of Risk Research*, Vol. 8, No. 2 (2005), pp. 145–156, Paul Slovic, 'Trust, Emotion, Sex, Politics, and Science: Surveying the Risk-assessment Battlefield', *Risk Analysis*, Vol. 19, No. 4 (1999), pp. 689–701 and Wouter Poortinga and Nick F. Pidgeon, 'Trust in Risk Regulation: Cause or Consequence of the Acceptability of GM Food?', *Risk Analysis*, Vol. 25, No. 1 (2005), pp. 199–209.
135 Baruch Fischhoff, 'Psychological Perception of Risk', pp. 463–492.
136 *Improving Risk Communication*, pp. 27–29.
137 Ibid., p. 165.
138 Ibid., pp. 164–165.

3 Methodological approach

1 For instance there are DSM surveys of terrorism in Northern Ireland by Ed Cairns which include the Enniskillen bombing of 1987. See Ed Cairns and Christopher Alan Lewis, 'Collective Memories, Political Violence and Mental Health in Northern Ireland', *British Journal of Psychology*, Vol. 90 (1999), pp. 25–33 More recently there are mental health reports on the Oklahoma bombing in 1995. See Carol S. North, Sara J. Nixon, Sheryll Shariat *et al.*, 'Psychiatric disorders among survivors of the Oklahoma City bombing', *Journal of*

the American Medical Association, Vol. 282 (1999), pp. 755–762. Yael Danieli *et al.* have released an 800-page volume for mental health professionals and first responders called *The Trauma of Terrorism* that contains numerous case studies on the psychosocial impact of terrorism including terrorism in Spain (ETA) and Algeria. See Yael Danieli, Danny Brom and Joe Sills (eds), *The Trauma of Terrorism* (New York: Haworth Press, 2005).

2 William E. Schlenger, Juesta M. Caddell, Lori Ebert *et al.*, 'Psychological Reactions to Terrorist Attacks: Findings from the National Study of Americans' Reactions to September 11', *Journal of the American Medical Association*, Vol. 288, No. 5 (August 2002), p. 581.

3 Lennart Sjoberg, 'The Perceived Risk of Terrorism', *Risk Management: An International Journal*, Vol. 7, No. 1 (2005), p. 45.

4 Gallup, 'Terrorism in the United States', *Polls Topics and Trends*, 2002, www.gallup.com, 21 November, 2006, cited in Lennart Sjoberg, 'The Perceived Risk of Terrorism', p. 45.

5 Lennart Sjoberg, 'Editorial: Asking Questions about Risk and Worry: Dilemmas of the Pollsters', *Journal of Risk Research*, Vol. 7. No. 7–8, October–December (2004), pp. 671–672.

6 Ibid., p. 671.

7 Irving L. Janis, *Air War and Emotional Stress. Psychological Studies of Bombing and Civilian Defense* (New York: McGraw Hill, 1951); Enrico L. Quarantelli, 'Images of Withdrawal Behavior in Disasters: Some Basic Misconceptions', *Social Problems*, Vol. 8, No. 1 (1960), pp. 68–79.

8 Ross H. Pastel, Collective Behaviors: Mass Panic and Outbreaks of Multiple Unexplained Symptoms', *Military Medicine*, Vol. 166, December (2001), pp. 44–46.

9 Edgar Jones, Robin Woolven, Bill Durodié and Simon Wessely, 'Civilian Morale during World War Two: Responses to Air-raids Re-examined', *Social History of Medicine*, Vol. 17 (2004), p. 463.

10 Janis, *Air War and Emotional Stress*, pp. 26, 35.

11 Jonathan Sime, 'The Concept of Panic', in David Canter (ed.), *Fires and Human Behaviour* (2nd edn) (London: David Fulton, 1980), p. 75.

12 Ira Helsloot and Arnout Ruitenberg, 'Citizen Response to Disasters: A Survey of Literature and Some Practical Implications', *Journal of Contingencies and Crisis Management*, Vol. 12, No. 3 (September 2004), pp. 98–111.

13 Sime, 'The Concept of Panic', p. 73.

14 Carol Fullerton, George Brandt and Robert Ursano, 'Chemical and Biological Weapons: Silent Agents of Terror', in Robert Ursano and Ann Norwood (eds), *Emotional Aftermath of the Persian Gulf War: Veterans, Families, Communities, and Nations* (Washington, DC: American Psychiatric Press, 1996), pp. 111–142; and Tim Cook, 'Against God-inspired Conscience: The Perception of Gas Warfare as a Weapon of Mass Destruction, 1915–1939', *War and Society*, Vol. 18 (2000), pp. 47–69.

15 Harshit Sinha, 'Plague: A Challenge for Urban Crisis Management', *Journal of Contingencies and Crisis Management*, Vol. 8, No. 1 (March 2000), pp. 42–54.

16 David Alan Alexander and Susan Klein, 'Biochemical Terrorism: Too Awful to Contemplate, Too Serious to Ignore', *British Journal of Psychiatry*, Vol. 183 (2003), p. 493.

17 John Peterson, 'Perception vs Reality of Radiological Impact: The Goiânia Model' *Nuclear News*, Vol. 31, No. 14 (1988), pp. 84–90.

18 See Arieh Shalev, 'Posttraumatic Stress Disorder among Injured Survivors of a Terrorist Attack. Predictive Value of Early Intrusion and Avoidance Symptoms', *Journal of Nervous and Mental Disease*, Vol. 180, No. 8 (1992), pp. 505–509 and

North *et al.*, 'Psychiatric Disorders among Survivors of the Oklahoma City Bombing', pp. 755–762.

19 Avoidance in non-terrorism incidents includes those who have been in a car accident and subsequently become less willing to drive. See Richard A. Bryant and Allison G. Harvey, 'Avoidant Coping Style and Post-traumatic Stress Following Motor Vehicle Accidents', *Behaviour Research and Therapy*, Vol. 33, No. 6 (1995), pp. 631–635.

20 Janis, *Air War and Emotional Stress*, p. 118.

21 Sinha, 'Plague: A Challenge for Urban Crisis Management', pp. 50–52.

22 *Improving Risk Communication*, p. 5.

23 P. Curran, P. Bell, A. Murray, G. Loughrey, R. Roddy, L. G. Rocke, 'Psychological consequences of the Enniskillen Bombing', *British Journal of Psychiatry*, Vol. 156, No. 4 (1990), pp. 479–482.

24 North *et al.*, 'Psychiatric Disorders among Survivors of the Oklahoma City Bombing', pp. 755–762.

25 Sara Freedman, Dalia Brandes, Tuvia Peri and Arieh Shalev, 'Predictors of Chronic Post-traumatic Stress Disorder. A Prospective Study', *British Journal of Psychiatry*, Vol. 174 (1999), pp. 353–359.

26 Janis, *Air War and Emotional Stress*, p. 111.

27 Ibid.

28 Ibid., p. 113.

29 Enrique Baca, Enrique Baca-Garcia, Maria Mercedes Perez-Rodriguez and Maria Luisa Cabanas, 'Short- and Long-Term Effects of Terrorist Attacks in Spain', *Journal of Maltreatment & Trauma*, Vol. 9, No. 1/2 (2005), pp. 157–170.

30 Henry A. Lyons, 'Terrorists' Bombing and the Psychological Sequelae', *Journal of the Irish Medical Association*, No. 67 (1974), pp. 15–19 and Pierre Verger, William Dab, Donna L. Lamping *et al.*, 'The Psychological Impact of Terrorism: An Epidemiologic Study of Post-traumatic Stress Disorder and Associated Factors in Victims of the 1995–1996 Bombings in France', *American Journal of Psychiatry*, Vol. 161, No. 8 (August 2004), pp. 1384–1389.

31 Janis, *Air War and Emotional Stress*, p. 113.

32 Paul Wilkinson, *Terrorism and the Liberal State* (London: Macmillan, 1977), p. 49.

33 Ibid., p. 59.

34 Walter Laqueur, *A History of Terrorism* (London: Transaction Publishers, 2001), p. 118.

35 Alexander and Klein, 'Biochemical Terrorism: Too Awful to Contemplate, Too Serious to Ignore', p. 491.

4 Israel and the Scud missile attacks during the 1991 Gulf War

1 Uzi Rubin, 'Historical Background', in *Theatre Ballistic Missile Defence: Progress in Astronautics and Aeronautics* (Lexington, NY: American Institute of Aeronautics and Astronautics, 2001), p. 22.

2 Zahava Solomon, 'Psychological Responses to Missile Attack – Israel during The Gulf War', in Ben Sheppard (ed.), *Jane's Special Report: Ballistic Missile Proliferation* (Coulsdon: 2000, Jane's Information Group), p. 167.

3 Asher Arian and Carol Gordon, 'The Political and Psychological Impact of the Gulf War on the Israeli Public', in Stanley A. Renshon (ed.), *The Political Psychology of the Gulf War: Leaders, Publics and the Process of Conflict* (Pittsburgh, PA: University of Pittsburgh, 1993), p. 228.

4 Ibid.

5 Casualty statistics taken from Arieh Y. Shalev and Zahava Solomon, 'The Threat and Fear of Missile Attack: Israelis in the Gulf War', in Robert J. Ursano and

Ann E. Norwood (eds), *Emotional Aftermath of the Persian Gulf War: Veterans, Families, Communities, and Nations* (Washington, DC: American Psychiatric Press, 1996), p. 150.

6 Eric Karsenty, Joshua Shemer, Alshech, Itzhik, Bruno Cojocaru *et al.*, 'Medical Aspects of the Iraqi Missile Attacks on Israel', *Israel Journal of Medical Sciences*, Vol. 27, No. 11–12 (1991), p. 606 and Zahava Solomon, *Coping with War-Induced Stress: The Gulf War and the Israeli Response* (New York: Plenum Press, 1995), p. 49.

7 Solomon, *Coping with War-Induced Stress*, p. 47.

8 Ibid., p. 47.

9 Arian and Gordon, 'The Political and Psychological Impact of the Gulf War on the Israeli Public', p. 228.

10 Rubin, 'Historical Background', p. 21.

11 Anthony H. Cordesman and Abraham R. Wagner, *The Lessons of the Modern War, Volume IV, The Gulf War* (Boulder, CO: Westview Press, 1998), p. 856.

12 Donald Silverberg and Esther Sofer, 'Role of the Tel Aviv-Jaffa Municipal Workers in the Treatment of Survivors of Missile Blasts', *Israel Journal of Medical Sciences*, Vol. 27, No. 11–12 (November–December 1991), p. 701.

13 Avraham Bleich, Shmuel Kron, C. Margalit *et al.*, 'Israeli Psychological Casualties of the Persian Gulf War: Characteristics, Therapy, and Selected Issues', *Israeli Journal of Medical Sciences*, Vol. 27, No. 11–12 (November–December 1991), p. 674.

14 Silverberg and Sofer, 'Role of the Tel Aviv–Jaffa Municipal Workers in the Treatment of Survivors of Missile Blasts', p. 702.

15 Uri F. Muller, Aviva L. Yahav and Galia Katz, 'Moving Places: A Glance at the Gulf War from the Sealed Room', *British Journal of Medical Psychology*, Vol. 66 (1993), p. 332.

16 Ibid.

17 Jenny D. Kark, Sylvie Goldman and Leon Epstein, 'Iraqi Missile Attacks on Israel: The Association of Mortality with a Life-Threatening Stressor', *Journal of the American Medical Association*, Vol. 273, No. 15 (April 1995), p. 1209.

18 Ibid, p. 1210. A separate study by Hart *et al.* believed that there was not an increase in cardiac mortality during the first missile attacks, but the paper does not provide statistics to support this supposition. The report also notes that the number of cardiac patients seen by the emergency room did increase, but this was put down to a lower threshold for referral. See Jacob Hart, Michael A. Weingarten, Adriana Druckman, Zeno Feldman and Aya Shay, 'Acute Cardiac Effects of "SCUD" Missile Attacks on a Civilian Population', *Medicine and War*, Vol. 9, No. 1 (1993), pp. 40–44.

19 Peretz Lavie, Avraham Carmeli, Lilach Mevorach and Nira Liberman, 'Sleeping under the Threat of the Scud: War-Related Environmental Insomnia', *Israel Journal of Medical Sciences*, Vol. 27, No. 11–12 (November–December 1991), pp. 681–686.

20 Twelve patients undergoing routine sleep diagnostic (polysomnograph) recordings at a sleep laboratory during the war had to be awakened from sleep in order to don the gas masks at the time of the missile attacks. Once the all-clear signal was given, all were able to return to sleep within 12 minutes without any evidence of stress-related sleep disturbances.

21 Jeffery Borkan, Pesach Shvartzman, Reis, Shmuel and Avgail G. Morris, 'Stories from the Sealed Rooms: Patient Interviews during the Gulf War', *Family Practice*, Vol. 10, No. 2 (1993), p. 190 Semi-structured interviews were conducted from 18 January until 28 February (the cessation of hostilities) by three family physicians at clinics in the geographic north, south and centre of the country.

22 Hasiden Ben-Zur and Moshe Zeidner, 'Anxiety and Bodily Symptoms under the Israeli Threat of Missile Attacks: The Israeli Scene', *Anxiety Research*, Vol. 4 (1991), p. 86.

23 Ephraim Yuchtman-Yaar, Yochanan Pere and Dafna Goldberg-Anabi, 'Israeli Morale during the Gulf War', *International Journal of Public Opinion Research*, Vol. 7, No. 4 (1995), p. 366.

24 Ibid. The questionnaires examined the 'political attitudes and democratic values of the Israeli public' by conducting a nationwide survey of over 1,200 individuals six weeks prior to Desert Storm and re-interviewed 418 respondents three weeks into the war as opposed to the 600 that had been originally intended. Other interviews could not be completed satisfactorily due to missile attacks interrupting the interview, some respondents being frightened, while others fled to safer areas. The study admits that the failure to reach the planned quota of interviews raises the question of whether the findings could be 'explained away'.

25 Data taken from Solomon, *Coping with War-Induced Stress*, p. 38.

26 Abraham Carmeli, Nira Liberman and Lilach Mevorach, 'Anxiety-related Somatic Reactions during Missile Attacks', *Israel Journal of Medical Sciences*, Vol. 27, No. 11–12 (November–December 1991), p. 677. The telephone survey of 595 subjects investigated the emotional reactions of the civilian population to missile attacks; specifically, the somatic expressions of anxiety were measured and related to expectations about future missile attacks.

27 Kark *et al.*, 'Iraqi Missile Attacks on Israel: The Association of Mortality with a Life-Threatening Stressor', p. 1209.

28 Ibid., pp. 1208–1209.

29 Bleich *et al.*, 'Israeli Psychological Casualties', p. 674.

30 Avi Bleich, Anat Dycian, M. Koslowsky *et al.*, 'Psychiatric Implications of Missile Attacks on a Civilian Population: Lessons from the Persian Gulf War', *Journal of the American Medical Association*, Vol. 268, No. 5 (August 1992), p. 615.

31 Zvi Rotenberg, Shlomo Noy and Uri Gabbay, 'Israeli ED Experience during the Gulf War', *American Journal of Emergency Medicine*, 12 January 1994, pp. 118–119.

32 Bleich *et al.*, 'Psychiatric Implications of Missile Attacks on a Civilian Population', p. 614.

33 Ibid.

34 Shalev and Solomon, 'The Threat and Fear of Missile Attack: Israelis in the Gulf War', p. 144.

35 Arian and Gordon, 'The Political and Psychological Impact of the Gulf War on the Israeli Public', p. 229.

36 Shalev and Solomon, 'The Threat and Fear of Missile Attack: Israelis in the Gulf War', p. 146.

37 Norman Milgram, 'Stress and Coping in Israel during the Persian Gulf War', *Journal of Social Issues*, Vol. 49, No. 4 (1993), p. 109.

38 Yuchtman-Yaar *et al.*, 'Israeli Morale During the Gulf War', p. 369.

39 Solomon, *Coping with War-Induced Stress*, p. 20.

40 Milgram, 'Stress and Coping in Israel During the Persian Gulf War', p. 10. The article cites A. Dolev, 'The Great Escape from the A Region', *Jerusalem Post (City Lights section)*, 10 January 1992, p. 3.

41 Arian and Gordon, 'The Political and Psychological Impact of the Gulf War on the Israeli Public', p. 245.

42 Borkan *et al.*, 'Stories from the Sealed Rooms', p. 190.

43 Milgram, 'Stress and Coping in Israel during the Persian Gulf War', p. 107.

44 Arian and Gordon, 'The Political and Psychological Impact of the Gulf War on the Israeli Public', p. 245.
45 Milgram, 'Stress and Coping in Israel during the Persian Gulf War', p. 107.
46 Shalev and Solomon, 'The Threat and Fear of Missile Attack', p. 148.
47 Ibid., p. 149.
48 Milgram, 'Stress and Coping in Israel during the Persian Gulf War', p. 105.
49 Charles Samuel, *Missile, Masks and Miracles* (Baltimore, MD: Leviathan Press, 2000), p. 24.
50 Cited in Solomon, *Coping with War-Induced Stress*, p. 10.
51 Samuel, *Missile, Masks and Miracles*, pp. 24–25.
52 See Rotenberg *et al.*, 'Israeli ED Experience During the Gulf War', p. 119 and Karsenty *et al.*, 'Medical Aspects of the Iraqi Missile Attacks on Israel', p. 607.
53 Rotenberg *et al.*, 'Israeli ED Experience During the Gulf War', p. 118.
54 Karsenty *et al.*, 'Medical Aspects of the Iraqi Missile Attacks on Israel', p. 607.
55 Jacob Lomranz, Steven E. Hobfoll, Robert Johnson, Nitza Eyal and Mina Zemach, 'A Nation's Response to Attack: Israelis' Depressive Reactions to the Gulf War', *Journal of Traumatic Stress*, Vol. 7, No. 1 (1994), pp. 64–68.
56 Ibid.
57 Ibid.
58 Arian and Gordon, 'The Political and Psychological Impact of the Gulf War on the Israeli Public', p. 247.
59 Yuchtman-Yaar *et al.*, 'Israeli Morale During the Gulf War', p. 373.
60 *Strategic Survey 1990–1991: International Institute for Strategic Studies* (London: Brassey's, 1991), p. 61.
61 Shalev and Solomon, 'The Threat and Fear of Missile Attack: Israelis in the Gulf War', p. 143.
62 Solomon, *Coping with War-Induced Stress: The Gulf War and the Israeli Response*, p. 4.
63 Shalev and Solomon, 'The Threat and Fear of Missile Attack: Israelis in the Gulf War', p. 143.
64 Milgram, 'Stress and Coping in Israel during the Persian Gulf War', p. 106.
65 Ahron Levran, *Israeli Strategy after Desert Storm: Lessons of the Second Gulf War* (London: Frank Cass, 1997), p. 2.
66 Solomon, *Coping with War-Induced Stress*, p. 27.
67 Casualty statistics taken from Shalev and Solomon, 'The Threat and Fear of Missile Attack', p. 150.
68 Borkan, 'Stories from the Sealed Rooms', p. 190.
69 Ibid.
70 S. Peterson, 'Missiles Bring War Home', *Christian Science Monitor* (internet edition), 30 July 1997. Online, available www.csmonitor.com/1997/0730/073097.intl.intl.2.html (accessed 29 April 2007).
71 Shalev and Solomon, 'The Threat and Fear of Missile Attack: Israelis in the Gulf War', p. 144.
72 Avigdor Klingman and Hagai Kupermintz, 'Response Style and Self-Control under Scud Missile Attacks: The Case of the Sealed Room Situation During the 1991 Gulf War', *Journal of Traumatic Stress*, Vol. 7, No. 3 (1994), p. 419.
73 Solomon, *Coping with War-Induced Stress*, p. 217.
74 Izhak Gilat, Thalma E. Lobel and Tsvie Gill, 'Characteristics of Calls to Israeli Hotlines during the Gulf War', *American Journal of Community Psychology*, Vol. 6, No. 5 (1998), p. 701.
75 Solomon, *Coping with War-Induced Stress*, p. 225.
76 Gilat *et al.*, 'Characteristics of Calls to Israeli Hotlines During the Gulf War', p. 703.

77 Solomon, *Coping with War-Induced Stress*, p. 225.
78 Cordesman and Wagner, *The Lessons of the Modern War*, p. 856.
79 *Strategic Survey 1990–1991*, p. 73.
80 Solomon, *Coping with War-Induced Stress*, p. 19.
81 Ibid., p. 38.
82 Theodore A. Postol, 'Lessons of the Gulf War Experience with Patriot', *International Security*, Vol. 16, No. 3 (Winter 1991–1992), p. 140.
83 Ibid., p. 146.
84 Representative Les Aspin, 'Understanding Technology on the Battlefield: Lessons for a Defense that Works', speech before the American Institute of Aeronautics and Astronautics, 1 May 1991, p. 2 and Eric Schmitt, 'Israel Plays Down Effectiveness of Patriot Missile', *New York Times*, 31 October 1991, p. A8 cited in Postol, 'Lessons of the Gulf War Experience with Patriot', p. 135.
85 Postol, 'Lessons of the Gulf War Experience with Patriot', p. 119.
86 Solomon, *Coping with War-Induced Stress*, p. 225.
87 Shalev and Solomon, 'The Threat and Fear of Missile Attack: Israelis in the Gulf War', p. 149.
88 Ibid.
89 Arian and Gordon, 'The Political and Psychological Impact of the Gulf War on the Israeli Public', p. 241.
90 Solomon, *Coping with War-Induced Stress*, p. 225.
91 Ibid., p. 24.
92 Arian and Gordon, 'The Political and Psychological Impact of the Gulf War on the Israeli Public', p. 228.

5 The Tokyo sarin attack

1 David Kaplan, *The Cult at the End of the World: The Terrifying Story of the Aum Doomsday Cult, from the Subways of Tokyo to the Nuclear Arsenals of Russia* (London: Random House, 1996), p. 15.
2 Daniel A. Metraux, *Aum Shinrikyo's Impact on Japanese Society (Japanese Studies)* (New York: Edwin Mellen Press, 2000), p. 4.
3 Ian Burma, 'Lost without a Faith', *Time*, 3 April 1995, p. 32. Soka Gakkai have become an established political force (winning seats in the legislature).
4 Metraux, *Aum Shinrikyo's Impact on Japanese Society*, p. 6.
5 Despite the sect's extensive financial resources, Aum lacked biological scientists of sufficient calibre to weaponise their biological samples. In contrast the chemical weapons programme was far more successful.
6 Anthony T. Tu, *Chemical Terrorism: Horrors in Tokyo Subway and Matsumoto City* (Fort Collins, CO: Alaken Inc., 2002), p. 175.
7 Kaplan, *The Cult at the End of the World*, p. 17.
8 Tu, *Chemical Terrorism*, p. 143.
9 The rudimentary delivery mechanism reduced the potential loss of life. Had Aum perfected an aerosol delivery mechanism, the sarin would have dispersed over a greater distance causing far more casualties. See Robyn Pangi, 'Consequence Management in the 1995 Sarin Attacks on the Japanese Subway System', *Studies in Conflict and Terrorism*, Vol. 25 (2002), p. 421.
10 Taken from Tu, *Chemical Terrorism*, p. 153.
11 Pangi, 'Consequence Management in the 1995 Sarin Attacks on the Japanese Subway System', p. 437.
12 Kyle B. Olson, 'Aum Shinrikyo: Once and Future Threat?', *Emerging Infectious Diseases*, Vol. 5, No. 4 (July–August 1999), p. 514.

13 Tetsu Okumura, 'Report on 640 Victims of the Tokyo Subway Sarin Attack', *Annals of Emergency Medicine*, Vol. 28, No. 2 (August 1996), p. 131.
14 Amy E. Smithson, 'Rethinking the Lessons of Tokyo', in A. E. Smithson and Leslie-Anne Levy, *Ataxia: The Chemical and Biological Terrorism Threat and the US Response* (Washington, DC: Henry L. Stimson Center, 2000), Report no. 35, pp. 71–111.
15 Ibid., p. 132.
16 Ibid., p. 163.
17 Ibid., p. 169.
18 Ibid.
19 David Brackett, *Holy Terror: Armageddon in Tokyo* (New York/Tokyo: Wetherhill, 1996), p. 147. The investigations into Aum's work on sarin were complicated by the fact that it was legal to make and possess sarin itself, primarily because the government had never passed a law making it illegal.
20 David Van Biema, 'Prophet of Poison', *Time*, 3 April 1995, p. 23.
21 Within a month of the attack, the Diet ratified legislation to tighten controls on the production and use of sarin and related chemicals through the 'Law Related to the Prevention of Bodily Harm Caused by Sarin and Similar Substances'.
22 Mark Mullins, 'The Legal and Political Fallout of the "Aum Affair"', in Mark Mullins (ed.), *Religion and Social Crisis in Japan: Understanding Japanese Society through the Aum Affair* (New York: Palgrave, 2001), p. 77.
23 Ibid., p. 72.
24 Ibid., p. 82.
25 Kaplan, *The Cult at the End of the World*, p. 246.
26 Brackett, *Holy Terror*, p. 136.
27 Ibid., pp. 135–136.
28 Murakami identified his interviewees through first scanning the media for the names of the victims. Twenty per cent of a list of 700 names acquired were identifiable. Out of this, 140 were positively identified of which 60 consented to be interviewed.
29 Haruki Murakami, *Underground: The Tokyo Gas Attack and the Japanese Psyche* (London: Harvill Press, 2001), p. 161.
30 See Olson, 'Aum Shinrikyo: Once and Future Threat?', p. 514 and Nozomu Asukai and Kazuhiko Maekawa, 'Psychological and Physical Health Effects of the 1995 Sarin Attack in the Tokyo Subway System', in J. Havenaar and J. Cwikel (eds), *Toxic Turmoil: Psychological and Societal Consequences of Ecological Disasters* (New York: Kluwer Academic/Plenum Publishers, 2001), p. 151.
31 David Alan Alexander and Susan Klein, 'Biochemical Terrorism: Too Awful to Contemplate, Too Serious to Ignore', *British Journal of Psychiatry*, Vol. 183 (2003), p. 493.
32 Tetsu Okumura, 'Report on 640 Victims of the Tokyo Subway Sarin Attack', *Annals of Emergency Medicine*, Vol. 28, No. 2 (August 1996), p. 131.
33 Kanzo Nakano, 'The Tokyo Sarin Gas Attack: Victims' Isolation and Post-Traumatic Stress Disorders', *Cross-Cultural Psychology Bulletin*, December 1995, p. 13.
34 Ibid.
35 Ibid.
36 Murakami, *Underground*, p. 61.
37 Brackett, *Holy Terror*, pp. 153–154.
38 Ibid., p. 152.
39 Kevin Fedarko, 'Another Shock to the System', *Time*, 10 April 1995, p. 27.
40 Kaplan, *The Cult at the End of the World*, p. 276.
41 Nakano, 'The Tokyo Sarin Gas Attack', p. 12.

42 'Most Nerve Gas Victims Still in Suffering', *Japan Times*, 28 January 1999. Online, available at http://search.japantimes.co.jp/cgi-bin/nn19990128a5.html (accessed 29 April 2007).
43 Noriko Kawana, 'Psycho-Physiological Effects of the Terrorist Sarin Attack on the Tokyo Subway System', *Military Medicine*, Vol. 166, Supplement 2 (2001), p. 23.
44 Murakami, *Underground*, p. 61.
45 Ibid., p. 100.
46 Ibid., p. 123.
47 Ibid., p. 34.
48 Ibid., p. 108.
49 Ibid.
50 Kaplan, *The Cult at the End of the World*, p. 255.
51 Robert Jay Lifton, *Destroying the World to Save It* (New York: Henry Holt, 1999), p. 233.
52 Kaplan, *The Cult at the End of the World*, p. 217.
53 Brackett, *Holy Terror*, p. 7.
54 Kaplan, *The Cult at the End of the World*, p. 255.
55 Ibid., p. 270.
56 Murakami, *Underground*, p. 100.
57 Pangi, 'Consequence Management in the 1995 Sarin Attacks on the Japanese Subway System', p. 433.
58 Murakami, *Underground*.
59 Kaplan, *The Cult at the End of the World*, p. 265.
60 Brackett, *Holy Terror*, p. 149.
61 Kaplan, *The Cult at the End of the World*, p. 255.
62 Van Biema, 'Prophet of Poison', *Time*, p. 23.
63 Pangi, 'Consequence Management in the 1995 Sarin Attacks on the Japanese Subway System', p. 433.
64 According to Kyle B. Olson and David Kaplan, in the days after the attack, Fumihiro Joyu's regular media appearances led to him becoming a 'teen heart-throb' and women's magazines ran articles praising Joyu's physique. See Olson, 'Aum Shinrikyo', p. 515 and Kaplan, *The Cult at the End of the World*, p. 274.
65 Brackett, *Holy Terror*, p. 163.
66 Nakano, 'The Tokyo Sarin Gas Attack', p. 15.
67 Louise Lemyre, Mélanie Clément, Wayne Corneil *et al*. 'A Psychosocial Risk Assessment and Management Framework to Enhance Response to CBRN Terrorism Threats and Attacks', *Biosecurity and Bioterrorism: Biodefense Strategy, Practice, and Science*, Vol. 3, No. 4 (2005), p. 317.
68 The JRA was formed around 1970 after breaking away from Japanese Communist League-Red Army Faction. The JRA was led by Fusako Shigenobu until her arrest in Japan in November 2000.
69 Tu, *Chemical Terrorism*, p. 137. The noxious odour was caused by trimethylphosphonate (the first-step reaction to sarin) spilling over the reaction container on 7 and 15 July 1994.
70 Murakami, *Underground*, p. 100.
71 Okumura, 'Report on 640 Victims of the Tokyo Subway Sarin Attack', p. 130.
72 Murakami, *Underground*, pp. 146–147.
73 Ibid., p. 162.
74 Nakano, 'The Tokyo Sarin Gas Attack', p. 14.
75 Murakami, *Underground*, p. 147.
76 Nakano, 'The Tokyo Sarin Gas Attack', p. 14.
77 Kawana, 'Psycho-Physiological Effects of the Terrorist Sarin Attack', p. 23.

78 Ibid., p. 26.
79 'Sarin Victims Say More Must Be Done', *Asahi Shimbun*, 20 March 2000, cited in Pangi, 'Consequence Management in the 1995 Sarin Attacks', p. 441.

6 September 11 attacks

1 Albert R. Roberts, 'Assessment, Crisis Intervention, and Trauma Treatment: The Integrative ACT Intervention Model', *Brief Treatment and Crisis Intervention*, Vol. 2 No. 1 (Spring 2002), p. 1.
2 One of the few mental health studies on the Pentagon attack is by Thomas Grieger *et al.* in the journal *Psychiatric Services*. See Thomas A. Grieger, Douglas A. Waldrep, Monica M. Lovasz and Robert J. Ursano, 'Follow-up of Pentagon Employees Two Years after the Terrorist Attack of September 11, 2001', *Psychiatric Services*, Vol. 56, No. 11 (2005), pp. 1374–1378. The paper that examined the mental health of the Pentagon staff two years after the attack identified that 14 per cent had probable PTSD and 7 per cent had probable depression.
3 *The 9/11 Commission Report: Final Report of the National Commission on Terrorist Attacks upon the United States* (New York: W.W. Norton & Company, 2004), p. 51.
4 Ibid, p. 56.
5 Phil Hirschkorn, Rohan Gunaratna, Ed Blanche and Stefan Leader, 'Special Report: Al Qaeda "Blowback"', *Jane's Intelligence Review*, Vol. 13, No. 8 (2001), p. 42.
6 *The 9/11 Commission Report*, p. 66.
7 Hirschkorn, 'Special Report', p. 45.
8 For instance, *Jane's Intelligence Review* ran a special report on Al Qaeda a month before the attacks. See Hirschkorn, 'Special Report', and Phil Hirschkorn, 'Convictions Mark First Step in Breaking up Al Qaeda Network', *Jane's Intelligence Review*, Vol. 13, No. 8 (2001), pp. 42–51.
9 *The 9/11 Commission Report*, p. 149.
10 Ibid., p. 173.
11 'Text of World Islamic Front's Statement Urging Jihad against Jews, Crusaders', *Al Quds al Arabi*, 23 February 1998 (translated by the Foreign Broadcast Information Service).
12 BBC News 24, 11 September 2001.
13 R. W. Apple, 'Nation Plunges into Fight with Enemy Hard to Identify', *New York Times*, 12 September 2001, p. A1.
14 James Risen and David Johnston, 'Intelligence Officials Think Group Headed by Bin Laden', *New York Times*, 12 September 2001, p. 3.
15 Stephen Evans, 'Ground Zero', in Jenny Baxter and Malcolm Downing (eds), *The Day That Shook the World* (London: BBC Worldwide Limited: 2002), p. 21.
16 'Bin Laden's Statement: "The Sword Fell"', *New York Times*, 8 October 2001, p. B7.
17 Fred Halliday, *Two Hours That Shook the World* (London: Saqi Books, 2002), p. 34.
18 Steven Simon, 'The New Terrorism: Securing the Nation against a Messianic Foe', *The Brookings Review*, Vol. 21, No. 1 (2003), p. 18.
19 Nick Fielding, 'Al Qaeda Leaders Reveal 9/11 Secrets', the *Sunday Times*, 8 September 2002, p. 1.
20 Ibid., p. 1.
21 'Correspondent: Clearing the Skies', *BBC2 Television*, 1 September 2002.

22 'Plane Controllers Recall 11 September', *BBC News Online*, 12 August 2002. Online, available http://news.bbc.co.uk/1/hi/world/americas/2188688.stm (accessed 7 May 2007).

23 Jim Dwyer, Eric Lipton, Kevin Flynn, James Glanz and Ford Fessenden, '102 Minutes: Last Words at the Trade Center; Fighting to Live as the Towers Died', *New York Times*, 26 May 2002, p. 3.

24 Ibid.

25 Ibid.

26 Wilfred D. Iwan, 'Collapse of the World Trade Center Towers: A New Type of Urban Risk', paper presented to *Asia's Premier Conference on Terrorism Risks*, Singapore, 24 January 2003. According to Wilfred Iwan, the towers were designed to take a wind load of 11,000,000 lbs, while the impact force of the 767 aircraft is calculated to be 1,000,000 lbs.

27 Ibid.

28 Andrew Pierce, 'Death Toll of Thousands and Hundreds of Burn Victims Feared', the *Times* (special supplement), 12 September 2001, p. 3.

29 Albert R. Roberts, 'Assessment, Crisis Intervention, and Trauma Treatment: The Integrative ACT Intervention Model', *Brief Treatment and Crisis Intervention*, Vol. 2, No. 1 (2002), p. 1.

30 '9/11 One Year Later: A Nation Remembers – Special Commemorative Edition', *American Media Inc.*, 2002, p. 60.

31 Rohan Gunaratna and Peter Chalk, *Jane's Counter Terrorism*, 2nd edn (Coulsdon: Jane's Information Group, 2002), p. 107.

32 Grant Wardlaw, *Political Terrorism: Theory, Tactics and Counter-measures* (Cambridge: Cambridge University Press, 1982), p. 34.

33 Sandro Galea, David Vlahov, Heidi Resnick, Jennifer Ahern, Ezra Susser, Joel Gold, Michael Bucuvalas and Dean Kilpatrick, 'Trends of Probable Posttraumatic Stress Disorder in New York City after the September 11 Terrorist Attacks', *American Journal of Epidemiology*, Vol. 158, No. 6 (2003), p. 520.

34 Ibid., p. 520.

35 Sandro Galea, Jennifer Ahern, Heidi Resnick and David Vlahov, 'Posttraumatic Stress Symptoms in the General Population after a Disaster: Implications for Public Health', in Yuval Neria, Raz Gross and Randall Marshall (eds), *9/11: Mental Health in the Wake of Terrorist Attacks* (New York: Cambridge University Press, 2006), pp. 19–44.

36 William E. Schlenger, J. M. Caddell, L. Ebert *et al.*, 'Psychological Reactions to Terrorist Attacks: Findings from the National Study of Americans' Reactions to September 11', *Journal of the American Medical Association*, Vol. 288, No. 5 (2002), p. 581. The term 'probable' was used because the PTSD diagnoses were made on the basis of screening instruments, not comprehensive clinical evaluations. The research was based on a sample of 2,273 adults including samples from the New York, NY, and Washington, DC and other major metropolitan areas. The epidemiological surveys were web-based and used a cross-sectional sample. The surveys were sent via e-mail from 12 October through to 12 November 2001.

37 Other major metropolitan areas examined were Boston, MA, Philadelphia, PA, Chicago, IL, Houston, TX, and Los Angeles, CA.

38 Ibid., p. 585. The 5.1 per cent adjusted probable PTSD of New Yorkers derived from logistic regression analyses taking into account the sociodemographic differences of race/ethnicity, age, sex and education characteristics that were distinct from the national average.

39 Schlenger *et al.*, 'Psychological Reactions to Terrorist Attacks', p. 585.

40 Ibid.

41 Roxane Cohen Silver, Alison Holman and Daniel N. McIntosh, 'Nationwide Longitudinal Study of Psychological Responses to September 11', *Journal of the American Medical Association*, Vol. 288, No. 10 (2002), p. 1235.

42 Albert R. Roberts, 'Assessment, Crisis Intervention, and Trauma Treatment: The Integrative ACT Intervention Model', p. 2.

43 'Situation Normal: Almost – 2002 Year End Report', *Pew Research Center for the People and the Press*, 2003, p. 2.

44 Baruch Fischhoff, Roxana M. Gonzalez, Deborah A. Small and Jennifer S. Lerner, 'Judged Terror Risk and Proximity to the World Trade Center', *Journal of Risk and Uncertainty*, Vol. 26, No. 2/3 (2003), p. 148.

45 Ibid., p. 139.

46 See 'Resilience or Panic? The Public and Terrorist Attack', *Lancet*, Vol. 360, No. 14 (2002), p. 1901 and Thomas Glass and Monica Schoch-Spana, 'Bioterrorism and the People: How to Vaccinate a City against Panic', *Clinical Infectious Diseases*, Vol. 34, No. 2 (2002), p. 217.

47 Ibid.

48 Jim Dwyer and Eric Lipton, 'Fighting to Live as the Towers Died', *New York Times*, 26 May 2002.

49 Guylène Proulx, 'Researchers Learn from World Trade Center Survivors' Accounts', *Construction Innovation*, Vol. 8, No. 1 (March 2003), pp. 1–3.

50 Ibid.

51 Ibid.

52 The subway system was completely closed around 10:20am and all tunnels and bridges into the city and some major highways were closed to non-essential traffic. There remained a limited bus service in some areas and passenger ferries, but many had to walk to get out of Manhattan.

53 Somini Sengupta, 'A Battered Retreat on Bridges to the East', *New York Times*, 12 September 2001, p. A11.

54 Richard Pérez-Peña, 'Trying to Command an Emergency When the Emergency Command Center Is Gone', *New York Times*, 12 September 2001, p. A7.

55 N. R. Kleinfield, 'Buildings Burn and Fall as Onlookers Search for Elusive Safety', *New York Times*, 12 September 2002, p. A1.

56 Anthony R. Mawson, 'Understanding Mass Panic and Other Collective Responses to Threat and Disaster', *Psychiatry*, Vol. 68, No. 2 (2005), p. 106.

57 Galea, S., Ahern, J., Resnick, H. and Vlahov, D. *et al.*, 'Psychological Sequelæ of the September 11 Terrorist Attacks in New York City', *New England Journal of Medicine*, Vol. 346, No. 13 (March 2002), p. 982. The survey entailed random-digit-dialling to contact a representative sample of adults living south of 110th Street, Manhattan, seven miles north of where the WTC stood.

58 Ibid.

59 Department of Health and Human Services, Mental Health: A Report of the Surgeon General (Rockville, Md.: Substance Abuse and Mental Health Services, National Institute for Mental Health). Cited in Galea *et al.*, 'Psychological Sequelae of the September 11 Terrorist Attacks in New York City', p. 985.

60 'Dead and Missing', *New York Times*, 26 December 2001, p. B2. Cited in Galea *et al.*, 'Psychological Sequelæ of the September 11 Terrorist Attacks in New York City'.

61 Ibid.

62 Robert J. Ursano, 'Post Traumatic Stress Disorder', *The New England Journal of Medicine*, Vol. 346, No. 2 (2002), p. 131 and Kenneth C. Hyams, Frances M. Murphy and Simon Wessely, 'Responding to Chemical, Biological or

Nuclear Terrorism: The Indirect and Long-Term Health Effects May Present the Greatest Challenge', *Journal of Health Politics, Policy and Law*, Vol. 27, No. 2 (April 2002), p. 279.

63 David Vlahov, Sandro Galea, Heidi Resnick *et al.*, 'Increased Use of Cigarettes, Alcohol, and Marijuana among Manhattan, New York Residents after the September 11th Terrorist Attacks', *American Journal of Epidemiology*, Vol. 155, No. 11 (2002), p. 988. The survey selected 1,008 individuals by using random-digit-dialling between 16 October and 15 November 2001. A total of 988 responses was used in the final analysis.

64 Ibid.

65 Brian Reade, 'Out of the Darkness: A Commemorative Issue', *Daily Mirror*, 11 September 2002, p. 11.

66 Sarah Kershaw, 'Even 6 Months Later, "Get Over it" Just Isn't an Option', *New York Times*, 11 March 2002. Online, available at http://query.nytimes.com/gst/fullpage.html?res=9C04E2D81639F932A25750C0A9649C8B63 (accessed 3 July 2008).

67 Joshua Miller, 'Affirming Flames: Debriefing Survivors of the World Trade Center Attack', *Brief Treatment and Crisis Intervention*, Vol. 2, No. 1 (2002), p. 89.

68 Galea *et al.*, 'Trends of Probable Post-traumatic Stress Disorder in New York City after the September 11 Terrorist Attacks', pp. 514–524.

69 Lynn E. DeLisi, Andrea Maurizio, Marla Yost, Carey F. Papparozzi, Cindy Fulchino, Craig I. Katz, Josh Alterman, Mathew Biel, Jennifer Lee and Pilar Stevens, 'A Survey of New Yorkers after the September 11, Terrorist Attacks', *American Journal of Psychiatry*, Vol. 160, No. 4 (2003), p. 782.

70 Richard J. McNally, Richard A. Bryant and Anke Ehlers, 'Does Early Psychological Intervention Promote Recovery from Post Traumatic Stress?', *Psychological Science in the Public Interest*, Vol. 4, No. 2 (2003), p. 46.

71 Ibid.

72 DeLisi *et al.*, p. 782.

73 Joseph Boscarino, Richard Adams and Charles Figley, 'Mental Health Service Use One Year after the World Trade Center Disaster: Implications for Mental Health Care', *General Hospital Psychiatry*, Vol. 26 (2004), p. 350.

74 Ibid.

75 Ibid.

76 Baruch Fischhoff, R.M. Gonzalez, D. A. Small and J. S. Lerner, 'Evaluating the Success of Terror Risk Communication', *Biosecurity and Bioterrorism: Biodefense Strategy, Practice, and Science*, Vol. 1, No. 4 (2003), p. 257.

77 Mark Schuster, 'What We Know about Public Opinion Post September 11', paper presented to the NATO-Russia Advanced Scientific Workshop on the Social and Psychological Consequences of Chemical, Biological and Radiological Terrorism', 25–27 March 2002. and Mark Schuster, B. D. Stein, L. H. Jaycox *et al.*, 'A National Survey of Stress Reactions after the September 11, 2001 Terrorist Attacks', *New England Journal of Medicine*, Vol. 345, No. 20 (15 November 2001), p. 1510.

78 Schuster, 'What We Know about Public Opinion Post September 11'.

79 Roxane Cohen Silver, E. Alison Holman, Daniel N. McIntosh, Michael Poulin, Virginia Gil-Rivas and Judith Pizarro, 'Coping with a National Trauma: Nationwide Longitudinal Study of Responses to the Terrorist Attacks of September 11', in Neria, *9/11*, pp. 45–70.

80 McNally, 'Does Early Psychological Intervention Promote Recovery from Post Traumatic Stress?', p. 48.

81 Ibid., p. 49.

82 Jerome C. Wakefield and Robert L. Spitzer, 'Lowered Estimates, but of What?', *Archives of General Psychiatry*, Vol. 59 (2002), pp. 129–130.

83 Miller, 'Affirming Flames', p. 88.

84 Leonie Huddy, Stanley Feldman, Theresa Capelos and Colin Provost, 'The Consequences of Terrorism: Disentangling the Effects of Personal and National Threat', *Political Psychology*, Vol. 23, No. 3 (2002), p. 505.

85 Russ Hoyle, 'A Year Later, a City Is Still on Edge', *New York Daily News*, 1 September 2002, p. 1. The poll interviewed 503 adults in New York City on 20–21 August by Blum & Weprin Associates. The margin for error was plus or minus 4.5 per cent.

86 Hoyle, 'A Year Later, a City Is Still on Edge', p. 1.

87 Erica Goode, 'Now, Fear of Flying Is More Than a Phobia', *New York Times*, 29 January 2002, p. F1.

88 Ibid.

89 Ibid.

90 Robert E. Bartholomew and Simon Wessely, 'Protean Nature of Mass Sociogenic Illness', *British Journal of Psychiatry*, Vol. 180 (April 2002), p. 304.

91 Ibid.

92 Robert Bliss, chief press officer, Massachusetts Turnpike Authority Department of Revenue, personal communication, 15 July 2002, cited in George M. Gray and David M. Ropeik, 'dealing with the Dangers of Fear: The Role of Risk Communication', *Politics and Public Health*, November–December 2002, p. 107.

93 Gerd Gigerenzer, 'Out of the Frying Pan into the Fire: Behavioural Reactions to Terrorist Attacks', *Risk Analysis*, Vol. 26, No. 2 (2006), pp. 347–351.

94 Silver *et al.*, 'Nationwide Longitudinal Study of Psychological Responses to September 11', p. 1240.

95 Ibid.

96 Leonie Huddy, Stanley Feldman, Charles Taber and Gallya Lahav, 'The Politics of Threat: Cognitive and Affective Reactions to 9/11', paper presented at the annual meeting of the American Political Science Association, Boston, 28 August–1 September 2002.

97 Ibid.

98 Huddy *et al.*, 'The Consequences of Terrorism', p. 494.

99 'Situation Normal: Almost – 2002 Year End Report', *PEW Research Center for the People and the Press*, 2003, p. 2.

100 'Terrorism in the United States'. *Gallup*. Online, available at http://www.galluppoll.com/content/?ci=4909 (accessed 19 January 2007).

101 Ibid.

102 Lydia Saad, 'Most Americans Say Lives Not "Permanently Changed" by 9/11', *Gallup*, 11 September 2006.

103 Ibid.

104 Ibid.

105 Ibid.

106 Fred Kaplan, 'Facing Terror/A City Tested/NY Mayor; In Crisis, Giuliani's Image Transformed', *Boston Globe*, 14 September 2001, p. A38.

107 Barry Shlachter, 'New Yorkers, Critics Praise Mayor Giuliani's Handling of Crisis', *Knight Ridder/Tribune News Service*, 14 September 2001, KR-ACC-NO: K1684.

108 Editorial, 'Retain Rudy?; The Mayor Has Been a Rock, but He Should Not Stay On', *Pittsburgh Post-Gazette*, 1 October 2001, p. A16.

109 Rudolph W. Giuliani, *Leadership* (New York: Miramax Books, 2002), p. 7.

110 Richard Pérez-Peña, 'Trying to Command an Emergency When the Emergency Command Center Is Gone', *New York Times*, 12 September 2001, p. A7.

111 Giuliani, *Leadership*, p. 6.
112 *Time*, 31 December–7 January 2002, p. 65.
113 Felicity Barringer and Geraldine Fabrikant, 'As an Attack Unfolds, a Struggle to Provide Vivid Images to Homes', *New York Times*, 12 September 2001, p. A25.
114 'A Scarred Capitol', *Economist*, 15 September 2001, p. 17.
115 Giuliani went to the Fire Department's command post to ask 'What should I tell people?'. The advice was that they had enough personnel to assist those in the WTC to leave the building and evacuees should then head north.
116 Shlachter, 'New Yorkers'.
117 David Beal, 'Seeking Leaders in a Time of Need', *St Paul Pioneer Press*, 15 September 2001, p. C1.
118 Giuliani, *Leadership*, p. 25.
119 Ibid., p. 366.
120 Sandra Mullins, 'The Anthrax Attacks in the New York City: The "Giuliani Press Conference Model" and Other Communication Strategies that Helped', *Journal of Health Communications*, Vol. 8 (2003), pp. 15–16.
121 Ibid.
122 Kaplan, 'Facing Terror'.
123 Stevenson Swanson, 'Since September 11, Giuliani Has Become "Rudy the Rock"', *Chicago Tribune*, 20 September 2001, p. 11.
124 Andrew Grossman, 'NY Mayor's Handling of Terrorist Crisis Resonates with Media', *Hollywood Reporter*, 25 September 2001.
125 Dan Barry, 'A Man Who Became More than a Mayor', *New York Times*, 31 December 2001, p. A1.
126 David Seifman, 'Rudy's Courage a Beacon for Us All – How Giuliani and His Team Led City out of Darkness', *New York Times*, 17 September 2001, p. 20.
127 *Time*, 31 December–7 January 2002, p. 44.
128 Vincent Covello, 'Risk Communications', paper given to the WIN Global 2003 conference, Las Vegas/Yucca Mountain, 16–19 June 2003.
129 David Ropeik, 'Risk Communications During a Terrorist Attack or Other Public Emergency', in *Terrorism and Other Public Emergencies: A Reference Guide for Media* (Washington DC: US Department of Health and Human Services, 2005), p. 11. Online, available at http://www.hhs.gov/emergency/media guide/PDF/11.pdf (accessed 18 April 2007).
130 Verena Dobnik, 'Singing after World Trade Center Brings Fame to New York Cop; Now He's Got a Record', *Associated Press*, 13 December 2001.
131 'Correspondent', BBC2 Television, 1 September 2002.
132 Elisabeth Bumiller with David E. Sanger, 'A Somber Bush Says Terrorism Cannot Prevail', *New York Times*, 12 September 2001, p. A1.
133 *The 9/11 Commission Report*, p. 326.
134 Apple, 'Nation Plunges into Fight with Enemy Hard to Identify'.
135 Ibid.
136 Shlachter, 'New Yorkers'.
137 Paul Reynolds, 'Washington Readies for War', in Baxter and Downing, *The Day that Shook the World*, p. 87.
138 Apple, 'Nation Plunges into Fight', Section A, p. 1.
139 Paul F. Deisler, Jr, 'A Perspective: Risk Analysis as a Tool for Reducing the Risks of Terrorism', *Risk Analysis*, Vol. 22, No. 3 (2002), p. 408.
140 Ibid.
141 Andrew Miga, 'Meehan, Neal Raise Doubts on Leadership of President', *Boston Herald*, 14 September 2001, p. 4.
142 Giuliani, *Leadership*, p. 353.

143 Beal, 'Seeking Leaders in a Time of Need'.
144 Mary McGrory, 'Beyond Recognition', *Washington Post*, 16 September 2001, p. B01.
145 Editorial, 'President Bush's First Win', *New York Times*, 17 September 2001, p. A14.
146 Reynolds, 'Washington Readies for War', in Baxter and Downing, *The Day that Shook the World*, p. 95.
147 Rob Watson, 'Analysis: Bush Hits the Right Note', *BBC News Online*, 25 September 2001. Online, available at http://news.bbc.co.uk/1/hi/world/americas/1562436.stm (accessed 29 April 2007).
148 'Address to a Joint Session of Congress and the American People'. Online, available at http://www.whitehouse.gov/news/releases/2001/09/20010920–8.html (accessed 7 May 2007).
149 'Address to a Joint Session of Congress and the American People'. Online, available at http://www.whitehouse.gov/news/releases/2001/09/20010920–8.html (accessed 7 May 2007).
150 Rob Watson, 'George W. Bush: Wartime President', *BBC News Online*, 2 October 2001. Online, available at http://news.bbc.co.uk/1/hi/world/americas/1574277.stm (29 April 2007).
151 Randall A. Yim, 'Homeland Security: Risk Communication Principals May Assist in Refinement of the Homeland Security Advisory System', testimony before the subcommittee on national security, emerging threats, and international relations, Committee on Government Reform, House of Representatives, United States General Accounting Office, 16 March 2004, p. i.
152 David Johnston and James Risen, 'A Nation at War: Domestic Security; New Signs of Terror Not Evident', *New York Times*, 6 April 2003, p. B1.
153 'Terror Alert Raised to High amid Fears Foreign Attacks Could Spread', *Associated Press*, 21 May 2003.
154 John Rollins and L. J. Cunningham, 'Post 9/11 National Threat Notification Efforts: Issues, Actions, and Options for Congress', *CRS Report for Congress*, 29 April 2005, p. 8.
155 Ibid., p. i.
156 Ibid., p. 1.
157 Yim, 'Homeland Security', p. 9.
158 Elaine Monaghan, 'All-American Survival Pack: What Everyone Needs', *The Times*, 12 February 2003, p. 15.
159 Federal Emergency Management Agency, *Are You Ready?: A Guide to Citizen Preparedness* (Washington, DC: 2002).
160 Baruch Fischhoff, 'Assessing and Communicating the Risks of Terrorism', in Albert H. Teich, Stephen D. Nelson and Stephen J. Lita (eds), *Science and Technology in a Vulnerable World* (Washington, DC: American Association for the Advancement of Science, 2002), pp. 51–64.
161 'American Public Opinion about Terrorism', *Gallup*, 19 April 2005.
162 Ibid.
163 'Modest Support for Missile Defense, No Panic on China', 11 June 2001. Online, available at http://people-press.org/reports/display.php3?ReportID=10 (accessed 7 May 2007).
164 Gigerenzer, 'Out of the Frying Pan into the Fire', p. 349.
165 Saad, 'Most Americans Say Lives Not "Permanently Changed" by 9/11'.
166 Gray and Ropeik, 'Dealing with the Dangers of Fear', p. 113.
167 Ibid.
168 Jeffrey M. Jones, 'Fear of Terrorism Increases amidst Latest Warning', *Gallup*, 12 February 2003.

7 2001 anthrax attacks

1 David Claridge, 'Exploding the Myths of Superterrorism', in Maxwell Taylor and John Horgan (eds) *The Future of Terrorism*, (London: Frank Cass, 2000), p. 145.

2 Ross Pastel, 'The Psychological Effects of the Anthrax Attacks in America', paper presented to the NATO-Russia Advanced Scientific Workshop on the Social and Psychological Consequences of Chemical, Biological and Radiological Terrorism, 25–27 March 2002.

3 'Anthrax Isn't Contagious; Anxiety Is', *Economist*, 20 October 2001, p. 57.

4 Michael D. Lemonick, 'Deadly Delivery', *Time*, 22 October 2001, p. 3.

5 Leonard A. Cole, *Anthrax Letters: A Medical Detective Story* (Washington, DC: Joseph Henry Press, 2003), p. 188.

6 Ibid.

7 Ibid.

8 Robert J. Blendon, John M. Benson and Catherine M. DesRoches, 'Using Opinion Surveys to Track the Public's Response to a Bioterrorist Attack', *Journal of Risk Communication*, Vol. 8 (2003), p. 89.

9 Ibid.

10 Monica Schoch-Spana, 'Educating, Informing, and Mobilizing the Public', in Barry S. Levy and Victor W. Sidel (eds), *Terrorism and Public Health: A Balanced Approach to Strengthening Systems and Protecting People* (New York: Oxford University Press, 2003), p. 121.

11 'No Rise in Fears or Reported Depression; Public Remains Steady in Face of Anthrax Scare', *Pew*. The research was conducted on 10–14 October 2001. Online, available at http://www.pewtrusts.com/pubs/pubs_item.cfm?content_item_id=785&content_type_id=18&page=p1 (accessed 7 May 2007).

12 Ibid.

13 'Survey Shows Americans Not Panicking over Anthrax But Taking Steps to Protect against Possible Bioterrorist Attacks', *Ascribe Inc. Newswire*, 7 November 2001. The survey was conducted via telephone between 24–28 October 2001and included a nationally representative random sample of 1,015 adults aged 18 or over. The margin of sampling error is plus or minus 3 percentage points.

14 Ibid.

15 Cass R. Sunstein, 'Terrorism and Probability Neglect', *Journal of Risk and Uncertainty*, Vol. 26, No. 2–3 (2003), p. 130.

16 Douglas Schaffer, G. Armstrong, K. Higgins *et al.*, 'Increased US Prescription Trends Associated with the CDC *Bacillus Anthracis* Antimicrobial Post Exposure Prophylaxis Campaign', *Pharmacoepidemiology and Drug Safety*, Vol. 12, No. 3 (2003), pp. 177–182. The differing prescription peaks of ciprofloxacin followed by doxycycline are consistent with the CDC's initial choice of ciprofloxacin followed by the preferred use of doxycycline once susceptibility patterns for anthrax were known. The use of the third drug, amoxicillin increased only marginally (by 12,000 in October).

17 Jeffrey M. Jones, 'Nine in 10 Americans Are Going about Their Business as Usual', *Gallup News Service*, 26 October 2001. Online, available at http://www.gallup. com/poll/releases/pro11026.asp (accessed 7 May 2007).

18 Blendon, *Harvard School of Public Health/Robert Wood Foundation survey project on Americans' response to biological terrorism, tabulation report*.

19 Kenneth Shine, 'For a Hearing on Risk Communication: National Security and Public Health' (testimony presented to the Subcommittee on National Security, Veterans Affairs, and International Relations, House Committee on Government Reform, Washington, DC: 29 November 2001.

20 Jeffrey M. Jones, 'Nine in 10 Americans', p. 88.
22 FBI, 'National Instant Criminal Background Check System (NICS) Information'. Online, available at www.fbi.gov/hq/cjisd/nics/index.htm (accessed 2 August 2002). Cited in George M. Gray and David M. Ropeik, 'Dealing with the Dangers of Fear: The Role of Risk Communication', *Politics and Public Health*, November–December 2002, p. 107.
23 Blendon, *Harvard School of Public Health/Robert Wood.*
24 Schoch-Spana, 'Educating, Informing, and Mobilizing the Public', p. 122.
25 Monica Schoch-Spana, 'Plenary Session: Building Bridges to the Future: Lessons Learned from Anthrax, 2001', presentation to the Society for Risk Analysis, 10 December 2003.
26 Ibid.
27 Cass R. Sunstein, 'Terrorism and Probability Neglect', p. 131.
28 Rima E. Rudd, John P. Comings and James N. Hyde, 'Leave No One Behind: Improving Health and Risk Communication through Attention to Literacy', *Journal of Health Communication*, Vol. 8 (2002), p. 107.
29 John Hobbs, Anne Kittler, Susannah Fox, Blackford Middleton and David W. Bates, 'Communicating Health Information to an Alarmed Public Facing a Threat Such as a Bioterrorist Attack', *Journal of Health Communications*, Vol. 9 (2004), p. 68.
30 Seth Borenstein, 'CDC Defends Anthrax Response', *Detroit Free Press*, 24 October 2001, p. 6A.
31 Christopher P. Weis *et al.*, 'Secondary Aerosolization of Viable *Bacillus Anthracis* Spores in a Contaminated US Senate Office', *Journal of American Medical Association*, Vol. 288, No. 22 (December 2002), p. 2857.
32 Ibid.
33 Susan J. Robinson and Wendy C. Newsletter, 'Uncertain Science and Certain Deadlines: CDC Responses to the Media During the Anthrax Attacks of 2001', *Journal of Health Communications*, Vol. 8 (2003), p. 26.
34 Bradly A. Perkins *et al.*, 'Public Health in the Time of Bioterrorism', *Emerging Infectious Diseases*, Vol. 8, No. 10 (October 2002), p. 1017.
35 Ibid.
36 Christine E. Prue, Cheryl Lackey, Lisa Swenarski and Judy M. Gantt, 'Communication Monitoring: Shaping CDC's Emergency Risk Communication Efforts', *Journal of Health Communication*, Vol. 8 (2003), p. 37.
37 Ibid.
38 Robinson and Newsletter, 'Uncertain Science and Certain Deadlines', p. 23.
39 Ibid., pp. 31–32.
40 Prue, 'Communication Monitoring', p. 45.
41 Colin W. Shepard, Montse Soriano-Gabarro, Elizabeth R. Zell *et al.*, 'Antimicrobial Post Exposure Prophylaxis for Anthrax: Adverse Events and Adherence', *Emerging Infectious Diseases*, Vol. 8, No. 10 (October 2002), p. 1128.
42 Ibid., p. 1126.
43 'Building Bridges to the Future: Lessons Learned from Anthrax, 2001', *RISK newsletter*, First Quarter 2004, p. 8.
44 Ivan Walks, 'Plenary Session: Building Bridges to the Future: Lessons Learned from Anthrax, 2001', presentation to the Society for Risk Analysis, 10 December 2003.
45 Carolyn M. Greene, 'Epidemiologic Investigations of Bioterrorism-related Anthrax, New Jersey, 2001', *Emerging Infectious Diseases*, Vol. 8, No. 10, (October 2002), p. 1054.
46 'Statement of Postmaster General/CEO John E. Potter', before the Committee on Governmental Affairs, United States Senate, 30 October 2001.

47 John Donnelly, 'Anthrax Crisis Tests Mettle of CDC Chief', *Boston Globe*, 11 November 2001, p. A1.
48 Interview with William K. Hallman, Associate Professor of Human Ecology and Psychology, State University of New Jersey, at the conference 'Communicating the War on Terror', London, 5–6 June 2003.
49 Peter M. Dull, '*Bacillus Anthracis* Aerosolization Associated with a Contaminated Mail Sorting Machine', *Emerging Infectious Diseases*, Vol. 8, No. 10 (October 2002), p. 1044.
50 Marsha L. Vanderford, 'Communication Lessons Learned in the Emergency Operations Center During CDC's Anthrax Response: A Commentary', *Journal of Health Communications*, Vol. 8 (June 2003), pp. 11–12.
51 Ibid.
52 Walks, 'Plenary session: Building Bridges to the Future'.
53 Lawrence K. Altman and Gina Kolata, 'Anthrax Missteps Offer Guide to Fight Next Bioterror Battle', *New York Times*, 6 January 2002, p. A1.
54 Schoch-Spana, 'Educating, Informing, and Mobilizing the Public', p. 123.
55 Hobbs *et al.*, 'Communicating Health Information to an Alarmed Public', p. 69.
56 Vincent P. Hsu *et al.*, 'Opening a *Bacillus Anthracis*-containing Envelope, Capitol Hill, Washington, DC, The Public Health Response', *Emerging Infectious Diseases*, Vol. 8, No. 10 (October 2002), p. 1041.
57 Shepard *et al.*, 'Antimicrobial Post Exposure Prophylaxis for Anthrax', p. 1126.
58 Hsu *et al.*, 'Opening a *Bacillus Anthracis*-containing Envelope', p. 1039.
59 Ibid., p. 1040.
60 Ben Pershing, 'As Anthrax Crisis Hit, Confusion Reigned', *Roll Call*, 25 October 2001.
61 Ibid.
62 Ken Fireman and Thomas Frank, 'Domestic Dissonance; Many Voices, Many Disagreements in War on Terrorism', *Newsday*, 25 October 2001, p. A6.
63 Ibid.
64 Ibid.
65 Diane Plumberg Clay, 'Mock Bioterror Attack Spurs US Preparedness', *Daily Oklahoman*, 22 October 2001, p. 3.
66 Pershing, 'As Anthrax Crisis Hit, Confusion Reigned'.
67 Ibid.
68 *The David Letterman Show*, NBC Television, 18 October 2001.
69 'Wimps – The Leaders Who Ran Away from Anthrax', *New York Post*, 18 October 2001, p. 1.
70 Paul F. Deisler, 'A Perspective: Risk Analysis as a Tool for Reducing the Risks of Terrorism', *Risk Analysis*, Vol. 22, No. 3 (2002), p. 408.
71 Rodney Jay C. Salinas, 'Live Now, Deliver Later', *Amerasia Journal*, Vol. 27/28, Part 3/1 (2002), p. 269.
72 David A. Shore, 'Communicating in Times of Uncertainty: The Need for Trust', *Journal of Health Communications*, Vol. 8 (2003), p. 14.
73 Ibid.
74 Blendon, 'Using Opinion Surveys to Track the Public's Response to a Bioterrorist Attack', p. 87.
75 Ibid.
76 Schoch-Spana, 'Educating, Informing, and Mobilizing the Public', p. 123.
77 Baruch Fischhoff, 'Assessing and Communicating the Risks of Terrorism', in A. H. Teich, S. D. Nelson, and S. J. Lita (eds), *Science and Technology in a Vulnerable World* (Washington, DC: AAAS, 2002). p. 54.
78 Shine, 'For a Hearing on Risk Communication'.

79 Ibid.
80 Sandra Mullins, 'The Anthrax Attacks in the New York City: The "Giuliani Press Conference Model" and Other Communication Strategies that Helped', *Journal of Health Communications*, Vol. 8 (2003), p. 16.
81 Ibid.
82 Jeffrey P. Koplan, 'Communication During Public Health Emergencies', *Journal of Health Communications*. Vol. 8 (2003), p. 145.
83 John Cloud, 'Search and Disrupt', *Time*, 22 October 2001, p. 46.
84 Ibid.
85 Schoch-Spana, 'Educating, Informing, and Mobilizing the Public', p. 122.
86 Michael Elliot, 'A Clear and Present Danger', *Time*, 8 October 2001, p. 40.
87 Hobbs *et al.*, p. 69 and Philip S. Brachman, 'The Public Health Response to the Anthrax Epidemic', in Levy and Sidel, *Terrorism and Public Health*, p. 114.
88 Brachman, 'The Public Health Response', p. 115.
89 Robinson and Newstetter, 'Uncertain Science and Certain Deadlines', p. 27.
90 Felicia Mebane, Sarah Temin and Claudia F. Parvanta, 'Communicating Anthrax in 2001: A Comparison of CDC Information and Print Media', *Journal of Health Communication*, Vol. 8 (June 2003), p. 51.
91 D. White, 'Scientists Rate the Stories: Experts Evaluate the Accuracy of Anthrax Coverage, 12 October, 2001. Online, available at http://www.poynter.org/content/content_view.asp?id=6431 (accessed 29 April, 2007).
92 Mebane *et al.*, 'Communicating Anthrax in 2001', p. 51.
93 Hobbs *et al.*, 'Communicating Health Information to an Alarmed Public', p. 68.
94 Rudd *et al.*, 'Leave No One Behind', p. 110.
95 Mebane *et al.*, 'Communicating Anthrax in 2001', pp. 59–78.
96 Ibid., p. 76.
97 Blendon, 'Using Opinion Surveys', p. 87.
98 D. Ricks, 'Experts' Warning: Ciprofloxacin Not the Only Anthrax Treatment', *Newsday*, 8 April 2002, p. A38, cited in Hobbs *et al.*, 'Communicating Health Information to an Alarmed Public', p. 69.
99 Blendon, 'Using Opinion Surveys', p. 91 and Mebane *et al.*, 'Communicating Anthrax in 2001', p. 51.
100 James M. Hughes and Julie Louise Gerberding, 'Anthrax Bioterrorism: Lessons Learned and Future Directions', *Emerging Infectious Diseases*, Vol. 8, No. 10 (October 2002), p. 1014.
101 Ibid.

8 Israel and the Second Intifada

1 Jeremy Pressman, 'Visions in Collision: What Happened at Camp David and Taba?', *International Security*, Vol. 28, No. 2 (2003), pp. 5–53.
2 Charles D. Smith, *The Palestinian and Arab–Israeli Conflict* (New York: Bedford/St Martin's Press, 2004), 5th edn, p. 494.
3 Pressman, 'Visions in Collision', p. 7.
4 Smith, *The Palestinian and Arab–Israeli Conflict*, p. 503.
5 Ibid., p. 506.
6 James F. Miskel, 'The Palestinian Intifada: An Effective Strategy', *World Policy Journal*, Winter (2004–2005), p. 48.
7 Assaf Moghadam, 'Palestinian Suicide Terrorism in the Second Intifada: Motivations and Organisational Aspects', *Studies in Conflict and Terrorism*, Vol. 26 (2003), p. 77.
8 Ibid., pp. 74–75.

9 Kirsten E. Schulze, *The Arab–Israeli Conflict* (London: Longman, 1999), p. 75.
10 Pressman, 'Visions in Collision', p. 26.
11 Ibid., p. 27.
12 Bob Zelnick, 'The Unnecessary Intifada', *Orbis*, Winter 2003, p. 13.
13 Andrew Kydd and Barbara Walter, 'The Strategies of Terrorism', *International Security*, Vol. 31, No. 1 (2006), p. 60.
14 Quoted in Hassan, 'An Arsenal of Believers', p. 38, cited in Andrew Kydd and Barbara Walter, 'The Strategies of Terrorism', *International Security*, Vol. 31, No. 1 (2006), p. 60.
15 Sergio Catignani, 'The Strategic Impasse in Low-Intensity Conflicts: The Gap between Israeli Counter-Insurgency Strategy and Tactics during the *Al-Aqsa Intifada*', *Journal of Strategic Studies*, Vol. 28, No. 1 (2005), p. 62.
16 Moghadam, 'Palestinian Suicide Terrorism in the Second Intifada', p. 65.
17 Smith, *The Palestinian and Arab–Israeli Conflict*, p. 506.
18 Catignani, 'The Strategic Impasse in Low-Intensity Conflicts', p. 1.
19 Nadav Morag, 'The Economic and Social Effects of Intensive Terrorism: Israel 2000–2004', *MERIA Journal*, Vol. 10, No. 3 (September 2006), pp. 120–141.
20 Ruth Pat-Horenczyk, 'Post-Traumatic Distress in Israeli Adolescents Exposed to Ongoing Terrorism: Selected Findings from School-Based Screenings in Jerusalem and Nearby Settlements', *Journal of Aggression, Maltreatment & Trauma*, Vol. 9, No. 3–4 (2005), p. 342.
21 Smith, *The Palestinian and Arab–Israeli Conflict*, p. 500.
22 Pressman, 'Visions in Collision', p. 40.
23 Smith, *The Palestinian and Arab–Israeli Conflict*, p. 506.
24 Ibid.
25 Miskel, 'The Palestinian Intifada', p. 54.
26 Zelnick, 'The Unnecessary Intifada', p. 13.
27 James Glanz, 'Hostage Is Freed after Philippine Troops Are Withdrawn from Iraq', *New York Times*, 21 July 2004, cited in Kydd and Walter, 'The Strategies of Terrorism', p. 49.
28 Arieh Y. Shalev and Sara Freedman, 'PTSD Following Terrorist Attacks: A Prospective Evaluation', *American Journal of Psychiatry*, Vol. 163, No. 6 (2005), p. 1189.
29 Shaul Schreiber, Ornah Dolberg, Agnes Leor, Helena Rapoport and Miki Bloch, 'Occurrence of PTSD in Injured Survivors of Suicide-Bomb Attacks', poster presented at the International Society for Traumatic Stress Studies 21st Annual Meeting, 2–5 November 2005.
30 Ornah T. Dolberg, Shaul Schreiber, Agnes Leor, Helena Rapoport and Miki Bloch, 'The Prevalence of PTSD among Survivors of Terror Attacks – A Report of 129 Cases', presented at the Israeli Psychiatric Association Annual Meeting, Haifa, April 2003.
31 Avraham Bleich, Marc Gelkopf and Zahava Solomon, 'Exposure to Terrorism, Stress-Related Mental Health Symptoms, and Coping Behaviors among a Nationally Representative Sample in Israel', *Journal of American Medical Association*, Vol. 290, No. 5 (August 2003), pp. 612–620.
32 Arieh Y. Shalev, 'Posttraumatic Stress Disorder among Injured Survivors of a Terrorist Attack. Predictive Value of Early Intrusion and Avoidance Symptoms', *Journal of Nervous Diseases*, Vol. 180 (1992), pp. 505–509.
33 Arieh Y. Shalev, 'The Israel Experience', p. 220 in Juan José López-Ibor, George Christodulou, Mario Maj *et al.*, *Disasters and Mental Health* (London: Wiley, 2005).
34 Irwin J. Mansdorf and Jacob Weinberg, 'Stress Reactions in Israel in the Face of

Terrorism: Two Community Samples', *Traumatology*, Vol. 9, No. 3 (September 2003), p. 159.

35 Arieh Y. Shalev, Rivka Tuval, Sarah Frenkiel-Fishman, Hilit Hadar and Spencer Eth, 'Psychological Responses to Continuous Terror: A Study of Two Communities in Israel', *American Journal of Psychiatry*, Vol. 164, No. 4 (April 2006), p. 667.

36 Arieh Y. Shalev *et al.*, 'Psychological Responses to Continuous Terror', p. 670.

37 Bleich *et al.*, 'Exposure to Terrorism', p. 612.

38 Yori Gidron, Yosi Kaplan, Avital Velt and Rozi Shalem, 'Prevalence and Moderators of Terror-Related Post-Traumatic Stress Disorder Symptoms in Israeli Citizens', *Israeli Medical Association Journal*, Vol. 6 (July 2004), p. 389.

39 Ibid., p. 388.

40 Eli Somer, Ayalla Ruvio, Erez Soref and Ilana Sever, 'Terrorism, Distress and Coping: High versus Low Impact Regions and Direct versus Indirect Civilian Exposure', *Anxiety, Stress, and Coping*, Vol. 18, No. 3 (2005), p. 178.

41 Mansdorf and Weinberg, 'Stress Reactions in Israel in the Face of Terrorism', p. 159.

42 Pat-Horenczyk, 'Post-Traumatic Distress in Israeli Adolescents Exposed to Ongoing Terrorism', p. 342.

43 Ibid., p. 32. The study noted that more adolescents exposed to terrorism, whether personally or indirectly, than non-exposed youth reported functional impairment (23 per cent, 25.1 per cent vs 11.8 per cent respectfully), somatic complaints (33.5 per cent, 26.6 per cent vs 21.5 per cent respectfully) and severe or very severe depression (16.6 per cent, 5 per cent vs 10.2 per cent respectfully).

44 Ilan Kutz and Avi Bleich, 'Mental Health Interventions in a General Hospital Following Terrorist Attacks: The Israeli Experience', in Yael Danieli, Danny Brom and Joe Sills (eds), *The Trauma of Terrorism* (New York: Haworth Press, 2005), p. 426.

45 Shalev, 'The Israel Experience', pp. 217–228.

46 Guy Stecklov and Joshua R. Goldstein, 'Terror Attacks Influence Driving Behaviour in Israel', *Proceedings of the National Academy of Sciences* (5 October 2004), p. 14551.

47 Ibid., p. 14555.

48 Ibid.

49 See David P. Phillips, 'Airplane Accident Fatalities Increase Just after Newspaper Stories about Murder and Suicide', *Science*, Vol. 21, No. 4357 (1978), pp. 748–750 and David P. Phillips 'Suicide, Motor Vehicle Fatalities, and Mass Media: Evidence toward a Theory of Suggestion, *American Journal of Sociology*, Vol. 85, No. 5 (1979). pp. 1150–1174.

50 Bleich *et al.*, 'Exposure to Terrorism', pp. 612–620.

51 Somer *et al.*, 'Terrorism, Distress and Coping', p. 178.

52 Bleich *et al.*, 'Exposure to Terrorism', pp. 612–620.

53 Correspondence with the author, 3 March 2008.

54 Rhonda S. Adessky and Sara A. Freedman, 'Treating Survivors of Terrorism While Adversity Continues', *Journal of Aggression, Maltreatment & Trauma*, Vol. 10, No. 1–2 (2005), p. 445.

55 Deena Yellin, 'Voice: Ten Years Later?', in Y. Danieli, D. Brom and J. Sills (eds), *The Trauma of Terrorism* (New York: Haworth Press), p. 605.

56 Shalev, 'Psychological Responses to Continuous Terror', p. 667.

57 Adessky and Freedman, 'Treating Survivors of Terrorism while Adversity Continues', p. 447.

58 Ibid.

59 Batya Ludman, 'Behavioural Responses to the Intifada', email, 16 April 2004.
60 Alan Kirschenbaum, 'Does Terror Terrorize? Community Resilience in Israel', *Gazette*, Vol. 69, No. 3 (November 1997). Online, available at http://www.-rcmp-grc.gc.ca/gazette/vol69no3/terror_e.htm (accessed 5 February 2008).
61 Marc Gelkopf, 'About Your Request', email, 15 April 2004.
62 Ludman, 'Behavioural Responses to the Intifada'.
63 Shalev, 'The Israel Experience', pp. 217–228.
64 Eli Somer, Eli Buchbinder, Maya Peled-Avram and Yael Ben-Yizhack, 'The Stress and Coping of Israeli Emergency Room Social Workers Following Terrorist Attacks', *Qualitative Health Research*, Vol. 14, No. 8 (October 2004), p. 1083.
65 Shalev, 'The Israel Experience', pp. 217–228.
66 Alan Kirschenbaum, 'Terror, Adaptation and Preparedness: A Trilogy for Survival', *Journal of Homeland Security and Emergency Management*, Vol. 3, No. 1 (2006), p. 14.
67 Ibid.
68 Ibid., p. 18.
69 Ibid., pp. 22–23.
70 Arieh O'Sullivan, 'Anti-Terror Advisor: Israelis Too Complacent about Security', *Jerusalem Post*, 8 April 2004. Online, available at http://www.jpost.com (9 April 2004).
71 Molly Moore, 'Fear of Reprisals Casts a Pall on Jerusalem: Israelis Desert Restaurants and Buses', *Washington Post*, 24 March 2004, p. A1.
72 Shalev, 'The Israel Experience', pp. 217–228.
73 Yori Gidron, Gal Reuven, and Sa'ar Zahavi, 'Bus Commuters Coping Strategies and Anxiety from Terrorism: An Example of the Israeli Experience', *Journal of Traumatic Stress*, Vol. 12, No. 1 (1999), p. 185.
74 Zelnick, 'The Unnecessary Intifada', p. 16.
75 Ibid.
76 Shalev, 'The Israel Experience', pp. 217–228.
77 Ibid., p. 15.
78 Ibid., p. 16.
79 Somer *et al.*, 'Terrorism, Distress and Coping', pp. 172–173.
80 Gelkopf, 'About Your Request'.
81 Ludman, 'Behavioural responses to the Intifada'.
82 Shalev, 'The Israel Experience', p. 225.
83 Gerald Cromer, 'Analogies to Terror: The Construction of Social Problems in Israel during the Intifada Al Aqsa', *Terrorism and Political Violence*, Vol. 18, No. 3 (2006), p. 397.
84 Ludman, 'Behavioural Responses to the Intifada'.
85 Susy Kovatz, Ilan Kutz, Gil Rubin *et al.*, 'Comparing the Distress of American and Israeli Medical Students Studying in Israel during a Period of Terror', *Medical Education*, Vol. 40 (2006), p. 392.
86 Ibid., p. 389.
87 S. Breznitz and Y. Eshel, 'Life Events: Stressful Ordeal or Valuable Experiences?' in S Breznitz (ed.), *Stress in Israel* (New York: Van Nostrand Reinhhold, 1983), pp. 228–261. Cited in Somer *et al.*, 'Terrorism, Distress and Coping', p. 178.
88 Shalev, 'The Israel Experience', pp. 217–228.
89 Bella Ben-Gershon, Alexandria Grinshpoon and Alexander Ponizovsky, 'Mental Health Services Preparing for the Psychological Consequence of Terrorism', in Damieli, Brom and Sills, *The Trauma of Terrorism*, p. 747.
90 Ibid., p. 749.
91 Somer *et al.*, 'The Stress and Coping of Israeli Emergency Room Social Workers Following Terrorist Attacks', p. 1079.

92 Somer *et al.*, 'Terrorism, Distress and Coping', p. 166.
93 Ibid.
94 Shalev, 'The Israel Experience', pp. 217–228.
95 Yellin, 'Voice: Ten Years Later?', p. 607.
96 Mansdorf and Weinberg, 'Stress Reactions in Israel in the Face of Terrorism', p. 155.
97 Shalev, 'Psychological Responses to Continuous Terror', p. 667.
98 Adessky and Freedman, 'Treating Survivors of Terrorism while Adversity Continues', p. 444.

9 Conclusion

1 Paul Wilkinson, *Terrorism and the Liberal State* (London: Macmillan Press, 1977), p. 47.
2 Andrew Lambert, *The Psychology of Air Power*, (London: RUSI, 1995), p. 5.
3 'Commuters describe Madrid Blast Chaos', BBC News, 11 March 2004. Online, available at http://news.bbc.co.uk/1/hi/world/europe/3500702.stm (accessed 13 March 2007).
4 Juan J. Miguel-Tobal, Antonio Cano-Vindel, Hector Gonzales-Ordi, Iciar Iruarrizaga, Sasha Rudenstine *et al.*, 'PTSD and Depression after the Madrid March 11 Train Bombings', *Journal of Traumatic Stress*, Vol. 19, No. 1 (2006), pp. 69–80.
5 Carmelo Vázquez, Pau Pérez-Sales and Georg Matt, 'Post-Traumatic Stress Reactions Following from the March 11, 2004 Terrorist Attacks in a Madrid Community Sample: A Cautionary Tale about the Measurement of Psychological Trauma', *Spanish Journal of Psychology*, Vol. 9, No. 1 (2006), pp. 61–74.
6 D. Fraquas, S. Teran, J. Conejo-Galindo, O. Medina, E. Sainz Corton, L. Fernando *et al.*, 'Posttraumatic Stress Disorder in Victims of the March 11 Attacks in Madrid Admitted to a Hospital Emergency Room: 6 Month Follow Up', *European Journal of Psychiatry*, Vol. 21, No. 3 (2006), pp. 143–151.
7 Alejandro López-Rousseau, 'Avoiding the Death Risk of Avoiding a Dread Risk', *Psychological Science*, Vol. 16, No. 6 (2005), pp. 426–428.
8 Gerd Gigerenzer, 'Out of the Frying Pan into the Fire: Behavioural Reactions to Terrorist Attacks', *Risk Analysis*, Vol. 26, No. 2 (2006), p. 351.
9 Keith B. Richburg, 'Madrid Attacks May Have Targeted Election', *Washington Post*, 17 October 2004, p. A16.
10 Luis Moreno, 'The Madrid Bombings in the Domestic and Regional Politics of Spain', *Irish Studies in International Affairs*, Vol. 16 (2005), pp. 65–72.
11 Alan Hamilton, 'Panic, Shoving, Fear of Fire and Bonding Below Ground', *The Times*, 7 July 2006, p. 7.
12 Ben Macintyre, 'In 56 Horrific Minutes, Familiar London Landmarks Became a Monument to Mass Murder', *The Times*, 8 July 2005, p. 4.
13 'The Bus Looked as if It Was Cut in Half by the Blast', *The Times*, 8 July 2005, p. 9.
14 Terry Kirby and Andrew Malone, 'Rush-Hour Bomb Attacks and Kill Dozens and Injure 700: "I Thought We Were All Going to die. I Was Waiting for a Fire"', *Independent*, 8 July 2006, p. 2.
15 Louise Jury and Arifa Akbar, 'For Hours, Convoys of Ambulances Took away the Victims: "I Heard Screaming ... People Were Trying to Get Out"', *Independent*, 8 July 2005, p. 9.
16 BBC News Online (2005), available at http://search.bbc.co.uk/cgi-bin/search/results.pl?scope=all&edition=d&tab=av&recipe=all&q=july+7+bombing+tube++mobile+phone&x=0&y=0 (accessed 17 December 2007).

17 See e.g. James Rubin, C. R. Brewin, N. Greenberg, John Simpson and Simon Wessely, 'Psychological and Behavioural Reactions to the Bombings in London on 7 July 2005: Cross Sectional Survey of a Representative Sample of Londoners', *British Medical Journal*, Vol. 331 (2005), pp. 606–611 and G. James Rubin, Chris R. Brewin, Neil Greenberg, Jamie Hacker Hughes, John Simpson and Simon Wessely, 'Enduring Consequences of Terrorism: 7 Month Follow-up Survey of Reactions to the Bombings in London on 7 July 2005', *British Journal of Psychiatry*, Vol. 190 (2007), pp. 350–356.

18 Arieh Y. Shalev, Rivka Tuval, Sarah Frenkiel-Fishman, Hilit Hadar and Spencer Eth, 'Psychological Responses to Continuous Terror: A Study of Two Communities in Israel', *American Journal of Psychiatry*, Vol. 164, No. 4 (April 2006), p. 667.

18 Rubin *et al.*, 'Enduring Consequences of Terrorism'.

19 Shalev *et al.*, 'Psychological Responses to Continuous Terror', p. 670; Rhonda S. Adessky and Sara A. Freedman, 'Treating Survivors of Terrorism while Adversity Continues', *Journal of Aggression, Maltreatment & Trauma*, Vol. 10, No. 1–2 (2005), p. 445.

20 Ibid.

21 Rubin, 'Psychological and Behavioural Reactions to the Bombings in London on 7 July 2005', p. 611.

22 Mark Schuster, B. Stein, L. H. Jaycox *et al.*, 'A National Survey of Stress Reactions after the September 11, 2001 Terrorist Attacks', *New England Journal of Medicine*, Vol. 345, No. 20 (November 2001), pp. 1507–1512.

23 Ibid., p. 606.

24 Ibid., p. 611.

25 Ibid.

26 Avraham Bleich, Marc Gelkopf and Zahava Solomon, 'Exposure to Terrorism, Stress-Related Mental Health Symptoms, and Coping Behaviors among a Nationally Representative Sample in Israel', *Journal of American Medical Association*, Vol. 290, No. 5 (August 2003), pp. 612–620.

27 Rubin *et al.*, 'Psychological and Behavioural Reactions to the Bombings in London on 7 July 2005', p. 613.

28 *Today Programme*, BBC Radio 4, 4 August 2005.

29 Ben Webster, 'Passengers Conquer Fears and Get Back on the Tube', *The Times*, 7 July 2006, p. 8.

30 Ibid.

31 Ibid.

32 Ben Webster, 'It's a Wrap: How the Clever Cyclist Can Get Round Train Ban', *The Times*, 10 April 2006, p. 5.

33 'Tourist Numbers Down on London', *The Times*, 13 February 2006, p. 3.

34 Liane Katz, 'UK Tourism Has Record Year despite London Bombs', *Guardian Unlimited*, 8 November 2006. Online, available at http://travel.guardian.co.uk/article/2006/nov/08/travelnews.uknews (13 March 2007).

35 Roger E. Kasperson and Jeanne X. Kasperson, 'The Social Amplification and Attenuation of Risk', in Howard Hunreuther and Paul Slovic (eds), 'Challenges in Risk Assessment and Risk Management', *Annals of the American Academy*, Vol. 545 (May 1996), p. 95.

36 Shalev *et al.*, 'Psychological Responses to Continuous Terror', p. 667.

Select bibliography

Abrahams, M., Why Terrorism Does Not Work', *International Security*, Vol. 31, No. 2 (Fall 2006), pp. 42–48.

Alexander, D. A. and Klein, S., Biochemical Terrorism: Too Awful to Contemplate, Too Serious to Ignore', *British Journal of Psychiatry*, Vol. 183 (2003), pp. 491–497.

Arian, A. and Gordon, C., The Political and Psychological Impact of the Gulf War on the Israeli Public', in S. A. Renshon (ed.), *The Political Psychology of the Gulf War: Leaders, Publics and the Process of Conflict*', (Pittsburgh, PA: University of Pittsburgh, 1993), pp. 227–250.

Asukai, N. and Maekawa, K., Psychological and Physical Health Effects of the 1995 Sarin Attack in the Tokyo Subway System', in J. Havenaar and J. Cwikel (eds), *Toxic Turmoil: Psychological and Societal Consequences of Ecological Disasters* (Dordrecht/New York: Kluwer Academic/Plenum Press, 2001), pp. 149–162.

Baca, E., Baca-Garcia, E., Perez-Rodriguez, M. M. and Cabanas, M. L., Short- and Long-Term Effects of Terrorist Attacks in Spain', *Journal of Maltreatment & Trauma*, Vol. 9, No. 1/2 (2005), pp. 157–170.

Ben-Zur, H. and Zeidner, M., 'Anxiety and Bodily Symptoms under the Israeli Threat of Missile Attacks: The Israeli Scene', *Anxiety Research*, Vol. 4 (1991), pp. 79–95.

Berry, N. O., 'Theories on the Efficacy of Terrorism', in Paul Wilkinson and A. M. Stewart (eds), *Contemporary Research on Terrorism* (Aberdeen: Aberdeen University Press, 1987), pp. 293–306.

Bleich, A., Dycian, A., Koslowsky, Z, Solomon, Z. and Wiener, M., Psychiatric Implications of Missile Attacks on a Civilian Population: Lessons from the Persian Gulf War', *Journal of the American Medical Association*, Vol. 268, No. 5 (1992), pp. 613–615.

Bleich, A., Gelkopf, M. and Solomon, Z., Exposure to Terrorism, Stress-Related Mental Health Symptoms, and Coping Behaviors among a Nationally Representative Sample in Israel', *Journal of the American Medical Association*, Vol. 290, No. 5 (August 2003), pp. 612–620.

Bleich, A., Kron, S., Margaht, C, Inbar, G., Kaplan, Z., Cooper, S. and Solomon, Z.., Israeli Psychological Casualties of the Persian Gulf War: Characteristics, Therapy, and Selected Issues', *Israeli Journal of Medical Science*, Vol. 27, No. 11–12 (November–December 1991), pp. 673–676.

Blendon, R. J., Benson, J. M. and DesRoches, C. M., Using Opinion Surveys to Track the Public's Response to a Bioterrorist Attack', *Journal of Risk Communication*, Vol. 8 (2003), pp. 83–92.

Brackett, D. W., *Holy Terror: Armageddon in Tokyo* (New York/Tokyo: Wetherhill, 1996).

Bradly, A., Perkins, A., Yeskey, K., Public Health in the Time of Bioterrorism', *Emerging Infectious Diseases*, Vol. 8, No. 10 (October 2002), pp. 1015–1018.

Breslau, N., Lucia, V. C. and Davis, G. C., Partial PTSD versus Full PTSD: An Empirical Examination of Associated Impairment', *Psychological Medicine*, Vol. 34 (2004), pp. 1205–1214.

Cairns, E. and Lewis, C. A., Collective Memories, Political Violence and Mental Health in Northern Ireland', *British Journal of Psychology*, Vol. 90 (1999), pp. 25–33.

Carmeli, A., Liberman, N. and Mevorach, L., 'Anxiety-Related Somatic Reactions During Missile Attacks', *Israel Journal of Medical Sciences*, Vol. 27, No. 11–12 (November–December 1991), pp. 677–680.

Cromer, G., 'Analogies to Terror: The Construction of Social Problems in Israel During the Intifada Al Aqsa', *Terrorism and Political Violence*, Vol. 18, No. 3 (2006), pp. 389–398.

Danieli, Y., Brom, D. and Sills, J. (eds), *The Trauma of Terrorism* (New York: Haworth Press, 2005).

Deisler, P. F., 'A Perspective: Risk Analysis as a Tool for Reducing the Risks of Terrorism', *Risk Analysis*, Vol. 22, No. 3 (2002), pp. 405–414.

DeLisi, L. E., Maurizio, A., Yost, M., Papparozzi, C. F., Fulchino, C. I., Katz, C., Altesman, J., Biel, M., Lee, J. and Stevens, P., 'A Survey of New Yorkers after the September 11, Terrorist Attacks', *American Journal of Psychiatry*, Vol. 160, No. 4, April (2003), pp. 780–783.

Dull, P. M., *Bacillus Anthracis* Aerosolization Associated with a Contaminated Mail Sorting Machine', *Emerging Infectious Diseases*, Vol. 8, No. 10 (October 2002), pp. 1044–1047.

Durodie, B. and Wessely, S., Resilience or Panic? The Public and Terrorist Attack', *The Lancet*, Vol. 360, No. 9348 (December 2002), pp. 1901–1902.

Fischhoff, B., Risk Perception and Communication Unplugged: Twenty Years of Process', *Risk Analysis*, Vol. 15, No. 2 (1995), pp. 137–145.

Fischhoff, B., 'Assessing and Communicating the Risks of Terrorism', in A. H. Teich, S. D. Nelson and S. J. Lita (eds), *Science and Technology in a Vulnerable World* (Washington, DC: American Association for the Advancement of Science, 2002), pp. 51–64.

Fischhoff, B., Psychological Perception of Risk', in D. Kamien (ed.), *The McGraw-Hill Homeland Security Handbook of Terrorism* (New York: McGraw Hill, 2006), pp. 463–492.

Fischhoff, B., Gonzalez, R. M., Small, D. A. and Lerner, J. S., Evaluating the Success of Terror Risk Communication', *Biosecurity and Bioterrorism: Biodefense Strategy, Practice, and Science*, Vol. 1, No. 4 (2003), pp. 255–258.

Fischhoff, B., Gonzalez, R. M., Small, D. A. and Lerner, J. S., Judged Terror Risk and Proximity to the World Trade Center', *Journal of Risk and Uncertainty*, Vol. 26, No. 2–3 (2003), pp. 137–151.

Fraquas, D., Teran, S., Conejo-Galindo, J., Medina, O., Sainz Cortú, E., Ferrando, L., Gabriel, R. and Arango, C., Posttraumatic Stress Disorder in Victims of the March 11 Attacks in Madrid Admitted to a Hospital Emergency Room: 6 Month Follow Up', *European Journal of Psychiatry*, Vol. 21, No. 3 (2006), pp. 143–151.

Freedman, L., Strategic Terror and Amateur Psychology', *Political Quarterly*, Vol. 76, No. 2 (2005), pp. 161–170.

Freedman, L., 'The Politics of Warning: Terrorism and Risk Communication', *Intelligence and National Security*, Vol. 20, No. 3 (September 2005), pp. 379–418.

Freedman, S., Brandes, D., Peri, T. and Shalev, A., 'Predictors of Chronic Post-traumatic Stress Disorder. A Prospective Study', *British Journal of Psychiatry*, Vol. 174 (1999), pp. 353–359.

Galea, S., Ahern, J., Resnick, H., Kilpatrick, D., Bucuvalas, M., Gold, J. and Vlahov, D., 'Psychological Sequelae of the September 11 Terrorist Attacks in New York City', *New England Journal of Medicine*, Vol. 346, No. 13 (March 2002), pp. 982–987.

Galea, S., Ahern, J., Resnick, H. and Vlahov, D., 'Post-traumatic Stress Symptoms in the General Population after a Disaster: Implications for Public Health', in .Y Neria, R. Gross and R. Marshall (eds), *9/11: Mental Health in the Wake of Terrorist Attacks* (New York: Cambridge University Press, 2006), pp. 19–44.

Galea, S., Vlahov, D., Resnick, H., Ahern, J., Susser, E., Gold, J., Bucuvalas, M. and Kilpatrick, D., 'Trends of Probable Post-traumatic Stress Disorder in New York City after the September 11 Terrorist Attacks', *American Journal of Epidemiology* Vol. 158, No. 6 (2003), pp. 514–524.

Garnett, J., 'Strategic Studies and Its Assumptions', in John Baylis, Ken Booth, John Garnett *et al.*, *Contemporary Strategy: Theories and Policies* (London: Croom Helm, 1975), pp. 3–21.

Gearty, C., *Terrorism* (Aldershot: Dartmouth, 1996).

Gidron, Y., Kaplan, Y., Velt, A. and Shalem, R., 'Prevalence and Moderators of Terror-Related Post-Traumatic Stress Disorder Symptoms in Israeli Citizens', *Israeli Medical Association Journal*, Vol. 6 (July 2004), pp. 387–391.

Gigerenzer, G., 'Out of the Frying Pan into the Fire: Behavioural Reactions to Terrorist Attacks', *Risk Analysis*, Vol. 26, No. 2 (2006), pp. 347–351.

Gillespie, K., Duffy, M., Hackman, A. and Clark, D. M., 'Community-based Cognitive Therapy in the Treatment of Posttraumatic Stress Disorder following the Omagh Bomb', *Behaviour Research and Therapy*, Vol. 40, No. 4, (April 2002), pp. 345–357.

Glass, T. and Schoch-Spana, M., 'Bioterrorism and the People: How to Vaccinate a City against Panic', *Clinical Infectious Diseases*, Vol. 34, No. 2 (January 2002), pp. 217–223.

Gray, G. M. and Ropeik, D. M., 'Dealing with the Dangers of Fear: The Role of Risk Communication', *Politics and Public Health* (November–December 2002), pp. 106–116.

Greene, C. M., 'Epidemiologic Investigations of Bioterrorism-Related Anthrax, New Jersey, 2001', *Emerging Infectious Diseases*, Vol. 8, No. 10 (October 2002), pp. 1048–1054.

Grieger, T. A., Waldrep, D. A., Lovasz, M. M. and Ursano, R. J., 'Follow-up of Pentagon Employees Two Years after the Terrorist Attack of September 11, 2001', *Psychiatric Services*, Vol. 56, No. 11 (November 2005), pp. 1374–1379.

Helsloot, I. and Ruitenberg, A., 'Citizen Response to Disasters: A Survey of Literature and Some Practical Implications', *Journal of Contingencies and Crisis Management*, Vol. 12, No. 3 (September 2004), pp. 98–111.

Hobbs, J., Kittler, A., Fox, S., Middleton, B. and Bates, D. W., 'Communicating Health Information to an Alarmed Public Facing a Threat Such as a Bioterrorist Attack', *Journal of Health Communications*, Vol. 9, No. 1 (2004), pp. 67–75.

Hoffman, B., *Inside Terrorism* (London: Victor Gollancz, 1998).

Huddy, L., Feldman, S., Capelos, T. and Provost, C., 'The Consequences of Terrorism: Disentangling the Effects of Personal and National Threat', *Political Psychology*, Vol. 23, No. 3 (September 2002), pp. 485–509.

Hughes, J. M. and Gerberding, J. L., 'Anthrax Bioterrorism: Lessons Learned and Future Directions', *Emerging Infectious Diseases*, Vol. 8, No. 10 (October 2002).

Hyams, K. C., Murphy, F. M. and Wessely, S., Responding to Chemical, Biological or Nuclear Terrorism: The Indirect and Long Term Health Effects May Present the Greatest Challenge', *Journal of Health Politics, Policy and Law*, Vol. 27, No. 2 (April 2002), pp. 273–292.

Janis, I., *Air War and Emotional Stress: Psychological Studies of Bombing and Civilian Defense* (London: McGraw Hill, 1951).

Janis, I. L. and Feshbach, S., Effects of Fear-Arousing Communications', *Journal of Abnormal and Social Psychology*, Vol. 48, No. 1 (1953), pp. 78–92.

Jehel, L., Paterniti, S., Brunet, A., Duchet, C. and Guelfi, J.D., Prediction of the Occurrence and Intensity of Post-traumatic Stress Disorder in Victims 32 Months after Bomb Attack', *European Psychiatry*, Vol. 18, No. 4 (June 2003), pp. 172–176.

Jenkins, B., *International Terrorism: A New Kind of Warfare* (RAND P-5326, 1974).

Jones, E., Woolven, R., Durodié W. and Wessely, S., Public Panic and Morale: World War Two Civilian Responses Re-examined in the Light of the Current Anti-terrorist Campaign', *Journal of Risk Research*, Vol. 9, No. 1 (2006), pp. 57–73.

Kaplan, D., *The Cult at the End of the World: The Terrifying Story of the Aum Doomsday Cult, from the Subways of Tokyo to the Nuclear Arsenals of Russia* (London: Random House, 1996).

Kark, J. D., Goldman, S. and Epstein, L., Iraqi Missile Attacks on Israel: The Association of Mortality with a Life-Threatening Stressor', *Journal of the American Medical Association*, Vol. 273, No. 15 (19 April 1995), pp. 1208–1210.

Karp, A., *Ballistic Missile Proliferation: The Politics and Technics* (Oxford: Oxford University Press, 1995).

Karsenty, E., Sgemer, J., Cojocaru, B. *et al.* Medical Aspects of the Iraqi Missile Attacks on Israel', *Israel Journal of Medical Science*, Vol. 27, No. 11–12 (1991), pp. 603–607.

Kasperson, R. E. and Kasperson, J. X., The Social Amplification and Attenuation of Risk', in Howard Hunreuther and Paul Slovic (eds), Challenges in Risk Assessment and Risk Management', *Annals of the American Academy*, Vol. 545 (May 1996), pp. 8–13.

Kawana, N., Psycho-Physiological Effects of the Terrorist Sarin Attack on the Tokyo Subway System', *Military Medicine*, Vol. 166, Supplement 2 (2001), pp. 23–26.

Keller, C., Siegrist, M. and Gutscher, H., The Role of Affect and Availability Heuristics in Risk Communication', *Risk Analysis*, Vol. 26, No. 3 (2006), pp. 631–639.

Kirschenbaum, A., Terror, Adaptation and Preparedness: A Trilogy for Survival', *Journal of Homeland Security and Emergency Management*, Vol. 3, No. 1 (2006), pp. 23–48.

Klingman, A. and Kupermintz, H., Response Style and Self-Control under Scud Missile Attacks: The Case of the Sealed Room Situation During the 1991 Gulf War', *Journal of Traumatic Stress*, Vol. 7, No. 3 (1994), pp. 415–426.

Koplan, J. P., Communication During Public Health Emergencies', *Journal of Health Communications*, Vol. 8 (2003), pp. 144–145.

Kovatz, S., Kutz, I., Rubin, G. J. *et al.*, Comparing the Distress of American and Israeli Medical Students Studying in Israel During a Period of Terror', *Medical Education*, Vol. 40, No. 4 (2006), pp. 389–393.

Kydd, A. and Walter, B., The Strategies of Terrorism', *International Security*, Vol. 31, No. 1 (Summer 2006), pp. 49–79.

Lambert, A. P. N., *The Psychology of Air Power* (London: RUSI, 1995).

Laqueur, W., *A History of Terrorism* (London: Transaction Publishers, 2001).

Lemyre, L., Clément, M., Corneil, W. *et al.*, 'A Psychosocial Risk Assessment and Management Framework to Enhance Response to CBRN Terrorism Threats and Attacks', *Biosecurity and Bioterrorism: Biodefense Strategy, Practice, and Science*, Vol. 3, No. 4 (2005), pp. 316–330.

Lofstedt, R. E., Risk Communication: Pitfalls and Promises', *European Review* , Vol. 11, No. 3 (2003), p. 417.

Lomranz, J., Hobfoll, S. E., Johnson, R., Eyal, N. and Zemach, M., 'A Nation's Response to Attack: Israelis' Depressive Reactions to the Gulf War', *Journal of Traumatic Stress*, Vol. 7, No. 1 (1994), pp. 64–68.

López-Rousseau, A., 'Avoiding the Death Risk of Avoiding a Dread Risk, *Psychological Science*, Vol. 16, No. 6 (2005), pp. 426–428.

Mebane, F., Temin, S. and Parvanta, C. F., Communicating Anthrax in 2001: A Comparison of CDC Information and Print Media', *Journal of Health Communication*, Vol. 8 (2003), pp. 50–82.

Metraux, D. A., *Aum Shinrikyo's Impact on Japanese Society (Japanese Studies)* (New York: Edwin Mellen Press, 2000).

Miguel-Tobal, J. J., Cano-Vindel, A., Gonzales-Ordi, H., Iruarrizaga, I., Rudenstine, S. *et al.*, PTSD and Depression after the Madrid March 11 Train Bombings', *Journal of Traumatic Stress*, Vol. 19, No. 1 (2006), pp. 69–80.

Miller, J., 'Affirming Flames: Debriefing Survivors of the World Trade Center Attack', *Brief Treatment and Crisis Intervention*, Vol. 2, No. 1 (Spring 2002), pp. 85–94.

Moreno, L., The Madrid Bombings in the Domestic and Regional Politics of Spain', *Irish Studies in International Affairs*, Vol. 16 (2005), pp. 65–72.

Murakami, H., *Underground: The Tokyo Gas Attack and the Japanese Psyche* (London: Harvill Press, 2001).

Nakano, K., The Tokyo Sarin Gas Attack: Victims' Isolation and Post-Traumatic Stress Disorders', *Cross-Cultural Psychology Bulletin* , Vol. 29 (December 1995), pp. 12–15.

National Research Committee on Risk Perceptions and Communication, *Improving Risk Communication* (Washington, DC: National Academy Press, 1989).

Neumann, P. R. and Smith, M. L. R., Strategic Terrorism: The Framework and Its Fallacies', *Journal of Strategic Studies*, Vol. 28, No. 4 (August 2005), pp. 571–595.

Neumann, P. R. and Smith, M. L. R., *The Strategy of Terrorism: How It works, and WHY IT FAILS* (Abingdon: Routledge, 2008).

North, C. S., Nixon, S. J., Shariat, S. *et al.*, Psychiatric Disorders among Survivors of the Oklahoma City Bombing', *Journal of American Medical Association* , Vol. 282 (1999), pp. 755–762.

Olson, K. B., 'Aum Shinrikyo: Once and Future Threat?', *Emerging Infectious Diseases*, Vol. 5, No. 4 (July–August 1999), pp. 513–516.

Pangi, R., Consequence Management in the 1995 Sarin Attacks on the Japanese Subway System', *Studies in Conflict and Terrorism* , Vol. 25, No. 6 (2002), pp. 421–448.

Pape, R., *Dying to Win: The Strategic Logic of Suicide Terrorism* (New York: Random House: 2005).

Perez-Sales, C. V. P. and Matt, G. Post-traumatic Stress Reactions Following from the March 11 2004 Terrorist Attacks in a Madrid Community Sample: A Cautionary Tale about the Measurement of Psychological Trauma', *Spanish Journal of Psychology*, Vol. 9, No. 1 (2006), pp. 61–74.

Peterson, J., Perception vs Reality of Radiological Impact: the Goiânia Model', *Nuclear News*, Vol. 31, No. 14 (1988), pp. 84–90.

Powell, D. and Leiss, W., *Mad Cows and Mothers' Milk* (London: McGill-Queen's University Press, 1997).

Prue, C. E., Lackey, C., Swenarski, L. and Gantt, J. M., Communication Monitoring: Shaping CDC's Emergency Risk Communication Efforts', *Journal of Health Communication*, Vol. 8, No. 1 (2003), pp. 148–151.

Renn, O. and Levin, D., Credibility and Trust in Risk Communication', in R. Kasperson and P. J. Stellen (eds), *Communicating Risks to the Public* (Dordrecht: Kluwer Academic, 1991), pp. 175–218.

Roberts, A. R., 'Assessment, Crisis Intervention, and Trauma Treatment: The Integrative ACT Intervention Model', *Brief Treatment and Crisis Intervention*, Vol. 2, No. 1 (Spring 2002), pp. 1–22.

Robinson, S. J. and Newstetter, W. C., Uncertain Science and Certain Deadlines: CDC Responses to the Media During the Anthrax Attacks of 2001', *Journal of Health Communications*, Vol. 8, No. 1 (2003), pp. 17–34.

Rogers, B., Amlot, R., Rubin, G. J., Wessely, S. and Krieger, K., Mediating the Social and Psychological Impacts of Terrorist Attacks: The Role of Risk Perception and Risk Communication', *International Review of Psychiatry*, Vol. 19, No. 3 (2007), pp. 279–288.

Ropeik, D. and Slovic, P., Risk Communication: A Neglected Tool in Protecting Public Health', *Risk in Perspective*, Vol. 11, No. 2 (2003).

Rotenberg, Z., Noy, S. and Gabbay, U., Israeli ED Experience During the Gulf War', *American Journal of Emergency Medicine*, Vol. 12, No. 1 (January 1994), pp. 118–119.

Royal Society, Risk Perception', in *Risk Analysis, Perception and Management: Report of a Royal Society Study Group* (London: Royal Society, 1992), pp. 89–134.

Rubin, G. J., Brewin, C. R., Greenberg, N., Simpson, J. and Wessely, S., Psychological and Behavioural Reactions to the Bombings in London on 7 July 2005: Cross-sectional Survey of a Representative Sample of Londoners', *British Medical Journal*, Vol. 331 (2005), pp. 606–611.

Rubin, G. J., Greenberg, N., Hughes, J. H., Simpson, J. and Wessely, S., Enduring Consequences of Terrorism: 7 Month Follow-up Survey of Reactions to the Bombings in London on 7 July 2005', *British Journal of Psychiatry*, Vol. 190 (2007), pp. 350–356.

Rudd, R. E., Comings, J. P. and Hyde, J. N., Leave No One Behind: Improving Health and Risk Communication through Attention to Literacy', *Journal of Health Communication*, Vol. 8 (2002), pp. 104–115.

Siegrist, M., Keller, C. and Kiers, H. A. L., 'A New Look at Psychometric Paradigms of Perception of Hazards', *Risk Analysis*, Vol. 25, No. 1 (2005), pp. 211–222.

Schaffer, D., Armstrong, G., Higgins, K. *et al.*, Increased US Prescription Trends Associated with the CDC *Bacillus Anthracis* Antimicrobial Post Exposure

Prophylaxis Campaign', *Pharmacoepidemiology and Drug Safety* , Vol. 12, No. 3 (2003), pp. 177–182.

Schelling, T., *The Strategy of Conflict* (Cambridge, MA: Harvard University Press, 1960).

Schlenger, W. E., Caddell, J. M., Ebert, L. *et al.*, Psychological Reactions to Terrorist Attacks: Findings from the National Study of Americans' Reactions to September 11', *Journal of American Medical Association* , Vol. 288, No. 5 (August 2002), pp. 581–588.

Schoch-Spana, M., Educating, Informing, and Mobilizing the Public', in B. S. Levy and V. W. Sidel (eds), *Terrorism and Public Health: A Balanced Approach to Strengthening Systems and Protecting People* (New York: Oxford University Press, 2003), pp. 118–135.

Schuster, M., Stein, B. D., Jaycox, L. H. *et al.*, 'A National Survey of Stress Reactions after the September 11 2001 Terrorist Attacks', *New England Journal of Medicine*, Vol. 345, No. 20 (November 2001), pp. 1507–1512.

Shalev, A. Y., Posttraumatic Stress Disorder among Injured Survivors of a Terrorist Attack. Predictive Value of Early Intrusion and Avoidance Symptoms', *Journal of Nervous Diseases*, Vol. 180 (1992), pp. 505–509.

Shalev, A. Y. and Freedman, S., PTSD Following Terrorist Attacks: A Prospective Evaluation', *American Journal of Psychiatry*, Vol. 163, No. 6 (June 2005), pp. 1188–1191.

Shalev, A. Y., Tuval, R., Frenkiel-Fishman, S., Hadar, H. and Eth, S., Psychological Responses to Continuous Terror: A Study of Two Communities in Israel', *American Journal of Psychiatry*, Vol. 164, No. 4 (April 2006), pp. 667–673.

Shepard, C. W., 'Antimicrobial Postexposure Prophylaxis for Anthrax: Adverse Events and Adherence', *Emerging Infectious Diseases*, Vol. 8, No. 10 (October 2002), pp. 1124–1132.

Sheppard, B. (ed.), *Jane's Special Report: Ballistic Missile Proliferation* (Coulsdon: Jane's Information Group, 2000).

Sheppard, B., Rubin, G. J., Wardman, J. K. and Wessely, S., 'Terrorism and Dispelling the Myth of a Panic Prone Public', *Journal of Public Health Policy*, Vol. 27, No. 3 (2006), pp. 219–245.

Shore, D. A., Communicating in Times of Uncertainty: The Need for Trust', *Journal of Health Communications*, Vol. 8, No. 1 (2003), pp. 13–14.

Silke, A. (ed.), *Terrorists, Victims and Society: Psychological Perspectives on Terrorism and Its Consequences* (Chichester: Wiley, 2003).

Silver, R. C., Holman, E. A., McIntosh, D. N., Poulin, M., Gil-Rivas, V. and Pizarro, J., Coping with a National Trauma: Nationwide Longitudinal Study of Responses to the Terrorist Attacks of September 11', in Y. Neria, R. Gross and R. Marshall (eds), *9/11: Mental Health in the Wake of Terrorist Attacks* (New York: Cambridge University Press, 2006), pp. 45–70.

Silverberg, D. and Sofer, E., Role of the Tel Aviv-Jaffa Municipal Workers in the Treatment of Survivors of Missile Blasts', *Israel Journal of Medical Sciences*, November–December 1991, Vol. 27, No. 11–12 (1991), pp. 701–703.

Sime, J., 'The Concept of Panic', in D. Canter (eds), *Fires and Human Behaviour*, Wiley, pp. 63–81.

Simon, S., The New Terrorism: Securing the Nation against a Messianic Foe', *The Brookings Review*, Vol. 21, No. 1 (Winter 2003), pp. 18–34.

Sjoberg, L., The Perceived Risk of Terrorism', *Risk Management: An International Journal*, Vol. 7, No. 1 (2005), pp. 43–62.

Slovic, P., Trust, Emotion, Sex, Politics, and Science: Surveying the Risk-assessment Battlefield', *Risk Analysis*, Vol. 19, No. 4 (1999), pp. 689–701.

Slovic, P. (ed.), *The Perception of Risk* (London: Earthscan Publications Ltd, 2000).

Slovic, P., Finucane, M. L., Peters, E. and MacGregor, D. G., Risk as Analysis and Risk as Feelings: Some Thoughts about Affect, Reason, Risk, and Rationality', *Risk Analysis*, Vol. 24, No. 2 (2004), pp. 311–322.

Solomon, Z., *Coping with War-Induced Stress: The Gulf War and the Israeli Response* (New York: Plenum 1995).

Somer, E., Ruvio, A., Soref, E. and Sever, I., Terrorism, Distress and Coping: High versus Low Impact Regions and Direct versus Indirect Civilian Exposure', *Anxiety, Stress, and Coping*, Vol. 18, No. 3 (2005), pp. 165–182.

Stecklov, G. and Goldstein, J. R., Terror Attacks Influence Driving Behaviour in Israel', *Proceedings of the National Academy of Sciences*, Vol. 101, No. 40 (2004), pp. 14551–14556.

Sunstein, C. R., Terrorism and Probability of Neglect', *Journal of Risk and Uncertainty*, Vol. 26, No. 2–3 (2003), pp. 121–136.

Thornton, T., Terror as a Weapon of Political Agitation', in Harry Eckstein (ed.), *Internal War: Problems and Approaches* (New York: Free Press of Glencoe, 1964), pp. 71–79.

Tu, A. T., *Chemical Terrorism: Horrors in Tokyo Subway and Matsumoto City* (Fort Collins, TX: Alaken, 2002).

Ursano, R. J., Post Traumatic Stress Disorder', *The New England Journal of Medicine*, Vol. 346, No. 2 (January 2002), pp. 130–132.

Ursano, R. J. and Norwood, A. E. (eds), *Emotional Aftermath of the Persian Gulf War: Veterans, Families, Communities, and Nations* (Washington, DC: American Psychiatric Press, 1996).

Vanderford, M. L., Communication Lessons Learned in the Emergency Operations Center During CDC's Anthrax Response: A Commentary', *Journal of Health Communications*, Vol. 8 (2003), pp. 11–12.

Wardlaw, G., *Political Terrorism: Theory, Tactics and Counter-measures* (Cambridge: Cambridge University Press, 1982).

Waters, J. M., Moving Forward From September 11: A Stress/Crisis/Trauma Response Model', *Brief Treatment and Crisis Intervention*, Vol. 2, No. 1 (Spring 2002), pp. 55–74.

Weis, C. P.. Intrepido, A. J., Miller, A. K. *et al.*, Secondary Aerosolization of Viable *Bacillus Anthracis* Spores in a Contaminated US Senate Office', *Journal of the American Medical Association*, Vol. 288, No. 22 (December 2002), pp. 2853–2858.

Wilkinson, P., *Terrorism and the Liberal State* (London: Macmillan, 1977).

Wilkinson, P., *Terrorism versus Democracy: The Liberal State Responses* (London: Frank Cass, 2002).

Index

Made in the USA
Middletown, DE
23 August 2016